UNMEDIATED

Essays on Media, Culture, Cinema

UNMEDIATED

Essays on Media, Culture, Cinema

SASHI KUMAR

Tulika Books

Published by
Tulika Books
35 A/1 Shahpur Jat, New Delhi 110 049
tulikabooks.wordpress.com

First published in India in 2014

ISBN: 978-93-82381-32-7

Printed at Chaman Offset, Delhi 110 002

For my mother

BHANUMATHY

Contents

Foreword

For as long as I have known him, Sashi Kumar has been inseparable from the Indian media, an organic presence and player in their evolution and transformation over the past three decades. Two things stand out about his media career. First, its versatility, unusual in its range even in a field used to mobility across platforms – he has been television newscaster, reporter and documentary producer; a newspaper's foreign correspondent; chief producer of a news agency's television experiment; pioneer entrepreneur of Indian news television; film critic, creative filmmaker and occasional actor; and founder of India's and South Asia's premier journalism school. The second thing that stands out is the consistently progressive, pro-people roles Sashi Kumar has played as journalist, writer and media entrepreneur.

As important has been his capacity to step back, and step outside the arena, to reflect on the larger, long-range issues concerning media, society and culture. These issues include the rising threats to free speech in India; the media's strengths, virtues, weaknesses and vices; their structural features, which tend to work against independence, diversity and quality; their cultural attributes and interactions; what the market does to the media; the opportunities offered and the challenges posed to all forms of the media by revolutionizing technology; regulatory questions; and indeed the very future of journalism in this digital age.

I have used media in the wider sense, advisedly. When journalists speak of the media, they almost always mean the news media, forgetting there is a huge media world out there that has little to do with news as we know it. It is as though virtually from the time he started out in the late 1970s, Sashi Kumar resolved to avoid narrowcasting his role as a journalist. After all, he came to professional journalism via the world of cinema, his journalistic writing beginning with film criticism: criticism of serious and 'new' Indian cinema to which he brought a fresh standpoint, and a sceptical and challenging voice. Even after he rooted himself firmly in the mainstream media, making a full-time career alternately in television and print journalism as a reporter and commentator on national and international affairs, he retained his affection, if not passion, for what brought him into the profession. From time to time, he ventured out as empathetic but sharp-edged critic, ironic commentator, and, to an extent, player in the world of cinema, music and other forms of cultural production.

An interesting outcome of this progressive versatility is this collection of his published contributions, which divides into three distinct reading experiences: reflections on journalism and the news media; meditations on theoretical issues arising in the cultural domain; and essays in film criticism and analyses of cinematic text. These articles were contributed over three decades to a variety of publications – *The Hindu*, *Frontline*, *Outlook*, *Tehelka*, *India Today*, *Seminar*, *Social Scientist*, *Business Today*, *Business World* and the *Al Jazeera* website. They also include some book reviews by, and interviews with, the author.

Sashi Kumar is a vigorous and unsentimental critic of the performance of the news media in India and globally. He has little time for the romantic notions, the pieties that feature in conventional, run-of-the-mill discourses on the freedom and independence of the press and television. He clearly sees Noam Chomsky's propaganda model, which sets out a theoretical basis for explaining and doing something about the media's role in 'manufacturing consent' for unjust and wrong-headed policies, as applying to the Indian situation. The use of irony, satirical as well as philosophical irony, in targeting the hyper-commercialization, blinkered vision, trivialization, dilettantism, 'homogenized' sameness and shallowness of a large part of Indian journalism is particularly suited to this criticism.

The essays offer expert insights on the failings of India's plethora of television news channels – and what seems at the surface to be an orgiastic excess of 24x7 news and news chatter. For example, what looks like diversity and intense competition in a supposedly free market is an illusion, fake-diversity, pseudo-competition for dishing out much the same fare, with 'more' turning out to be 'less'. This observation comes with explanatory power, a nuanced analysis of how and why it is so.

There is this important insight on how the market affects the media:

> The market, including in print and television, has become segmented and stratified, so that it is less and less one of mass media. The media themselves have become more and more class-conscious, with little going for those below a set threshold of purchasing power. The lower you are on the social and economic scale . . . the less relevant you are to the media either as subject or consumer.
>
> Absence of cross-media restrictions in India has paved the way for monopolies straddling different sectors like print, television, radio and cybermedia. Profit maximization, rather than any commitment to the citizen's right to be informed, drives the news media.

Such 'class consciousness', which works to distance and alienate the news media from hundreds of millions of India's working people who suffer multiple forms of deprivation and exploitation, manifests itself in the shrinking of space for rural India – so much so that 'there is hardly any evidence today of that vast hinterland and its preponderant society and culture on television screens across the country'.

Some of these essays were written more than two or even three decades ago, but the assessments and insights they offer do not seem dated at all. They seem, in fact, to connect seamlessly with the more recently written essays, which testifies to the deep-going and enduring nature of the structural features and tendencies observed and analysed in this collection.

All this must not lead to the impression that Sashi Kumar the critic has a negative attitude to India's news media. He places high value on the historical tradition of a relatively independent press, on the democratic aspects of the recent development of all forms of the news media – print, broadcast and digital, in totality, on the exciting opportunities offered by new technology, and on innovative and creative work in the field. He is a great believer in the democratic roles – which, in my understanding, are chiefly the credible-informational and the critical-investigative-adversarial functions – that the news media, or, more accurately, influential sections of them, can play and have been playing to varying degrees in India. And he is a tiger when it comes to defending free speech, attacking censorship of all kinds and opposing the demand for external regulation of the news media (although he concedes that 'the media . . . have only themselves to blame for bringing things to such a pass').

Sashi Kumar's opposition to external regulation proceeds from the premise that freedom of the press in India is fragile, compared with what has been internalized over 'centuries of trials and tribulations' in the United Kingdom and what has been 'firmly written into the Constitution' in the United States. Any attempt to dilute or weaken this fragile freedom, which is neither internalized nor explicitly protected by the Constitution, would be dangerous, and it is in the context that he asserts that 'regulation of content by a statutory body is at best a euphemism for censorship'.

The arrangement he favours is credible self-regulation by the media, recognizing of course that this is easier said than put in place. He also favours a deeper and more potent role for the statutory Press Council of India – with a fresh mandate, and expanded to cover print, broadcast and online media – in addressing 'the lack of real pluralism', facilitating 'diversity in the media space' and enabling 'a multi-tiered milieu that caters to different segments of the people'. I too believe this is an issue of central importance but it rarely finds more than a passing mention in the Indian debate on media reform.

In a recently written essay for *Frontline*, Sashi Kumar looks appreciatively at the Leveson Inquiry and prescription, which is an arrangement for credible and independent (that is, independent of the media and of politicians) self-regulation underpinned by law. But he warns that this model of regulation, which is 'fine-tuned to the sensitivities of British society', must not be distorted or over-read to allow it to become a dangerous tool in the hands of the government 'to clip the wings of the news media here in India'. Anyone who values media freedom and independence will find it hard to disagree with this approach to the challenging issue of regulation.

My knowledge of cinema is highly limited, with my interest confined to the art and creativity of a handful of great filmmakers, including Sergei Eisenstein, Satyajit Ray and Akira Kurosawa, and the process by which outstanding literary works, such as *War and Peace*, *The End of the Affair*, *The Guide*, *The English Patient*, *The Remains of the Day* and, most recently, *Midnight's Children*, are transformed, felicitously or for worse, into cinema. But as a lay reader, I found the film criticism and analyses of cinematic text offered in this collection educative as well as interesting as a literary form.

Our film critic is at his best while writing about India's 'new cinema'; his critique is original, nuanced and a pleasure to read. While the new cinema, when it comes into its own, 'tends to revel in its rebel image', its real character and content fail to live up to this self-image – because 'it is essentially a broad conglomerate of films, diffused and indeterminate both in its choice and handling of formal content, and in its social context'. As for stance and content, Sashi Kumar, who seems to hint at the imitativeness and lack of originality of much of India's new cinema, regards 'the use of the epithet "narcissists" for filmmakers of this cadre' as 'not entirely baseless'.

Equally important is the weak connection with social context:

> While the New Cinema in our country . . . steers carefully clear of the path trodden by its starkly escapist and abstracted commercial counterpart, it does not seem so concerned about its social relevance. It is this that ultimately qualifies and limits its role as rebel, and circumscribes its viewing to minority, even exclusive, audiences. It is this erraticism again, which makes the commercial industry itself look askance at this development as a prodigal variant, still seeking its bearings.

Here too there seem to be a few exceptions that prove the rule. But even a Ray film (*Pather Panchali* aside), while being 'a marvel of technical finesse and aesthetic flow . . . does not seek to provoke a questioning process or engender thinking on its social content and context'. This important and persuasive critique was written in 1979 but I suspect it applies just as well to much of twenty-first century 'new cinema'.

Finally, a word on Sashi Kumar's theoretical interests and concerns in the domain of culture. The central theme of the essays in this category is the tendency towards hegemonization of mass culture round the world and what to do about this. This process, which undermines creativity, has gone quite far. It is, in fact, 'representative of the essential ingredients that make up the modern Americanized worldview: a kind of divine right theory of leadership in any global action; cultural chauvinism in the sense of universalizing all that is American;

and an exclusive prerogative to hold dear the nation-state concept'. It seeks to shape the form and content of mass media, especially television and cinema. The technology of the information revolution, which is accessible to the developing world, offers scope for genuine diversification, leap-frogging development, and the opportunity to 'break free of a leviathan structure that straddles the globe', but unfortunately, 'the development priorities of a major portion of the world tend to keep the benefit of this technological advantage at bay'. Policy and political choices are of the essence here, working wittingly or unwittingly on the side of hegemonization. But the point about the analysis is the qualified optimism underlying it: 'the liberating potential of the information technology' can be realized by India and other developing countries, but political will and the setting of progressive development priorities will be the key.

Over the past decade-and-a-half, I have shared Sashi Kumar's keen and sustained, even over-riding, interest in the education of young men and women for the profession of journalism. The neglect of journalism education and training has been one of the traditional weaknesses of India's press and broadcast news media, and the neglect has proved costly over the long term. Led by Sashi Kumar, a few of us drawn from the media and academic fields have worked together as trustees to establish and develop the Asian College of Journalism in Chennai. This post-graduate institution, established and administered by a not-for-profit public trust or foundation, has an ambitious mission: to provide students drawn from a diversity of backgrounds from all over India and, to an extent, from other South Asian countries with a 'world-class journalism education adapted to the specific needs of India and other developing countries in Asia'. The work of developing a J-school of a new type for India and the wider region has proved most rewarding. We have been particularly struck by the number of young people who, year after year, come to a field where the monetary rewards are not high, where cynicism is widely supposed to rule, in a spirit of idealism and public service. I expect this work in progress, a new chapter in our author's remarkable media career, to find reflection and resonance in his next collection of essays.

Chennai
October 2013

N. RAM
Chairman, Kasturi & Sons Ltd.;
Publisher and former Editor-in-Chief,
The Hindu Group of Publications

Preface

This compilation is drawn from my published work from the late 1970s to the present. It is informed by my exposure to, quest and passion for, practice in, and contemplation on *the media* as a broad category of culture and the ecology, and including film, print, television, radio and the net. It is informed too by my brief engagement, in between, with advertising across different media, and an entrepreneurial phase of establishing and running a satellite and cable TV enterprise at the cusp of the transition from the analogue to the digital.

The twin pulls that have dominated and endured this hitchhiker's journey across a variegated media-scape are journalism and cinema. The one has found some repose in the college of journalism I am now involved with, where thoughts and discussions about the news media in their current state of uncertainty continue to stimulate as much as exercise the mind. As for the other, cinema, there is a restless and helpless awareness of the deficit between technological innovativeness and craftsmanship that shock and awe, but don't quite break through into a new realm of artistic consciousness, and the conceptual highs that the international masters of an earlier generation – including from the erstwhile Soviet Union and the Eastern Bloc where the best filmmakers seemed at their creative best in negotiating state subsidies and state censorship at the same time – took the medium to.

Looking back, it is amusing how one thing led to another in an unintended sequence connecting the dots of my media career. I had been writing on films for *The Hindu* for a few years (the early essays in this volume), alongside presenting English news and making documentary films for television and dabbling in advertising across the media for the extra money it brought (I was multitasking in the media for as far back as I can remember and long before convergent, digital multimedia made it so much simpler) when, out of the blue one day in late 1983, the then Editor of the paper, G. Kasturi, called for me and asked me whether I would set up and man its West Asia bureau. I would, but didn't it make a difference that I had no experience of international or political reporting? He was confident it didn't, and that I would measure up to the task. I chose not to disagree. Would I then tour the region to decide the best location for the bureau? I did, and zeroed in on Bahrain as the apt monitoring post for the Gulf and the Levant.

As I remember, until then I had only one published piece somewhat related to the job on offer – a longish feature in *The Hindu* on the impact of Gulf money on Kerala. I was however an avid follower and active supporter of the Palestinian movement. Maybe the Editor had read my article and thought that, more than films, that was the kind of thing I should be writing about; maybe he had got wind of my interest in the Palestinian cause too, and more than didn't mind it. Anyway, that posting took me beyond parsing the filmic frame into the wider world of proper journalism.

While based in Bahrain, travelling and filing reports on issues like the Iran–Iraq war, the politics of the oil cartel, offshore banking, Arab nationalism, the Israeli–Palestinian conflict, expatriate Indian labour and continual US meddling in the region, I chanced upon a redoubtable Palestinian, Ahmed Suleiman, who happened to be the chief of Radio Bahrain, and who rued the poor-cousinly treatment of his people by the Gulf Sheikhs as much as he resented the news broadcasts on his channel being all delivered by Britishers. In me he found not only a kindred spirit, but also an opportunity, at long last, to break the British monopoly of the airwaves. It was a new experience for me to collate, prepare and present radio news, but familiar too, in terms of the straight and narrow official path the state-owned broadcaster, whether in India or in Bahrain, was expected to take.

The eventful sojourn in Bahrain was cut short by enticing news from India about a defrosting of the government-controlled television medium (there were no private channels yet), allowing for a bigger role by outside producers, and greater critical latitude and freedom in programming. I was invited to build and head the television arm of the news agency, Press Trust of India (PTI), but arrived there via a detour of a few months to Bombay and a short stint in charge of the Ambani-owned television serial and entertainment programming outfit, Mudra Videotech. It was a fascinating peep into the show-swirl of the small screen that was gathering momentum, but one that left me convinced that news, not soap, was my métier.

PTI-TV was exciting, gruelling and rewarding. It soon became the prominent programming banner on national television. We carved niche-slots on the economy (*Money Matters*), culture (*Tana Bana*), national politics and international affairs. Research, investigation, depth of treatment, breadth of field coverage and consistently high production values were the defining features of the brand. Our distinctive offering was a series of documentaries, some in many parts, on a range of international issues. It took me, among other places abroad, to the Soviet Union as it was staring at its own collapse and dismemberment; to Romania just after the fall of Ceausescu; to both sides of Germany shortly before and after the wall came down; to Sri Lanka several times to record the plight of the Tamil people caught between a chauvinistic, intolerant and cruel Sinhala state, and a ruthless LTTE leadership, both proto-fascist in their own ways; on a multi-national whistle-stop shooting tour for a series on a grand idealistic theme of universal disarmament.

The rigorous ground work, extensive location shooting, sleepless nights of editing and post-production, and the thought and care given through it all to ensure that perspectives were never distorted, seem a far cry from the nightly boisterous brawl goaded on by the anchor that passes for studio news debate and discussion these days. News bulletins no longer have packaged stories – that is, self-contained capsules of field footage edited and voiced-over to give the viewer a succinct, rounded and accurate account of the given news item. They resort, instead, to facile impressionistic opinions by the reporters, or guests in the studio or outside. Comment pips fact every inch of the way. The information that is conveyed lacks credibility, is speculative or half-baked. This, in fact, is peculiar to television in India. Reputed international news channels, including public service broadcasters like the BBC, continue to rely on pre-packaged, autonomous capsules to tell the story. Packages, though, entail crew and travel and shoot and post-production costs, all of which can be saved if they are substituted by studio prattle.

PTI-TV's programme inventory, in its range and thematic concerns, provided a good indication of the kind of fare befitting an enlightened public broadcaster, as distinct from a propagandist and pedagogic government channel. It was around this time, in the late 1980s, that the new, independent possibility in this direction – opened up by direct broadcast satellite (DBS) technology – dawned on me, and I began to think in terms of a national, even pan-South Asian equivalent of public service television to be set up by PTI-TV. That was really the genesis of *Asianet.* I developed a blueprint for the project which seemed to find favour with the management and a good section of the news agency's board of directors. But when a decision was inordinately delayed, I decided to cut loose and concentrate the limited resources I could muster, in the absence of the institutional backing of PTI, in Kerala, where we set up the *Asianet* TV channel and cable company as twin entities in the early 1990s. In the initial years, programming on *Asianet* reflected the public-interest broadcast philosophy with which I had set out on this business, and maintained a healthy mix that leaned more on knowledge and information than mere entertainment – and was not any the poorer for it, registering steady commercial growth year on year. But that is another story . . .

I hope this rushed recollection prefacing the collection of essays before you will help better place the 'voice' that speaks to various aspects of the media and mediated culture in them.

I am indeed very happy that N. Ram, at once my mentor and my friend, acceded to the publisher's request to write the Foreword to this volume. It could really not have been anyone else.

I would like to thank *The Hindu* archives for locating the articles of the earlier period, and the Editor of *Frontline*, Vijay Shankar, for his timely intercessions in making them available for this book.

It was my wife Radhika's idea to gather my published pieces on the media together into a book. I must thank her too for getting me to work on it. Not that I had much to do once my sister, Indu, undertook its publication by Tulika. The credit for painstakingly putting it all together goes entirely to the editorial team at Tulika Books, particularly Rani Ray, Shad Naved and Rakhi Sehgal. I am grateful to all of them.

Chennai SASHI KUMAR
March 2014

Essays on MEDIA & CULTURE 1992–2014

An Eye to China

Impressions of a modern ancient nation

They call him 'Damu' in China. Tradition puts him down as Bodhidharma, the third son of King Sugandha of Kanchipuram, who embraced Buddhism and became the twenty-eighth patriarch in the line of Buddha, propounded the philosophy of Dhyan Buddhism, set sail for China around AD 517 and arrived in Canton after a three-year voyage.

Buddhism then was already practised – and had royal patronage – in China. However, Bodhidharma was to wrest it out of its normative, ritualistic shell, and infuse into it an inner philosophical dynamism and discipline that, over the next five generations, evolved into a body of doctrines identified as Chan Buddhism in China and its later variant, Zen Buddhism, in Japan and Korea.

This saga of the contemporary Zen boom also throws an interesting sidelight on the martial forms, paintings and crafts of China. For instance, one learns that it was Bodhidharma who founded the Shaolin monastery – the mystic take-off point for an entire crop of oriental novels in the Bruce Lee and Ninja traditions, and where to this day, the master and the disciple rise with the birds to go through a strict regimen of yogic training and Wu-shu martial practice; that the Japanese Noh theatre, and the masque forms and Manichaean attributes of the traditional Chinese theatre, have echoes of the Kathakali dance-form; that the essential distinctiveness of the great Japanese film-maker Ozu lay in his success in transmitting Zen Buddhist stillness and meditativeness into his celluloid frames.

It was this intrepid missionary and traveller, Bodhidharma, that Doordarshan set out to capture in a full-length docu-feature, fleshing him out afresh from scriptures, texts, oral traditions and fables – a task made possible through the scholastic labour of the Chinese professor Tan Chung, now at the Centre of East Asian Languages in Jawaharlal Nehru University, New Delhi.

It was this mission that took a Doordarshan crew, with me in tow, to China. When I arrived in Beijing the crew had been in China for over two months on the trail of Bodhidharma, travelling extensively to and filming the sites of his many wondrous but plausible (and, by modern reckoning, some equally fantastic but implausible) feats. The final leg of the shooting in Beijing was to be in the studios of CCTV where the famous encounter between Bodhidharma and Emperor Wu of the Liang dynasty (AD 527) – seen as a watershed and, in a sense of Bodhidharma's chronicle rather than of history, as the *terminus a quo* of Dhyan Buddhism in China – was to be canned. I was there because by a quirk of facial resemblance, I was cast as Bodhidharma.

Damu, or Thamu as it sounds in Chinese, seems more a concept than a well-delineated figure in the subconscious; a folk hero of a misty and mystic past still pervasive in reach. The only other Indian who vies with him for an abiding presence in the average Chinese mind is Raj Kapoor, whose *Awara* (both the film and the song) is a kind of fixture the Indian visitor has invariably to grapple with. Once the ice is broken and you are identified as 'Hindu' comes the *Awara* test; if you do not know the tune, they will hum it and you can just fill in the words. In many of the newly mushrooming karaoke bars, where visual sequences and a matching music track are played on a large TV screen and you pay 10 or 20 yuan to fill in the song through a crooner's microphone, a pop version of the *Awara* song is a constant theme. Unfortunately, Dr Kotnis does not evoke anywhere near the same degree of recognition, though there is some space dedicated to him and his work in the Museum of the Revolution near Tiananmen Square. (Kotnis was a member of the Indian doctors' team that went to China in 1938 to help victims of the war with Japan, and died there.)

We are in Beijing the week before Premier Li Peng's visit to India, and the Bodhidharma shooting, understandably, takes a back seat in CCTV's priorities. They are preoccupied with preparations for the visit. The average Chinese – literate and used to newspaper-reading – is aware of the visit, but there seems to be little awareness of its historic nature as perceived from the Indian side. When we point out that the visit takes place after thirty-one years marked by some difficult phases in the India–China relationship, the reaction is one of polite surprise. We suspect it has to do with a natural discretion in discussing politics with foreigners, but are surprised at how strongly, even vituperatively, they come out on such issues as corruption in Chinese society, nepotism and unfair privileges in the upper echelons.

On India there are no strong views, or any sense of vexation or obsession (that is, when someone is familiar with the problem at all) with the border issue. Nor is there anything approximating to a national animus (now fast receding even in India) towards an adversarial neighbour. The common reaction, on the other hand, was to see the two cultures as a continuum. But the Pakistanis were apparently more paranoid about the Li Peng visit. Pakistan's Prime Minister rushed a letter through a special emissary to Li Peng who in turn promptly assured Islamabad of Beijing's unswerving relationship.

This sense of dichotomy between popular perception and a possible official line makes for an interesting dualism when it comes to dealing with the United States and Japan. In both cases a studied ambivalence seems to be in vogue. With Carla Hills and her infamous Super 301 looming like a spectre on an economy committed to reforms and opening up, the US boycott of China already in force, and visiting US Senators taking the Chinese officialdom unawares by their dramatic tantrums and self-righteous stance on human rights, the Beijing leadership seems increasingly hard put to keep in focus the fact of 30 per cent of its foreign trade being with the US alone.

The latest irritant, which in a sense impinges on India and made the Li Peng visit more significant, is the resolution in the US Congress on Tibet, and the increasingly strident tone this issue is taking in public forums and lobbies in the United States. The presence of the Dalai Lama (whose political stature has grown since he won the Nobel Peace Prize) and of a sizeable Tibetan refugee population in India draws New Delhi willy-nilly into the picture, as the Chinese are only too aware.

A shift in Sino–American relations, necessitated by the US's hegemonistic zeal (in the wake of Eastern Europe, West Asia and the Soviet Union), is subtly but distinctly visible. Not that there is any evidence of the earlier capitalist-roader variety of anti-Americanism. But the occasional pinpricks in statements, if not in action, and write-ups in *China Daily* seem a fair pointer in this direction.

There is, simultaneously, a move to come to terms with Japan as a potential ally, economically. But here history and the past need a lot of smoothing over. Thus the paradox of daily reports of economic and cultural delegations exchanging visits between the two countries, while the traumatic memories of Japanese war atrocities on the Chinese and Koreans hog prime time on TV.

If Washington has trained its sights on China as the last great bastion of socialism, it is fairly certain it will not be a walk-over here. Whatever the ideological pros and cons of socialism with Chinese characteristics and the policy of economic reform, life and society here are a far cry from that of the want and lack of choice that characterized the Soviet Union or many of the East European nations even before the present chaos. Markets are vibrant; shops are full with a stunning variety of goods sold day in and day out in a frenetic trade that leaves no doubt about the purchasing power.

While foreigners use the designated foreign exchange currency, there is no problem and hence no black market in hard currency (the current real rate in Moscow is 90 roubles to the dollar). All this exists alongside state subsidies in housing, heating, education, public transport and medicare.

If, however, the overall impression is of an economy and society of self-assurance, China is not without its internal problems. The sceptics do not fail to point out that all talk of socialism is largely notional in an economy that, in fact, has crossed over to the free market. More disturbing is the disquiet and growing frustration among the youth, a symptom of which was the upsurge in Tiananmen Square and other parts of the country in the summer of 1989. A measure of the appeasement of those sections is available in the continual reports of crackdown on corruption. A day before we left Beijing, *China Daily* spoke of some 80,000 cases of bribery and abuse of power detected by a special cell set up for the purpose. And Tiananmen seems to have cast a long shadow over contemporary life and society. It is one issue on which it is difficult to draw out a Chinese.

But when a nerve snaps the pent-up anger comes through: that it was a spontaneous upswell against the bureaucracy, not some US-inspired or remote-controlled misadventure; that they could never believe the tanks would crush students and ordinary people the way they did; that they unleashed on students and shopkeepers the Tibetan police, which has a reputation for ruthlessness (this was in Chengdu in Sichuan Province where I was recently for an international TV festival). On our way to the Forbidden City in Beijing where emperors of many dynasties lived, our driver points to the complex where the present Chinese leadership lives – and says: 'This is the Forbidden City, not what you are going to see.'

There is a reading that the Chinese leadership sees Tiananmen also as a product of premature liberalization and western ideas of democracy. But this does not really tally with our experience. Among those who would talk about it at all, there was no one who thought it was (or, in any case, should have been) against the ideology of the system. On the contrary, it was to them a strike against the degeneration and the distortions in the system. However, one unmistakable consequence of Tiananmen Square is a relook at Mao Zedong and his principles, bringing the doctrine of current reforms to the touchstone of Maoism. The 'he was 70 per cent right and 30 per cent wrong' position notwithstanding, both the leadership and the people, if for different reasons, seem to be going over Chairman Mao's thoughts again for possible clues to a situation where, as one Chinese official put it, the enemy is not so much outside as within.

First published in *Frontline*, 17 January 1992.

Cultural Onslaught

Mass media, globalization and the state

Flash forward just a couple of decades into the twenty-first century: a massive alien invasion threatens human civilization. A vile electronic nimbus hiding within it arrays of fighter spacecraft and devilish creatures of the other world hangs menacingly above the earth's surface. A cloudburst, and all humanity would perish in a flash. The counter-offensive is led by no less than the President of the United States, who happens to be an ex-fighter pilot and who requisitions the Air Force of all countries in the world for the task. Much daredevilry and spatial action later, the day is saved and the future is restored to mankind. Since all this happens on the fourth of July, the President goes on to announce that henceforth that day would mark not just American independence but world independence. The film itself, of which this is the theme, is among Hollywood's three biggest blockbusters of last year – with audiences, not only in the US but also in a good portion of the rest of the world, lapping it up.

This celluloid celebration of the great American destiny would be laughable were it not uncomfortably close, in its megalomania and hegemonizing instinct, to the quixotic Star Wars project of President Reagan. It is representative of the essential ingredients that make up the modern Americanized world-view: a kind of divine right theory of leadership in any global action; cultural chauvinism in the sense of universalizing all that is American; and an exclusive prerogative to hold dear the nation-state concept. With the cloak-and-dagger mindset of the Cold War era yielding to the coke-and-hamburger sales pitch of a unipolar, market-friendly world, the United States now seeks to provide our times with a new homogeneous model of culture and civilization. And as we move from the industrial into the information society, it seeks to leverage the main instruments of this new society, namely the electronic media and computerization, to its purpose. That such leverage can at once become an act of imperial power was driven home to us in the war against Iraq – when video, computer, avionic and missile technologies, all combined to make it a militarized video game.

Essentially, then, the US role and influence in shaping the form and content of mass media are aimed at ascertaining its ascendancy well into post-industrial civilization. Even in the latter phase of industrial society, the US had seized the initiative in organizing production on principles of standardization and segmentation, exemplified in the assembly line of the Ford car factory in Detroit.

By the 1920s Fordism, as it came to be called, had become not just a byword for capitalist development and productivity, but also a grand new model of social organization with universal implications. It had taken on the proportions of a world-view that could be praised or caricatured – and we have a tragicomic portrayal of it in Chaplin's *Modern Times* – but not ignored.

Among Fordism's unlikely supporters was Antonio Gramsci who in his *Prison Notebooks* essay, 'Americanism and Fordism', welcomes it as a necessary restructuring not only of the capitalist system but of the working class itself. It was debatably the inspiration for Stalinist planning and industrialization. So pervasive was the idea of its applicability that Aldous Huxley, in his science-fiction work, *Brave New World*, conjures up a future dominated by a Fordism that is an amalgam of American capitalism and Soviet communism, and where the presiding deity is Ford himself and whose *My Life and Work* (1922) is the bible of the times.

Americanism thus came into its own in a modern mass culture sense as something synonymous with Fordism, and its emphasis on the mass rather than the individual, leading to mechanization and dehumanization. It is the same social conditioning that throws up the idea of the robot – a word coined by Czech writer Karel Čapek in 1917 from the Czech word meaning serf or bonded labourer – as a substitute for the mechanized and labouring but unfeeling human being. It is again the same context that is explored by Walter Benjamin in his landmark essay, 'The Work of Art in the Age of Mechanical Reproduction' (*Illuminations*, 1935), where he stands traditional aesthetics on its head and defines cinema in terms of mass media.

As Fordism went into a tailspin with a new fillip to consumerism and wasteful expenditure in the post-1945 boom years, automation and eventually computerization, robotics and television were, by the 1970s, setting the stage for the communications revolution. The automobile sector shifted to the periphery and communications moved centre stage in US industry. Marshall McLuhan, who was opposed to Fordism, lost no time in supplanting it with his confusing model of the global village. His theory was a curious mixture of romantic reaction and futuristic technology. Even as he harked back to a pre-Fordist, even pre-Gutenberg community, he had an intuitive – if no more – sense of the media technology that would come to hold sway in future.

McLuhan's global village premise or hope, however, is loosely confused with the current globalization in the media. What in fact has been happening is a reversal to Fordist principles: a concerted US appropriation of the mass media with a view to organizing it precisely along lines of Fordist industrialism, to subserve the same end of an Americanized world-view. The advent of direct broadcast satellite (DBS) technology in the mid-1980s and its newer variant of digitized direct-to-home (DTH) technology have opened up the skies to the US-centric mass media's power play.

State-run television, or network television as conventionally understood, has not been able to withstand this invasion on TV signals, which cut across geopolitical boundaries. Indeed these signals have hastened the dismemberment of the Soviet Union, led to the collapse of East Europe and the crumbling of the Berlin Wall. What a US sitcom like *Dallas* did, when beamed across the Wall, to fuel a revolution of rising consumerist expectations in East Berlin, is already a case study of the powerlessness of the nation-state before the onslaught of the new medium. What these signals do to distinct cultural contexts, local communities and traditions, and towards engendering an amorphous generation of youth virtually cut off from meaningful family life with standardized demands and aspirations, are worrying imponderables.

Cinema too has more or less fully subscribed to this Americanization. The narrative has returned with a vengeance, avant-gardism is dead, all formal experimentation has collapsed, the new wave is at low ebb, and Hollywood rules the roost. The globalized electronic media have fallen into the stranglehold of a transnational oligopoly that has, and promotes, a more or less overlapping Americanized world-view. Within the United States itself, as Noam Chomsky and Edward Herman point out in their brilliant analytical study, *Manufacturing Consent* (1988), there is an implicit and unstated collusion of consensus among the practitioners and players in the media – endorsed by North American business and administration – not to deviate from, much less subvert, the tried and tested US propaganda model.

Chomsky and Herman delineate five essential characteristics of the model: (1) recognition of ownership size, ownership concentration and profit motivation of the dominant mass media firms; (2) advertising as the primary income source of mass media; (3) reliance by the media on information provided by government, business and experts funded by these primary sources and agents of power; (4) flak as a means of disciplining the media; and (5) anti-communism as a national religion and control mechanism. These features are not formalized into a systematic code (as in the Fordist mode of production) because, as Chomsky and Herman explain, the US media do not function in the manner of the propaganda system of a totalitarian state. Rather they permit – indeed, encourage – spirited debate, criticism and dissent, as long as these remain faithfully within the system of presuppositions and principles that constitutes an elite consensus, a system so powerful as to be internalized largely without awareness. However, the same urge and need that gave rise to Fordism as a means of organizing industrialism as an expression of the Americanized world-view inform the global play of mass media – particularly global electronic media – today.

The standard bearers of this implicit exercise to represent the world in the American image are also the pioneers of the direct broadcast technology era. Rupert Murdoch and Ted Turner characterize the dominance and universalization of the US-centric electronic media. Murdochism, in a generic sense, is to this first flush of the global information revolution what Fordism was to the later phase of industrialism. And as the information society is still in the process of being organized, its formative elements comprise both the technology of the mass media and how that technology is consumed by the masses. The evolving technology of mass media does offer the scope to break free of a leviathan structure that straddles the globe. The convergence of the main sectors of the information era – broadcasting and cinema, print and publishing, and the computer industry – as well as the ongoing integration of video and computer and the use of cyberspace, all make the emerging technology one of a dynamics of diversification. This does not lend itself easily to containment or straitjacketing into any uniform, universal idiom, but then the development priorities of a major portion of the world tend to keep the benefit of this technological advantage at bay. And therein lies the paradox of our times.

The technology of the information revolution is accessible to us in the developing world almost simultaneously as it emerges in the west, unlike the industrial revolution experience which left us struggling and straggling behind a vast technology gap. Indeed there would seem to be a historical opportunity here to quantum-leap the technological hiatus and proceed almost abreast of the west into the information era. But real and imaginary concerns about appropriate paths of development keep us from decisively converting technology to our advantage. Meanwhile, as we demur, and remain tentative and reactive in our response to technology, the lead on the other side again threatens to leave us behind. The liberating potential of the information technology thus goes unrealized by default.

The haphazard growth of the electronic media in India, in both the government and private sectors, typifies this ambivalent and reactive attitude of the state. The mushrooming of cable in response to DBS technology was largely ignored until it impinged on political and electoral prospects. The belated intervention in the form of a Cable Act (1995), which continues to be a paper exercise, has hardly made any difference, in terms of regulation or quality standardization, to the situation on the ground. Meanwhile, the push and pull of the market, and the entry of foreign and big Indian business have made the scene murkier. Similarly, in the name of comprehensive media legislation, satellite television too hangs in the balance; the initial spurt of independent indigenous initiative seems to be facing a growing challenge from global media sharks, and, with the government inexplicably shy of ensuring a level playing field, it is anyone's guess which way the balance will tilt. The state appears unsure even about the measures it has taken, as if not willing to go the whole hog. Thus there is a current governmental formulation on the use of DTH encrypters – which is rightly a deterrent against any immediate entry of DTH technology into the country – that leaves everyone guessing about whether it means denial or delay, and whether, in either case, it is a sell-out to this or that media lobby.

In fact, the government's *bona fides* in this field tend to be suspect because they set out the electronic media for special treatment. There is a lot of hair-splitting when it comes to recognizing the electronic media, which purveys information as much as entertainment, as part of the fourth estate. And while the government is fairly categorical in assuring the print media that it will not brook any foreign investment or participation in that sector, there are no such protective noises when it comes to the electronic media. There is similar hair-splitting about regulation (as against control), overlooking the fact that in just about any country in the world – and most notably in the 'mother of all democracies', the United States – there are strong guidelines in place in this vital sector. Thus the electronic media mayhem in India continues, leaving the state trying to cope with it.

At the same time, given the nature of the current Indian polity and the composition of the United Front government, crucial issues pertaining to this area have been thrown up in the public domain, however belatedly. Hints of collusion and spurious efforts at creating a *fait accompli* by backdoor entry were evident in the initial Foreign Investment Promotion Board (FIPB) nod given by the Industry Ministry to a Murdoch venture setting up a fully owned cable distribution and software generation company in India. The move was aborted when the Information Ministry woke up to what was happening behind its back and the Cabinet Committee set aside the proposal. But as the government moves to introduce comprehensive media legislation in the budget session of Parliament, hectic behind-the-scenes lobbying seems to have hijacked meaningful discourse on the issue. An Indian variant of manufacturing consent among the foreign players seeking entry, and the indigenous channel that is part of or has the backing of a political party and sections of the government, seems to be at play. And while the initial stance of the nodal Information and Broadcasting Ministry – or at least of the Minister – seems defiantly set against such a pushover (even if it is couched in terms of defence of Doordarshan), it remains to be seen whether it will not be eroded by arguments that cleverly confuse globalization in the media with economic liberalization. Indeed it is a kind of disingenuity where the comprador mentality of the Murdochites is sought to be passed off, even celebrated, as advocacy of a free information regime – or even a freer world. The new colonies of the information era would be those that offer at once the best scope for cheap software as material and large-sized markets. From an Americanized world-view, India qualifies eminently as a vast media hinterland.

First published in *Frontline*, 21 February 1997.

For Democratic Media Space

Information without transformation is just gossip. – Tarzie Vittachi

The space for rural India has shrunk so drastically in the television dispensation that has come to be since the mid-1980s, that there is hardly any evidence today of that vast hinterland and its preponderant society and culture on television screens across the country. Were one to deduce India purely from the collective contemporary televisual experience, one would come up with a vast city-state – much as envisioned by Plato or Aristotle – with a premium on the good life for the privileged, which was also the dominant middle class.

Television's known and demonstrative role in rearranging our sense of time and space, fragmenting our cognitive faculty, is compounded, in this context, by literally pushing into oblivion the overwhelming reality of India, which is rural India, so that it becomes a dark mass that exists around and outside the four corners of the television frame. No voices from that darkness really register on this screen; conversely, no concern for what goes on out there is allowed to disturb the cocooned relationship that the viewer and the viewed have forged between themselves. The screen has become the wish-fulfilling touchstone of the appetites and aspirations of that burgeoning middle class, which, in neo-colonial terms, is the counterpart of the comprador mentality that looks up to the universally flaunted value systems of the supreme colonizer of our times – the United States of America. The aggressive and almost self-propelled process of colonization itself is all the more insidious because it is not so much in the physical realm of a land or its natural resources, but in the mind of the people.

The wayward trajectory of the global media in the overarching scheme of globalization has been the subject of a number of informed analyses and critical studies. These not only confirm our worst suspicions, but also offer us useful insights into the shift in the role and purpose of the media as privileged sections of human civilization settle into the information age. Noam Chomsky, in his work (co-authored with Edward Herman) with the self-explanatory title, *Manufacturing Consent* (1988), exposes the implicit and illicit collusion between the US administration and the US media in promoting and perpetuating a US-centric view of the world, and an active pursuit of interventionist foreign policy that subscribes to that view.

A study by Robert McChesney (also co-authored with Edward Herman, 2001) points to the appropriation of the global media by some three or four dozen large transnational corporations through a spate of acquisitions, mergers and joint ventures, and the creation of oligopolistic markets. In another work, *Rich Media, Poor Democracy* (2000), McChesney works the theme of the converse relationship between the prosperity of the media and that of democracy in the US, in a context where hypercommercialized content limits the ability of Americans to act as informed citizens. Ben Bagdikian, in his classic study titled *The Media Monopoly* (1983), shows how the ten top US corporations control almost everything we see, hear and read – so that the US, in addition to its self-arrogated role of policing the world, casts itself as a centralized corporate ministry of information, not unlike many totalitarian dictatorships. To counter this alarming trend, Bagdikian urges grassroots activism and a return to public broadcast philosophy.

The French scholar Pierre Bourdieu in his slim but profound analysis, *On Television and Journalism* (1988), points to the agenda-setting role of television, and observes how we are getting closer and closer to the point where the social world is primarily described – and in a sense prescribed – by television. He and others have also looked at television's innate tendency to be trivial and reductive; its complicity in bestowing counterfeit intellectualism on those unable to acquire that status by right or merit; its helpless dependence on the ratings game; and the paradox of standardization and homogenization in content – rather than difference and variety – that competition engenders.

Much of this discourse on television and the media seems also in general to assume, with Francis Fukuyama (in his latest book, *The Great Disruption*, 1999), that the transition to an information society has already been made and that the tenets of a new post-industrial age are operative. In this new economy, Fukuyama observes,

> services increasingly displace manufacturing as a source of wealth. Instead of working in a steel mill or an automobile factory, the typical worker in an information society has a job in a bank, software firm, restaurant, university or social service agency. The role of information and intelligence, embodied in both people and increasingly smart machines, becomes pervasive and mental labour tends to replace physical labour.

Fukuyama's characterization of modern society in terms of the great disruption brings to a head a schematic train of thought that emphasizes rupture rather than continuity in history and society, hazarded by empirical society-watchers such as Alvin Toffler who, through a series of works since the 1970s, pushed the idea of a Third Wave of computer-using societies replacing the earlier industrial age, just as the industrial age itself displaced the preceding agricultural era; or Daniel Bell who in 1973 suggested that with the emergence of a new white-collar workforce, the old industrial system is behind us; or, again, the Massachusetts Institute of Technology's Media Lab founder Nicholas Negroponte's dizzy vision of a digitally-taped-and-determined world. This newfangled post-industrial school of thought utilizes, as Dan Schiller (1996) points out,

> its exceptionalist premise (the uniqueness of information and its production) to invoke a comprehensive but indemonstrable historical rupture, and therefore to draw back decisively from the predominating social relations of production and into schematic and false models of social development. Information itself was given an aura of objectivity.

In all of this discourse, moreover, one searches in vain for a linkage that incorporates predominantly rural societies, such as India, into the new scheme of things. Extant media punditry also leaves the preponderant part of the world's largest democracy – that is, rural India – out in the cold.

It would seem that with all its warts and contradictions, global television, which has coopted urban India, is a cultural commodity that circulates in one orbit while rural India continues to plod in another, and ne'er the twain shall meet. Seen thus, modern television in India seems a grand aberration that has missed the bus. At a theoretical level, that television as an instrumentality that mediates modernity can play such tricks on reality has, interestingly, been projected by philosophers such as Feuerbach ([1841] 1989), for whom a distinctive attribute of the present age is that it prefers the sign to the thing signified, the copy to the original, representation to reality, appearance to the essence – so much so that illusion only is sacred, truth profane.

A great insight into this theme is the critique of modern society by the French thinker Guy Debord, who was a product of the Situationist International group that emerged into prominence in the late 1960s. Debord's exposition, titled *The Society of the Spectacle* (1967), almost intuitively captured the essence of images detached from everyday aspects of life, and although the complexity and seemingly far-fetched nature of his ideas saw him largely reviled during his lifetime, there is now a (much-needed) rethinking on their relevance. In societies where modern conditions of production prevail, Debord sets out his proposition, all of life presents itself as an immense accumulation of spectacles. Everything that was directly lived has moved away into a representation. The spectacle, he continues, as the concrete inversion of life is the autonomous movement of the non-living. Debord enthusiasts go to the extent of calling his *Society of the Spectacle* the *Capital* of the new generation, and compare how, just as Marx wrote *Capital* to detail the complex and subtle economic machinations of capitalism, Debord set out to describe the intricacies of its modern incarnation and the means by which it exerts its totalizing control over lived reality.

This autonomous and spiralling growth of an alienative virtual-global middle-class television culture that is at once self-perpetuating and self-serving, and that ignores the peasantry as a class and ruralness as a lived condition, could be seen as facilitated by what economist Prabhat Patnaik, in the realm of the political economy, critiques as a misleading perception of a total retreat of the state. To paraphrase Patnaik in this context, the so-called retreat is a feint that disguises a city-biased intervention by the state and, like in the economy, the information society is witnessing . . . a transition from one paradigm of state intervention to another.

The iron hand of the US administration in systematically pursuing its goal of hegemony in the information era under the velvet glove of free-enterprise championship has been chronicled by Herbert Schiller (in his essay, 'Striving for communication dominance: a half century review', in the collection, *Electronic Empires*, 1998), to illustrate his point that the US (capitalist) state, contrary to many reports, is alive and, if not well, at least still in charge. Schiller also implicitly challenges the rupture or great disruption theorists by pointing to the continuity through the latter half of this century of government initiative, support for and promotion of information and communication policies by the US. Indeed the *cause célèbre* of free flow of information became a convenient alibi for the administration to propel the US into information ascendancy. As early as 1946, Assistant Secretary of State William Benton made it clear that

> the State Department plans to do everything within its power along political or diplomatic lines to break down the artificial barriers to the expansion of private American news agencies, magazines, motion pictures and other media of communications throughout the world. . . . Freedom of the press – and freedom of exchange of information generally – is an integral part of our foreign policy.

An estimated 1 trillion dollars have been spent over the last fifty years to ensure US domination of information technology. The creation of the communications satellite undertaking, COMSAT, was a direct action by the state to elbow out its ally Great Britain, which commanded undersea cable, from the race. In sum, as Schiller observes, the US state has played a pivotal role in achieving and maintaining US global cultural–informational domination over the last fifty years, a domination enduring to this day. This has been a fully conscious and deliberate effort carried out by each administration, from Truman's to Clinton's. State-led growth into global pre-eminence of a US information superstructure puts the US in a position better than any other country to multiply the potency of its hard and soft power resources through information (Nye and Owens, 'America's Information Age', 1996; Joseph S. Nye was formerly Assistant Secretary of Defence for International Affairs and William A. Owens, former Vice-Chairman, Joint Chiefs of Staff).

The use of the free flow of information slogan by the US for its hegemonic design is, needless to say, a mockery of the debate on the New World Information and Communications Order of the 1970s or the McBride Commission Report's

(1980) concern about an information-rich North versus a South at the receiving end. That discourse too is hijacked as new and emerging markets (read developing countries) are road-rollered into submission through the mechanism of the World Trade Organization (WTO) and a series of agreements to liberalize trade and information technology (signed in December 1996), telecommunications (February 1997), and financial services (December 1997) under its auspices.

Even if the latest round of the WTO in Seattle was stymied by a combination of grassroots activism – achieved, interestingly, through use of the tools of information technology, including the internet and Palm Pilot – and organized resistance by the developing countries, the fact that North American markets are drying up and that relatively stricter regulatory systems are in place in the European Union makes the South, with some 2.5 billion television consumers, an urgent destination for corporate conglomerates of the information sector. And within the South, Asia, where the growth of cable and satellite television is projected to leap to 206 million units by the year 2004 (from 44 million in 1994), is a prime market.

A study in contrast would be the Indian state's total lack of any initiative and largely helpless response in the new order of cable and satellite television, especially since the advent of direct broadcast (DBS) technology in the mid-1980s. Taking advantage of the silence in the over-a-century-old and largely obsolete Indian Telegraph Act (1885) on the reception of satellite signals and their distribution through cable, a rash of small cable operators surfaced, setting up dishes in their backyards or rooftops and distributing foreign channels (Cable News Network or CNN, and the Gulf War gave their business a head start) to the cluster of homes served by them. The rapid proliferation of this cable television operation in turn soon drew indigenous television entrepreneurs, with Hindi (Zee) and southern regional channels (Sun and Asianet) showing the way in the beginning of the 1990s.

Over this last decade, the number of television channels received in India has risen to over 70, even as larger, corporatized cable networks tend to take over or replace the smaller operators who set the ball rolling in the first place. Television's share of media ad-spend has also risen progressively to reach 40 per cent, in keeping with the trend in the neighbouring Southeast Asian economies, with the privately owned satellite channels eating considerably into the revenues of the state-owned Doordarshan channels. This cablewala-led transformation of the television scenario in India – with its inbuilt city bias in networking and programming terms – has become a *fait accompli* to which the government continues to react in confused and tokenist terms.

With the perceptible, if unstated, shift by Doordarshan from its public broadcast mandate, to compete with the plethora of independent channels by imitating their formula of commercially successful programming, and with the commercial channels all drawing from the same bag of programme-mix, we have a near-uniformity of fare across state- and private-owned television which negates the pluralism that such a development should have engendered. Switching channels, one gets more and more of the same – so that, by the law of diminishing returns, more begins to be less. This sameness is limiting, not only in terms of the audience addressed (a city-bred middle class), but also in terms of the horizon of information the media survey.

Under identical pressures of ratings and raking in revenues, the competition between channels becomes a frenetic wild goose chase that throws up little that is new or different. Even news ,or that whole area we call television journalism, is no exception to this behaviour; if anything, peer pressure and a vying-for-the-same-story syndrome ensure that from the order of the headlines to what is centre-staged as current affairs over a given period of time, no channel departs from the essential content of its competitors. It is, as Bourdieu (cited earlier) describes, a circular circulation of information among the channels, a game of mirrors reflecting one another that produces a formidable effect of mental closure.

An insensitive, extreme manifestation of such behaviour, of course, is the prerogative of western, particularly US, media, where hours, days, weeks and months of prime television time are consumed in titillating coverage of an O.J. Simpson case or the romantic gore of Diana's death or *l'affaire* Monica Lewinsky – even as mass-scale starvation and death in Somalia, or the ravages of ethnic strife and war in Bosnia, or human suffering on a similar scale in any part of the world other than the First World pass them by, meriting only casual and certainly far less passionate attention.

The electronic media in this part of the world too, however, avidly share this voyeuristic interest in, and trial by media of, persons who have little to do with the context or lives of the public here. This tailism is no doubt partly dictated by the one-way informational flow and the dependence on foreign visual news agencies, but it also betrays the urge to belong to that metropolitan culture and its inner-city preoccupations.

If this craving for bonding with a pan-national, television-generated community (which could be characterized, in Fukuyama's terms, as investment in social capital) is endemic to the game of globalizing information, what is more worrisome is the manner in which intellectuals in society – who, one imagines, would be a *cordon sanitaire* or a court of last resort against the numbing and dumbing effect of television – fall a prey to the lure of the media. Indeed intellectuals should at best be adversarial to, or at least keep a safe distance from, mass media. But the growing tendency of intellectuals to flirt with the media, or vice versa, is taking its toll on intellectualism itself on the one hand, and infusing the media with a false sense of power over intellectuals on the other. The problem of the mass media making inroads into intellectual space is one that exercises intellectuals themselves.

In the words of Jacques Derrida (1992):

> What certain academics should be warned against is the temptation of the media. What I mean by this is not the normal desire to address a wider public, because there can be in that desire an authentically democratic and legitimate political concern. On the contrary, I call temptation of the media the compulsion to misuse the privilege of public declaration in a social space that extends far beyond the normal circuits of intellectual discussion. Such misuse constitutes a breach of confidence, an abuse of authority – in a word, an abuse of power.

When academics seek or accept the imprimatur of intellectualism outside of their community or peer assessment and from the mass media, especially television which can quickfix fast-thinking and glib-mouthed thinkers and subject experts in the course of a single chat show, not only is the domain of original thought and serious study compromised (already, in India, the honorific of a doctorate has been devalued with politicians routinely having the title affixed to their names by one obliging university or the other), but their moral stature and power to move against the current or oppose the herd mentality is also rendered vulnerable.

This media-induced heteronomy (understood as the loss of autonomy by being subject to external influence) in academia is a matter of serious concern to Bourdieu (*On Television and Journalism*, 1998). A good historian, he says, is someone good historians call a good historian. But heteronomy begins when someone who is not recognized as a historian (a historian who talks on television about history, for instance) gives an opinion about historians – and is listened to. He cites the study of the French literary field during the Occupation by Gisèle Sapiro, which shows that the more people are recognized by their peers and are therefore rich in specific capital, the more likely they are to resist. Conversely, the more heteronomous they are in their literary practices, meaning drawn to market criteria, the more inclined they are to collaborate. Bourdieu's verdict is that such heteronomous individuals constitute the Trojan horse through which heteronomy – that is, the laws of the market and the economy – is brought into the field.

Where the intellectual community stands, or should stand, vis-à-vis the mass media is important not only because that is the reservoir of knowledge that can make sense of and, if necessary, intervene and counter the superficial excesses of information in the new era (one should hold steadfast to the distinction between knowledge and information in this new context), but also in terms of locating the media in the public sphere as against the private or reserved space intellectuals occupy.

In his classic definition of the public sphere, which merits being quoted at length to appreciate the total concept, Jürgen Habermas (1974) calls it

> a realm of our social life in which something approaching public opinion can be formed. Access is guaranteed to all citizens. A portion of the public sphere comes into being in every conversation in which private individuals assemble to form a public body. They then behave neither like business or professional people transacting private affairs, nor like members of a constitutional order subject to the legal constraints of a state bureaucracy. Citizens behave as a public body when they confer in an unrestricted fashion – that is, with the guarantee of freedom of assembly and association and the freedom to express and publish their opinions – about matters of general interest. In a large public body this kind of communication requires specific means for transmitting information and influencing those who receive it. Today [1974], newspapers and magazines, radio and television are the media of the public sphere. We speak of the political public sphere in contrast, for instance, to the literary one, when public discussion deals with objects connected to the activity of the state.

The way the mass media have actually turned out, however, their public sphere identity is putative rather than real, driven as they are by the market and catering as they do only to the concerns of this market-based consumer. This is even more so as the media becomes globalized, and for those already functioning as such – like CNN or the British Broadcasting Corporation (BBC) World Service – the viewership size actually shrinks further to a minuscule elite across the world. The globalized part of the print media too is as elitist (and must know English, to boot), with studies showing that the average gross personal income of subscribers to *The Financial Times* outside of the United Kingdom, numbering some 130,000, is $120,000 and that of the 64,000 readers getting *The Wall Street Journal* in Europe is a staggering $196,000.

The odd attempts to realize the media as a democratized public sphere, even if they have been isolated instances at the fringe – like the experiment with Aboriginal television in Australia or the ongoing tussle between the indigenous Maori people and the Government of New Zealand for control over the airwaves – become redeeming case studies to cling to in this scenario.

The community television initiative in Ernabella, southern Australia, in 1985 was entirely by local aboriginals who raised the funds among themselves (a surcharge of 10 cents on all soft-drink sales by the local store raised a good part of the capital), and evolved a mix of programmes that reflected their folklore, magical rites and local problems which they produced on their own, as well as other programmes relating to aboriginal issues acquired from media institutions specializing in this area or recorded off mainstream telecasts such as those of the Australian Broadcasting Corporation (ABC).

Although the success of the Ernabella model inspired other and larger schemes for an alternative aboriginal television regime in Australia, particularly under the Broadcasting in Aboriginal Communities Scheme (BRACS), they turned out to be accommodative in nature rather than a space for aboriginal assertion. A more ambitious scheme by the Central Australian Aboriginal Media Association (CAAMA) to intervene in the federal government's licensing of satellite television in the Northern Territory became, initially, a *cause célèbre* of sorts – especially in the process of its struggle in the mid-1980s to muster the $6 million required for the licence fee. The Imparja service, as it was called, catered to over 60 per cent of all aboriginal groups and looked like the new hope of aboriginal articulation; but within a few years (and the beginning of the 1990s) the hope had turned sour as the station was driven by the market into dependence on subsidy by the federal government, and its programming staff and content became overwhelmingly white.

The co-founder and director of CAAMA, an aboriginal woman, who quit her post in 1991, summed up the experience:

> Our original aim was to get some control over the satellite so that we could use it to suit our purposes. . . . We wanted to see a lot of black face, people speaking our local languages. . . . We were especially interested in using it for educational purposes . . . but look at Imparja now, it's no different to any other commercial TV station. . . . In a way, it has become what we tried to stop.

In New Zealand the Maori people, who constitute 30 per cent of the population, are staking their claim for equal participation in, and control over, use of the airwaves with the whites, or *pakehas* as they are called. Theirs is a larger and more original case, based as it is on their right under the Treaty of Waitangi of 1840, signed between their chiefs and the British Crown, which gives them total authority over all their resources. The interesting thrust of the Maori argument seems to be that the airwaves over a country are as much part of its people's resource as land or any other natural resource, and that entitlement to it is automatic under the Treaty. Indeed the New Zealand government is not about to buy this argument, and it had in fact sought to preempt any dilution of its control over broadcasting by a piece of legislation which, while talking about the need for representative public broadcasting, forbade resort to the judicial process to correct any distortions. The whole issue continues to be hotly contested in the Waitangi Tribunal and other courts, and even though winning the battle for the Maoris' cause is an uphill task, their demand opens up a whole new possibility of a basic right to airwaves. In such redefinitions and reassertions seem to lie the clue towards renegotiating a truly democratic media space.

First published in *Frontline*, 21 January 2000.

Television: An Extension of Our Times

We are, on the one hand, told that we have stepped out of the industrial age into the era of the information or communications revolution. On the other, we are warned that all talk of such an abrupt transition is, at best, simplistic and, at worst, a devious ploy to undo the scientific, materialistic underpinnings of history. Be that as it may, what does seem apparent is that information and communications technology (ICT) is in the driver's seat, even if the direction in which it is taking the world is not clear. It is also fairly evident that the industrial revolution was patently unequal, as much in its process as in its result, providing the tools of mechanized production to an industrializing North and denying it to a resource-exploited, often colonized South, thereby creating the much talked-about, yawning gap between the two. The instruments of the ICT revolution were, in contrast, accessible to the developing countries close on the heels of their prototyping in the developed world. The technologies of cinema, broadcast and the computer came to us almost on par with the west, raising fond hopes of a historic opportunity to bridge the North–South divide.

The Direct Broadcast Satellite (DBS) technology too was available to India and South Asia almost simultaneously as in the west, in the mid-1980s. It was the CNN offering of the Gulf War of 1991 – a war whose conduct and coverage tended to merge in popular consciousness as a grand militaristic video game – that gave a fillip to Cable and Satellite (C&S) in the region. The initiative came from below, from the small-time cable operator whose grey-market entrepreneurship set the cabling rolling. If there was no law yet that enabled or regulated C&S TV, there was no law against it either. The only piece of legislation that had some bearing on the situation was the century-old Indian Telegraph Act of 1885, which forbade transmission of wireless signals except by, or with the explicit permission of, a state agency. But the Act was silent on the reception of wireless signals. Cashing in on that silence, the cable-wala, as he came to be called, quickly strung cables across rows of houses, set up a ramshackle head-end and control room somewhere in between, and brought images of the war to his subscribers who, until then, were on an almost exclusive diet of terrestrial, state-run, Doordarshan programming. It must, however, be pointed out that this groundswell of a cable revolution came at a time when the state-run television itself was breaking out of its paternalistic pedagogic mould, and allowing independent producers reasonable space and say in what came to be identified as the glasnost and perestroika phase of Doordarshan – perhaps its finest moments, just before it was swamped by a host of independent satellite channels.

If the modest neighbourhood cable operator showed the way, he was soon to lose out to a second wave of organized cable networks, who acquired a formal 'right of way' for cabling from local governments or authorities, built large head-end farms that housed several dishes, and catered to hundreds and soon thousands of homes from each such facility. The big players, some of them global and already in the channels business in the region, were soon on the cable scene, and, through a series of buy-outs, mergers and forced strategic alliances, established their monopolistic sway over distribution. Through it all and well until the recent move towards a Convergence Act, which conceals more than it reveals, the state remained a bemused spectator, alternately marvelling at the freewheeling growth of this new sector and ruing the absence of any regulation. Even in the early 1990s, agents of established and aspiring multinational corporations (MNCs) in the mass media were active in new and emerging markets, with an eager eye for acquisitions and alliances. With Europe and North America saturated, and much of the rest of the world having stringently regulated information regimes or insufficient purchasing power to sustain a mass media free market, they zeroed in on Asia and particularly India – where a 'free sky' policy prevailed by default – as the preferred investment destination. Indigenous capital and intitiative in the region were soon striking deals with the visitors. The very first channels to have a larger South Asian presence, Zee and Star TV, were quickly drawn into the Murdoch orbit. Zee's Subhash Chandra worked out a favourable, if complicated arrangement with Murdoch's News Corp, with a buy-back option on shares which he exercised in 1999. The Hong Kong Chinese entrepreneur Li-Ka Shing, who launched the pan-regional AsiaSat broadcasting satellite platform, and on it, the channel Star TV (Satellite Television Asian Region), was to hand it over on a golden platter to Murdoch.

The trajectory that propels the mass media into an MNC business also predetermines its content. Wrested from its region-specific or 'national' moorings, the cultural product tends to become fairly homogenized, standardised fare. While invoking the alibis of free market demand and competition, an inexorable supply-side process is set in motion. Indeed, 'Murdochism', in this generic sense, is a throwback to 'Fordism', which was the hallmark of American industrialism. Henry Ford's car factory at Detroit exemplified the latter phase of the industrial revolution, just as Manchester and textile manufacture typified the earlier period. The assembly-line production method, period-specific planning and organizational principles introduced here were to become a pervasive model of twentieth-century industrialism, so much so that even Stalin relied on the Fordist model in the industralization of the Soviet Union, even if Charlie

Chaplin's brilliant caricature of it, as the worker programmed to fix nuts and bolts on the frenetic assembly line in *Modern Times*, exposed its dehumanizing character. Ford's cryptic offer that 'any customer can have a car painted any colour that he wants as long as it is black' sums up the notional rather than real choice in such a dispensation.

Signals from the Skies

In much the same manner, Murdochism, in a generic sense, sets the agenda and the menu for television today. There is a makebelieve of choice in the fare purveyed while the reality is that a set of stereotypes, which emphasizes cosmetic 'commonalities' of a virtual class of global television viewers and ignores or wishes away the ground reality of 'differences' in cultural context and experience, is perpetuated. This homogenizing thrust is reinforced by the ongoing 'convergence' of the three broad sectors of (i) broadcasting and the movie industry, (ii) the newspaper and publishing industry and (iii) computer and cyberspace – all of which could, in the not-too-distant future, be delivered to the consumer on a single screen. There is then the rather intimidating prospect of a supervening leviathan-like information structure encompassing people across the world, irrespective of national boundaries, and regional, cultural or social differences.

The collapse of the Soviet Union and much of the erstwhile Eastern Bloc was hastened as much by DBS TV signals from the skies as by the contradictions on the ground. Satellite signals and footprints did not respect geopolitical boundaries, and it was no longer possible to limit the medium or its message to the confines of the nation-state. The American serial *Dallas* and its received image in the former German Democratic Republic is a case in point. The good-life-in-the-west projected by the serial, a life of runaway conspicuous consumption, became a critical reference for viewers in East Germany (where it was beamed from West Germany and widely viewed) about the American way of life. As early as 1982, the French Culture Minister, Jack Lang, was calling *Dallas* cultural imperialism. And, even as Marxists saw in the excesses of *Dallas* a critique of capitalism, the average East German contrasted it with his own system, where the basic necessities were provided by the State, but where he felt he was denied the leisure-bound, luxurious life his western counterpart enjoyed. The revolution of rising expectations that brought the Berlin Wall crumbling down soon yielded to the harsh reality of East Germans becoming virtual refugees in a new, unified Germany.

However different the social and cultural context in South Asia, the fragility of a system that denies basic necessities to the vast majority of the population, even as consumerism on television further alienates its miniscule beneficiaries from the vast silent mass, cannot be overstated. The sheer increase in the number of satellite TV channels over the last decade has not meant any real pluralism in content, democratization in terms of access or empowerment, or any real advance in enabling an Indian identity of diversity. What we get as we switch channels is more and more of the same so that, to wit, by the law of diminishing returns, more becomes less. John Tusa, former managing director of the BBC, sees this new television experience as a series of paradoxes:

> more choice but less diversity; more information, but less knowledge; more action but less news; more gratification but less satisfaction: more viewers but fewer audiences; more entertainment but less engagement; more immediacy but less depth; more in the present, less in the past; more unto the minute, but less tradition; more on demand, less to wait for.

If this trend continues, Tusa goes on,

> then television and radio would have largely ceased to be media of expression and communication as we have come to know them, and would instead have become more like any other public utility. TV and radio on tap; programmes on demand; running hot and cold information, entertainment and education . . . gas, water, electricity, the media – all will be just a question of guaranteeing a safe, reliable and massively increasing supply at ever-decreasing cost.

There is growing confusion about whether television, even as a news medium, is an agency of representation or a consumable in the market. It seems to be both. The wall-to-wall, wraparound presence of the medium today makes it more and more difficult to draw a distinction between a reality out there and its representation in the TV box. It is, rather, all about a composite representative reality that is the given, and that is all-inclusive and all-consuming. There are echoes here of Feuerbach in the nineteenth century (in his preface to the second edition of *The Essence of Christianity*), when he says that the present age prefers the 'sign to the thing signified, the copy to the original, representation to reality, the appearance to the essence', and concludes that 'illusion only is sacred, truth profane'. 'Nay sacredness', Feuerbach elaborates, 'is held to be enhanced in proportion as truth decreases and illusion increases so that the highest degree of illusion comes to be the highest degree of sacredness.' Heidegger later observed that a distinctive attribute of the twentieth century is that it sees the world in terms of representations. It is relevant here, by way of elaboration, to invoke Roland Barthes' concept of 'meaning' – even the Eiffel Tower being described by him as a 'pure, virtually empty, sign that means everything'. Barthes makes a case for meaning in its own right; he is opposed to the idea of depth hiding any significant or unravelled meaning and declares, 'myth hides nothing'. Depth and height become irrelevant, the surface reality is all that matters. As Susan Sontag put it, 'In the post Nietzchean tradition there are neither depths nor heights, there are only various kinds of surface, of spectacle.' Barthes privileges the spectacle as 'the universal category through whose forms the world is seen'.

The spectacle as the driving force of modern society was the obsessive and singular theme of Guy Debord, one of the best minds of the Situationist International movement of the late 1960s. Debord's *Society of the Spectacle*, written in 1967, has since remained a relatively obscure piece of work. It is, however, being resituated now as a prescient forecast of a TV-driven society, even being called the 'Capital of the new generation'. Debord's central proposition is that, 'in societies where modern conditions of production prevail, all of life presents itself as an accumulation of spectacles'. He further notes, 'everything that was directly lived has moved away into representation'.

The accumulation of spectacles Debord talks about is there for all to see. There is increasing awareness of what this visual clutter – the complete space it occupies and the frenetic pace it dictates – is doing to our lives and our sensibilities. In a refreshing new study, *Media Unlimited*, Todd Gitlin, professor of culture, journalism and sociology at New York University, points out how the United States is caught in the maelstrom of this image torrent, and how American images and sounds become omnipresent as American imperialism.

The disjuncture between lived reality and represented (or mediated) reality is also a function of the way the medium works, its rules of the game, and the peculiar way in which peer and market pressures operate on it. When, for example, we observe in the course of a daily editorial review in a TV or newspaper organization that we have 'missed' a story, what we mean is not there was a news development which all of us failed to identify or report. Indeed, we pursue our profession in the unerring faith that if none of us saw it or reported it, it did not exist – reminiscent of the Sumerian idea as far back as 2000 BC that what is not recorded does not exist ('*Quod non est acts, no est in memdo*'). What we therefore mean when we refer to a 'missed' story is that another channel or newspaper had a story that we did not. That this is a rare eventuality is itself a tribute to the consensus, cross-checking and mutual agreement that inform much of the news that makes its way to the news-desk. The 'press club' syndrome plays its own role in ensuring that the bulk of the news is the same across channels and newspapers, and that barring the occasional exclusives and scoops, there are no surprises.

Increase in the numbers of newspapers or channels makes little difference to the way this game is played, and does not necessarily mean any significant increase in the volume or variety of news output. It does not widen our news horizons. On the contrary, as the distinguished French sociologist Pierre Bordieu points out in his incisive study, *On Television and Journalism*, it becomes a game of mirrors with every channel or newspaper making sure that it has what the rest have. As a result, says Bordieu, there is only 'circular circulation of information', which leads to a 'formidable effect of mental closure'. Dealing with such standardized fare, moreover, journalists often tend to pride themselves over small differences in the detail or treatment of the same story – differences which may have escaped the viewer's attention altogether. Peer pressure thus homogenizes, rather than differentiates, news content.

The Medium's Temptations

In a post-Cold War, unipolar world, the so-called globalization of the information sector is tantamount to accession and celebration of an Americanized worldview, which incorporates regional variants to the extent that they subscribe to the larger scheme of things. The process by which that larger scheme is forged in the United States has been described in the path-breaking work by Noam Chomsky and Edward Hermann, tellingly titled *Manufacturing Consent*. There is in the US, the authors argue, an implicit nexus between the mainstream media and the administration in 'manufacturing' consent on crucial matters of war and foreign policy, which safeguards the US-centric global agenda. They point out that the US media invariably subscribe to a 'propaganda model', which is arrived at through a series of news 'filters'. There are five such definitive filters: (1) size, concentrated ownership, owner wealth and profit orientation of the dominant mass media firms; (2) advertising as the primary source of income; (3) the dependence of the media on information provided by the government, business and 'experts' funded by these primary sources and agents of power; (4) 'flak' as a means of disciplining the media; and (5) anti-communism as a national religion and control mechanism. The acquisitions and mergers that mark the telecommunications industry, the Hollywoodization that has virtually killed or subsumed every other cinema in the world, the neo-colonial drive by the US into new information markets (South and Southeast Asia and China) – all point to all-round American ascendancy in the information age. From Truman to Bush, the US has pursued supremacy in the information sector as a conscious plank of its foreign policy, spending over three trillion dollars since the Second World War to achieve this.

Today, in the aftermath of the iniquitous and shameful invasion of Iraq by the Coalition of the Willing – the label 'Coalition of the Killing' is of course more appropriate – we are left stunned by another spectacle of death and destruction. TV screens gave us a ringside view of this gladiatorial display by the US, the UK and their disparate gang of flunkies. What, however, we will eventually not be able to get over is the alacrity with which the dubious category of 'embedded journalists' became complicit in the war game. The soldiers in uniform were almost sedate compared to these embedded eager-beavers in fatigues from CNN or BBC, and their counterparts at the studio end, who let their excitement run amuck, throwing all norms of credible – not to mention unbiased or even-handed – reporting to the desert winds. They were as breathless about the Bedouin tribes they passed in the desert as about the false claims about the taking of Basra or Um Qasr, in take one itself. Faced with competing and conflicting versions – because there were alternative versions like Al Jazeera and Abu Dhabi TV for a change – they were glib in putting out constructs that explained their mis-reporting in the first instance: it's not that Basra was not or could not be taken, but there were Baathist elements holding out, using the people as human shield; it's not that the people did not want to hail the invaders as liberators, but they were wary after the 1991 experience when, after such a demonstration of support, the US forces left, and left them high and dry to face the wrath of the regime. But now that Saddam has been ousted and they have the run of the place, why are the crowds chanting that the US troops go home? Because, you must understand, they have had a miserable life all these years of sanctions and deprivation; it takes time to get them used to democracy…

And through this charade every appearance of Saddam Hussein, whether on Iraqi TV or in a Baghdad neighbourhood, as instantly and invariably suspect, until the prolonged absence of any categoric denial by Pentagon would evoke a half-hearted suggestion that it could indeed be Saddam and not his dupe. Every appearance of the BBC reporter in Baghdad was accompanied with a reminder to us by the studio anchor that his movements and his report are monitored by the Iraqi authorities; on the other hand, we were never told that the embedded journalists had undertaken to follow a list of over 50 rules, set out by the coalition army, in their reporting.

As the invasion progressed, the camaraderie between the officers in uniform and the embedded media mongers became demonstrably more and more infectious in the official briefings and short field interviews, so much so that you often had brigadiers or generals suggesting that such and such a development or achievement for the invading forces would be 'a good news story", and the reporter nodding in agreement. The montages and signature tunes that herald each fresh bulletin or special report of the invasion on CNN and BBC have the flourish of conquest; what follows furthers that mood. After the dust settles in Iraq, a bout of frank media-bashing seems very much in order. Shooting the messenger is no doubt an unpardonable crime from the media point of view. But when the messenger begins to shoot from the hip?

One can, of course, turn the whole argument around and ask why one should expect CNN or BBC to be any different in times of war than the Indian or Pakistani media and their respective coverages of, say, the Kargil war. After all, American and British troops in Iraq are pretty much their boys on the war front. Why do we assume supranational objectivity by the western media when our own approach has always been intensely nationalistic? Indeed the hoary tradition and legacy of the Indian press we cherish is its nationalistic beginnings and the role it played in the independence movement. Post-independence, we have continued to equate the journalistic calling as the call of the nation, unmindful of whose call it actually turns out to be. Come globalization, and we are suddenly confused. The nation-state, we are told, is dead in the era of

Direct Broadcast Satellite communications, because these satellite signals do not respect geographical boundaries. But by a sleight of hand, the US state is the only nation-state around. Its preoccupations become the obsession of the media in the rest of the world. This process is abetted by the fact that news sources and footage for television privilege the American way of life over the rest. Thus, in a process of fatuous tailism, O.J. Simpson and Monica Lewinsky become prime-time obsessions for days on end as much in India as in the US, even as pathetically malnourished children in Somalia or elsewhere in Africa, or starvation deaths in Andhra or Orissa in our own country, move out of the headlines and eventually out of the news altogether, during the same period.

The recent emergence of the Gulf-based satellite TV channel, Al Jazeera, as an alternative voice at odds with such an orchestrated media and the arm-twisting that goes on behind the scenes to bring it in step with the rest, has raised a whole set of new and interesting issues that the media manipulation machinery in the US is working overtime to tackle. Robert McChesney, in his study (also co-authored with Edward Herman), points to the appropriation of the global media by some three or four dozen large transnational corporations through a spate of acquisitions, mergers and joint ventures, and the creation of oligopolisitc markets. In another work, *Rich Media, Poor Democracy*, McChesney works the theme of the converse relationship between the prosperity of the media and the prospect of democracy in the US, in a context where the hypercommercialized content limits the ability of Americans to act as informed citizens. Ben Bagdikian, in his classic study, *The Media Monopoly*, shows how the ten top American corporations control almost everything we see, hear and read, so that the US, in addition to its self-arrogated role of policing the world, casts itself as a centralized corporate 'ministry of information', not unlike many totalitarian dictatorships.

The breathless tempo of television journalism tends to make it largely an unremitting succession of conditioned reflexes with little time or space for fresh thought or a logical chain of reasoning. The tyranny of sound bites reduces it to a language game that cannot handle complex or difficult concepts. Todd Gitlin cites a study done by Kiku Asdotto in 1998 showing that the average weekly sound bite on US TV networks from a presidential candidate shrank from 42.3 seconds in 1968 to 9.8 seconds in 1988 and to 7.8 seconds in 2000. A major media reform in the public interest advocated by Ben Bagdikian is the mandatory provision of prime-time opportunity to local and national candidates standing for elections, with fifteen-minute minimums to avoid slick sound bites with little content. Viewers conditioned by mainstreaming messages also tend to take the sting out of political debates. In a study of televised political rallies in Italy in the 1960s, Umberto Eco shows how, in an attempt to package proposals suitably for the average TV viewer, the representative of the Communist Party ended up saying pretty much the same things as the campaigner of the rival Christian

Democratic Party. The differences between the two all but disappeared as each tried to be as reassuring and neutral as possible.

Much of the discourse on television and other media seems to assume, with Francis Fukuyama (in his latest book, *The Great Disruption*), that the transition into the 'information society' has already been made and that the tenets of the new, post-industrial age are operative. In this new economy, observes Fukuyama,

> services increasingly displace manufacturing as a source of wealth. Instead of working in a steel mill or an automobile factory, the typical worker in an information society has a job in a bank, software firm, restaurant, university or social service agency. The role of information and intelligence, embodied in both people and increasingly smart machines, becomes pervasive and mental labour tends to replace physical labour.

The Fukuyama characterization of modern society in terms of a 'great disruption' brings to a head a schematic train of thought that emphasizes rupture rather than continuity in history, put forth by futurist writers like Alvin Toffler who, through a series of works since the 1970s, pushed the idea of a 'Third Wave' of computer-using societies replacing the earlier industrial age, just as the industrial age itself displaced the preceding agricultural era.

Daniel Bell suggested in 1973 that, with the emergence of a new white-collar work force, the old industrial system is behind us; while the MIT Media Lab founder Nicholas Negroponte propagated his dizzy vision of a digitally-taped-and-determined world. All this new-fangled post-industrial school of thought utilizes, as Dan Schiller (1996) points out,

> its exceptionalist premise (the uniqueness of 'information' and its production) to invoke a comprehensive but undemonstrable historical rupture, and therefore to draw back decisively from the predominating social relations of production and into schematic and false models of social development. 'Information' itself was given an aura of objectivity.

Aggressive, intrusive and pervasive television has also made inroads into intellectual and academic space in a manner that is taking its toll on intellectualism on the one hand, and giving the medium a vain sense of power over intellectuals on the other. As Jacques Derrida warns,

> What certain academics should be warned against is the 'temptation of the media'. What I mean by this is not the normal desire to address a wider public, because there can be in that desire an authentically democratic and legitimate political concern. On the contrary, I call temptation of the media the compulsion to misuse the privilege of public declaration in a social space that extends far beyond the normal circuits of intellectual discussion. Such misuse constitutes a breach of confidence, an abuse of authority – in a word, an abuse of power.

When academics seek, or accept, the imprimatur of intellectualism outside of their community or peer group, especially from television which can quickfix fast-thinking and glib 'thinkers' in the course of a single chat show, not only is the domain of original thought and serious study compromised, but their moral stature and power to move against the current is rendered vulnerable. This media-induced heteronomy (or loss of autonomy by being subject to external influence) is explained by Pierre Bordieu thus: 'A good historian is someone good historians call a good historian. But heteronomy . . . begins when someone who is not recognized as a historian (a historian who talks on television on history, for instance) gives an opinion about historians – and is listened to.' He cites the study by Gisele Sapiro of the French literary field during the Occupation which shows that 'the more people are recognized by their peers, and are therefore rich in specific capital, the more likely they are to resist. Conversely the more heteronomous they are in their literary practices, meaning down to market criteria, the more inclined they are to collaborate.' Bourdieu concludes that such individuals 'constitute the Trojan horse through which heteronomy – that is the laws of the market and economy – is brought into the field'.

Noam Chomsky has also pondered on this issue of the appropriation of intellectuals by the mass media as an agent of the state. 'The media', he says,

> can turn to academic experts to provide the perspective that is required by the centres of power, and the university system is sufficiently obedient to external power so that appropriate experts will generally be available to lend the prestige of scholarship to the narrow range of opinion permitted broad expression.

Academia must engage with the media selectively and on its own terms. That, or as Andy Warhol predicted, in the future everyone will be famous for fifteen minutes.

First published as a three-part article in *The Hindu*, 18 May, 25 May and 1 June 2003.

Making Sense of CAS

V. Sridhar interviews Sashi Kumar

Millions of television viewers in the four metropolitan cities await the implementation of the Conditional Access System (CAS) with fear of the unknown. CAS, which is being touted by the government as a mechanism to liberate viewers from the caprices of turf-grabbing cable TV operators, has instead caused fears that viewers are being thrown to the wolves. The deadline for the first phase of implementing CAS is 14 July [2003]. The issue of charges for channels, particularly the pay channels, is only one of many concerns that consumers face. The price and the terms on which viewers will be able to instal set top boxes (STBs) in order to view the pay channels remain an imponderable. Many viewers wonder whether they will be able to view their favourite channels at all.

While these issues rankle viewers, other issues of greater significance have remained largely obscured in the rush to the deadline. Cable TV, which made its appearance in India in the early 1990s and quickly spread across the country, thanks to the enterprise of the local cable TV operator, is now a different kind of business. Its scale, and the presence of almost 100 channels, mean that the small cable TV operator no longer calls the shots. Instead, multi-system operators (MSOs), who act as distribution hubs, have acquired a clout that oftentimes extends to the political realm as well. Several of the bigger broadcasters have acquired a stake in MSOs, spelling a vertical integration. Given this, the fear of the rise of oligopolies is very real.

Sashi Kumar, Chairman of the Media Development Foundation, which runs the Chennai-based Asian College of Journalism, has been a familiar face on TV for over two decades, initially familiar to TV audiences as a news presenter on Doordarshan, well before cable TV arrived in India. During the mid-1980s, as Chief Producer, he played a key role in the Press Trust of India's foray into the television medium. Prior to this he had a stint in the print medium, being The Hindu's *West Asia correspondent, based in Bahrain. In 1993, still the early days of the cable revolution in India, he promoted Asianet, one of the first regional-language channels in the country. A film and media critic of repute, he has been a keen observer of the way the medium of television has unfolded in India.*

Although Sashi Kumar believes that CAS is broadly a step in the right direction, he is critical of the Bharatiya Janata Party-led government pushing CAS in haste. He points out that the government is rushing CAS through with a view to draw dividends in the coming round of elections. CAS, as it is being implemented, is also likely to push the industry along oligopolistic lines. He believes that the small cable TV operator, who played an important role in the cable revolution in India, is fading away, being increasingly replaced by cartels of MSOs, often acting hand in glove with broadcasting companies. He contests the notion that CAS will result in greater choice for viewers and save them from the tyranny of the cable TV operator. Instead, the viewer's choice of channels will be within a narrow range of options that will be decided in an arbitrary manner, which may well have adverse implications for Indian democracy.

Excerpts from an hour-long interview he gave V. Sridhar are set forth below.

How do you view the CAS in the context of the way TV, particularly cable TV, has grown as a medium in India in the past decade? How do you think CAS will unfold?
The evolution of cable TV has been a series of *faits accomplis*. The cable revolution in India was heralded by the small cable TV operators after the first Gulf War brought CNN into Indian homes. That small cable operator is now nowhere in the picture. By a slow process, through a series of aggrandizements, the small operator is now a part of a larger cable operators' business. He is lost somewhere in this whole scheme run by MSOs and cable TV operators. It is a part of the way the cable revolution has happened in this country that during the last decade the small operator has been marginalized in the metropolises and big cities, which is where the bulk of the cabling is. So we are left with only the big players – some of them indigenous and some of them with links to multinationals. Some MSOs have channels of their own, implying an axis of sorts. We do not have any law against cross-media holdings in this country; in any case, even in the west, cross-media dispensations seem to be collapsing, as indicated by the recent dismantling of rules governing cross-holding by the Federal Communications Commission (FCC) in the United States. So we have the big players, the sharks, who are trying to control cable operations in the country.

So, do you see the MSO segment coalescing into the broadcasting end of the business by companies extending their reach across the two important segments of the industry?
Yes. There will be cross-media holdings; for example, Siticable (the cable network) and Star (the broadcaster). Zee is another example of a broadcaster extending operations into the MSO segment. These tie-ups indicate vertical integration in the industry. But while we are told that this is the way technology evolved in the west, and while it is true that this is a technological imperative in some sense, the point is that in all the developed countries the basic infrastructure was enabled or facilitated by the state. Maybe this was done in the private arena, but there were rules and legislation that put in place the enabling provisions which facilitated the creation of the infrastructure, particularly the highways.

In India we do not have the highways for cables. Much of the optic fibre network laid by Bharat Sanchar Nigam Ltd (BSNL) or private parties is being wasted. So, what do we see in the name of cabling? We see cables strung across trees or poles, and we do not know whether taxes are paid for using these. Cable operators use our terraces to station their equipment. It is a ramshackle operation, except that the operation is on a much larger scale than earlier. The situation is similar to placing toll gates without building a highway. The cart has been put before the horse. CAS and other sophisticated concepts are being talked about without the government having created or facilitated the building of a cable network. The channel for the super-highway should have been created first. This would have enabled combining several utilities on a single cable system – for TV, electricity and other applications which require cabling. We had fifteen to twenty years to do this, but we have not done it.

In Kerala, when I was with Asianet, we ran cables on electricity poles, running 1 metre below the wires carrying power. We thus created the super-highway. If the state government thinks that the cable operation is becoming a Frankenstein's creature, it has the option to nullify the contract or of imposing conditionalities to protect consumers. In the case of CAS, I do not see the government being equipped to do this. The CAS issue shows that the government has a warped view of its priorities. I think CAS is actually a bit of a joke. To insist that we have to implement it here and now because, otherwise, we will miss the boat or lose out on bringing in new technology, is sheer nonsense. We do not have the STBs readily available. It is clear that we do not have enough STBs to cater to the needs of the four metropolises from 15 July. What is this hurry about?

What is the government trying to achieve through CAS?
It is clear that the hurry to implement CAS is political. The cable TV operator is being wooed in a pre-election situation. This is because he will carry the must-carry Doordarshan channels or the other channels that carry the propaganda of the party in power. Moreover, he is being wooed because he carries election propaganda and video material for political parties in many states. Today, because people are so obsessed with TV, spending most of their time indoors, their participation in political rallies (particularly among the middle classes) is dwindling. In this situation, the cable TV operator's role becomes a crucial component of campaigning.

What impact will CAS have on the industry? Is CAS pushing the industry along oligopolistic lines?
The industry is really moving along oligopolistic lines – towards cartels and lobbies that operate on behalf of these cartels; lobbies have always been political appendages of cartels. TV is getting less and less diversified, and more and more homogenized, consolidated and cartelized. That obviously means that the

small cable TV operator is nowhere on the scene. The small operators who are subscribing to the MSOs will find themselves acting as slaves to this technology. The CAS is technology-driven and technology-determined, and therefore, the person who is switching this system on and off in a room somewhere literally calls the shots. An important implication of this is that the democratization effect that the cable TV dispensation promised at one time (in terms of liberating us from the monopoly of Doordarshan) has actually swung the other way. On the one hand, we appear to have moved away to a far more commercialized and commoditized situation in which oligopolies are dominant. That is far more dangerous than the mindless and senseless monopoly of Doordarshan.

However, on the other hand, CAS does seem to rationalize (at least on paper) the situation in which many viewers are asking: Why should I be seeing 70 channels in 15 languages, 14 of which I do not understand anyway? Why can't I just watch what I want? Why can't I insulate myself and my children from channels that I think are showing obscenity, and sex and violence? So, CAS is supposed to enable us to pick and choose channels, apart from the bouquet of free channels. That makes sense to an extent, in terms of the consumer-is-king concept. But the problem is, we do not know whether all of the channels will be available to viewers from all the cable operators. For instance, if I want to watch Kairali in Chennai, I will get it only on Hathway, not Sumangali. Will this change when the CAS dispensation comes into force? Will MSOs who are also associated with channels be even-handed in distributing rival channels? Will those pictures continue to be hazy and less clear than their own channels? Moreover, the subscriber cannot switch between MSOs, at least not without incurring an additional cost for the STB. These are moot points.

There are several other unanswered questions. Is it mandatory for the MSO to carry all channels? If so, what is the definition of all? Every channel which can be received on a dish in Indian territory – is that the definition? We do not even know the number of channels that we can get. What will happen to the regional channels in the four metros? Can someone in Chennai get an Oriya channel? Will that be free or will it be a pay channel? The government says that cable TV operators will have to provide thirty free-to-air (FTA) channels. Who is going to determine which of the channels will be aired free? Is it to be on the basis of the population mix in the cities? Or is it to be determined on the basis of the population mix in the target group that the MSO or the cable TV operator is serving? I think there is far too much arbitrary power left in the hands of the MSO or the cable TV operator at this point in time. Is it mandatory for MSOs to create a dish farm which will enable them, necessarily, to capture all satellite signals that are carried into the country? This means that the MSO must have a huge dish farm. Logically, only the big cartels and oligopolies can do this. The field is weighted towards the big players. Unfortunately, many of the finer details about these matters have not come into the public realm.

Many of the issues have not been even discussed. Why this hurry? Why 14 July? I do not understand the logic. They [the government] should have gone through a learning process to begin with, discussed and debated the issues, and then arrived at a decision on how to implement CAS. I am not saying that CAS should not be implemented. In fact I think it is necessary in order to rationalize this market. But first the highway should have been in place, and the state should have had a direct or indirect role in creating the wherewithal for reaching the signals. Instead, the ongoing frenetic discussion and excitement is only on issues related to the last mile, that is, from the cable TV operator to the TV viewer. How does the signal reach the super-highway? That issue is not in the picture at all.

The government, you mentioned, is pushing CAS for political reasons. And CAS, it appears from what you say, is pushing the industry along oligopolistic lines . . .
I think a cable operator-driven cartel (or pressure group) seems to be prevailing at this point in time. Although there are the political reasons that I mentioned earlier, I think there is also the element of enlightened self-interest of the government. Doordarshan has been suffering during the last several years of cable operations because its signals are just about the worst in a cable bouquet. The government probably thinks CAS will rectify the situation and that the must-carry channels of Doordarshan will be clearer now. Doordarshan was always shunted to the S-band and did not get a decent distribution by channel operators. The government, because of the greater transparency and accountability that is a feature of CAS, probably believes that it will be able to monitor things so that this actually happens.

The government also appears to have taken on some of the big broadcasters who have been critical of the government. For instance, some channels said strong things about the government's role in Gujarat. If the government is not democratic-minded or liberal in terms of its information regime (in real terms, not as rhetoric), then it would try and restrict the scope for such channels. Once you have a gateway principle, which is what CAS is based on, you can place your guards and you can monitor who is delivering what.

What does CAS have in store for broadcasters?
Broadcasters are no saints. They have been remiss in the way they have gone about informing the public or advertisers about their reach. They have been bluffing, lying through their teeth. Their claims of the number of connections have always been exaggerated; they multiply the number of connections by five to arrive at viewership figures for their channels. They think advertisers are taken in by these figures. I don't think advertisers take the broadcasters' claims seriously. But in the absence of any other figures, they hedge their bets and put their advertisements on each of the channels.

The segmentation of the market started happening even before CAS was on the agenda. Among advertisers, the logic that larger reach automatically means large revenues is no longer valid. Advertisers understand that there is no point in advertising a consumer durable or an item of conspicuous consumption on a medium with a long reach like Doordarshan; probably 90 per cent of the viewers cannot afford the item. It probably makes better sense to put the advertisement money into a niche channel (even a narrowcasting channel) which has a better reach among those with the purchasing power. This kind of segmentation has been taking place for some time; there has also been segmentation along linguistic lines, and it has also happened in terms of rural and urban markets.

Broadcasters have tended to gloss over this when they sold themselves to advertisers, taking advantage of the confused scenario. This is the beginning of the end of that bluff regime, and it will show up who is what. Therefore broadcasters are a little wary about CAS, but one must see this as a part of the process if the government does go ahead with CAS.

The next step, we understand, is going to be DTH (direct to home), which is a swing in the other direction. That is meant to cater to the needs of a segmented market. DTH does in the air what CAS does on *terra firma*. It is a more sophisticated system, but one which still has free-to-air and pay channels operating on a K_u band transponder, which has been forbidden so far. Once DTH comes, the rich could afford it. There could even be pay-per-view and other sophisticated concepts that will come into play in a DTH regime.

I don't see why the government is in a hurry to introduce CAS. Perhaps the cable operators told the government, give us at least one or two years' time because DTH, which is likely to come soon, is sounding our death knell. But that is not the way it has happened in the west; there, both cable and DTH coexist. Despite these fears, the market in India is huge and constantly expanding. I don't think the cable and TV markets have been saturated, and there is no need for this paranoia.

How does CAS compare with the DTH option? It is reported that Star TV is aiming to go the DTH way while Zee has developed its reach through its MSO operations on the ground.

Zee is also planning to go the DTH way. It also has a licence and it has been given a letter of intent, and so have Star and Doordarshan. It is good that Doordarshan is getting into DTH. It is high time it started earning more revenues instead of doing charity for everyone. DTH will also be competitive, but operating in a rarefied atmosphere.

I think cable will continue to be relevant to the mass of viewers in townships, semi-urban and rural areas, apart from a good proportion of the lower end of urban viewers. Cable has deeply penetrated urban slums. For these people these changes will be very important.

Is this the end of the road for the small cable operator?
I think the small operator is gone. But I do not find myself weeping for him because the cable business has become a question of taking territory. There are big sharks in the picture now and they are moving in with huge investments. In the run-up to the process of acquiring territory, there is a lot of *goonda*ism and mafia-like activity because these operators want to capture turf. This hectic activity of capturing turf has been fuelled by the out-of-the-blue 14 July deadline.

I also think that the cable operation is increasingly operating in a seller's market. Initially it was clearly a buyer's market because there was a demand for this service. Over time, there was increasing tension between buyers and sellers. Now it is becoming a seller's market, in the sense that choices for consumers are only notional. I do not think it is practical for cable operators to be mandated to carry the signals of all the channels. Is the government going to say these are the 100 channels (30 free-to-air and 70 pay) that are mandatory? I do not see any such list forthcoming.

I was shocked by the large advertisement issued recently by the government (DAVP), which uses your and my money. It looks like an advertisement for which the cable operator should be paying. It even mentions cable operators by name, claiming that they have promised this and that, and that it is likely the consumer will pay less. It is like a public interest advertisement issued by a multinational edible oil company which claims its product will prevent cardiac arrest. . . . This ad is a bit like that, on behalf of the cable TV operators. It indicates a kind of complicit attitude in this whole issue.

It is said that CAS will result in lowering broadcasters' reliance on advertising revenue. Broadcasters claim that subscription rates in India are among the lowest in the world and that this is no more viable.
To be fair, it must be said that we in India pay far less for a cable regime with these numerical (I would not say in terms of variety) choices. But it is also true that India is an exception. I do not think there is a free sky regime anywhere in the neighbourhood – not in Singapore or Malaysia, which are highly regulated regimes. Except in Europe and America, nowhere do viewers get to see 60 to 70 channels. We cannot suggest mindlessly that we should go the way the west went, in terms of determining whether the system should be ad-driven or subscription-driven. Our social conditions are different, our purchasing capacities are different, the cable penetration is uneven, there is multi-linguism, and the whole cultural situation is so different.

I think there is still tremendous scope for advertisements supporting the television dispensation because traditionally, the proportion of ad-spend in the electronic media has been 60 per cent, the remaining going to print and other media. In India, it has been the other way around. Sixty per cent of ad-spend is still on print, only 40 per cent (maybe going up to 45 per cent now) is being spent on the electronic media. This difference of 10 to 15 percentage points still remains to be acquired by the electronic media. Obviously, there is far greater scope for advertising in TV. We are not talking about taking a piece of the existing cake alone; the cake itself is expanding. Therefore, there is no need to worry about subscription as a great source of revenue. This is why the big broadcasters have been careless about the number of connections that cable operators provide them. Now, I think, because of the number of channels, broadcasters see more competition within the segments.

One of the new developments in India is the arrival of the news channel as a viable economic entity. Conventional wisdom was that news is required to drive a channel, but that it cannot be sustained independently through advertisement revenues. But that is changing because of the law of diminishing returns operating on movies and teleserials. News, particularly live 24-hour news portrayed as drama, has itself become entertainment. News channels are thus viable profit centres. There have been many entrants in this field. Tomorrow there may be women's channels, or even health or children's or fashion, with many competing channels offering similarly focused fare. When this kind of segmentation happens, it is necessary to bring in the subscription angle.

I do not agree that the primacy of the subscription channels – which is what you see in the cables in the west – is *ipso facto* relevant to us because the DTH regime already exists there. When DTH comes here the whole system will be in flux again because DTH can handle the segmentation. There is also the other aspect relating to value-driven services on cable, which we have not really examined. That could be the greatest subscription source. You could have telephony, internet, voice mail, home security alarm systems, all of which are value-added services that cable operations at a technologically sophisticated level offer to consumers. What this means is that with the same installed capacity in terms of the cable network, the operator can get more by way of subscriptions. Therefore, the cabling network means establishing the infrastructure for all this to happen.

So, the issue is not just advertisement revenues against small levels of subscription revenues, as is being claimed by some. The operator is basically being given the turf on which he or she is going to become a bigger and bigger player. These players are also going to control much of the information and communication that is purveyed and exchanged in homes. The MSO is going to become the immediate information and communication technology (ICT) supervisor in some sense. This has serious implications for the next five to ten years.

This also has implications for a functioning democracy . . .

Absolutely. I think some wise people in the government have noted this and have worked to bring in this regime. It is necessary, at some level, for the state to intervene or to facilitate, but for the right reasons. If it is done wrongly, it can hit the ruling party just as hard as it can hit those in the opposition. The single biggest worry about CAS is the rush. There is a shortage of set top boxes (STBs). At least, they can be imported. Some time could have been given so that the STBs would have been in operation for a while in a free regime, by which time prices would have come down. People who are going to buy an STB today are going to look foolish five years later. We are also not clear as to how the cable operator is going to charge for the STB. There are many unresolved questions. These could have been resolved if there was time.

We are told that consumers have to articulate their grievances to an SDM (Sub-Divisional Magistrate) or a Commissioner of Police. Consumers are being asked to ask for more trouble. Imagine the police having to see whether you or the cable TV operator is right. TV-watching is supposed to be a leisure-time activity; instead, the system is going to be more intrusive and problematic.

How do you look at CAS in terms of the government's stated rationale that this is a consumer-friendly measure? Subscription rates are expected to go up significantly. Do you think there could be a backlash from consumers?

Unfortunately, it is not a one-point agenda on which viewers can join together to fight. If I want to enlist support because I am not able to watch a particular channel, my neighbours may not be interested in seeing that channel. So it is a very difficult organizational concept.

But could there be a backlash in terms of price? Consumers may say, we do not want this at this price.

That is likely, but it depends on the way prices go. The government's thinking on this appears to be that the consumer may not end up paying more than Rs 200 a month for the FTA and a decent bouquet of pay channels. But I doubt this, although I do not think that prices will go up tremendously – unless the price of the pay channels is pitched high. However, it is not as if any of the channels are indispensable.

The CAS will put the onus of creating better brands – brands which the consumer cannot do without – on the channels. They can no longer get away by doing what the others are doing. Apart from small and cosmetic differences, all of them are doing the same thing. In reality, what happens is that if a viewer has missed a channel for a week, he or she stops missing it. It is a case of out of sight, out of mind. I would like to see how many of these channels want to become pay channels and at what price. Some of them, surprisingly, may prefer to be in the FTA mode. They may not want to get exposed as channels with a narrow viewer base if they offer their fare as a pay channel; in the FTA mode they may still be able to get away with their claims of viewership. A pay channel can always shift back into the FTA mode, but that would be like getting its nose rubbed in the mud twice over. It may be better for a channel to remain FTA, assess its prospects in the context of how the other pay channels are faring, and then launch it in pay mode. Each channel, I suppose, knows what its real viewership is – at least, it has a very good approximation. CAS will give them an opportunity to do some hard-nosed stocktaking to decide whether they want to continue as FTA and derive the advantage of maximum advertising revenue, or try and introduce the pay concept and wait it out.

I would think that the multinational corporations, those like Murdoch's Star TV, will be willing to take the latter route, because they always work on such long credit lines that they are willing to fund and fund and wait it out. They could also be the ones who would do the test ballooning in this case and create a culture of pay channels in India as well. Some of this carries social stigma, especially among the middle class. If I do not have a particular channel at home, it is interpreted as my unwillingness or inability to pay for it.

You talked about the move to an oligopolistic situation. What would be the elements of such an oligopoly?
Pricing is an obvious issue. It is likely that pay channels will come together and seek to protect their profits by agreeing on some kind of unified pricing. They could get together and decide that there should be no distress sale. At some level, the business functions like a club. In terms of technology too, we could expect oligopolistic behaviour. The MSOs could get together and decide as a cartel to get only a particular kind of STB, not necessarily the best. They could decide on an optimal level of technology that they consider good enough for the Indian market. This has always happened in India. In the name of appropriate technology, consumers are shortchanged and inferior goods are passed on at a higher price.

Another important aspect of CAS relates to the quality of signals that is supplied by MSOs to viewers. Is there a way of testing signal quality? I would like the government and the state apparatus which is now implementing CAS, to ensure that minimum levels of quality of signals are provided by the MSOs. There are parameters for colour, sound and quality of signals that can easily be monitored. Are these yardsticks going to be applied? The government has not put any deterrents to ensure that MSOs deliver quality service.

I think the script is being written by the oligopolies in the cable business; the government is merely mouthing that script. I do not think the government has even understood the issues independent of these players. We saw on TV a leading MSO repeatedly bailing out the Union Minister for Information and Broadcasting. In short, on CAS, the tail is wagging the dog.

First published in *Frontline*, 4 July 2003.

Restrained Accounts

Book review: H.Y. Sharada Prasad, *The Book I Won't Be Writing and Other Essays*, Chronicle Books, Delhi, 2003.

It is easy enough to guess why Sharada Prasad will not be writing the one book expected of him. It goes against the grain of the man who, through the two decades that he was adviser in the personal office of three Indian Prime Ministers, consistently kept a low profile, bringing to his role a scholarly dignity that was more implicit than stated. It would not be like him at all to be telling us about the prime ministerial goings-on he was privy to all those years. The reasons he himself cites, in his introductory self-exculpation, have more to do with a self-abnegatory modesty. He feels inadequate, he says, to the task of capturing the complex personality of Indira Gandhi. In any case, he adds cryptically, so many attempts have been made on her life. The biographic landscape is for him a minefield littered with fatuous hagiographies on the one hand, and gross muckraking of the M.O. Mathai variety on the other. It is best to keep off. He finds a model of such abstinence in Kathleen Hill, who was personal private secretary to Winston Churchill and six other British Prime Ministers, and kept all that she saw and heard on the job precisely that – personal and private.

It is tempting, however, to second-guess the kind of book that would have emerged should Sharada Prasad have taken the biographic or autobiographic plunge. The motley reminiscences, musings, observations and reflections that constitute the *Other Essays* part of the title (that is, all of the book except the eponymous first essay) give us occasional, if fairly leading, clues about where his abiding loyalties lie. Abiding, because they are not just an occupational commitment, but arise from his deep faith in the one family and the three Prime Ministers in the cause of the nation. Of the three, the Indira Gandhi period must be the asparagus of his memory; he had never actually worked with Jawaharlal Nehru and by the time Rajiv Gandhi was in his prime-ministerial prime, a yuppie set of advisers was already hogging the limelight. There were, in between, the few months spent with Morarji Desai, for whom he has not one unkind or mischievous word. Even if he holds the years spent in the Prime Minister's Office (PMO) generally close to his chest, we catch stray glimpses now and then of what went on in the inner sanctum. We learn what Indira

Gandhi thought of Margaret Thatcher after their first meeting; we learn that she was already shifting her political preference to Rajiv Gandhi from Sanjay Gandhi towards her last years; that she doodled all over her notes (a Cleopatra profile being her favourite); that she once had telepathic communication with the Kanchi Sankaracharya; that she differed with Nehru over Kerala; and that she felt she could reach out to the people over the head of the press.

His approach to the Emergency rule invoked by Indira Gandhi is somewhat circumspect. While it does seem to have left a bad taste, he prefers to fast-forward to the happy ending, when the people forgave Indira Gandhi and re-elected her. On dynastic rule he is less ambivalent, devoting an entire article to listing genealogical succession in various spheres of life – film, music, cricket, law, medicine – and asking why politics should be an exception. This is not the only instance in the book where he is impatient with Nehru dynasty baiters, although he does point out that while Motilal Nehru and Gandhi did pave the way for Jawaharlal Nehru's succession, Nehru himself could not have groomed Indira Gandhi as Prime Minister because he could not possibly have had foreknowledge that Lal Bahadur Shastri, who was his decided successor, would only have a short stint. Interestingly, in another essay where he is mulling over Rajmohan Gandhi's *The Good Boatman*, which deals with how M.K. Gandhi managed to steer the boat safely to independent nationhood, much of the discussion is again on the question of who will be Gandhi's anointed successor. Here, significantly, C. Rajagopalachari (who, Rajmohan Gandhi recounts, was also in the race along with Sardar Patel) was automatically out of the reckoning once his daughter married Gandhi's son. While Sharada Prasad seems in agreement with the end-result that saw Nehru donning the role, had Gandhi been genealogically inclined, surely things might have been quite different.

Sharada Prasad believes that the Prime Minister, in our parliamentary democracy and cabinet system, is far more than *primus inter pares* or first among equals. He or she is the undisputed boss who calls all the shots. His description of the alienation and isolation that sets in and erodes absolute power has the feel of having almost shared the experience up close, even if at second remove. In what also reads like a fascinating account of the process of hubris, he narrates how the leader

> becomes more inaccessible and unforthcoming, forgets his obligations to colleagues, often hurts and humiliates them, grows more and more suspicious, loses touch with grassroots workers in the party, hears only what he wants to hear, is carried away by media praise of his decisiveness and astuteness, gets trammelled by administration to the neglect of policies, and forms an exaggerated picture of his indispensability. And misleaders (in the party, in the civil services, in intelligence) keep assuring him of his popularity. All this leads to defeat, either in the party or at the hustings.

The anecdote about how, at the instance of Indira Gandhi, he finds himself in Anand Bhavan in Allahabad one summer, making an inventory of personal items long stowed away in a locked almirah of Jawaharlal Nehru, gives us an idea of the contrasting sensibilities of father and daughter. The prize discovery in the almirah was urns containing the ashes of Motilal Nehru, Swarup Rani Nehru and Kamala Nehru. Sharada Prasad's excitement over Jawaharlal's umbilical nostalgia is dampened, however, by Indira Gandhi, who quickly and quietly has the urns immersed in the Sangam. Indira Gandhi made fewer concessions to sentiment than her father, is his resigned comment.

On subjects removed from the corridors of power, we see the author visibly relax and become more felicitous. There is engaging variety not only in what he chooses to address (each week, because the bulk of the essays appeared as weekly columns in *The Asian Age*), but also in his tone, tenor and narrative style. There is the self-reflexive counsellor introspecting on advice and advisers, on bureaucracy and diplomacy. There is the informed and concerned citizen mulling over our education system, our scientific temper, the status of our children, gender discrimination, the VIP menace and the Bill Gates hype; the laid-back, vintage raconteur telling us, tongue-in-cheek, how he heard Prince Philip call Queen Elizabeth 'sausage', or quoting a not only erudite but challenging (and unintelligible, there lies the dig) theory about *Time* by a professor–scientist from Madras. There is, too, the scribe-turned-sour who has a mouthful to say about contemporary journalistic practices: the journalist thinks he knows all there is to know about things that happen. He also thinks that others are interested in what he thinks. Or, again:

> Looking back over the last forty years, I would say that our journalists do not go very well prepared to press conferences. Many do not even know how to put a question pointedly but with courtesy and concern for grammar and logic. . . . Just when a correspondent seems to be getting somewhere, another cuts in to ask something wholly unconnected. There are too many casual artists, too many with known loyalties to parties and links with individual politicians. Then there are Hindi journalists with a deep deprivation complex. Others want to show off their punditry and ask questions with numerous clauses and sub-clauses.

He has mixed feelings about television ('I am crotchety in my approach to TV'). He credits Indira Gandhi with heralding the television age in India, albeit reminding us of the pun of the times that Nehru was a visionary, Shastri a revisionary and Indira Gandhi a televisionary. He himself prefers radio for his news (in addition to newspapers) and music, but admits that the idiot box has him sitting up engrossed in cricket and football matches, and wandering around the house bleary-eyed for the effort.

The most delightful three pages of the book are a take on the spate of apologies (assumedly for past war crimes and misdemeanours) that marked the turn of the century. This rambunctious little piece, called 'The Apology Epidemic', is Sharada Prasad at his puckish best or, to put it in parlance matching the performance, Sharada Prasad unplugged. He has all creatures and creators, great and small, on their knees, begging forgiveness for every act of omission or commission in the collective memory of mankind. Among them, various Old Testament characters apologized to various women whom they had *known* in the style of latter-day American Presidents. While much of his writing is peppered with his wry wit, nothing prepares us for this kind of hilarity from one whose general image and demeanour hardly suggests such gay abandon. But then, why should we have expected any different, or less? As he himself observes elsewhere in the book, pointing to the perils of physiognomy, 'The face does not necessarily give us a clue to a person's innermost thoughts or tell us much about his tastes and sense of values.' And sense of humour, he might add.

The mellower reminiscences of those whose friendships he made and valued are as moving as they are engaging. They are no more than thumbnail sketches, but like the few deft strokes of the consummate artist, they suffice to evoke the essential traits of the persona. These are evolved and fulsome relationships, and their accounts are distilled and restrained, never effusive. Living or dead, all of them inhabit a world of old-world charm and repose. Their lives constitute the touchstone on which the fluctuating values of changing generations could be tested. Like in a surreal dance, Sharada Prasad weaves his way through that pantheon – A.K. Ramanujan, Sadasivam and M.S. Subbulakshmi, Sivarama Karanth, R.K. Narayan, Mallikarjun Mansur, Raghubir Singh, K.K. Hebbar, R.K. Laxman, D.G. Tendulkar and the relatively less famous Santokhba, the prodigious scroll painter of epics.

All in all, it is an invaluable read. Where he is deliberately politically obtuse, he seems to suggest that you read between the lines. Through it all, if there is one thing he would like the reader to bear in mind, it is that he writes as an essayist (the buried-in-the-issue variety), rather than as a chronicler or a fleet-footed journalist. As he writes at will, occasionally dipping into his stock of quotations, he would rather not be hurried – for, if the bell rings, why must I run? It is a meditative reverie that seeks to be left alone.

First published in *Frontline*, 18 July 2003.

The News According to Star

The fault, dear Brutus, is not in our stars,
but in ourselves . . .
– *Julius Caesar*

In what looks like a trial by the media even as the jury is out, the prosecutors could well find themselves in the dock. The issue is compliance or otherwise by Star News with the recently revised equity rule for a television news channel uplinking from India. The thrust of the case against Star is that it is making a monkey of whatever regulatory authority is in place, as a recent editorial in *The Hindu* (17 July 2003) put it. But then the reactive, ad hoc nature of such regulation through new guidelines and rules lends itself to no less. It seems to be a case of half a regulatory loaf being worse than no bread.

On the face of it, there seems nothing illegal about the way Star has gone about structuring its equity afresh. In seeking to subscribe to the new stipulation that an Indian news channel cannot have more than 26 per cent foreign equity, Star has taken recourse to two shell entities: Media Content and Communications Services (MCCS) and Touch Telecontent. It has packed them with Indian investors who together hold the mandatory minimum 74 per cent of a ridiculously low equity base of Rs 1 lakh – being raised now, we are told, to Rs 4 crore. But when a business venture of such size and scale, which has been investing and billing hundreds of crores of rupees in the Indian market ever since the advent of independent satellite television in 1993, finds itself – midstream – having to divest the bulk of its equity holding in one channel in response to new guidelines, how else would we expect it to proceed? The idea of a Broadcast Regulatory Act was given up years ago. The Convergence Bill has been on the anvil for a long time, with no closure in sight. The government's Conditional Access System (CAS) directive to cable TV hangs fire. This is part of the problem of seeking to legitimize a string of *faits accomplis*, which mark the evolution of cable and satellite (C&S) television in India. When we expect Star to satisfy not just the letter but also the spirit of the new rules, we must, in all fairness, examine whether it is being given a fighting chance to get into the spirit of it.

It is one thing – the only thing for anyone who cares for journalism – to oppose Rupert Murdoch and all that he stands for in the media. It is quite another to use Murdochism as an alibi to protect and promote the business interests of a newly emerging, indigenous media cartel. It is one thing to argue for a clear and transparent legal regulatory framework for the Indian broadcast media, which for a long time did not have the constitutional (Article 19) protection that the press has enjoyed since 1950. It is quite another to use columns of print or channel time to push for such regulation in a specious and self-serving manner so that the reader, willy-nilly, is implicated in what is essentially corporate media competition for market share. We were just about recovering from the excesses of the advertorial – news-space in a paper being put on sale – in the inimitable style of *The Times of India*, which raised agonizing questions about where news ends and advertising begins. Now we are being treated to the sorry spectacle of the other side of an important story being censored in news columns. Standing the issue of news versus advertisement on its head, it has taken a full-page ad in the form of an 'Open Letter' in some national dailies (see page 9 of *The Hindu*, 21 July 2003), for us to read the news according to Star.

Star, of course, fudges the issue by drawing attention to the popular impact of its bouquet of about a dozen channels, including such mega-shows as *Kaun Banega Crorepati*, when only the question of uplinking for Star News is at stake. More pertinently, the Open Letter advertisement asks whether Star acquires the stigma of a foreign investor only when its erstwhile partner Zee and news-content provider NDTV are no longer with it. The more troubling part, however, is the revelation that letters to the editor sent by Star to *India Today* and *The Times of India*, in response to articles published on the Star News equity issue, were not published. The letters, carried in the advertisement, make the point that the two publications owe it to their readers to disclose their vested interest in the matter: *India Today*'s affiliate company, Aaj Tak, is in direct competition with Star in Hindi news, and *The Times of India* group's affiliate Radio Mirchi is a competitor to Star in FM radio. The Star advertisement highlights the issue of conflict of interests. What is clear is that some of our venerable media players, as interested parties in the fray, have failed to live up to the basic tenets of fair, balanced reporting and professional ethics. What is particularly galling is that it has taken someone from the Murdoch stable to rub this in.

One cannot, therefore, avoid being wary of the sudden emergence of the Indian Media Group (IMG) on the scene. This initiative, for the first time, cuts across the print and broadcast sectors, and bands together many of the big players in some kind of a pseudo *deshi–videshi* struggle. It seems to make too much of a public cause of powerful private interests. While there can be no quarrel with the group's call for a regulatory authority to administer a to-be-formulated policy for foreign investment in the media and to handle complaints, the call for stricter regulation is too narrowly focused on uniform foreign investment rules across print, television and radio. Some of the regulations proposed by the group are disingenuous. One is outright atrocious: to avoid *de facto* control by a foreign company, 51 per cent of the rights should vest in one Indian family or group. It sounds very much like a call to the state to come to the aid of the free market in protecting and sustaining monopolies in the news media. In any case, how on earth does a government ensure that 51 per cent of equity in a public limited company remains with one Indian family or group?

The logic that a uniform regulatory policy should apply to print and broadcast is not borne out by the disparate trajectories and stages of growth of the two media sectors in India. Nor is it borne out by the experience of several developed countries, which have no, or minimal, rules for print, but fairly detailed regulations for broadcast. The IMG must be seen for what it is: a high-profile pressure lobby seeking to enshrine its constituents' special interests as rights in a national media policy. While there is certainly a role in a democracy for such lobbying for a consensual policy, the government must cut through the clutter of demands and keep the larger objective of the public interest in focus. This it must do in evolving a benign and forward-looking, but effective legal regulatory system for the broadcast media. The system must be transparent and fair, and must enable freedom of expression, diversity and competition to thrive.

Internationally, the two main planks of protective broadcast media regulation are restrictions on foreign investment and on cross-media holdings. It is noteworthy that some of those in the forefront of the campaign against Star News have themselves been fierce champions of liberal foreign equity participation in the print media. What is more, they have set the trend for cross-media holdings in the country. While the level and scope of foreign equity participation in the print media, at least for now, have been settled, we have not been through a democratic debate on the pros and cons of cross-media holdings in our context. Should legislative intervention or executive action become necessary in future to tackle this as yet another *fait accompli*, it is not hard to imagine another somersault of positions across the board.

There is a tendency in India to tail what happens in the United States on such matters. In the US, it would seem that the issue of cross-media holdings has been resolved for the time being with the three–two ruling by the Federal Communications Commission (FCC) dismantling the bulk of restrictions. However, this has met with a good deal of opposition. The FCC has been inundated with letters and e-mails of protest from the public. There has also been mounting opposition in Congress, so much so that it might require a presidential veto to keep intact the FCC's drastic alteration of the rules of the game. It is instructive and amusing to learn that in the acrimonious lead-up to the FCC ruling, even the Murdoch-owned Fox News channel, an exemplar of chauvinistic and hawkish journalism, ran the opposition's advertisement campaign: Murdoch wants more. Much more. Unless we act now, Rupert Murdoch will get his way.

First published in *The Hindu*, 28 July 2003.

If the Salt Loses Its Savour

For a while now, we are being treated to the idea and the distracting sight of the free press purely as a function of the free market. The value addition that cover pages of newspapers acquire as fancy wrapping paper, and the tease with which pages inside and pullouts mollycoddle sundry bimbos or walk the fashion ramp seem the general direction of this paradigm shift. In this welter of pin-up, pop-up and keyhole, news is (just about) an also ran.

The trivialization of news and tabloidization of newspapers is, of course, a sorry story. But what is intriguing is the sleight of hand by which different newspapers competing in the free market do not give us a differentiated cultural product, but by and large homogenized, standardized fare. Operating under identical pressures, different newspapers chase the same set of stories and there is, at the end of the day, an implicit consensus on what will make it into the pages the next morning – often even in terms of the hierarchical ordering of the news on the same page or across pages. This is more obvious in the broadcast media where, on switching channels during news time, you find even the headlines cast in the same running order. The daily news template is of course set by the complex chain of news collection and collation, but is finally a collective, consultative exercise that is part of an unstated press club syndrome.

Sharing and comparing notes, rather than competing in the market, marks the process of arriving at the bulk of the daily news menu. It is a process that also sets the agenda for the reader or viewer because he has – with the exception now of the internet which opens up a whole new, even if not easily verifiable, realm of information – little other means of knowing any better. There is an old Sumerian saying (*c.* 2000 BC), *Quod non est in actis, non est in memdo*, or: What is not recorded, does not exist. So it would seem with the all-pervasive news media of our times. After all, when the news editor at the daily editorial meeting laments that we missed the story, what he means is that another paper or channel carried it; he has not the faintest idea if something out there went unreported by all of the media. Into this already pre-set and restricted discourse comes the page-three phenomenon writ large in the media, further narrowing the scope for substantive news.

The reader or viewer – or consumer, to the market-driven media – is at the receiving end of a collusive oligopoly that uses market competition as an alibi to perpetuate its control. A recent example of the big Indian media converting a right cause into a dubious, self-serving one was in the context of the anti-Murdoch campaign, when the 26 per cent limit on foreign direct investment in a news channel uplinking from India was put to the test, with Star News seeking to short-circuit it with shell companies and some legal subterfuge. Banding themselves as the Indian Media Group, the big media players rose to protect their home turf and recommended a number of measures to keep Murdoch at bay, among them one that was rather disingenuous: that at least 51 per cent rights in an Indian media venture should vest in one Indian family or one Indian group.

Where the oligopolistic press turns upon itself is in the no-holds-barred cover-price war to grab more market share. The plummeting cover price in a section of the mainstream press is not, of course, an unqualified boon for the reader. In the process he is, at second remove, being put at the mercy of the advertiser. In a scenario where advertisement revenues far outrun circulation revenues, where the marketing department rather than the editorial team is at the helm of the organization, where the working journalist is systematically marginalized, the primacy of news is already at stake. The heavy reliance on advertisement further segments the media market, and creates a disjuncture between reach and advertiser demand. This is easily evident in the television media after the Direct Broadcast System (DBS) came into force in the late 1980s, and numerous independent, free to air cable and satellite channels became available to the Indian viewer. Over the years, Doordarshan, which has the single largest geographic and viewership reach, has been consistently losing advertisement revenue to private and niche channels that cater to a miniscule section of the population, but which has the purchasing power to buy the goods and services advertised on them. Reach has to be qualified in terms of purchasing power to attract the advertiser, and therefore the media, to that segment of viewership. Something akin to this may also be in store for the print media in an artificially maintained low cover-price regime. The precarious economics of the newspaper industry already points to the danger of spiralling low-priced circulation without commensurate advertising revenues; after a point, every additional copy can drag the paper into the red. The trick is of course to maintain a healthy balance between advertisement and cover-price revenues, and to not let the advertiser run away with the paper.

Cutting across class, cultural and language segmentation is the larger reality of a city-centric media which leave the vast rural population out in the cold or with nothing but the city to aspire to. Indeed, if a time capsule were to be buried today with samplings from contemporary media, and, assuming a flash forward in time of a few centuries, a future civilization were to discover it and try to infer what India might have been like at the dawn of the twenty-first century, it would probably conclude that it was a vast city-state. The glaring gap between the representational and the real, between the citizens' right to be informed and the media's market persona, may, in the long run, have rather serious implications for the concept of the freedom of the press itself. It is a freedom constructed on the Fundamental Rights chapter (Article 19) of our Constitution, and zealously guarded against periodic attempts at encroachment by the executive, legislature and judiciary. Whenever this freedom was in peril, civil society has risen with the press to protect it. It devolves on the press to continue to merit the moral and constitutional high ground that society accords it. It forfeits its privileged status if it acts like just another consumable in the market. There may be no immediate escape from a corporatized media in our context. But surely journalism must continue to be at the centre of it. For, if the salt loses its savour . . . ?

First published in *Tehelka*, 1 January 2005.

Appropriation of the Media

Book review: *Who Owns the Media?: Global Trends and Local Resistances*, edited by Pradip N. Thomas and Zaharom Nain, Malaysia, 2005.

Who owns the media? We suspect we know the answer to that question even as we launch into this collection of essays. But the collusive, battening, disembodied and overarching nature of that ownership is frightening in its different manifestations across the world. The tone is set by media scholar Robert McChesney as he takes on the self-righteousness with which the free market appropriates the media: in the corporate view, their privileges were won by seemingly immaculate conception, and should be regarded as natural and inviolable thereafter.

The frenzied phase of acquisitions and mergers, through the first half of 2000, already set up a new ownership pyramid (forget the inverted pyramid that journalism goes by) with nine transnational corporations controlling everything we see, hear and read in the represented world. Technological convergence has dovetailed into vertical integration in the industry, and corporate consolidation has spawned gigantism on an unprecedented scale, so much so that, as Peter Chernin, President of Newscorp, points out: 'There are great arguments about whether content is king or distribution is king. At the end of the day scale is king.'

The global institutions created to ensure equitable and democratic media, where they do not subserve the grand privatization agenda, have been elbowed out of the way. Sean O'Siochru takes stock of the ascendance of the trade paradigm, and the sidelining of the ITU (International Telecommunication Union) and UNESCO (United Nations Educational, Scientific and Cultural Organization), much of their role now being handled by the WTO (World Trade Organization). The worldwide web has remained outside the purview of the UN system, with ICANN (Internet Corporation for Assigned Names and Numbers), the body that assigns names and numbers for the internet's IP address and Domain Name System, literally operating under the US Department of Commerce.

Cees J. Hamelink looks at how the notion of intellectual property rights has been hijacked from its original public interest context to become a restrictive trade practice, so that a few mega-companies become the global gatekeepers of the world's cultural heritage. He urges a return to first principles, reminding us that intellectual property rights (IPR) are construed as human rights in the Universal Declaration of Human Rights, and commends the example of Larry Lessig who argues that a copy right must entail a copy duty to make the right holder accessible to the public.

In Eastern and Central Europe, as Slavko Splichal points out, a new nexus between the state and the corporate sector has proved lethal for independent media. But it is a heady, win-win mix for both partners – more political power for the state and more profit for the firm. Berlusconi's state-cum-media power pack in Italy typifies this new brand of political capitalism.

For the Caribbean, globalization in the media means a stronger dose of Americanization. Dealing with this experience, Hopeton Dunn notes that even by the mid-1980s, the region was inundated by US-led transnational corporations who had already set up as many as 1,723 branches there. But this acute neocolonial thrust has had its recoil in distinctive cultural assertions that, in turn, reach out to the world; like Reggae music with its indigenous Rastafarian inspiration, or the peculiarly Caribbean assimilation of cricket which, as C.L.R. James contextualizes it, moves Beyond a Boundary into society and politics.

The situation gets murkier as we move on to Africa where regulation and, often, censorship are posed as developmental imperatives, and where the local media has not yet been subverted or supplanted on a large scale by foreign investment. William Heuva, Keyan Tomaselli and Ruth Teer-Tomaselli analyse the classic trilemma faced by countries in southern Africa: accelerating service delivery by attracting foreign investment versus moving towards universal service with little economic returns versus retaining a measure of national sovereignty.

Looking at the rest of Africa, Francis Nyamnjoh finds both overt state control and an undercurrent of resistance. He cites the reputation of Radio Trottoir as the poor man's bomb and weapon of the powerless across a swathe of African states. Again, the internet, with the multiplier effect of the tam-tam at the village level, has proved an effective tool of resistance in much of the continent. Ordinary Africans, says Nyamnjoh conclusively, have refused to celebrate victimhood.

The media mayhem in Latin America is vividly captured by Ana Fiol. Out there in the backyard of the US, the media are enmeshed in the prop-up-and-destruct game the US administration plays with the local political leadership, even as they carve out large domestic and export markets for their cultural products. That the region is fertile ground for media is evident from the second-ranking global firms that have emerged from here: Televisa from Mexico, the Globo group from Brazil, the Venevision Cisneros group from Venezuela and the Clarin group from Argentina. For all that, and there lies the dig, the media capital of Latin America continues to be Miami, Florida.

Among the other significant area studies in the collection is one by Yuezhi

Zhao who describes how the state-subsidized and party-controlled media in China are neatly reinventing themselves as advertisement-based, market-driven enterprises. Zaharom Nain and Wang Kim recount the travails faced by the Malaysian media under Mahathir Mohamad and the relative tolerance of the current administration.

Pradip Thomas, who has co-edited the compilation, has a rather superficial and inadequate piece on the Indian media scene, but redeems himself with another researched and informative input on the innovative ways in which privatization is pursued, including debt–equity swaps that have meant sale of local assets for a song.

Standing on par with McChesney at the head of this body of work is Dan Schiller, who raises the implication of the glut that follows the hype of digital capitalism. Overall, it is a fascinating, if at times slightly bumpy, *tour d'horizon* from which we can draw a poor sense of comfort – that we are not alone in this crisis of our media.

First published in *The Hindu*, 8 March 2005.

The Information Revolution and the Emerging Media Ecology

Since the early 1990s, the spectre of a new revolution has been haunting us. Variously called the Information revolution or the Information and Communication Technology (ICT) revolution, it assumes a paradigmatic shift in production processes and relations, the emergence of a new knowledge-based economy, and a quantum leap from an industrial society into an information society. It is an epochal change, anticipated as far back as the 1970s in Alvin Toffler's metaphor of a Third Wave, in Daniel Bell's evocation of an emerging white-collar workforce replacing blue-collar industrial labour, in MIT (Massachusetts Institute of Technology) Media Lab founder Nicholas Negroponte's dizzying vision of a digitally determined world. It has sparked a combative post-industrial discourse that came to a head with Francis Fukuyama's dire predictions of an end of history and a great disruption.

In the first flush of this revolution, there were tantalizing opportunities conjured up for developing economies like India. Here was our historic chance to bridge the north–south divide that the industrial revolution had left us chafing under. Since the principal and popular instruments of the Information revolution – the electronic media and the computer – came to us close on the heels of their application in the west, we could, suddenly, transcend the technological lag of the industrial epoch and move forward abreast of the developed world. In any case, endism in history, and *rupture* rather than *continuity* in the political economy (*à la* Fukuyama), meant that we could all start afresh on a clean slate.

A later variant of the same theme, and in fashion now, is flatism: that all the world is a level playing field with easy enough exits and entrances. Thomas Friedman's history-in-a-hurry of the globalized world in the twenty-first century seeks to reconfigure the world as flat in this sense. It is a queer mix of anecdotal empiricism and suspended disbelief which seems to make out that the bonding of exclusive IT enclaves – in different countries at different stages of development – into a global supply chain makes the world one big happy family. It would be merely a harmless, idiosyncratic proposition if it were not so callously indifferent to the lived lives of the masses of real people outside this virtual flatland.

Stretching the flatness figure of speech to the media of our times takes us into postmodernist territory, especially in terms of the flattening of heights and depths into one surface sweep. Susan Sontag (1966) has pointed out that in the post-Nietzschean tradition there are neither depths nor heights; there are only various kinds of surface, of spectacle. Roland Barthes too rubbishes the idea of depth as a repository of any concealed meaning, and Jean Baudrillard's take on television as a mirror metaphor reinforces the surface-spectacle dimension of the media. Depth has yielded to breadth and we 'surf' television channels across a shallow expanse. Seeking our way through the dense clutter of images, we find ourselves stumbling on the prescient aphorisms of Guy-Ernest Debord. In his *The Society of the Spectacle* (1967), Debord observed: 'In societies where modern conditions of production prevail, all of life presents itself as an immense accumulation of spectacles. Everything that was directly lived has moved away into a representation.'

'The spectacle as the concrete inversion of life', Debord declared in another burst, 'is the autonomous movement of the non-living.' Or again, 'the specialization of images of the world is completed in the world of the autonomous image, where the liar has lied to himself.' Scholars like Pierre Bourdieu note how Debord, whose work has remained relatively obscure, was way ahead of his time, and how relevant he is to our understanding of the organic role of contemporary media. *The Society of the Spectacle* has even been called the *Capital* of the new generation and one Debord enthusiast (A.H.S. Boy) explains the comparison: 'In the same manner that Marx wrote *Capital* to detail the complex and subtle economic machinations of capitalism, Debord set out to describe the intricacies of its modern incarnation, and the means by which it exerts its totalizing control over lived reality.'

The peculiar manner in which the tension between *the represented* and *the real* is abstracted by the represented subsuming or *becoming* the real is not a new problem. As far back as 1841 we had Feuerbach, in his preface to *The Essence of Christianity*, pointing out that his era prefers the image to the thing, the copy to the original, the representation to the reality, appearance to being. In our own context, Dushyanta, in Kalidasa's *Shakuntala*, laments the trick memory has played on him thus:

> Like one who doubts the existence
> of an elephant who walks in front of him
> but feels convinced by seeing footprints,
> my mind has taken strange turns.

More recently, Heidegger held that a distinctive attribute of the twentieth century is that it sees the world in terms of representation; and postmodern studies are suffused with the idea of a mediated universe that is autonomous and self-fulfilling. Marshall McLuhan was coming to haunt us with a vengeance. The medium was the message – and self-obsessively so.

Postmodernist empathy with the media takes a new turn with the shift from analogue to digital technology. In the new pixellated media environment McLuhan's (1964) soothsaying finds fresh meaning, as when he talks of a dispersed media structure whose centres are everywhere and margins are nowhere. The constructs and methods of the analogue world are jettisoned as we plunge headlong into this digital realm. In the process, the hierarchization of text and the logical cause-and-effect sequencing of content give way to a simultaneity and multiplicity of information bytes. In the dominant medium of television this change is manifest in the altered role of the screen as a site where *montage* and *collage* combine at the same time. Live and taped talking heads; intervening fast-cut visuals and reportages; layers and tiers of discrete information delivered as charts, financial text or animated graphics; insets on the stock or commodities market; news update scrolls; commercial pop-ups; and a medley of sound and musical effects – all vie at once with one another for your attention. That is the look of the new-age television screen, and it demands fairly developed multitasking and non-linear ingestion capabilities on the part of the viewer.

The digital-driven speed of the media has converted what used to be seen and experienced as a seamless flow across channels into what Todd Gitlin (2003) calls a torrent. The sheer pace of it is self-defeating because there is less and less time and space to even pay attention to it, let alone assimilate the barrage coming at us without let or pause. Attention spans have dwindled to ridiculous lows and the turnover of media-generated celebrities seems to keep pace with the rapid rate of obsolescence of the technology itself. The future that Andy Warhol spoke of, when everyone will be famous for fifteen minutes, may well be here.

Celluloid cinema too seems reconciled to a makeover where the depth, resolution and tone of film negative stock defer to the speed, malleability and, above all, cost-saving of digitization. The distribution and exhibition ends are likely to conflate with the prototyping of digital release, whereby satellite-fed signals of a new film are tapped and simultaneously screened by appointed cinema theatres.

The Information revolution, then, with the media as its shifting eye of the storm, is in the melting pot, constantly redefining and reframing even the objective conditions in which it plays itself out. Coming to terms with this evolving media ecology can at best be tentative and open-ended. As first- and second-generation beneficiaries (or victims, depending on how you look at it) in the thick of it, we do not have the benefit of distance to assess how it will all turn out. But it does appear that new dynamics are at work in the information sector, which, combined with the impetus to globalization and the free market, have put us on a course of whose direction we need to have some sense.

Two determining features riding tandem in this flux-ridden media situation are convergence and corporatization. Convergence, in the MIT's Media Lab definition of the term, implies a coalescing of what were hitherto three separate segments: (i) broadcasting and the movie industry, (ii) the print and publishing industry, and (iii) the computer industry – into a single electronic delivery screen of the future. As it turned out, this became a model for business consolidation with forward and backward integration. The turn of this century saw a frenetic spate of mergers and takeovers, the first half of 2000 alone recording deals totalling 300 billion dollars. When the dust settled, nine transnational corporations were in control of the global media market: General Electric, AT&T and Liberty Media, Disney, AOL–Time Warner, Sony, Newscorp, Viacom, Vivendi, Bertelsmann. They were also, for the most part, vertically integrated, to combine related businesses and convergent technologies. They are now a formidable oligopoly with – as media scholar and activist Robert McChesney points out – cross-holdings of one another's shares and interlocking boards of directors, and therefore not really in competition among themselves.

In his work with the telling title, *Rich Media, Poor Democracy* (2000), McChesney points to the converse relationship between the prosperity of the media and the prospect of democracy in the United States, in a context where hypercommercialized content limits the ability of Americans to act as informed citizens. Ben Bagdikian, in his classic study *The Media Monopoly* (1983), shows how, with the control of the media market by primarily US multinational corporations, the United States sets itself up in the world as a supervening ministry of information. International and multilateral institutions like UNESCO (United Nations Educational, Scientific and Cultural Organization) and ITU (International Telecommunication Union), which by law and convention dealt with the media, have been sidelined, and their role has been appropriated by US-controlled mechanisms like the WTO (World Trade Organization) and ICANN (Internet Corporation for Assigned Names and Numbers). While the aggressive role of the WTO in telecommunications and intellectual property rights issues is by now well known, it is instructive to find that ICANN, which assigns names and numbers for the internet and Domain Name Systems (DNS), is registered as a not-for-profit private sector corporation under Californian law, bringing it under the control of the US Department of Commerce.

Paradoxically, it was the Direct Broadcast Satellite (DBS) technology of the mid-1980s, which liberated television from the control of national governments, that also abetted the process of dismantling communist governments in Europe and paved the way for a unipolar world of US supremacy. The collapse of the Berlin Wall, and of much of the erstwhile Eastern bloc, was hastened as much by DBS signals from the sky as by internal contradictions on the ground. The US television serial *Dallas* and its received message in the former German Democratic Republic is a case in point. Beamed across the wall from West Germany, the serial had a wide, if surreptitious, viewership in the East. Unfortunately, with the limited exposure of a closed society, those who watched the ostentatious lifestyle and lavish consumerism depicted by the soap thought that what they saw was what they would get in the West. And even as Marxists saw in the excesses of *Dallas* a critique of capitalism, for the East German

– subsidized or free housing, gas, mass transportation, health care and education notwithstanding – they constituted the good life in the West denied to him in his system. *Dallas* is cultural imperialism, the French Culture Minister Jack Lang had declared in 1982. The revolution of rising expectations that brought the Berlin Wall down soured, of course, when the bulk of East Germans found themselves as refugees in the new unified Germany.

Successive US administrations in the period since the Second World War have consciously promoted American ascendancy in the information sector as a centre plank of their foreign policy, spending as much as 1 trillion dollars till the end of 1990 towards this end. As early as 1946, Assistant Secretary of State William Benton made it clear that

> the state department plans to do everything within its power along political or diplomatic lines to break down the artificial barriers to the expansion of private American news agencies, magazines, motion pictures and other media of communications throughout the world. . . . Freedom of the press – and freedom of exchange of information generally – is an integral part of our foreign policy.

That this was a specious concern for free flow of information, a US-centric version of it, became obvious when the Reagan administration quarrelled with UNESCO for its espousal of the New World Information and Communications Order (NWICO) and quit the organization, followed dutifully by the United Kingdom. The US even elbowed UK, its ally, out of the race by setting up the communications satellite undertaking, COMSAT, which effectively neutralized the British command over undersea cable.

Behind the rhetoric of freedom of information was the ambition to preside over an information superstructure that would place the US in a position, as Nye and Owens have noted, better than any other country to multiply the potency of its hard and soft power resources through information (Joseph S. Nye was formerly Assistant Secretary for Defence for International Affairs, and William A. Owens, former Vice Chairman, Joint Chiefs of Staff). By the same token, behind the corporate control of the media in the US is the proactive presence of the US administration. Contrary to popular perception, multinational media corporations have not flowered out of the free market but are products of state-led growth. The nexus between the state and the firm, which in any other market would be decried as protectionism or interventionism, becomes in the US a compact as much of liberty as of profit. The media that results cannot but carry this qualification. Noam Chomsky and Edward Hermann, in their incisive work, *Manufacturing Consent* (1988), describe how the mainstream US media constitute a propaganda model defined through a series of five filters: (1) size, concentrated ownership, owner wealth and profit orientation of the dominant mass media firms; (2) advertising as the primary source of income; (3) dependence of the media on information provided by the government, business, and experts funded by these primary sources and agents of power; (4) flak as a means of disciplining the media; and (5) anti-communism as a national religion and control mechanism. Irrepressibly buoyant and bold on all domestic issues, the US media tend to consensually freeze when it comes to US foreign policy or the American way of life, irrespective of whether the rest of the world wants or needs it.

The Indian media, happily, have acquitted themselves better on this score. Virtually nothing is taboo for the press here – a good section of it is not squeamish even on sensitive issues like Jammu and Kashmir – and even excesses are excused as a small price to pay in the cause of democracy. The few overt attempts by the state to control the press, most notoriously during the period of Emergency imposed by Indira Gandhi, have ended as misadventures, and actually made it stronger and more resilient. But over the last few years, one cannot help feeling that the market is running away with the media. Apart from the pressures of globalization and liberalization, the advent of the independent Cable and Satellite (C&S) regime may have played a significant role in driving the media into the arms of the market.

C&S television, enabled by Direct Broadcast Satellite (DBS) technology, came to India almost by default. The first Gulf War of 1991, fought as much on camera as for the camera, was offered to the world as DBS signals up there, ripe and ready to be picked. A number of low-budget entrepreneurs set up receiver dishes and conveyed CNN images of the war to subscribing households along cables strung across high-rise buildings in cities and towns. The cable revolution had begun – just like that. Each of these cable operations mushrooming across the country catered typically to not more than a hundred homes. By the time the government began to sit up and take note, it was already a changed scenario. There was nothing the state could do, either, to prevent satellite television beaming into homes, because it did not contravene any law. Government monopoly over the electronic media was grounded in the faith that the old Indian Telegraph Act of 1885 gave the state exclusive right for wireless transmission. But the Act was silent – because it could not have foreseen the possibility so far back – about the reception of wireless signals.

With the proliferation and rapid spread of cable networks, it was only a question of time before alternative channels, programming initially in Hindi and the south Indian languages, made their appearance. Since they could not uplink to their satellites from Indian territory, they used uplink stations abroad, from as far away as Russia to facilities closer in the region, in Hong Kong, Philippines and Singapore. From those ad hoc beginnings, C&S has today grown into a mammoth industry. The anonymous *cablewalas* who first showed the way have been taken over, for the most part, by bigger players. Many of them find themselves handling last-mile operations for the big cable companies. As the competition for eyeballs among the satellite channels began hotting up and as television began to stake a claim for a larger share of the advertisement spend, the print media went into a spin trying to reinvent themselves. In the ensuing race to the bottom between tabloidized print and dumbed-down television, the net loser has been the reader and the viewer.

Although, between the two, television must appear more irredeemable, it is in fact print that seems to be in a tailspin from where there is no escape in sight. With price wars having reduced the cover prices of most newspapers to token amounts, reliance on advertisement revenues is fostering a dependency syndrome that may be difficult to shake loose. Also, in a situation where the reader as subscriber is not the main or even a substantial source of revenue, his right to be informed as a citizen vies with his role as a consumer in the market for the paper's attention. That the advertiser is more interested in the reader as consumer than as empowered citizen does not make things easy.

This fatal attraction of the market and consequent alienation from civil society has serious implications for the future of the media themselves. Although in India the freedom of and for the media are not specifically stipulated in the Constitution (unlike in the United States where the First Amendment forbids Congress from making any law that abrogates the freedom of the press), they are a derivative right by Article 19 in the Fundamental Rights chapter guaranteeing freedom of expression. Courts have repeatedly reaffirmed this right and civil society has stood shoulder to shoulder with the media whenever they were under threat – whether from the executive, the legislature or the judiciary. Should the media place themselves purely at the mercy or bidding of the market, they would forfeit their right to the moral and statutory high ground they have enjoyed all along as a fourth pillar of democracy. It therefore devolves upon the media to reconnect with the public as more than consumers, just as it is a challenge for the people to reclaim the media for themselves.

In television, technological renewal makes the essential difference. After two decades of DBS technology, we are already into DTH (direct to home) transmission in India. Subscription revenues in the DBS regime accrue to the distributor as cable operator rather than to the programmer as television channel. Subscription management in this system has been a blind man's buff with rampant underdeclaration of customer lists by cable operators, and payment irregularities and losses through the network chain. DTH could change all that, and establish a more direct relationship between what the viewer pays and what he gets. With both technology and the advertiser sorting the vast, amorphous viewership into tiered and profiled purchasing-power segments, a fragmentation takes place that may actually work against dumbing down or least-common-denominator programming, with fare that seeks to meet different levels of expectation and sophistication of different target groups.

In the process, however, television becomes less and less a mass medium or broadcaster, and more and more a narrowcaster. It is a model of the medium that runs counter to its normative national role of an integrating social agent. Already, we have less and less of each other in our regional-language C&S channels. Television is no longer a site for multicultural expression as it was in the heyday of Doordarshan, when, for example, it was possible to get to see films in different Indian languages, subtitled for a cosmopolitan viewership, on the same national channel. On the other hand, structural devolution has debunked the Delhi-centric, paternalistic model, and set in motion a regional idiom of the electronic medium which is an enterprising mix of the local and the global. In this new axis, the nation-state is no longer the primary framework of reference. The global village has come full circle.

First published in *The Hindu*, 11 October 2005.

Mandi House Memoirs

Book review: Bhaskar Ghose, *Doordarshan Days*, Penguin/Viking, Delhi, 2005.

Bhaskar Ghose's *Doordarshan Days* reads a bit like the story of King Midas. All he touched turned into gold, but his nemesis was built into the boon. At the end of it, the golden period of Doordarshan – its much-vaunted *glasnost* and *perestroika* phase – turned out to be an aberration, sweet reform soured before our eyes. In his recounting of those heady years, Ghose holds forth in the first-person singular with such frank immodesty that we can begin to see where the problem lay.

Not that he even suspects that he might have been more a part of the problem than the solution. Instead, we are treated to an identification parade of bureaucrats and ministers who were the spoilers and villains of his piece of action: A.S. Grewal, Suresh Mathur, S.S. Gill, Krishna Kumar, H.K.L. Bhagat, Singh Deo, V.N. Gadgil and (et tu, Brute?) Gopi Arora. If only they had let him be, he and Doordarshan would have blazed a different trail, and left all those private channels taking away the public broadcasters ad revenues far behind gaping in wonder.

If only all this were true. The fact remains that Doordarshan ended up where it did and when it did because the Direct Broadcast Satellite (DBS) technology of the mid-1980s made it impossible for the state, even more authoritarian than in India, to continue to monopolize the electronic media. That Bhaskar Ghose was to Doordarshan what Romi Chopra was to Apna Utsav (even if Ghose has a dig at the Apna Utsav syndrome in his book), and both sought to showcase India rather out of context. That, much as he laments the commercialization of Doordarshan, it was he who led it inexorably in the direction of the market.

Only two persons from his Doordarshan days measure up to Bhaskar Ghose's unreserved praise – Madan Mohan and Radhikant Basu. As Chief Engineer of Doordarshan, Madan Mohan was, by all accounts, a quiet, resourceful and innovative technocrat, and the opposite, if anything, of Ghose's own flamboyance. In him Ghose found both a mentor and a salver of his troubled mind. Radhikant Basu, who took over his mantle, rushed forward from where Ghose left off. And when he in turn left Doordarshan to join Rupert Murdoch, and made a string of a mess of Star TV and then the Tara channels, the cycle of self-deceit and tall claims was complete.

Ghose does say, in his postscript, that this is not a definitive history of Doordarshan. But in the absence of one, this easily makes do as a quick-fix chronicle. And in any case these days, when it is in fashion to rewrite even definitive histories, there is just so much you can quarrel with a meek attempt to shift blame or pass the buck for what could not be.

First published in *Business Today*, 6 November 2005.

Localization of Indian Broadcasting

One of our finest poets and cultural icons, A.K. Ramanujan, had a quotidian sense of India. One way of defining diversity for India, he said, is to say what the Irishman is said to have said about trousers. When asked whether trousers were singular or plural, he (the Irishman) said, 'Singular at the top and plural at the bottom.' It is interesting to explore whether, or to what extent, this lived plurality at the local level is reflected in the numerous regional television channels that have proliferated in India over the last decade.

Discounting half-baked theories and subliminal deductions, and construed at a flatly empirical what-you-see-is-what-you-get level, there is little to show that the regional-language television has begun to engage with even a strand of the vast and fascinating weave of the composite Indian experience.

It all set out to be quite different. When Direct Broadcast Satellite (DBS) technology came to India in the early 1990s, close on the heels of its advent in the west, it was the south of the country that first liberated itself from the thraldom of state-run television. Doordarshan (India's state-owned television) was obsessively Hindi- and north-centric, with a mindset that saw the south, comprising four distinct states across the Vindhya ranges, as an amorphous mass situated somewhere in the back of the beyond. Asianet and Sun TV, which emerged on the scene in quick succession, were pioneering moves to give Kerala and Tamil Nadu, and the sizeable diaspora of Malayalis and Tamilians, a televisual identity of their own. Entrepreneurs in Andhra Pradesh and Karnataka followed suit with their own independent channels, and the Cable and Satellite (C&S) revolution panned out to other regions of the country from the crucible of the south.

The promise held out in the first flush of this regionalization of the electronic media soured quickly as content and style of programming began to subscribe to the meta-model of Americanized television fare. The languages were different, but the genres were the same. There was not a hint of the vast Indian hinterland as the regional urban sensibility aspired to that of the global metropolis and of the inner city. It was glocalism perversely cast – leapfrogging from the local to the global without a moment for the terrain in-between.

Paradoxically, even as the television of the region was turning its back on the region, a process of miscegenation in politics was moving regional political parties to the national centre stage, heralding a new era of coalition governments.

But much of this was lost on much of regional television as it chorused with the dominant English channels in caricaturing the not-so-Anglophile regional satraps staking their claims in Delhi. A Lalu Prasad Yadav or a Mayawati, more often than not, are the butt of jokes even when they make a political point in deadly earnest. Rival channels in a language or a state are either directly owned by political parties, or openly hitched to one or the other party, and this strongly colours their portrayal of what is happening in their region. The viewer is often left trying to figure out, not just differing versions of a news story but one story that glaringly contradicts another. Nowhere is this contradiction as head-on or stark as in Tamil Nadu, where the DMK's (Dravida Munnetra Kazhagam) Sun TV and rival AIADMK's (All India Anna Dravida Munnetra Kazhagam) Jaya TV are so obsessed with one another that both seem to have lost sight of the viewer.

Situations of crisis have tended to be exacerbated, rather than responsibly reported, by regional television. The build up to hysteria of the Bharatiya Janata Party's *Ramjanmabhoomi* movement (and the *rath yatra* that led to the destruction of the mosque at Ayodhya), the anti-Muslim riots in the wake of the Godhra train incident in Gujarat in 2002, and recent remarks about premarital safe sex by film star Khushboo being torn out of context and pilloried in Tamil Nadu, are some instances of the populist agitprop role of local television.

What local entertainment television does to its mother tongue is another sordid chapter. In the south, channel after channel gives you the same breathless talk-, game- or song-show host inflecting good old Tamil, Telugu, Malayalam or Kannada into a hybrid American pop dialect that is as unsettling as it can be insulting to any native language sensibility. This deracination is compounded by a new and rapidly growing trend to push Hollywood dubbed into the regional language on prime cinema time. Cinema is what we thought we ourselves had aplenty. But our celluloid fare, with its local and often rural milieu, is not seen as attractive to the burger-and-cola-fed appetites of urbanizing TV viewers. Add to this the fact that every language with a television face becomes dominant at the expense of numerous other languages which, without the critical numbers or influence, are languishing at the margins – and we have a sense of the slow poisoning afflicting local language and local culture, courtesy local TV. There are an estimated 850 languages in daily use in India (*Ethnologue Report of India*), and already many of them are faced with extinction and some, in a desperate bid to survive, are merging with the stronger variants.

The stratified growth of local-language television has made for a more segregated and blinkered viewership. In the days when Doordarshan sought, even in its dowdy manner, to fulfil its public interest broadcast mandate, it became, at least occasionally, a common platform where one part of India could see, hear and understand another. Films in regional languages telecast with subtitles on Doordarshan, for instance, allowed us a syncretic glimpse of local-specific cultures and concerns. With the regional-language channels ploughing their exclusive furrows and Doordarshan in a state of limbo, there is no television equivalent of a social integer in India. The validity of an integer in a context where the concept of the nation-state is itself *passé* is, of course, another discourse.

The regional-language channels continue to draw and grow on an expanding advertisement pie composed of a handful of established, big-budget national and regional advertisers, and numerous fresh spenders, at several local tiers in the field. In many languages, the number of players seems to have far exceeded the logic of the market, but the shake-out, long hinted at, has not happened. An indication of the uncovered gap of both their influence in the market and their potential for advertisement revenues lies in the statistic that with nearly 40 per cent of the total viewership, they account yet for less than 20 per cent of the total ad-spend in the television sector.

The latest National Readership Survey, which shows that the Indian-language press is growing at a much faster pace than the English press, seems to emphasize that the local lure is real not only for television but for the older print media as well, and that newer regional markets are opening up. Radio and telecommunications in the private sector also seem set to go local and develop a neighbourhood identity. The two rounds of FM radio licensing, in which over 300 private players have won bids to run stations in over 90 zones across India, are creating a new buzz that seems to proceed from the margins to the centre rather than the other way round. But the real breakthrough would be in the technological dispersal that digitization implies. With the expansion of broadband capacities, the liberalization of last-mile connectivity, the unbundling of the local loop and fibre-to-the-home set to become a reality in middle-class India, often cutting across the urban–rural divide, there is bound to be a churning process that unleashes energies which are latent in different locations of the country. The emergent structure need not be one whose centre of gravity is the metropolis or the big city. It could rather be a multinodal, evolving and open-ended model that integrates in some significant measure the semi-urban and rural hinterland. This vision of a technologically converged yet devolved telecommunication regime can of course quickly evaporate into thin air, if the handful of big corporations who are already eyeing this virgin opportunity are allowed to set the terms of a mock-cartel competition and walk away with chunks of the cake.

What is being missed in the current saga of privatization of the information–communication–entertainment (ICE) sector is that the wherewithal of reach is in the public domain and, in a democratic reckoning, must belong to the people. The airwaves or radio spectrum over India must be construed as much a natural resource as her rivers or mineral deposits. The pathways of overhead or underground cabling that crisscross vast tracts of land must be seen as based on the principle of a right of way over public, and therefore commonly owned, property. The recent move by the AIADMK government in Tamil Nadu to take over the private cable TV network and operations in the state, whatever its partisan motives, is illustrative of a normative and legitimate role of the state in regulating infrastructure in this realm. It was widely welcomed – including, quietly, by political allies of the DMK, the party against whom it was targeted – as addressing the haphazard and monopolistic growth of cable television in Tamil Nadu.

With all-round penetration of cable television hovering around 60 per cent in the state, dominant control by the family of one political group and a large business house effectively meant that they determined the channels that will be distributed, and, further, that they decided which of them will be on prime band and which on the lesser band. The fate of a new channel, even if in Tamil, depended on the whim and fancy of a couple of such multisystem operators, or MSOs, who had the bulk of the state wired up. Often, new channels seeking distribution were required to pay high carriage costs. Fees down the cable chain, including what must be paid by the last-mile cable operator and by the subscriber, were stipulated by the MSO.

This monopolistic position was, in the first instance, appropriated by a mix of political, money and muscle power, and not acquired through fair or competitive trade practice. Central to this appropriation is the right of way for cabling along public pavements and across public roads, which is based on local body clearances and varies from place to place in the state. Indeed, in the cities and towns, these cables are strung across high-rise buildings or intervening props, be it a tree, a lamp-post or a pole erected for the purpose along the pavement.

Cable and Satellite (C&S) networks can not only purvey the numerous TV and audio channels, but also potentially offer value-added features like internet, voice mail, electronic home shopping, home security alarm systems and a host of other services to the home, and should ideally be seen as part of an infrastructure-building exercise. Governments at the state level should ideally play a role in ensuring that such a vital infrastructure is not hijacked for partisan political ends and ensure that it remains in the public sphere.

Alongside these manifest developments in, and concerns about, the ICE sector, a quieter, local-specific presence being felt is that of the community radio. Restricted as yet largely to academic campuses, its grassroots potential as an instrument of empowerment has been driven home dramatically in the wake of the recent tsunami disaster. To inhabitants along a stretch of the Tamil Nadu coast, a community radio-like set-up served as an early warning against the killer waves, and it has now become a model widely espoused by NGOs to target far-flung communities in different areas. At a time when the private corporate FM radio is set to make local waves, opening up the community radio to public-spirited initiatives and players would be a welcome countervailing influence. For this to happen, the skewed and narrow bureaucratic mindset that the radio, given its bottoming-out reach, is more politically and socially sensitive – and therefore more vulnerable – than the other electronic media must yield to an appreciation of its transformative quality in a community environment by providing actionable information.

For too long now, *babu*-dom in India has been dabbling in pulp psychology about the way radio can make or mar the lives of what are seen as lower denominations of impressionable, naïve listeners. Therefore, goes the argument, the need for vigil over the medium. Indeed the same illogic has been applied to keep news and current affairs outside the purview of licensing for FM radio, so much so that FM sans news is today a laughable anomaly in a context where tidbits of news assail us at every step of our daily lives – from the ubiquitous mobile phone, from internet, from the host of local, national and international TV channels, from other radio offerings like World Space, BBC, broadcasts from neighbouring countries, and so on.

The record of the Indian regional-language satellite and cable TV may indeed be sullied in communally, or multiculturally, sensitive situations. But the response surely does not lie in a Canute-like attempt to halt the technology waves. Nor does it lie in the idea, peddled by some bureaucrats, of a regulation of content tantamount to pre-censorship, as the experience of cinema – the only media sector thus far subject to pre-censorship – teaches us. The perversity and deviousness with which the average Indian cinema has all these years dodged the censors, and managed to pack the screen with sex and violence far worse than the censorship code was meant to prevent, is clinching proof of the futility of such preemptive laws. The creative spirit, even where it plays foul, cannot really be put down by the letter of the law. What is required is an enlightened and enabling framework with a truly representative body of professionals setting, and subscribing to, a code of self-regulatory guidelines, and where peer pressure and accountability become natural deterrents against deviant behaviour.

First published in *Seminar*, No. 561, May 2006.

Chintha Ravi and *Ende Keralam*

I remember it as another of those happenings that made Asianet – the brainstorming session we had at our office in Chennai about fifteen years back, about a travelogue on the channel. It was a slot waiting to be filled because we had the traveller–chronicler par excellence right in our midst, as part of the core group of friends and well-wishers who implicitly believed in, and was part of, the channel's initiative.

I remember too with some pride that the marathon series was christened by me: *Ende Keralam* – as in Ravi's Keralam.

It was clear from the very beginning that it would be a modern *Pilgrim's Progress*-like account of Ravi's personal rediscovery of Kerala. He would travel and tell, in his inimitable style. And we would get a different, truer feel of our Kerala. Beyond the grand narrative of historians. Beyond the ornate descriptions of poets. Beyond its romantic ensnarement in film songs. Beyond the Pavlovian picture-postcard response of green paddy fields, blue backwaters and multihued sunsets. Beyond the kitsch Kathakali masks crucified on walls across middle-class Malayali homes within and outside the state.

Ravi set out, somewhat in the manner of a footloose and idyllic *flâneur*, on his journey across Kerala – from the north to the south of the state. Both the journey and his telling of it have the sense of an anecdotal drift. His have-camera-will-travel-and-shoot approach gives the series, and every moment in it, a freshly minted quality. The pace is an unhurried, leisurely contrast to contemporary breathless television. As much as the picture and sound, the spaces in between are restful and contemplative. The gentleness of his being, the grasp of his mind – free of rancour and wary of certitudes, and his essential humaneness inform the body of the work.

The nearly two hundred episodes of *Ende Keralam* constitute a continuum of particulars. The series shuns universalization. People, places and situations are strung along as Ravi chances upon them. This does not make it any less relevant or abiding. It is an unpremeditated engagement with the here-and-now where one sees and hears the present ticking before the chronicler. The chaste, transparent engagement makes luminous and enduring what the camera-eye beholds.

Over the years, and with many repeat telecasts, the series has acquired a unique mnemonic value – as many characters, big and small, that peopled it have passed on, and some places and landmarks it featured have changed beyond recognition. With each viewing, as the here-and-now moves further and further back into the realms of the there-and-then, as some presences in the frame become absences in real life, Proustian memory takes over from where the travelogue has left off – shifting the entire experience to a different plane.

Ende Keralam is a distinctively writerly text – not only in terms of the voice-over of the sound track, but also in its visual language. Ravi seeks to use his camera as naturally and unselfconsciously as a pen, much like the *camera stylus* aspiration of the French New Wave cinema. He creates an engaging tension between his lucid camera language and his commentary track in the measured, magisterial Malayalam that only he can write. The result is a sense of Brechtian alienation which prevents the material at hand lapsing into soppy nostalgia. The quotidian and the commonplace seem to flower under his benign gaze, and demand and deserve our attention with his authorship.

I remember *Ende Keralam* as all this, and for all this . . .

Memories of the series spill over from the small screen into what its assorted camp followers referred to simply as the flat – where Ravi stayed during his post-production work in Trivandrum, and where late-night soirees were marked by loud fracas and very occasional fisticuffs. Through it all Ravi sat like an ancient-modern Buddha, contemplating the growing volatility around him with a mild frown.

These days, I have yet another reason to remember *Ende Keralam*. It is the name of a restaurant specializing in ethnic Kerala cuisine close to my house in Chennai. I have found the fare unpredictable the few times I have eaten there; sometimes delicious, at others less so. But I must remember to take Ravi there some day.

In death, as in life, Ravi subverts temporality. Did he disappear over the horizon of space, or did his Kierkegaardian hourglass of time run out on him? If travel and traversing space are the metaphors of his essential persona, his cultivated stillness on a scale of time makes a mockery of spatial distancing. We are left contemplating his life like he did a painting – as process rather than product, almost replaying in his mind the artist's brush and palette, simultaneously filling in and emptying the space framed by the canvas before him. Line and colour and tone separate the traversed canvas from the untouched stretch of neutered stillness.

He was sentient in a strange way. He responded with cerebral warmth and concern to the seasonal therapeutic and deleterious breezes that waft across Kochi and Malabar. He had the manner of one who knew all oft and less travelled roads. He sat in the front of the vehicle next to the driver, as if bracing for the road ahead rushing forward to embrace him. He sensed impending rain even when he was closeted indoors. He liked furniture that breathed and became a dynamic participant, not just a part of a room. He had a keen tactile sense of materiality. His aesthetic was always on fresh ground, never stale, slovenly or syrupy. He heartily endorsed John Abraham's round abuse of the clichéd and cloying celebration of Kerala's green-and-blue-hued nature in the visual arts and cinema.

He had the equivalent of colour blindness when it came to expressing musical tunes. Worse, actually, because he reduced all Malayalam film songs into a standard Gregorian-like chant. So the one thing you didn't want to venture into was to ask him to sing. Even on the rare occasions when, in a final gesture of condescension, he would sing along with his friends (and quite a few evenings progressed into, and climaxed in, singing bouts), his would be the lone voice stubbornly sticking out with its set drone. But then he couldn't have been tone deaf either, because the musical tracks for his documentary and cinematic work were unexceptionable. This is one mystery I never quite cracked about Ravi.

The other thing you made little headway in with Ravi was to get him to badmouth anyone. And what is social discourse in Kerala without a cynical negation of the other? But there really were no villains in his life. He could be irritated, angry, lose his temper, but there was never any malicious afore or afterthought. There was no petty jealousy or one-upmanship with anyone. He was incapable of *schadenfreude*. Faith in the basic goodness of people – all people – was his default setting. Enmity with Ravi could thus be a self-defeating, frustrating exercise for those who bore it. For his part, he was nonplussed that the rest of the world was not like him. I have sometimes perversely egged him on to give vent to his prejudices or to direct his ire against someone I did not like. But he would not yield. Was he genuinely bereft of prejudice? Or was it the easiest, the most natural thing for him to seek to be in consonance with everyone around him?

He always occupied humanistic high ground. He stayed above the fray as petty politics in all realms played out around him. He was uniquely able to temper Marxist praxis with a Buddhist sense of distance and contemplation in his life and work. He stepped into filming, writing, discussion or thought as if into a continuum – like a dip each time into the flow of being and becoming. For this chronic traveller, departures and arrivals are both meeting points in a circularity of meaning and iteration. They are not so much descriptive accounts of places as ethnographic explorations. Sacred and secular monuments are brought to the touchstone of lived lives and lifestyles. They are never objectified or showcased as exotica. The footloose *flâneur* at once distilled the sights into signs and meanings.

He did not wear his intellect on his sleeve. It was part of his daily banter, suddenly revealing perspectives and dimensions even he would find exciting. When we were with him – even as we made light of the occasion – there was, unknown to us, a constant priming of the senses towards better, more fulsome critical understanding. There was more that was tacit than explicit in that sharing of awareness. Just as in his simple, trusting friendship.

The first part of this essay was written in June 2008 and published as an introduction to Ravi's book in 2009, while Ravi was still alive; the second part is the text of a talk at a meeting held to condole Ravi's death, in July 2011.

Media in the Melting Pot

As a copycat shoe act at a press conference it was a pale imitation of the original. Muntazer al-Zaidi aimed better, threw with robust force, and might have got his target but for George Bush's proverbial ducking skill. Jarnail Singh's shoe last week carefully avoided its mark. As is apparent from the television footage played *ad nauseam* since the incident, the senior scribe of the Hindi daily *Dainik Jagran* did not mean to hit the Indian Home Minister, P. Chidambaram. Nor, ostensibly, to become the news himself at the press conference he had gone to cover.

An agitated exchange between the journalist and the Minister culminated in Singh, almost desultorily, flipping his shoe across the table between them and on to the dais. At issue was the clean chit given by the country's Central Bureau of Investigation (CBI) to Jagdish Tytler, a prominent leader of the Congress Party, accused of inciting the riots against the Sikh population in the capital in the wake of Prime Minister Indira Gandhi's assassination by her Sikh bodyguards in 1984.

Chidambaram did not have to dodge the curious object that arc-ed safely away from him and fell by the side. But the fudge-and-dodge of his party and government in bringing those guilty of that carnage to book over the last twenty-five years were again up for the community's ire. A rash of street rallies and demonstrations erupted in Delhi and Punjab, the native state of the Sikhs. Tytler and his Party colleague Sajjan Kumar, also implicated in the case, were forced to withdraw as Congress candidates from Delhi in the polls to the Indian Parliament this month [April 2009].

Jarnail Singh's Sikh identity and sense of victimhood perhaps got the better of him in the situation. But overnight, media circles were agog with the implications of – to pun – Jarnailism versus Journalism. Beyond the immediate comic worry about whether footwear would any more be allowed into press conferences, the news media were awakening to a larger, more discomfiting doubt: whether clinical objectivity, balance and detachment as vaunted virtues of the profession were things of the past.

That doubt had surfaced dramatically in the television coverage of the terrorist attack on Mumbai last November [2008], when channels vied with one another in compromising security operations, in sabre-rattling against Pakistan and in generally rubbishing politicians as utterly contemptible. It was left to the government, paradoxically, to inject some sobriety into this free-for-all, by making it clear that it was not about to oblige the media by going to war with Pakistan.

A strong undercurrent of political and peer reaction against the media flying off the handle, and becoming part of the problem, did have some demonstrative effect. For a brief period, television news channels did appear a shade subdued and chastened. But with elections being announced, the tone is again growing strident.

There is, of course, no case for any ivory-tower journalism that gazes with equanimity at the seething, full-blooded and bloodying process that Indian elections have become. Journalists here cannot but get their hands dirty in their coverage of this ground-level churning of votes on and across caste, religious and community lines. From the dominant Congressism of the Nehruvian age through a tenuous bipolar phase, the national electorate now seems set to devolve into multiple regional party formations, each of them decisive in its own way in the new era of coalition politics. This bottoming-out of the franchise has, on the one hand, segmented it into numerous sectarian vote-banks, and, on the other, led to miscegenation and loosening social hierarchies.

The English-language television news channels find themselves getting more raucous and earthy to cope with this changing electoral demographic. The mainstream national English dailies and periodicals, for the most part, try and stay above the fray, even as they have grown more trivia- and tabloid-obsessed. These two news media together form the privileged, influential creamy layer of the fourth estate, which seeks to set the agenda in terms of a national–global consciousness. But in a polarized polity, the trend is not so much top-down as bottom-up.

In the regional languages of India there is a media scramble on to identify and occupy the niches that constitute the multi-party system. Local-language newspapers run by, or loyal to, one or the other political party have been buttressed by the recent spurt in the growth rate of the regional press, which in turn is sustained by urbanization, growing social mobility and the success of national literacy campaigns bringing newer readers into their fold. Their television counterparts also reach out to the illiterate sections, and therefore become that much more valuable as platforms to fetch votes and bond constituencies.

There is little place for professional news value in this scheme of things. A stark example of partisan news ruling the roost is the south Indian state of Tamil Nadu. Both the major political parties of the state, the Dravida Munnetra Kazhagam (DMK) and the All India Anna Dravida Munnetra Kazhagam (AIADMK), run television channels in the local Tamil language, directly or by proxy. In the name of news and current affairs, the two channels, for the most part, talk to and taunt each other.

Other Tamil channels too, similarly, are glib and aggressive mouthpieces of their respective parties. They are all in campaign mode round the clock and round the year, not only during elections. Caught in this crossfire, the only option the neutral Tamil viewer has is the state-owned television, Doordarshan, where, unfortunately, the editorial mindset is to sanitize to such an extent that no news is good news.

The smaller neighbouring state of Kerala is a study in contrast. With full literacy and sparkling development indices, the state has near-saturation news-media penetration and coverage, in both print and television. The Congress Party and the Communist Party of India (Marxist) (CPI[M]), which head the two coalition formations that alternate in government in successive elections, have their own newspapers and television channels. But they both strive for a semblance of credibility even among their cadres.

In any case, the dominant newspapers and channels here are professional business entities which may have political sympathies one way or the other, but are careful to appear even-handed to their large and ideologically disparate readership or viewership. With the rightist Bharatiya Janata Party (BJP) having only a marginal presence, the political discourse in the state has conventionally been left-of-centre. Ideologically, the differences between parties on the same side of the political spectrum are narrow, and cast more in terms of one-upmanship in their secular and progressive agendas. This lack of differentiation becomes all the more manifest on television during elections, when spokespersons of these political parties tend to soft-pedal extreme positions in a bid to be acceptable to the bulk of the viewers and end up saying pretty much the same thing in different words. They cannot be too careful in a state where a 1 per cent vote-shift makes or unmakes governments.

Voters in the northern states do not have to grapple with such subtleties. The election themes of the right, centre and left, and of national and regional parties are writ large and acrimoniously contested in the media. But for all the hypermedia atmospherics, no direct linkage has been established between media – particularly television – visibility and electoral success. Whether that will change with television channels panning out as extended forums of regional political parties, remains to be seen. For now what is certain is that the Indian media, like Indian politics, is in the melting pot.

First published on the *Al Jazeera* website, 12 April 2009.

Electoral Media Mix

When cyberdom comes, they say, we won't need to be out there braving the weather campaigning, attending rallies, or waiting in queues with all and sundry to cast our votes. We will be logged in, clued on, and will exercise our franchise with a tap on the keypad, a click on the mouse or a touch on the computer screen, from the comfort of our homes or offices. It will be a smooth, clinical, disinfected, disembodied affair. Welcome to the electoral utopia of the future.

Happily for us, we are digital divides away from that terrible prospect for our democracy. But television, as a halfway house, gives us a sense of what is to come. A good part of that great outdoor fiesta that is Indian elections has already moved indoors and collapsed within the four corners of the TV frame. This is the domesticated, made-for-TV part of our electoral process, targeted at the cocooned, growingly cynical and disenchanted middle classes.

The political cast of candidates and party spokespersons here are like marionettes at the ends of invisible electronic threads, mouthing their sound bytes, or whipping up spleen and animus according to the unstated script and format of the particular show they are on – with the anchor or moderator playing agent provocateur or ringmaster, as the case may be.

What should be on the ground is on air (apart from, that is, flying footwear). And the abstraction tells. A pow-wow on an English-language news channel is nowhere near anything substantive as it is rhetorical.

Arch rivals, daggers drawn, cannot help but let on that they are on backslapping terms in the real world. Show hosts and reporters, for the most part, either make you laugh or make you angry. When they are not gasping for things to say, they have bitten off more than they can chew and, in either event, end up sub-articulate. It's thumbs up all the way to dumb down.

The physicality and dynamics of ground events themselves lapse into kitsch in the TV gaze. I have never ceased to marvel at a surreal drama I pass by so often in Chennai on a stretch of footpath near the Chepauk cricket stadium. Tucked safely away from the Secretariat and Assembly complex, this is the designated venue for political demonstrations in the city. The attendance for an event ranges from a handful to a pandal-full, depending on who is organizing it. The leaders blasting into the public address system invariably have their backs turned to the audience, and seem, at first sight, to be addressing the passing traffic – until you realize that they are performing for TV cameras on the roadside in front of them. The entire gathering appears to be consensually pitching for wider reach of the airwaves. The electric possibility of the moment is taken over by an electronic casting about for a dispersed constituency.

Larger mobilizations by political parties for their election meetings present a more daunting spectacle. Saturation multi-camera coverage, often by and for their own captive TV channels, is now part of the ritual fanfare. It does not seem to matter that the fiery speech from the dais is lost on any section of the rally the camera trains on. The masses, surging and waving towards the camera sweeping over them, provide a peculiar Brechtian, alienative relief.

For all that, regional-language television captures the spirit and feel of the polls far more intimately than English-language channels, which somehow seem to be at one remove from it all. This is but natural in a sense, because elections in India are after all fought in the Indian languages and not in English. But the Delhi-centric channels have been slow to recognize the growing regional idiom in national politics. As that awareness is suddenly upon them, we see them hastily clambering up the learning curve; and often it is not a pretty sight.

As a Lalu Prasad Yadav or a Mayawati move on, in their estimation and treatment, from caricatures to consummate politicians and accomplished administrators; as the polity pans and bottoms out; as the political margin moves towards the centre – a reality check is forced upon them. Newer and more raucous voices reflecting lived realities intrude into the cultivated buzz of the studio chatterati and demand fresh responses.

A fractured political landscape perhaps needs a segmented TV market to match. And, from the look of it, what used to be a national–regional vertical axis in both politics and the TV news media has shifted into a horizontal roll-out of multiple constituencies. Even if Manmohan Singh had accepted Advani's call for a national debate on TV, and both of them had pretended as much, the national political consciousness is no longer polarized between two conventional national parties.

First published in *Outlook*, 11 May 2009.

We, the Media

The issue boils down to this: Do the media have a mandate, or responsibility, to safeguard the moral health of the vulnerable, younger age groups in society? The media's role in gathering and purveying information, we know, is not always enlightening or empowering. It can be innocence-shedding, voyeuristic, even corrupting. But should the media consciously become a moral agency and set up a virtual barrier, a *cordon sanitaire*, between virtue and vice, and monitor it with a vigilant eye?

The Japanese computer rape game is an open and shut case. It is pathologically perverse and has no right to exist in any sane setting. Precisely because it is so abhorrently aberrant, should the media be throwing any light on it, or drawing any attention to it?

We are familiar with the media's conspiracy of silence when it comes to facts upsetting our cocooned sense of what is right and normative. We therefore know little about the victims of the US invasion of Iraq. Even as the civilian victims are rendered a mortality statistic, the soldiers who die (and these deaths are no less unfortunate) have full-blooded identities with portfolios of courage and patriotism.

In the same context, the media have carefully and consensually shunned graphic depiction of the torture we now know of at Abu Ghraib. Interestingly, one outraged Flickr user and blogger, who goes by the pseudonym 'legofesto', responds to this blackout by mainstream media by recreating, from photographs and eyewitness accounts, the methods of torture at Abu Ghraib using Lego toy figures. Unlike the Japanese rape game, this toy metaphor becomes a powerful protest against squeamishness blocking media exposure of gross violation of human rights and dignity. Are our young minds to be insulated from knowledge of such iniquities with abetment through silence by the media?

Social and moral codes and filters, no doubt, delineate the media space, as against a freewheeling Tower of Babel anarchy. The freedom of expression guaranteed by Article 19 of the Indian Constitution is qualified by reasonable restraints. But what do the gatekeepers of the media let in, or keep out? Will a sanitized, formal public-media sphere keep the vulgarity out of our lives and those of our children? How do we control the diversified expressions of the media digitally exploding around us? Or the freewheeling cyberspace, the nooks and crannies of which host the pornographic?

Yes, what Guy Debord called the Society of the Spectacle is becoming a minefield of what-might-hit-you-next uncertainties. The media are in a state of flux, and long-held notions about journalistic principles are being questioned. Journalistic objectivity, for instance, is increasingly seen as a red herring for the status quo, especially where a new form of political capitalism takes over the media. Silvio Berlusconi in Italy and Thaksin Shinawatra in Thailand leveraged their media empires to capture political power. In India today, we see a mushrooming of television channels propagating one or the other political party's agenda. Objectivity, then, can only be a byproduct of colliding subjectivities across the media spectrum. Drawing moral lines in this welter of mediated information and disinformation, short of a consensual common minimum agreement on what is absolutely not on, can only complicate the picture even more.

As newer forms of the media – blogs, social media, citizens' journalism – assail the battlements, as it were, of the traditional mainstream media, a spontaneous democratization is redefining the purview of the fourth estate. This invariably upsets the value systems of the day and is prone to a degree of vulgarization. Victorian or brahminic values, for instance, tended to be scandalized by the sartorial and scatological affronts of mass media like cinema and television as the language turned realistically foul and the dress provocatively skimpy. It may be this bottoming-out that partly earns for the news media the charge of peddling sex and sensation. True, there is a problem; but it is partly generic to the evolving ecology, and should not be stretched to convey that the fourth estate is a fifth column of anti-social, immoral subversion.

The best that can be done is to engage critically with the media; and, to paraphrase Gandhi, be the media you want to change. Technological convergence and digitization make this possible. There are no entry barriers. Segmentation in the media sector is unleashing diverse and dispersed constituencies. The field is opening up for intervention and participation.

The young, from being victims, should become beneficiaries of this vast media-churning. They have a stake in the media commons, and must be equipped to constitute and transform it. Deconstructing and engaging with the media must become a part of curricular learning even at the school level. The age of the ubiquitous media demands no less.

First published in *Business World*, 1 February 2010.

Decade-end Thoughts

E.L. Doctorow's novel *Ragtime* (1975), subsequently made into a film, is set in the turn of the last century. The magician Houdini, the finance capitalist J.P. Morgan, automobile baron Henry Ford who symbolized the height of the industrial revolution, anarchist–feminist Emma Goldman, Freud, Jung, and a number of lesser luminaries rub shoulders with one another against the background score of Scott Joplin's ragtime music and the backdrop of rising resentment against racism in the United States. Doctorow effortlessly invokes the stalwarts and the major events of the era to evoke a peculiar but masterly blend of fact and fiction. There is the promise of imagination ahead. As Khalil Gibran sang, how could we lose faith in the justice of life, when the dreams of those who sleep upon feathers are not more beautiful than the dreams of those who sleep upon the earth?

Towards the end of that century, Eric Hobsbawm gave us a reality check of hopes belied and despaired for the twenty-first century, because he thought it was spiralling out of the reach of the common man. In his interview-mode analysis of what has gone by and what is to come, published as *The New Century* (2001), Hobsbawm stopped short of fully endorsing Isaiah Berlin's verdict that the twentieth century was the most terrible century in western history but pointed to an uncertain future where a few privileged nations barricaded themselves in and against the demands and aspirations of the rest of the world; where globalization and liberalization served the richest sliver of the human population, and became empty catchwords for those outside its pale; and where digital technology provided access and information but no real stakes in power and wealth.

Be that as it may, as the first decade of the twenty-first century draws to a close, it is tempting to imagine how a new novelist might draw on the major players and events of the last ten years in an epoch-setting, modern counterpart of Doctorow's *Ragtime*. It would be a formidable task, because the facts of this first decade of the new century are already stranger than fiction. An Osama bin Laden defies the creative imagination, and the manner of the strike on the twin towers on September 11 – and all that went into and before it – is the stuff of several novels. And all that followed slips into the surreal because it defies basic cause-and-effect sequence or logic. Because bin Laden has disappeared into thin air, Saddam Hussein becomes the alternative scapegoat and weapons of mass destruction (WMD) the bogey to fix him. America and its allies invade Iraq, and, after much killing and destruction, cannot find any hidden WMD. So they go for the next best thing that is hidden – Saddam himself. They pull him out of his underground burrow, try him in a kangaroo court and string him up. The rest of the story is about desperately trying to keep the volatile remnants together and, equally desperately, to bail out before the country collapses into civil war.

This master-narrative is the axis on which the first decade of this century has spun. As part of the spin, another ridiculous illogic stares the world in the face. Bin Laden becomes synonymous with Islam, and Islam becomes synonymous with terrorism – the black plague of this era. We will, we know, have to live with that untruth for a long time to come, as religious profiling takes us a few centuries backward. Paradoxically, the religions themselves seem to be seeking to be profiled by growingly assertive external markers, including the hijab and the purdah.

Other dramatis personae and events vie for attention with this central plot. Bush gives way to Obama, who initially stokes the romance of blackness in power. But with the global economy taking a nose-dive and the US economy being the worst off for it, and by pursuing a domestic economic and foreign war policy that looks like a cosmetic job done on Bush's, the historic gains of that electoral achievement seem frittered away.

Meanwhile, interesting configurations and contestations across the world add to the tension and the drama. Countries in Latin America are experimenting with newer forms of socialism and already predicting the end of what had set out to be the American century. In Russia, where socialism is already a faded memory, corrupt oligarchs jail corrupt plutocrats to prevent them emerging as a political threat. The European Union is an uncomfortable sight of coercive cohabitation in which the partners would rather sue one another for divorce. Israel gets more aggressive as the Palestinian cause becomes *passé* even among the Arab nations. African states don't really help in exploding the stereotype of internecine strife of genocidal proportions and corruption eating into the vitals of the system even before the system is in place. Iran and North Korea, we are urged to believe, are agents of a nuclear apocalypse. Pending that atomic obliteration, tsunamis, earthquakes and floods come as sharp, painful spikes in a dangerous graph of climate change, and take their periodic toll. Amidst all this, a lonely Aung Sang Suu Kyi, for long ploughing her lonely furrow in Burma, suddenly bursts upon our moral conscience – much like Nelson Mandela earlier.

On our subcontinent, the attack on Mumbai makes 26/11 a grisly sequel to 9/11. The Tamil cause in Sri Lanka, wrested from its self-appointed champion, the Pol Potist LTTE (Liberation Tigers of Tamil Eelam), is put in the vindictive hands of a proto-fascist Sinhala state. China is the bar India must seek to better in its newfound role as one of the world's emergent economic leaders, even as we set our sights on United Nations' Security Council membership. Farmers continue to commit suicide with reassuring regularity, and social and economic inequity and deprivation provide the static background buzz that tells us the system is live and ticking.

If a touch of the spy stuff was missing in all this, it takes us by storm towards the end of the decade with WikiLeaks and its unlikely hero, Julian Assange. Unlikely, because a rape rap doesn't quite sit well on a hero. But the impact of the material he put out in each instalment registers like on a Richter scale. The corridors of power suddenly find themselves exposed to the public realm. As world leaders run for cover, seek to limit the damage, silence Assange and plug the leak, we suddenly realize that digital information technology can invert the hierarchy and put the governing class at the receiving end.

Our own *desi* subplot of a leak that shook and displaced the powerful comes as a spicy finish to the decade. Nira Radia and her telephone chats are becoming as much the voyeurs' as the law enforcement agencies' delight. We hear and see journalists cosying up to corporates, corporates fixing policies, policies acquiring price tags, politicians looting the exchequer. A rash of scams surfaces, and suddenly the political milieu is a minefield across which everyone is stepping warily. A nice note on which to leave these pompous marauders as we bid goodbye to 2010. What a decade! Can any novelist, any fabulist, serve up anything better than it actually was?

First published in *Outlook*, 10 January 2011.

A Vintage Recollection

Book review: S. Muthiah, *A Madras Miscellany: A Decade of People, Places and Potpourri*, East West Books, Chennai, 2011.

The global village of Marshall McLuhan's imagination was a technologically distilled utopia where everyone and everything would be familiar and on sure ground – a network of personalized interrelationships, like in a village. The real world that has overtaken that vision may seem more like a digitally taped dystopia of anonymous multitudes in a state of perpetual anomie. But not for S. Muthiah. Week after week he cuts through the clutter and clamour of modern and modernizing Chennai, and leads us to the quiet refuge of his weekly column, 'A Madras Miscellany', where people, places and events acquire identity, context, lineage and meaning, connecting the dots, each time, of a little narrative.

He has been at it for over a decade now. The city itself has continued to transform during this period in terms of its demographics, architectural skyline, social dynamics, cultural milieu and varied lifestyles. But far from being disoriented by this welter of change, Muthiah picks up the threads of continuity whenever and wherever he can find them, and traces them as far back as they will take him. The littleness of the effort is deceptive. The bits and pieces of information he snaps up are the twigs and leaves of a mnemonic nest he has been patiently building for long. It is an unhurried, serendipitous work in progress, open-ended and perhaps never meant to be complete.

As a compilation 1,200-plus pages long, however, these disparate anecdotal tidbits take on the size and scale of a tome. The weekly modest deposits, we now see, have grown into a rich memory-bank from which one can draw at random. To use a book-cricketing metaphor, the open-any-page-and-read value of the publication makes it a unique proposition. Cover to cover, the columns appear in the same sequence as they did in *The Hindu* from mid-November 1999 to mid-November 2009. But the chronology of the matter in hand in between shuttles back and forth from the present to the recent past to the colonial.

Its dispersed, non-linear structure makes the experience of engaging with the book almost digital, and opens up, to the tech-savvy mind, the potential of an electronic video game-like version. Or an online avatar where interactivity with the reader, or the mutualization that N. Ram, Editor-in-Chief of *The*

Hindu, writes about in his Introduction, comes into its own in real time. The author will no doubt be aghast at such possibilities, having shunned the computer and the mobile phone as devices too modern for his taste and trade, and stayed with his time-tested Olivetti to churn out his weekly labour of love. The postman knocks to deliver or correct information, and the telephone at home suffices to stay in touch.

Not surprisingly, there is a vintage quality to the recollection and to the telling of it. Those peopling these pages tend to be more patrician than plebeian. No parvenu has a place here. Nor is there much tolerance for the quotidian. Like the persona, the locations and occasions the author evokes may have greater resonance in an initiated peer circle. But the lay reader is not left behind. The excitement of rediscovery is as fresh and tingling each time, in each essay. By his very act of remembering, Muthiah redeems his chosen or given subjects from the proverbial shortness of public memory, to make them snippets of material for his patchwork city lore.

Somewhere in these pages, he makes an oh-for-the-subaltern pass at the genre. But his approach is hardly that. The work does not, of course, seek or pretend to be a definitive historical account either. The factoids, flashbacks and memorabilia are too dispersed across time and space to add up to be a sum of their parts. But as potted history of a Chennai that was Madras, this is both a reader's and a collector's delight.

Tailpiece: As one who grew up in Madras of the 1960s and is yet to come fully to terms with the twenty-first-century metropolis it has become, this reviewer is easily drawn into the period mood Muthiah so instinctively creates. And, leveraging this opportunity, the reader–reviewer turns postman to knock for the author's help in cracking a fifty-year-old obsessive doubt. Who was the Montieth of Montieth Road in Egmore? It used to be a quiet, tamarind tree-lined residential street sated with the smell of the ripe fruit in summer. A future column, one fondly hopes, will tell.

First published in *The Hindu*, 7 June 2011.

Brand Anna and the Media

It would, of course, be an insult to the intelligence and concern of the cross-section of society flocking to the streets against corruption, to call it a rabble roused by the media. The credit for bringing things to this pass goes, perhaps even more than to Anna Hazare, to the government strategists who thought up the incredibly foolish plan of taking him into preventive custody, and soon found themselves at a loss to handle a detenu determined to overstay his welcome in Tihar jail. Hazare and his cohorts could not have asked for a better opening to this second round of their campaign for a Jan Lokpal Bill. The government, which has clearly lost the plot, now seems reduced to a face-saving role in a Hazare script.

For the media, this is no doubt a delectable situation replete with possibilities. And indeed, the generally barbed coverage fully befits the occasion. But then, in the race for eyeballs a section of the media – some television channels in particular – gives the impression of sprinting ahead of the story and dragging it along behind. What defies the imagination, even as it stretches journalistic credibility, is that the messengers become the lead players, directing the route the story will take, conjuring up twists and turns where there are none, and keeping the illusion of news-in-the-making breathlessly alive.

This hybrid genre of agitprop news television is by now a familiar, even if never pretty, sight in India. The type depends on a number of props to keep the buzz buzzing. Hyperbole is its figure of speech. The Hazare movement is instantly catapulted into a revolution, the second war of independence, the Arab Spring of South Asia. Nothing short of the entire nation, we are repeatedly told, is watching. So the man on the street or the VIP in the studio speaking to the TV channel is *ipso facto* speaking to the nation. It does not matter that the channel in question may only have a low, single-digit viewership. If there is a lighter side to Benedict Anderson's concept of nation as imagined community, this must be it.

The relationship between such media and their essentially middle-class consumers is becoming uncomfortably incestuous. When respondents cluster around a camera for a *vox pop*, they are not so much required to offer their independent view on an issue as add to the chorus of opinion orchestrated by the channel. A photo op masquerades as a movement. Dissident voices get short shrift. It is more like a recruitment drive than a professional journalistic exercise to seek and purvey news. Increasingly, the channels' role seems to be to trigger and promote a form of direct democracy by the middle class. Politics and politicians are routinely debunked; even representative democracy does not seem to make the grade.

No channel in the league seems able to resist this strange, aggressive, white-collar evangelism. On the contrary, the more strident and hawkish ones in the pack seem to set the tone and tenor of the discourse, and the rest follow helplessly as if driven by some inexorable law of the market. It is all so oracular and self-referential. The positions taken are almost always maximalist and hardly ever nuanced. A ratings mindset demands that the pot be kept boiling.

Arguably, the media promote such media friskiness in the middle class at its own peril. A revolution of rising expectations, even if not alarmist at present, may prove more and more difficult to cope with in the long run. Apart from the implicit risk to human sensibility of relentless, adrenaline-pumping media fare, the law of diminishing returns is bound to kick in sooner or later. Truth-telling, which is at the core of journalism, may then become vulnerable to the market dictate of giving the people what they want – an argument that already serves as an alibi for dumbing down and tabloidization in the news media. And, as Reuven Frank, former president of NBC, pointed out, giving the people what they want is a dope pusher's excuse. Journalism, surely, is a higher calling.

Anna Hazare and his struggle for an effective Lokpal Bill against corruption are not creations of the media. But there is a gnawing sense of a convergence of the civil society, which sustains the man and his movement, and the media market. It is at this meeting point that brand Anna takes shape, independent of its author. It is this brand that drives the media into its high-pitched hard-sell. It is a rare confluence of a big cause and huge profit. The irony is that the man who, more than most, paved the way for such freewheeling market-friendliness suddenly finds himself estranged and isolated. Brand Manmohan was for long celebrated by the middle classes he had enriched and pampered. But suddenly his government is the butt of their ire and new expectations abound.

First published in *Outlook*, 29 August 2011.

Musings on the Media in the Dock

Much of the media, says Justice Markandey Katju, the new Chairman of the Press Council of India, is of very poor intellectual level. That would be, even for a former judge, a judgmental statement – except that sections of the media concerned seem hell-bent on proving him right. Setting out to prove how seriously responsible it can be, the Indian Broadcast Editors' Association (BEA) issued ten guidelines on how the birth of Aishwarya Rai Bachchan's first child should be covered by TV channels. If the media obsession with an event that necessitated such a preemptive code is a measure of the intellectual level obtaining in the sector, the benefit of the doubt goes to Justice Katju.

On the other hand, Justice Katju may have got it all wrong, because intellectualism and the media have little to do with each other. If anything, they are antithetical to each other. Some of the best thinkers of our time – Noam Chomsky, Jacques Derrida, Pierre Bourdieu, to name a few – have dwelt on how the media compromise, coopt and corrupt intellectuals, and why they must resist the temptation of the media.

Be that as it may, Justice Katju's more substantive case for expanding the scope and powers of the Press Council, and for regulation of the news media, calls for critical reflection. The main thrust of his argument is that when politicians and bureaucrats, professional bodies such as the Medical Council of India and the Bar Council of India, and auditors are subject to such regulation, and when even judges of High Courts and the Supreme Court can be impeached, there is no reason why the press alone should claim exemption. He persuasively cites the example of regulatory frameworks in democracies and media dispensations in western countries. Self-regulation, he points out with a flourish, is an oxymoron.

But it is precisely the exceptionalist premise of the free media that sets it apart from other institutions and agencies, and makes it a *sine qua non* of democracy. In a democracy, the first three pillars – the executive, the legislature and the judiciary – are constitutionally accountable to the people. The government is responsible through the legislature; legislators have to seek their mandate from the people; even judges, as we were recently reminded, can be impeached by parliament. It is only the fourth pillar of democracy, or the fourth estate, that is not institutionally or constitutionally accountable. And indeed, that is the way it should be. For if the fourth pillar were to be so accountable, it would lend itself to the systemic oversight of one or more of the other pillars, and would therefore cease to be a free press in the true sense of the term.

The Italian philosopher Umberto Eco explains this exclusive privilege of the media in terms of a conundrum. Mass media, he says,

> can influence the political life of a country by creating opinion. But the traditional powers cannot control or criticize the mass media other than through the media itself; otherwise their intervention becomes a sanction – either executive, legislative or judiciary – which can happen only if the media commits crimes or appears to lead to the formation of political and institutional imbalance.

Eco, however, hastens to add: 'Since the media . . . cannot be exempt from criticism, it is a condition of health for a democratic society that *the press put itself on the stand*' (emphasis added). A natural instinct for self-preservation through self-regulation would, in this scheme of things, best guarantee an unfettered and responsible media freedom.

The situation we have today, though, has the appearance of a profligate news media perforce being put in the dock. The profligacy is seen as being so generic that when a court of law fines a television channel Rs 100 crore, as damages for showing the wrong photograph (of the complainant, Justice P.B. Sawant, who, incidentally, was a former chairman of the Press Council of India) with a report on judicial corruption, it hardly creates a ripple in the public sphere. The sense, if anything, is that the irresponsible, opinionated and corrupt media are finally getting their just deserts.

The media, no doubt, have only themselves to blame for bringing things to such a pass. Their disconnect with the public, which has been in the making for some time now, has eroded the moral and institutional high ground the media have thus far enjoyed, so much so that talk of reining them in through firm measures does not appear misplaced. It is fertile ground to sow seeds of doubt about the continued efficacy of self-regulation, and to raise the demand for a regulator other than of and by the media themselves.

The context and the track record of press freedom in India, however, demand a second look at the idea of an external regulator. Freedom of the press here is not as unquestionably a given as it is in the UK or the US. An unbridled press synonymous with democracy, as we know it, evolved over centuries of trials and tribulations in England, and is now an ingrained part of its political and social psyche. A free press is firmly written into the Constitution of the US: the First Amendment specifically forbids Congress from making any laws that abridge the freedom of the press.

There is no such implicit internalization of, or an explicit constitutional prescription for press freedom in the Indian situation. It is essentially inferred and derived from Article 19(1) (a) and (g) in the Fundamental Rights chapter of the Constitution, which speaks of the right to freedom of expression and movement, as well as the right to practise any trade or profession, within reasonable restraints. The Emergency of 1975 was the most serious but not the only attempt to thwart this freedom. Draconian laws against the press have been mooted by succeeding governments but foiled by the joint resistance of the media fraternity and the people. The legislature and the judiciary too have borne down on and beleaguered journalists in the name of breach of privilege and contempt of court. Freedom of the press here, thus, is not an inviolate or settled right that can be taken for granted. It may therefore be prudent to tread softly in terms of statutory regulation lest it become another mechanism to wield pressure on the media.

The indication from the public discourse thus far on the intended regulation is that it is likely to have a deterrent slant, and be directed at the news content purveyed by television and print media. Regulation of content by a statutory body is at best a euphemism for censorship. On the other hand, a forum to address and remedy grievances through a process of mediation, much like the Press Complaints Commission in the UK, would be unexceptionable. The law of the land, and the civil and criminal courts, must handle the rest. That the legal route is cumbersome and that justice is routinely delayed cannot become a selective alibi only against the press, and for regulation.

In fact, much of the distortion and prejudice circulating in the news media, particularly television, harks back to the lack of real pluralism in the sector. Stiff entry barriers and whimsical distribution costs have skewed the market in favour of a club of big players who collectively push the same consumerist values and a narrow class agenda. It is the structural disparity in the sector that is crying out for reform and regulation. If the Press Council can move to facilitate diversity in the media space and enable a multitiered milieu that caters to different segments of the people, it would at once pave the way for a more congenial and equitable media setting, and save itself the tedious and dubious prospect of cracking the whip to bring errant media practitioners to heel.

The Press Council, even to attempt this, will have to be recast with the necessary mandate, and expanded to include print, broadcast and online media. Technological convergence makes it redundant to have separate bodies attending to the different forms of the media. The media, and media freedom, have become indivisible, and must be dealt with as such. Media organizations, on their part, must re-establish their credibility and link with the people, to continue to assume the freedoms that define the democratic press. They must, equally importantly, carry out a self-reality check to see whether their obsession with the business of the media is driving this definitive journalism of the media out of their market.

First published in *The Hindu*, 22 November 2011.

The Exercise of Hegemony and the Need for a Counter-Hegemony Initiative in Contemporary Culture and Media

Fredric Jameson, in his *Cultural Logic of Late Capitalism* (1984), captures three critical historical junctures of capitalism and their respective cultural tempers: the market capitalism of the 1840s whose cultural logic was realism; the monopoly capitalism of the 1890s whose expression was modernism; and the latest and current phase of multinational capitalism of the 1940s which brings what, for many of us, may be the uncomfortable realm of postmodernism. Scholars like Vivian Sobchack have extrapolated on this schema to propose the dominant cultural instrumentality of each of these phases: the photographic, exemplifying the mood of realism under market capitalism; the cinematic, dominating the sensibility of modernism under monopoly capitalism; and the electronic, pervading the contemporary postmodern phase.

The shift from the cinematic to the electronic is subsumed in the larger transition from the analogue to the digital, which is perhaps the definitive technological change of our time and marks the essential dynamics of the information revolution, which, we are told, has succeeded or superseded the industrial revolution. It is a change with the potential to subvert the hierarchic ordering of the world as we know it. The non-linear takes over from the linear; the margins move into the centre; the tyranny of the written text is challenged by visual and acoustic modes of knowledge furtherance and sense perception. To put it another way, digital technology draws us to see, hear and experience our context first-hand, rather than read about it at one remove. The new technology weaves a sensorium around us that approximates our natural cognitive experience.

The electronic, on the rebound, alters the terms of the cinematic. Digitization is taking over both the production and – with satellite simulcasts – the exhibition of cinema, rendering obsolete the processing and printing of film raw stock. Digital surround sound in the modern cinema, or in home theatre, disperses the myriad components of the audio track so that they come to us from different directions, spatially matching the visual source of the voice or sound on the screen. The visual, meanwhile, strives to be expressed as 3D (three-dimensional) or HD (high definition), although, with variations in the aspect ratio, it continues to be confined to the rectangular screen. The change, perhaps, will be complete when the visual breaks out of its rectangularity and simulates the panoptic ken of the human eye.

The churning that accompanies the transition into the digital realm is yet to settle down, and has thrown up a mix of new perceptual and conceptual elements which seek to challenge the perspectives and values that are a given at this point. These constitute a cultural newspeak that requires us to press the reset button and reconfigure the world.

Flatism is perhaps the more tendentious of these concepts. In the post-Nietzschean tradition, as Susan Sontag (1966) tells us, there are no heights or depths – only various kinds of surfaces and spectacles. Roland Barthes (1972) goes further and rubbishes the idea of depth as a repository of any concealed meaning. Jean Baudrillard's (1989) mirror metaphor holds up the idiosyncratic end of the proposition. Régis Debray (1996) calls the contemporary realm a media-sphere that privileges the letter against the spirit, extension in space against comprehension, space against duration, surface against content. The mediological sensibility, he says, is not given to going to the bottom of things, keeping instead to faces, surfaces and interfaces. The operative jargon of the new media seems to prop up this new surfaceism: after all, we surf, rather than delve into, television channels and the internet. The setting thus was ripe for Thomas Friedman (2005) to script his anecdotal adventure of flattening the world into a continuum of information technology enclaves – a level playing field, as he saw it, with easy enough entrance and exit options.

Before Friedman declared the world flat, Francis Fukuyama (1993, 1999), with more scholarly effort, had both declared history dead and announced a new order on a clean slate. Endism, however, did not get as much play as Flatism, and Fukuyama's *The End of History* and *The Great Disruption* turned out to be flashes in the pan at the turn of the new century. But it was unsettling enough that he could grab intellectual and media attention, and seize the popular imagination, even if fleetingly, for propositions that were outlandishly *sui generis*.

Another set of ideas privileged by the information age is a version of the futurism propounded by Marinetti as far back as 1909, with its celebration of speed. We declare that the splendour of the world has been enriched by a new beauty: the beauty of speed.[1] Speed in the media morphs, in Todd Gitlin's (2003) gaze, into a torrent – which, combined with the digital parsing of sensibility, leads to the rhetoric of sound bytes and a regime of sparse attention spans. Speed introduces an aesthetics of blur to photo, video and typography, and incentivizes techniques like stop-framing, shutter motion and out-of-focus shots. The trend, for Gitlin, is reminiscent of the spirit of impressionism in painting: the visual style introduced by the French impressionists in the 1870s to convey the instant of motion, the instant *in* motion, recorded as if the artist's hand were in motion, has now reached typography, the representation of language itself.

The known iconizing impulse of the mass media breaks up, in this digital future, into a realm of flitting attention and fleeting reputations where, as Andy Warhol mocked, everyone will be world-famous for fifteen minutes. Speed and futurism combine also to pace up the rate of technological obsolescence in the digitized media. The state of the art is in constant renewal, and the new quickly yields to the newer in gadgetry – more up to the moment, versatile and affordable than what went just before.

The explosion of information that marks the age and the compression of this vast data through digitization place a huge demand on the human capacity for assimilation, making it necessary to resort to what the French biologist and futurist Joel de Rosney calls a dietetics of communication.[2] The need to pick and choose optimally, nutritionally, from the surfeit fare on offer out there for our consumption leads to the ratings mindset that rules mass media and culture. Ratings become not only the rationale for allocation of advertising budgets, but also the filter by which the popularity of cultural products are hierarchized. The bestseller and countdown lists in books and music, for instance, determine the universe of our reading and the repertoire of our heard melodies. Works outside these shortlists do not make it to our notice and, for all practical purposes, do not exist. The tyranny of ratings, as Pierre Bourdieu (1998) points out, takes a toll on our intellectual potential because it is so subservient to popular demand. It circumscribes our intellectual horizons. Contrast this, he says, with the fact that well until recently, the greatest accomplishments in literature, science or mathematics actually went against the grain of the popular.

It is also a phase when thinkers or clairvoyants who lived in advance of their times are being posthumously rediscovered for their prescience about the information age that is suddenly upon us. The oracular aphorisms of Marshall McLuhan (1994) and Guy Debord (1967, trans. 1994) seem to come into their own in this era. In particular, Debord's *Society of the Spectacle*, written in the late 1960s, bears an uncanny resemblance to what obtains today. In societies where modern conditions of production prevail, he wrote, all of life presents itself as an immense accumulation of spectacles. Everything that was directly lived has moved away into representation.

The process of reality being abstracted by its representation, which has dogged literature and philosophy down the ages, acquires a kind of criticality in the information age. A.K. Ramanujan (2005) cites the plight of King Dushyanta in Kalidasa's *Shakuntala* as his memory plays tricks on him – like one who doubts the existence of an elephant who walks in front of him but feels convinced by seeing footprints. The elephant in the room goes unrecognized; it takes its footprints, after it has left, to re-member, reconstruct its presence. Cognition, in the traditional Indian definition, integrates the *pratyaksha* (that which is manifest) with what is arrived at through *anumana* (inference), what is remembered through *smriti* (memory) and what is reported as *aptavakya* (eyewitness account). Representative reality takes over lived reality when direct, unmediated perception – or the capacity to see the obvious, the manifest, i.e. *pratyaksha* – is supplanted by the secondary constructs of *smriti*, *anumana* or *aptavakya*.

In nineteenth-century Europe we had Feuerbach, in his *Essence of Christianity* (1989), lamenting in similar vein, that his era prefers the image to the thing, the copy to the original, the representation to reality, appearance to being. The representative ritual of the eucharist, where the faithful partake of the body and the blood of Christ, acquires a larger-than-real dimension as it becomes a coded expression of the hierarchy of the church. In fact Régis Debray[3] has argued that representative values are often ascribed *post facto*. The French Revolution, he observes:

> invented the Enlightenment as a meaningful rallying round a cause; and the Catholic magisterium invented (one century after Jesus) the New Testament. The womb comes after the child, who shapes it in his own measure. The words of the Prophet are put in his mouth posthumously, all this according to the law of the precursor, the one of whom one knows afterward that he came before.

In his reflective study *Media Manifestos* (1994, trans. 1996), Debray arrives at a pervasive videosphere as the latest revelation in a palimpsest where a print- and publishing-centric graphosphere and scripture-dominated logo-sphere are the preceding layers, in that order. Moreover, he recognizes that this sphere is as determined as the biosphere, noting that a good politics can no more prevent a mass medium from functioning according to its own economy than it can prevent a severe drought. There may be consensus about the purpose of the sciences of life – viz., to prevent illness, increase longevity, mitigate suffering and better the quality of life; the manipulation of embryos and *in vitro* fertilization have to do with the genetic legacy of the species. There may not be a similar agreement about the objective of the sciences of culture because they are not subject to the equivalent of a bioethics. But they should be, suggests Debray, because like the genetic legacy of the species, they are the cultural legacy of communities. (He even raises, *inter alia*, the question whether mediology can become to semiology what ecology is to biosphere.) The new visual, sound and sign technologies are geared, instead, to globalize a sole political economy of videospheric consciousness which risks fostering harsh conditions for those who deviate from or disturb its status quo. These are technologies of standardization, rather than difference and divergence. Their product, says Debray, is of uniform value, just like power output – whether from sun, water, wind or atom – is all expressed as kilowatt/hour.

If Fordism typifies the industrial revolution at its height, its counterpart in the information revolution is Murdochism. Both systems ply standardization and homogenization. Ford intruded into the family, home and even the body of workers to ensure that they were physically and mentally fit to give of their best. Their sexual lives were monitored, their alcohol intake was reined in by prohibition and their morality was under constant scrutiny. As Gramsci writes in his *Prison Notebooks* (1996):

> American industrialists are concerned to maintain the continuity of the physical and muscular–nervous efficiency of the worker. It is in their interest to have a stable, skilled, labour force, a permanently well-adjusted complex, because the human complex (the collective worker) of an enterprise is also a machine which cannot, without considerable loss, be taken to pieces too often and renewed with single new parts.

Gramsci astutely forecast both the surveillance state and the intrusive information age when he observed:

> The attempts made by Ford with the aid of a body of inspectors to intervene in the private lives of his employees and to control how they spend their wages and how they lived, is an indication of these tendencies . . . these tendencies are yet private, but they could become, at a certain point, state ideology.

And they did, so much so that the citizen, even in liberal democracies, has been deconstructed, classified and archived in databases that serve both the profit agenda of the market and the security alarmism of the state. They are, moreover, insinuated into the practice of contemporary media and pop culture. The genre of Reality TV, which is a rage today, is a showcasing, for the most part, of the private phobias, maladjustments or mismatches in relationships between members of a social group or a family, for the entertainment and vicarious participation of viewers. All that happens behind closed doors and would normally be considered private, is displayed under the intense, unrelenting scrutiny of cameras for the public to behold. This is a modern spectacle, a psychological-thriller equivalent of the lion and the gladiator in the stadium. Pulp psychology rules the roost. The candid camera – both its jocular and sting variety – does not respect any limits of privacy. Even the internet, although purportedly a realm of anonymity, seems to end up constructing the self as a commodity by showcasing it as a cybershop window or web page, and by publicizing the personal through what seems a process of compulsive social networking.

The Hollywood blockbuster *Independence Day*,[4] of 1996, is a pointer to how technology in the garb and gizmohood of science fiction sublimates an implicit hegemonic intent into a noble and altruistic theme – in this case, a future unification of humankind occasioned by threat from an extraterrestrial enemy. The plot is about an alien invasion of the earth. No less than the President of the USA, who happens to be a fighter pilot, leads the counter-offensive. The forces he commands are drawn from across all nations of the world – a unanimous international fighting force. After much spatial blitzkrieg, the world is saved from being colonized, or destroyed, or whatever it is those weird aliens had set out to do. The rub comes at the end. In a state of the world address just before this historic victory, the President announces, as if fulfilling a long-nourished aspiration of peoples across the world, that henceforth the fourth of July would be celebrated not as American independence day but as world independence day. The telling-ness of the title kicks in. The film was one of the highest grossers ever until 1996 and, significantly, collected more overseas than within the US. Its success, like its theme, was emphatically global.

The hegemony operative here is what the scholar on media and cultural studies, Aida Hozic (1999), calls neo-Gramscian. It is persuasive rather than coercive. The hegemon presents its own interests as universal and objective, and thereby creates willing followers of its own vision. Hozic contrasts this with the neo-realist hegemony model of *Pax Americana*, where the dominant state calls the shots and determines the shape of inter-state relations.

Hozic's study of the curious intersection of Hollywood, Silicon Valley and the Pentagon ('Uncle Sam Goes to Siliwood: Of Landscapes, Spielberg and Hegemony'[5]) offers useful insights into how technology and its fetishization bring these unlikely partners on the same page, and subserve a hegemonic agenda. Computer companies like Silicon Graphics in the California belt, that earlier depended on the US military establishment for funding and research and development (R&D) work, began to turn, in the 1990s, to Hollywood for work. Even by the late 1970s Hollywood was in the process of a makeover, having stepped out of the producer-and-director-driven studio system into the more difficult turf of distributors and merchandisers. The star system and the exorbitant fees commanded by stars prompted a rebel group, including George Lucas and Steven Spielberg, to seek low-budget alternatives – to substitute the star with his virtual-digital equivalent. Lucas's *Star Wars* (1977) and Spielberg's *ET* (1982) were the first expressions of this dissidence. Stars were replaced with technology and special effects. Lucas's ILM (Industrial Lights and Magic) and Spielberg's DreamWorks SKG also initiated changes in the mode of production and distribution, restoring, on the one hand, the producer as key functionary, and adopting, on the other, a union-friendly approach. Spielberg, observes Hozic, was able to get the best animators to work for him because he allowed them authorial entitlement and a share of the profits.

From these independent beginnings, the digital technology-driven cinema has now become a cultural assertion of the US military–industrial complex. The technologies of simulation and image generation were similar for the Pentagon and Hollywood. The line between videogaming and electronic warfare blurred to such an extent that the theatre of war became a virtual theatre of the absurd for Baudrillard ([1991] 1995) when he declared that the Gulf War never took place – so unilateral, simulated and hyper-real was its conduct. The Hollywood–Pentagon mix provided volatile hits on the screen, unleashing sci-fi monoliths singlehandedly redeeming US humaneness from dystopias. These digital, special effects-suffused filmic products with their techno-icons also lent themselves better to licensing rights and branding, and to a corollary retail chain of merchandising.

Hozic points out that the dual-use technology regime under the Clinton administration, intended to promote a civilian–military industrial base, gave a fillip to this nexus, and further diffused the difference between entertainment, surveillance and warfare. Systems for monitoring ozone data are used in digital imaging for special effects; submarine sound detection technology is used in music recording; image generation technology, which served in missile rehearsal, has been turned into a part of computer-game software. The civilian aspect of dual-use technology by no means extended to the freewheeling public sphere as we know it; it was showcased in flight simulators or submarines or virtual-reality war games installed in theme parks and malls – or such other ostensibly public spaces which were enclaves of private profit. This Disneyfication and its variation of game/theme parks were essentially a process of private property masquerading as public space.

Hozic explains how a digital alliance of academic institutions in the Silicon Valley belt, R&D establishments like the Media Lab of the Massachusetts Institute of Technology, and corporate sponsors including Disney, Sony, Philips, Nintendo, Lego, Sega, Nike, Microsoft, Intel and Viacom – has built on the Silicon Valley–Hollywood–Pentagon nexus, to create diverse cultural products delivered online and offline.

Globally, Hollywoodization not only sealed the wellspring of the French New Wave of the late 1950s to early 70s, but also systematically infiltrated and deracinated the mainstream national cinemas of the world – so much so that today the dubbed Hollywood film sits pretty, like a strange but familiar cultural squatter, on prime-time television, cutting across national and local languages and cultures, whether in Europe, Asia, the Middle East or Africa. It is no longer quaint, let alone anachronistic, to see and hear American characters on the screen spout Tamil or Telugu or Hindi as the Hollywood meta-narrative unspools in such disparate ethnic settings.

Hollywood adversely impacts the local cinema industry both in terms of the market and creative expression. Voices of concern have already been raised in Kerala against Hollywood products further eroding an already precarious industry ravaged by high star-system-driven costs. Given the expatriate extent, even if narrow, of this Malayalam market, it may not get to the situation in neighbouring Karnataka where the industry has imposed a blanket ban on films dubbed into Kannada from any language. The Tamil cinema, with its wider film-friendly mass market base, has shown greater resilience, and added dubbed Hollywood to its indiscriminate if robust mix that spans the countryside with idealized feudal *katta panchayats* (kangaroo courts), middle- and upper-class city-centric milieus, and the hybridization that globalization brings to different segments of society.

Bollywood, while continuing to leverage its unique selling proposition of the song-and-dance item number (as it is called), has tailed Hollywood into the metropolitan mindset of consumerism and conspicuous consumption, and readjusted its sights to make the upper middle class and its non-resident Indian (NRI) counterpart its principal constituency. Whereas the original inspiration in Hollywood for the hi-tech, sci-fi, special-effects movie was as a counter to the bane of the star system, in both Bollywood's and Kollywood's (as Tamil filmdom is called) imitative versions, the star undergoes a prosthetic transmogrification and becomes a technological extension of himself. The robotized Rajnikanth of the Tamil film *Enthiran*[6] and cyborgized Shahrukh Khan of *Ra One*[7] in Hindi mark a self-transcendence from super-stardom to supra-stardom.

There is hardly any ruralness in the mainstream Hindi cinema of today. The rite-of-passage leitmotif of the 1970s and 80s by which the village rustic, as he moves into the city, at once sheds his innocence and becomes socially mobile, is no longer a thematic concern – precisely when, by all statistical accounts, urbanization is at its most acute in India.

Satellite delivery makes it no longer necessary to replicate hundreds of release prints of a film and cart the reels in cans to the theatres. Digital dissemination should ideally make for a de-massification of the medium, and enable devolved distribution and reach. What has happened instead is that the traditional multi-tiered exhibition system – with the A class circuit of theatres in cities, B class in townships and semi-urban areas, and C class temporary touring sheds in the villages – has collapsed, and is being rapidly replaced by a bundling of screens in the expensive and exclusive one-stop-shop facility of the multiplex.

The market, including in print and television, has become segmented and stratified, so that it is less and less one of mass media. The media themselves have become more and more class-conscious, with little going for those below a set threshold of purchasing power. The lower you are on the social and economic scale, seems the moral and the model, the less relevant you are to the media either as subject or as consumer.

Absence of cross-media restrictions in India has paved the way for monopolies straddling different sectors like print, television, radio and cybermedia. Profit maximization, rather than any commitment to the citizen's right to be informed, drives the news media. Real and imagined threats to freedom of the press are conjured up to keep the media market protected and yielding huge returns.

Lobbies for both maintaining and dismantling foreign direct investment norms in the Indian news media are essentially driven by the profit mantra – the one to keep their empires protected and competition at bay, the other to make fresh market forays with powerful foreign alliances. Both, though, are quick to cite the principle of freedom of the press or danger thereto, to press their claims. The ludicrous extent to which the bogey of press freedom can be invoked strikes home when big media houses editorially deplore the latest Wage Board recommendations on the salary structure for working journalists as a threat to a free press. What takes the cake, however, is the disingenuous attempt by the media baronage, a few years back, to make heredity and family an insurance against foreign invasion. Setting themselves up as the Indian Media Group, the members of this cartel had the gall to suggest to the government that, in order to prevent foreign infiltration in the print and broadcast sectors, mandatory 51 per cent rights should be vested in one Indian family or one Indian group.

This is not to suggest that there is no threat to the Indian media from outside. With saturation of the US and European markets, transnational heavyweights have been eyeing the Indian market as the new frontier. The big-ticket acquisitions and mergers that marked the US media scene in the late 1990s are now happening here. An investigative audit of Murdoch's diverse holdings in India, both direct and through Indian proxies, and across different sectors of the media, may well present an alarming picture of information and cultural control. (Indeed a timely exercise for a concerned neutral body like, say, the Press Council of India, would be to map the media in the country to ascertain who owns what, and how.) But the indigenous big media have been fatuous and self-serving in their response to the foreign investor at the door.

The growth of the television industry in India is peculiarly skewed and distorted by entry barriers, not in terms of access to satellite transponder or facility to uplink, but at the market-ruled distribution end. The distribution fees charged by the mega cable TV and DTH operators are exorbitant and vary whimsically, in the absence of any set tariff card, from channel to channel. As a result, small and even medium-sized ventures don't have a fighting chance of making it to the charmed circle of a national DTH or digital cable-served viewership, or even of being carried in the prime or adjacent bands in the analogue cable networks.

The situation makes a mockery of the 1995 Supreme Court ruling[8] that airwaves are public property. They seem, for all practical purposes, more like private property. This, in effect, defeats the purpose of licensing – for how does it benefit a channel to have the right to telecast without the means to be seen? In a context where hundreds of channels – over 700 at last count – are jostling for popular notice, the state should be building the infrastructure network, the information super-highway, to handle this traffic equitably and efficiently. Instead, a few big DTH and cable TV players have set up their own carriageways with their own tollbooths, charging rates that are prohibitive for the bulk of the traffic.

The government, if anything, has compounded the problem by making the financial profile required of applicants for new TV channels more demanding. The net worth qualification of an applicant for a news channel has been raised steeply, from Rs 3 crores to Rs 20 crores, and for non-news channels from Rs 1.5 crores to Rs 5 crores. The new norms, ostensibly intended to keep away non-serious applicants, weigh heavily in favour of moneybags and high net-worth entities rather than professionals in the field. Not unsurprisingly, the extant industry takes no objection to these changes, its only quarrel being with the penal clause of possible revocation of a channel's license if it violates, five times over the ten-year contractual period, the prescribed codes of programming and advertising.

With much of the turf taken, the hope of the independent, democratic media turns to the internet, with its promise of liberated bandwidths and devices like audio podcasts and Internet Protocol Television (IPTV), to provide cross-media versatility. India, with less than 10 per cent of its population having access to the net, may yet be on the wrong side of the digital divide. But the rate of growth in connectivity here is among the fastest in the world. According to a recent industry estimate (KPCB[9]), the year-on-year growth during the period 2007–10 was of the order of 43 per cent. It may not be farfetched to imagine a not-too-distant future where the plural energy of Indian culture unleashed on the net blazes a different and unique trail. But that hope needs to be tempered by what we see happening to the internet in a country like the United States, with near 80 per cent penetration and a longer experience with the medium.

In a very recent joint study, John Bellamy Foster and Robert McChesney (2011) take stock of the role and implications of the internet twenty years after it was made available to the public. Their finding, alarmingly, is that what once held the promise of an open public sphere is slowly being taken over by giant monopolies. In fact digital capitalism, it turns out, is more vicious than other forms of capitalism because it creates greater and more acute market concentration. The KPCB study cited earlier confirms this trend. The US mega-quartet of Apple, Google, Amazon and Facebook predominates the internet.

Apple's revenue in 2010 was $76,283 million and its market value in 2011 stood at $373 billion. Through iTunes, it has 87 per cent of the market share in digital music downloads and some 70 per cent of the MP3 player market. Google is a not so close second with revenue in 2010 of $29,321 million and market value in 2011 of $177 billion. But it controls 70 per cent of the search engine market and has a far greater global spread, with at least 80 per cent of its over 1,000 million monthly unique visitors in August 2011 coming from outside the USA. The corresponding figures for Amazon are $34,204 (revenue in 2010) and $108 billion (market value in 2011). Facebook's market value in 2011 was $77 billion (the revenue figure is not available), whereas eBay had a market value of $42 billion the same year and revenue of $9,156 in 2010. Microsoft, Intel and Cisco are among the other big players with monopoly clout.

The big players create the most visible and repeat-hit hot properties on the net, and erect barriers to prevent others from eroding their business concentration. What they have redeemed, fenced off and developed is where consumers aggregate and transact business the most – the rest of the net seems relative *terra incognita*. Michael Wolff of *Wired* magazine has shown how the concentration grows and accretes, and does not disburse or diffuse, over the so-called long tail that Chris Anderson (the founder of *Wired*) enthused about: the top ten websites accounted for 31 per cent of US page views in 2001, 40 per cent in 2006 and close to 75 per cent in 2010.

This array of organized monopolistic power contests the liberative power and potential of the internet as a space that enables and empowers peer-to-peer activities, the open source movement, user-driven knowledge domains like Wikipedia, browsers like Mozilla Firefox, sites with a nose for anything under wraps like WikiLeaks (which took the corridors of power across the world by storm and is struggling to outmanoeuvre a concerted financial blockade), and the viral power of social sites, for mass mobilization.

Foster and McChesney (2011) call this the paradox of the internet, akin to, they elaborate, the Lauderdale paradox in economics which deals with the conflict of interests between public wealth and private riches – where public wealth is understood as all that man desires as useful or delightful for him, and private riches as all that man desires as useful or delightful for him that exist in a degree of scarcity. Thus it is scarcity that makes the difference and helps make private riches out of public wealth. If what is naturally and plentifully available – like air, water or food – were rendered scarce, they would acquire an exchange value as against their use value. The Lauderdale paradox went through many hands and filters, including Ricardo and John Stuart Mill, and Marx adapted it to argue – and this became a key element of his *Capital* – that the conflict between use value and exchange value is germane to capitalistic production.

Marx, further, drew on Edward Gibbon Wakefield's take on the political economy of colonization. Wakefield found that the free availability of land in the new colonies, like America, Canada and New Zealand, created a shortage of wage labour because workers could set themselves up independently as subsistence farmers. The solution to the problem was to artificially inflate the price of land and encourage absentee landlordism, thus keeping land out of the reach of potential wage labour or the mass of the people. Similarly, by creating and developing select enclaves of heavy traffic and commerce in the internet space, the digital capitalist seeks to create artificial scarcity and high exchange value for them. Against this, the use value of the vast freewheeling realm of the net has to be redeemed and reinstated.

At another level, these virtual walled gardens in cyberspace are a throwback to the enclosure movements in England and Wales where open land that belonged to the community at large was systematically taken over and, even without physical fencing, began to be owned in severalty – a euphemism for the many who cornered it in what E.P. Thompson (1963) calls a plain enough case of class robbery. The striking difference, of course, is that the appropriators on the net today are fewer in number, far more concentrated and far more totalizing in their control.

On the other hand, from the Seattle protests against the World Trade Organization (WTO) in 1999, up until the Occupy Wall Street movement of 2011, the net has become the agency par excellence for popular mobilizations against the big and the powerful. Its viral virtual energy can be harnessed to topple absolutist regimes, as the Egyptian and Tunisian experiences have shown. The natural champions of such a netscape should be those in the vanguard of the knowledge economy – the organic intellectuals, in the Gramscian sense, of this era. Not coincidentally, we find the intellectual as a potential counter-hegemon being invoked repeatedly in a succession of works by the intellectuals themselves – almost like a self-awareness of their manifest responsibility. Foucault, Derrida, Bourdieu, Said, Chomsky – all have dwelt on the role of the intellectual in reframing contemporary society. When they succumb to the laws of the market (and become, as Bourdieu puts it, heteronomous) or capitulate to the temptation of the media, they legitimize and subserve the prevailing hegemonic forces. But where they do not lend themselves to be coopted by the market and position themselves, consciously and concertedly, against the current, they may well trigger the force to reverse it.

Notes

[1] Filippo Tommaso Marinetti published his futurist manifesto ('The Founding and Manifesto of Futurism') in the French paper *Le Figaro*, in February 1909. Primarily a movement in the arts, it was breathlessly excited about technology and the future, and impatient with intellectuals, museums, libraries, feminism and all utilitarian cowardice. Futurism dovetailed into fascism as Marinetti himself became an acolyte of Mussolini.

[2] French biologist and cyber-analyst Joel de Rosney revels in neologisms like cybionte, conceived as a global super-organism of which we are all neurons. The internauts themselves organize the global metacomputer realm, and its denizens constitute a pronetaire who, like Marx's proletariat, unite as a productive force of change.

[3] Debray's *Revolution in the Revolution?* was an iconic work, inspired by Che Guevara, on guerrilla warfare in Latin America. When he was taken into custody in Bolivia, Jean-Paul Sartre, expressing solidarity before a mass audience in Paris on 30 May 1967, said, as reported by *Le Monde*: 'Régis Debray has been arrested by the Bolivian authorities, not for having participated in guerrilla activities but for having written a book.' He turned to contemplation of a different kind in later life, creating the discipline of mediology, which sought to view history by hybridizing technology and culture (interview to *Wired* magazine).

[4] The film was directed by Roland Emmerich. The cast included Will Smith as a fighter-pilot and Bill Pullman as President Thomas Whitmore. The combined gross box office collection in the US and outside was $816,969,000. It won the Oscar for visual effects in 1996.

[5] Siliwood, in the title of Hozic's article, 'Uncle Sam Goes to Siliwood', conveys the mix of Silicon Valley and Hollywood.

[6] *Enthiran*, which cost $36 million and was directed by S. Shankar, was released on 1 October 2010, along with its dubbed versions: *Robot* in Hindi and *Robo* in Telugu.

[7] *Ra One*, budgeted at $30.5 million, and scripted and directed by Anubhav Sinha, was released on 26 October 2011.

[8] The Supreme Court ruling – given on 5 February 1995 by Justice P.B. Sawant and Justice S.

Mohan, in the case *Union of India vs. Cricket Association of Bengal* – says that airwaves or frequencies are a public property; their use has to be controlled by a public authority in the interests of the public and to prevent the invasion of their rights; since the electronic media involves the use of the airwaves, this factor creates an inbuilt restriction on their use as in the case of any other public property.

[9] The study, 'Internet Trends 2011', by the venture-capital firm Kleiner Perkins Caufield Byers (KPCB), was released at the Web 2.0 summit in San Francisco, California, in October 2011.

References

Barthes, Roland (1972), 'Myth Today', in *Mythologies*, New York: Noonday Press.

Baudrillard, Jean (1989), 'The Ecstasy of Communication', in Mark Poster, ed., *Jean Baudrillard: Selected Writings*, Stanford University Press.

Baudrillard, Jean (1995), *The Gulf War Did Not Take Place*, Bloomington: Indiana University Press; a collection of three essays – 'The Gulf War will not take place', 'The Gulf War is not really taking place' and 'The Gulf War did not take place' – originally published in the French paper *Liberation* and in the British *Guardian* between January and March 1991.

Bourdieu, Pierre (1998), *On Television and Journalism*, London: Pluto Press.

Debord, Guy Ernest ([1967] 1994), *La Société du spectacle* (French), Paris: Buchet Chastel; *The Society of the Spectacle*, translated by Donald Nicholson-Smith, New York: Zone Books.

Debray, Régis ([1994] 1996), *Manifestes médiologique* (French), Paris: Gallimard; *Media Manifestos: On the Technological Transmission of Cultural Forms*, translated by Eric Rauth, London/New York: Verso.

Feuerbach, Ludwig (1989), *The Essence of Christianity* (translated), Amherst, New York: Prometheus Books.

Foster, John Bellamy and Robert W. McChesney (2011), 'The Internet's Unholy Marriage to Capitalism', *Monthly Review*, Vol. 62, Issue 10, March.

Friedman, Thomas (2005), *The World is Flat: A Brief History of the Globalized World in the 21st Century*, UK/US: Penguin/Allen Lane.

Fukuyama, Francis (1993), *The End of History and the Last Man*, New York: Avon Books.

Fukuyama, Francis (1999), *The Great Disruption: Human Nature and the Reconstruction of Social Order*, New York: The Free Press.

Gitlin, Todd (2003), *Media Unlimited: How the Torrent of Images and Sounds Overwhelms Our Lives*, New York: Metropolitan/Owl.

Gramsci, Antonio (1996), *Selections from the Prison Notebooks*, Hyderabad: Orient Longman.

Hozic, Aida A. (1999), 'Uncle Sam Goes to Siliwood: Of Landscapes, Spielberg and Hegemony', *Review of International Political Economy*, Vol. 6, No. 3, Autumn.

Jameson, Fredric (1984), 'Postmodernism, or, the Cultural Logic of Late Capitalism', *New Left Review*, 146, July–August.

McLuhan, Marshall (1994), *Understanding Media: The Extensions of Man*, Cambridge, MA: The MIT Press.

Ramanujan, A.K. (2005), *Uncollected Poems and Prose*, USA: Oxford University Press.

Sobchack, Vivian (1994), 'The Scene of the Screen: Envisioning Cinematic and Electronic Presence', in Hans Ulrich Gumbrecht and K. Pfeiffer, eds., *Materialities of Communication*, Palo Alto, CA: Stanford University Press.

Sontag, Susan (1966), 'On Roland Barthes', in *Against Interpretation*, New York: Farrar, Strauss and Giroux.

First published in *Social Scientist*, Vol. 39, Nos. 11–12, November–December 2011, pp. 33–40.

Arab Spring and the Social Media

The revolution will not be televised,
Will not be televised, will not be televised,
The revolution will be no rerun brothers,
The revolution will be live.

The Gil Scott-Heron song of the 1970s has, over the succeeding decades, become a mixed metaphor of sorts, invoking at once the mutuality and the disjuncture between the media and historic moments of political upsurge. We have seen military coups and putsches in Africa, Asia and Latin America acquire a media coefficient, with the broadcasting station becoming as much a seat of power to be targeted as, and even before, the parliament or the presidential building. We have seen airwaves unleashed in the mid-1980s by the new Direct Broadcast Satellite (DBS) technology – wireless television signals that do not respect national boundaries – sweep away the hitherto insulated communist regimes of East Europe.

Moving into the globalizing and unipolar era, we have seen a brazen counter-revolution (even if it collapsed in two days) by the United States-backed Venezuelan oligarchs, fuelled by their private-owned TV channels, against Hugo Chavez's democratically elected government in 2002. We have seen, too, a spate of colour-coded revolutions, ranging from the Tulip Revolution of 2005 which typifies those of various hues in the Commonwealth of Independent States (CIS), culled out of the former Soviet Union, to the anti-Mahmoud Ahmadinejad Green Revolution in Iran of 2009 and the pro-Thaksin Shinawatra Red Shirt movement in Thailand in 2010 – which are seen as engendered by the newfound connectivity and virtual community capabilities of the user-driven digital cyber media, cumulatively dubbed the social media of our times.

The Arab Spring, the latest in the series, takes the social media determinism hypothesis to a new high, and into contending camps arguing respectively that the revolution will and will not be tweeted. The buzz generated online at such momentous junctures is certainly more than mere static, and transforms, by novel means such as hashtagging, into a concerted agenda with a burgeoning agitated engagement around it. Twitter, Facebook, YouTube, wikis, blogs, vlogs and podcasts not only mirror, but also feed into the dynamics on the ground, in terms of mass mobilization, unblinking blow-by-blow chronicling of direct action, signalling flash strikes and demonstrations and tactically staggering them to outwit the police, coordinating succour to those involved in street battles and piercing the smokescreens that the authorities raise around such situations. In Tunisia, Egypt, Yemen, Syria, Jordan, Libya, Bahrain and other Arab countries, the digital social media became so imbricated in the people's movements, kindled by the fire that consumed the Tunisian street vendor Mohammed Bouazizi in his iconic act of self-immolation in December 2010, that the sense was not so much of an online chatterati with a ringside view of the action driving the traffic as of cyber-agit propagandists driving the action themselves. In the jargon of the medium, the twitterati it seemed had become, or been overwhelmed by, the tweeple.

The twitterati–tweeple differentiation, in a manner of speaking, digitally parallels the liberalization–democratization dichotomy in the Arab world – where liberalization was a top-down initiative launched in the late 1980s by regimes in tandem with traditional oligarchs coopting an emerging economic elite, and thereby keeping grassroots popular democratic churning at bay. This calibrated liberalization saw fairly free parliamentary elections being held in Jordan (1989) and Yemen (1990); the Syrian parliament accommodate seats for 60 new independent candidates (1990); robust and competitive local elections being conducted in Algeria (1990); and even saw rigid Saudi Arabia experiment with a 60-member consultative body, the *majlis ash-shura*, and a code of basic civil rights, the *al-hukum al-asasi*.

By the mid-1990s, however, the regimes on this path had reached their respective thus-far-no-further threshold and had taken a U-turn into a counter-phase of active de-liberalization, marked by draconian laws against the press, suspension of elections and clampdowns on the opposition, particularly the Islamists. The process was uneven across the region, but broadly, if paradoxically, the regimes that were legatees of Arab nationalist, Baathist or Nasserite takeovers seemed quicker than the rest to cut short the liberalization exercise because it was seen as opening up the space for Islamist groups to flex their muscle. The Gulf kingdoms, on the other hand, continued with a gradualist liberalization of a beneficent patriarchal variety: in July 2002, Qatar drafted a new Constitution with provision for secret ballot by the population, including women; Bahrain released political prisoners and held out assurances of elections.

In sum, as Holger Albrecht and Oliver Schlumberger point out in their essay 'Waiting for Godot: Regime Change without Democratization in the Middle East' (2004), this qualified liberalization helped a permutation and cooptation in the structure of the governing elite, thereby avoiding regime change by change in regime. It did not, and was never meant to, lead to democratization. On the contrary, as the cited authors observe, the common denominator of all these changes in the functional logic of these regimes is that they served to foreclose the emergence of autonomous rival forces.

The regimes managed to keep things from spilling over on to the street by soft-pedalling the structural adjustment programmes in the 1980s, and by rampant NGO-ization of society since then, so that class-based protests by trade unions or the peasantry were marginalized and Islamization seemed the only oppositional act in town. Thus the Arab street, as it came to be called, was stereotyped in the western consciousness as a rallying point or the barometer of pan-Arab sentiment, rather than a site of local specific struggles. Asef Bayat, in his article 'The Street and the Politics of Dissent in the Arab World' (*Middle East Report*, Spring 2003), discusses how this sweeping orientalist Arab-street fixation misled western policy makers and media into strange assumptions and stranger deductions. In the aftermath of 9/11 and the looming threat of the US war on terror, the expectation was that the Arab street would rise in support of Osama bin Laden. When the street did not stir, the conclusion was that it did not matter any more, rather than that the street may not be in empathy with bin Laden. *The Economist* declared the death of the Arab street, and Condoleezza Rice, the then US National Security Adviser, went on to postulate that since Arabs, *sans* street power, could not liberate themselves, the US must deliver them from their despots. In the narratives of the western media, Bayat cryptically concludes, the Arab street is damned if it does and damned if it doesn't.

Bayat goes on to recount how the Arab street responded very differently and defiantly to the Israeli invasion of the West Bank in the end of March 2002, and to the US-led invasions of Iraq and Afghanistan. Millions of Arab citizens poured out on to the streets of West Asian capitals in a massive show of solidarity and strength, often defying local laws and authorities. There was a coordinated boycott of American and Israeli goods, including McDonalds, Kentucky Fried Chicken (KFC), Starbucks, Nike and Coca-Cola. Coca-Cola, which lost between 20 and 40 per cent of its market share in many Arab countries, was replaced by the Iranian Zam Zam Cola, which sold ten million cans in the Gulf kingdoms in just four months. A counter-cola market thrived briefly with Zam Zam being exported to European states, including Belgium and Denmark. Another brand, Mecca Cola, surfaced in Paris, and two million bottles were sold in two months to European Arabs. All this pointed to the political and economic potency of the Arab street.

Cyberactivism was in its early days although it had proved crucial and decisive in organizing the Seattle protests against the World Trade Organization (WTO) towards the end of 1999. The incipient internet did not yet have the digital social media complement: Wikipedia had just been launched (2001); and Facebook and YouTube were yet to hit cyberdom. Indeed a recent article in *The Economist* ('How Luther Went Viral', 17 December 2011) reminds us that social media as a genre or phenomenon is not unique to the digital era, and was marked by the same irrepressible energy and frisson five hundred years before Facebook. When Martin Luther nailed his 95 Theses against papal indulgences to a church door in Wittenberg in October 1517 – heralding the Reformation – they were swiftly disseminated by a set of retail media, including printed pamphlets, woodcuts and ballads, to became common currency across Germany and Europe in a matter of weeks.

There was already, at the dawn of this century, an established practice of agitation and indignation on the Arab street, spawned by a variety of what Bayat calls small media. Audio and video cassettes of popular, if controversial, Islamist folk heroes – such as the Egyptian theologian Yusuf al-Qaradawi (in exile in Qatar since the 1960s and well until the recent upsurge when he returned to Cairo); Sheikh Abd al-Hamid Kishk (whose hilarious Friday sermons were a huge draw until they were proscribed by President Hosni Mubarak in the 1980s); the Lebanese Ayatollah Fadlallah, considered the spiritual mentor of the Hizbollah; and the Egyptian television evangelist Amir Mohammed Khalid – were widely circulated. They jostled and vied for attention with a repertoire of hot-selling recordings and albums by a constellation of Arab icons – ranging from the adulated, evergreen divas Umm Kulthum of Egypt and Fairuz of Lebanon, to the Moroccan satirist Ahmed Sanoussi, and the more contemporary stars of Egyptian pop and fusion, Amr Diab and Mohammed Munir. The undercurrent of aspirational Arab-hood and political identity in this eclectic spread of rhetorical, satirical and musical work heaved again to the surface with the Israeli action in the West Bank in 2002, when these cultural products were in popular demand afresh.

When it came to internal domestic criticism in the authoritarian regimes of the region, the creative media seemed to pack more punch than the formal news media, which, when not run by the state, was under its systematic scrutiny. The Egyptian film *The Yacoubian Building*, made in 2006 based on Alaa Al Aswany's novel of 2002, is a powerful allegory on a society corroding from within. Set in and around an old Armenian building in the centre of Cairo, the film deals boldly with the quotidian and larger moral challenges faced by its disparate residents, who include, in the description of the director Marwan Hamed,

> a corrupt politician, an autocratic womanizer, a destitute young woman who lives on the roof of the building and is sexually abused at work, a talented student who mutates into an Islamic terrorist after he is denied the opportunity to study at the police academy because his father works as a janitor and has a low social status, a journalist who suffers because of his homosexuality, and a shoeshine boy who rises to become a Member of Parliament and misuses religion to pursue his own interests.

That recipe was bad enough, sampling as it did real-life characters and situations in Egyptian society. The conservative sections and the ruling class of Egypt came down heavily on the film, with 112 members of parliament demanding cuts. But the box office gave it a rousing welcome, and a follow-up television serial of the same story the next year made *The Yacoubian Building* almost a household name and an oblique precursor of Tahrir Square. For, to quote its director again,

> The film is a document of the time we live in because it shows very openly what many are thinking in secret. . . . Corruption has eaten its way into all areas of Egyptian life. A dialogue between the skirt-chasing, ageing grandee Zaki and the exploited young Busayna towards the end of the film sums up its allusive potency. 'If you can't find good in your own country,' Zaki tells Busayna, 'you won't find it anywhere else.' 'Then you will know why we hate Egypt,' is Busayna's tormented reply.

Not all creative gambits paid off like *The Yacoubian Building* did. The first graphic novel in Egypt, *Metro*, produced by Magdy El Shafee in 2008, about a computer engineer's futile fight against a system darkly and hopelessly corrupt, was banned by the authorities. Magdy was taken to task for testing public morals, subjected to a long trial, convicted and fined. This censorious atmosphere notwithstanding, a corpus of new and pioneering writing emerged, its authors strongly informed – even shaped – by the internet and hazarding a different language: among them Ahmed Alaidy whose novel *Being Abbas El-Abb* (2006) deployed a new hybrid vocabulary; Mohammed Aladdin who wrote up all of his 60-page novel, *The Gospel According to Adam* (2006), in one paragraph; Mansoura Ez Eldin with her oneiric brinksmanship in *Maryam's Maze* (2007) and *Beyond Paradise* (2009); and the graphic artist Ahmed Negy whose face and T-shirt designs became familiar in the Tahrir Square tumult.

The digital social media that burst on the scene with the YouTube-tagged Sidi Bouzid campaign after Mohammed Bouazizi's self-immolation (in that coastal town of Tunisia), merged into the chant 'Ben Ali, out' on Facebook and diverse other online forums, and then spread virally to feel and feed the pulse of the revolt as it expanded into the streets and public squares of Egypt, Libya, Syria, Jordan, Morocco, Yemen, Bahrain and other Arab states, are generally approached as exogenous to the social and cultural logic of each situation. The same fallacies applied in taking stock of the Green Revolution in Iran were in evidence here. There is a body of analysis now questioning the assumption that social media played a decisive role in the pro-Mir Hossein Moussavi and anti-Ahmadinejad rallies after the Iranian elections of 2009, on the grounds that the preponderant volume of tweets and online messaging were in English and not Persian, aimed at western rather than local netizens, and therefore unlikely to have intervened in or crucially impacted the course of events on the ground. The online excitement around the event, ostensibly, was greater among the observers than the participants.

The Arab Spring, on the other hand, seems to have integrated the social media in far greater measure. But it still appears to hover above the ground reality like a universalizing tech-veneer, unable to acquire a *raison d'être* in terms of each specific context. This is perhaps partly a function of the nature, scale and pitch of internet technology, which lends itself to a non-hierarchized and loosely networked cyber flatland. But without the underpinnings that relate them to local practice, custom and lore, do they tend to freewheel into a global rather than local realm and consciousness?

Brian T. Edwards, in his article 'Tahrir: Ends of Circulation' (2011), reflects on this tension informing the digital social media. What are the ends of circulation? he wonders.

> Does the digitally enabled circulation of revolutionary images, ideas, even advice – and in literary production of forms, genres, motifs – end in places like Cairo, where it is incorporated into a local idiom and national context? Or, is it precisely the abstraction and compression of representations of local meanings – a necessary precondition for forms to make their way across publics, from one mode in the circularity matrix to another – that allows them to flow globally, where they might achieve various ends?

The application of the social media across the Arab states was also uneven for reasons of connectivity, censorship and local politics. Digital media as a player in the protests was more vibrant and visible in Tunisia and Egypt. It was relatively subdued in Libya where the state controlled the internet, and in Yemen with its low internet penetration. Syria, with only 15 per cent of its population online, seemed to produce more noise because the pro- and anti-Assad forces were at loggerheads with one another. The opposition has also accused Twitter and Facebook of lending a helping hand to the Assad regime by blocking tweets and posts in the country. There were similar hurdles to free circulation of social media in the region, with other regimes too resorting to time-, location- and content-specific blocks.

In Egypt the social media initially bypassed the Muslim Brotherhood, which subsequently emerged as the group with the best electoral prospects. Cadres of the Brotherhood stayed away from the Day of Rage protest of 25 January 2011, which was mobilized in good part by Twitpic, Facebook and YouTube, and for which more than 90,000 people signed up on Facebook alone. By 28 January, the government was cracking down on this mobilization through the internet and mobile phones by pressuring operators to suspend services in selected locations. Opposition groups, particularly the Baradei Action for Change, countered this attempted blackout by hitting the streets and exhorting people to join them, to the slogan 'Down with Mubarak'. The authorities responded by imposing curfews and driving the protesters back indoors and, ironically, to their computer keyboards with a vengeance. The regime could not, apparently, keep them away from both the streets and their computers at the same time. Thus it went until 10 February, when Vice-President Omar Suleiman announced Mubarak's resignation. In the weeks leading up to his ceding power, there was an estimated tenfold increase in the tweets on the situation. Videos on the protest consumed gigabytes of YouTube space, the top two dozen fetching nearly 5.5 million views.

There were, through all this, the flash narratives of net heroism. The Tunisian activist blogger Salim Amamon was pitchforked from Ben Ali's jail to Minister of Youth and Government, a position he gave up soon. The Egypt-based Facebook group 'We are all Khalid Said', commemorating the young man who had been killed by the police in 2010, had over 80,000 followers on 27 January 2011, the day before the massive Friday turnout – which was a sudden spike from the 20,000 who had registered the previous day. *The New York Times* ran front-page stories in February 2011 about an Egyptian who named his newborn daughter Facebook and another eulogizing Google's Egyptian chief, Wael Ghonim, for waging the revolution via Facebook groups.

But sobering thoughts temper the enthusiasm. The key social platforms mediating the Arab Spring – Facebook, Twitter and YouTube – belong to US-based private corporations. Indeed, e-diplomacy is the latest plank in US foreign policy, of which information hegemony and control have been an integral part since the end of the Second World War. Some of these media organizations were also complicit with the regimes in removing videos from, or cutting access to, their sites at critical junctures. In some of the Gulf states, Skype was completely blanked out. There are reports of Egyptian youth planning to sue internet companies that colluded with Mubarak. The issue of censorship becomes intriguing with news of Twitter agreeing to be accommodative to requests from governments and organizations to remove tweets that run foul of the law of their lands. As this came just a month after Saudi prince Walid bin Talal took a $300-million stake in Twitter, and in the light of Facebook's market foray with a $5-billion initial public offering, it may not be just cussed conspiracy theory to see a pattern in these developments.

The social media were combative against, buttressed by and dovetailed into the dominant mainstream pan-regional media, Al Jazeera. The channel's programme *The Stream* aggregated citizen journalism and a lot of the activist social media. Soon after Mubarak ceded power, Wadah Khanfar, managing director of the channel, acknowledged the mediatory role of the citizens of Tunisia and Egypt: 'The youth of the Middle East [West Asia], choosing universal values from within while embracing tolerance and diversity – they are our reporters.' Al Jazeera also re-broadcast its social media-generated content to the US through Free Speech TV, a non-profit satellite network accessed by an estimated 35 million homes there.

The nature and scope of the agency of the social media in the Arab Spring, given the continuing flux in the region, is a developing story. But the reading in western capitals that this leavening of aspirations across the region, leveraged by cutting-edge digital media, is *ipso facto* a popular demand for the western liberal democratic model, is proving premature and misplaced with Islamist parties best placed to win the elections marking regime change in each country. The medium is clearly not the message in this case. Are the assorted social media manufacturing a public sphere, or people-hood, that cuts across the traditional categories of the *ummah* (Islamic nationhood) or the *millet* (the minorities), or that challenges the *assabiyah* (tribal or clan affiliation) factor even while upholding the *sharia* as the ultimate arbiter?

The distinction between liberalism, with its emphasis on individual liberty, human rights and the rule of law, and democracy, understood as combining the principles of equality, majoritarian rule and sovereignty of the people, may make a difference to that question. The rhetoric of the social media, typically, has been stridently western liberal, and impatient with the deliberative representative process organic to the political ethos of the Arab states. The street scuffles breaking out in Egypt and Tunisia between the Islamists, who probably see themselves as the democratic heirs of the Arab Spring, and the freewheeling protesters – many of them poster boys and girls of the social media – who are wary of a counter-revolution by the remnants of the old regime in league with the Islamists, keep the margins of the movement, even where it has been successful so far, restless. The social media, as is its wont, flocks to the dizzy fringes of the movement, and roots for dramatic and drastic changes. In the process, it may well be getting ahead of itself and not helping the crystallization of the transition it has helped usher in.

First published in *Frontline*, 23 March 2012.

Just Let the Press Be

It is open season on the political class and the news media. But then again, it is more like a chase of one's own tail. A self-righteous, delusional, Anna–Baba NGO-ized fringe sets out to stigmatize politics and parliamentarians; the news media salivate at the prospect, and rush to provide the arena and become the cheerleaders of the slanging match. The same media, in their turn, are at the receiving end of political, and some judicial, ire for what they do, don't do and won't do. Legislative action and judicial activism nevertheless take their cues from what the media ferret out and place in the public realm – and so it goes in circles, as vicious as they come.

Some of the blame in this game no doubt sticks, and is well deserved. Parliamentarians with criminal records are parliamentarians with criminal records. But that does not detract from the representative essence of an operative democracy. As Rousseau realized well over three centuries ago, representative democracy may not be the best form of government, but it is far better and safer than direct democracy with its populist hangman psyche that the Hazareites and Ramdevites baying for the blood of the political class typify. In any case, as the political scientist Ernest Barker reminded us in his *Reflections on Government* (1942), democracy is about leaders representing the will of the people, however inadequately, as against fascism which is about people representing the will of their leaders – as the motley crowds gathering under the cult banner of the Anna or the Baba suggest.

The thrust of the Lokpal cause is to tackle corruption in the political class, the administration at all levels and, somewhat more cautiously, in the judiciary. It does not, cannot, audit the performance of the political representative, or set out to correct the deficits or excesses of such representation. That is for the representatives' constituency, the voters, to decide and act upon through the exercise of their franchise, or, if it comes about in the future, through the right of recall of legislators who fail them. Arguably, it is not even the remit of the Lokpal exercise to ensure a standardized and universal morality in public life, because the understanding and degree of moral integrity can vary with the context and from public person to public person. Surely, in a democracy, morality is at best a benchmark to aspire to and not a matter for a legal bench.

The current missionary zeal in the nation to codify, sanitize and regulate across the board may, instead of deepening democracy, end up cribbing it, and drift unwittingly towards a totalitarian ethos. Ernesto Laclau, in his work *On Populist Reason* (2005), cites the essay 'The Question of Democracy' (1988) by the influential French philosopher Claude Lefort, on how modern democracy is predicated on what Laclau calls a revolution in the political imaginary, by which a hierarchical society centred on the king as point of unity of power, knowledge and law was disincorporated by the emergence of the place of power as essentially empty. In the words of Lefort:

> the locus of power becomes *an empty place*. . . . The phenomenon implies an institutionalization of conflict . . . the important point is that democracy is institutionalized and sustained by the *dissolution of the markers of certainty*. It inaugurates a history in which people experience a fundamental indeterminacy as to the basis of power, law and knowledge.

To overdetermine democracy may be to render it a pale shadow of itself; the sense of flux must be kept alive so that democracy is freewheeling and vibrant, and does not lapse into its guided, ethnic or other hybrid variants, familiar to us even in our neighbourhood. The implication in all this can be paraphrased into the well-worn Americanism: if it ain't broke, don't fix it.

The Chairman of the Press Council of India, Justice Markandey Katju's prescription for a regulated news media regime seems one such misplaced, if well-intentioned step towards reform that can actually de-democratize the fourth estate. Paradoxically, the Katju effect on the press can be as problematic as the Anna effect on politics. Paradoxical because Justice Katju, unlike Anna and Co. whose disgust at politics and politicians is manifest, is no adversary of the media. He has sprung to the defence of journalists under threat, whether from the state or from mafia of one or other variety. And yet, one cannot help notice an overhang of judicial intolerance in his expectations of the media.

Justice Katju is understandably exercised over the aberration and trivialization in media practice, in a context where tidbits of the flippant and the sensational get preference over stories of impinging social and economic reality that are crying to be told. There can be no quarrel, either, with the fact that paid news, corporate cronyism *à la* the Radia affair, libellous insinuation, voyeurism, violation of privacy and all kinds of subjectivities masquerading as journalistic objectivity threaten to drag the media unceremoniously down from the moral high ground they think they occupy.

That threat, a real possibility, itself would be their just deserts. The temptation to fix the media through an external regulatory authority may well seem a fashionable urge, much in the same vein as caricaturing and debunking politics is the hobby-horse of a section of the middle class. But it could mean a dangerous departure from the long-nurtured and cherished principle of the freedom of the press as the *sine qua non* of our democracy. Inasmuch as the fourth estate constitutes the fourth pillar of democracy and is therefore, by implication and extension, as relevant as the three other pillars (the executive, the judiciary and the legislature), in terms of the checks-and-balances aspect of the principle of separation of powers envisaged by the Constitution, any administrative tampering with it can have serious consequences for the larger democratic project itself.

The tendency of the first three pillars to bear down on the fourth is not new. There have been several instances in the past when the executive and the legislature, both central and state, have sought to muzzle the press by draconian laws or by invoking the privilege motion. The judiciary, for its part, keeps the press guessing about where legitimate criticism ends and contempt begins, in terms of scandalizing or lowering the authority of the courts. But the present conjunction of forces against the free press is a worrisome portent. The Supreme Court decides, in what senior jurists consider judicial overreach, to set up a five-member constitution bench headed by the Chief Justice, to go into the question of setting guidelines for media reporting; the decision, at the time of writing, is pending. A member of parliament from the ascendant Rahul Gandhi camp, Meenakshi Natarajan, moots introduction of a private member's bill in the Lok Sabha which invokes the bogey of national security to bring in a tough media regulator.

The learned judges may well decide to tread softly, or not at all, on the turf of the fourth estate. Spokespersons of the Congress Party have been quick to disown the private member's bill as a personal and private affair of the member concerned; in any case it has nowhere near a fighting chance of making it through the house and the whole thing may just be a trial balloon. But it is the signal of intent in these moves and the censorious mood they reflect vis-à-vis the news media which suggest what the credo of the freedom of the press may be up against in India.

Justice Katju has been at pains to point out that Meenakshi Natarajan and he may not be on the same page on the issue, because he stands for regulation, not control – which ostensibly is what the private member's bill spells. But this hairsplitting distinction is little solace for the press, because the chances are that the one will in effect mean just the same as, or inexorably lead to, the other. Less nuanced, if somewhat nonplussing, are his sundry *obiter dicta* which are acquiring the semblance of a body of Katju-isms: about the intellectual equipage of the majority of Indian journalists being very poor; about 90 per cent of Indians, no less, being fools because, among other things, they vote on caste and community lines, and believe in astrology to boot; about Salman Rushdie being a poor and substandard writer and our being drawn to the likes of him probably because we suffer from a colonial inferiority complex.

Justice Katju's take on external regulation for the press is not, of course, of a piece with such a general, sweeping and perhaps gratuitous airing of views, and needs to be taken more seriously – not least because of its consequences for the practice of journalism in the country. He seems to make a case for a coequal reading of Article 19(1) (a) in the Fundamental Rights chapter of the Constitution, which guarantees freedom of speech and expression, and Article 19(2), which qualifies the freedom with reasonable restrictions. People keep harping on the first and deliberately overlook or underplay the second, he says. But surely it is the right rather than the qualification that is fundamental and makes freedom of the press a derivative article of faith; the clause of restraint should not be allowed to take away from the robust, enabling spirit of the clause of freedom.

His contextual justification that the media have become very powerful and must hence be regulated is as problematic. It is akin, after a fashion, to the Malimath Committee on reform of the criminal justice system, upending, in its report in 2003, the long-held principle of innocent until proved guilty in criminal jurisprudence and, if anything, privileging presumption of guilt instead – informed, no doubt, by the imperative of tackling the humongous menace of terrorism and an extraordinary-times-need-extraordinary-measures mindset to match. The media today are both on a roll and at the receiving end as never before. They have exposed scam after scam of mindboggling order; pulled up and pulled down public figures and those running our lives one way or the other – often deservedly, sometimes unfairly; and collectively constitute a formidable scrutiny of public – and, alas, sometimes private – affairs. Nothing has been as effective, we know, as a combination of media exposé and blitz for quick administrative corrective action or redressal, sometimes forced by judicial intervention. This, then, is the time to celebrate the media and egg them on to a sustained interrogation of all that is rotten around us, not to deter or dampen their righteous enthusiasm.

The same media, at the same time, by their corrupt and irresponsible ways, also become the villain of the piece. Where, in the process, they run foul of the law of the land, they must obviously face the consequences. It may however be unfair to subject them generically to a special regulatory mechanism when, in the first instance, their rights are only those of any citizen under the Constitution: to free expression. Reasonable restraint too should then apply to them only as much as to any citizen, no more and no less. When Justice Katju asks why, if lawyers, medical professionals or chartered accountants can have regulatory bodies supervising them, media practitioners should not, he may be begging the question, because the freeness of the news media in a country is the litmus test of its democracy. The journalist is not necessarily a professional with prerequisite formal training (although it may help), subject to occupational codes, in the strict sense that a member of the Bar Council or the Medical Council or the association of chartered accountants is. This is self-evident, especially at a time when the journalist as citizen and the citizen as journalist are both redefining the practice of journalism, and when user-generated blogs and the digital social media are pressuring mainstream journalism from the margins. The difficulty of the analogy comes into sharper focus if we imagine a regulatory body for poets or artists, or indeed for professors in universities against sowing anarchic or disruptive seeds of ideas in the minds of their students.

This is not to gloss over the ethical and moral lapses of the media which direly affect their credibility, and, in some instances, betray the public trust. But these are matters for the media to tackle themselves; and they must, with a sense of urgency, if they are not to become redundant as the fourth estate. We already find peer pressure and peer exposure replacing the thick-as-thieves complicity that for long marked media behaviour. Critical comments about one another's sins of commission and omission are slowly emerging from an unhealthy convention of mutual conspiratorial silence. Media professionals should perhaps organize themselves into a watch group which audits media performance, and challenges unfounded, misleading or malicious journalism – much like the FAIR (Fairness and Accuracy in Reporting) exercise in the United States. This could proceed apace, and independent of, the news media organizations instituting an internal regulatory mechanism which sets down a code of practice where the 'don'ts' are minimal, specific and taboo, and the 'dos' more recommendatory and guideline in nature.

It is important not to see grey as black in the process. Yellow journalism is one such grey area (*sic*). While certainly not journalism with best foot forward, the yellow press often becomes a catchment area for stories that turn into scoops. The Indian experience is replete with examples of the small, local, sensation-seeking language press coming up with clues and cues that the bigger regional or national media pick up, not always with acknowledgement, to turn them into their investigative news breaks. Away from neat categories, therefore, a free press yellowing and fraying at the edges is closer to the reality. After all, one of the most prestigious awards for journalism in the world was instituted by, and is named after, the iconic original baron of yellow journalism, Joseph Pulitzer, who also founded the top-notch institution of journalism education, the Columbia Journalism School, at the turn of the last century.

The case for untrammelled journalism is not one for unlimited business of the media. In fact no one seems inclined to bell the fat cats in the media. There is little talk, amidst all the media nay-saying, of the need for cross-media restrictions and reining in monopolies in the sector. Policy frameworks and decisions are literally tailored for the big players, and a handful of multinationals – Murdoch, Disney and Ambanis being the biggest of them – has already cornered the bulk of the market. The latest stiffening of licence fees and qualifications for start-up TV channels is strongly weighed against the small or medium media entrepreneur, and takes the big-is-beautiful principle in the sector to a new high. For the business of media, journalism is just another means of making profit – that is, where it is not too small a part of a massive holding driven and dominated by entertainment to even matter all that much. In the corporatized paradigm, even paid news may be a risqué transaction rather than a morally repugnant aberration, and those who thought up this novel way of monetizing news may be wondering what the fuss is all about. How disingenuously corporate interests appropriate the rhetoric of the freedom of the press was recently on display when they raised the alarm that the Majithia Wage Board award for journalists posed a threat to that freedom.

The increasing mismatch between journalism as a socially purposeful calling and media as big business is already vitiating the free press regime. It evokes the disjuncture and tension between media as press and democracy that Robert McChesney flags in his work *Rich Media, Poor Democracy* (1999). The approach to reform in the sector, by do-gooders and cynics alike, mistakes the wood for the trees. It is the distortions of the media market that need to be targeted: segmentation of the market according to the purchasing profiles of consumers; cartelization by the major groups; cover-price wars which inevitably end up devaluing the quality of journalism on offer; tiered distribution on cable and direct-to-home (DTH) platforms which determine differential access to the media, and clearly discriminate against small and medium enterprises; undoing the licence to telecast by making it impossible to telecast through a prohibitively priced and unregulated distribution regime that is monopolized by a select club of the richest in the league.

The new aggrandizing media market, however, is a product of the economic reforms under the auspices of liberalization and globalization, and nothing is likely to be done to upset it, or to address the disparities and iniquities it breeds, in a situation where the market dictates to the state. Journalists, then, become the fall guys, the ones to blame and fix for a media gone horribly wrong. Freedom of expression, their stock-in-trade, is not a proprietary software allowed them by media owners. It is as much their occupational life-breath as it is the oxygen of democracy. Inasmuch as this freedom exercised by the fourth estate has a check-and-balance role vis-à-vis the performance of the executive, the legislature and the judiciary, it should be seen as implicitly subsumed in the separation of powers – a basic and unalterable feature of the Constitution. On balance, despite periodic provocations from sections of it, it is in keeping with the spirit of the Constitution and the finest traditions of democracy to just let the press be.

Our first Prime Minister was perspicuous, seeing the complexity of his choice even as he rooted for a hands-off-the-press policy. Addressing the Newspaper Editors' Conference in December of 1950, Pandit Jawaharlal Nehru said:

> To my mind, the freedom of the Press is not just a slogan from the larger point of view, but it is an essential attribute of the democratic process. I have no doubt that even if the government dislikes the liberties taken by the press and considers them dangerous, it is wrong to interfere with the freedom of the Press. By imposing restrictions you do not change anything; you merely suppress the public manifes-

tation of certain things, thereby causing the idea and thought underlying them to spread further. . . . I would rather have a completely free Press with all the dangers involved in the wrong use of that freedom than a suppressed or regulated Press.

First published in *Frontline*, 1 June 2012.

Manufacturing Dissent

Ever since the end of the Second World War, the United States has taken itself mighty seriously as a champion and enforcer of the freedom of information and the press across the world. Already in 1946, Assistant Secretary of State William Benton declared that the State Department would do everything within its power, along political or diplomatic lines, to break down the artificial barriers to the expansion of private US news agencies, magazines, motion pictures and other media of communication throughout the world. 'Freedom of the Press – and freedom of exchange of information generally – is an integral part of our foreign policy.' What those political lines were became clear enough during the Reagan years, when the US quit UNESCO in a huff over the demand from emerging and developing nations for a New World Information and Communications Order (NWICO) as codified by the McBride Commission report, which sought to upend the one-way information flow from the North to the South. The diplomatic lines resorted to were often of the gunboat variety, impatient with social and cultural differences that resisted US media consumerist fare.

The crusade was as disingenuous as it was unilateral because it really was more about prising open unwilling markets to the business of US media than about any ideologically inspired democratic concern for freedom of the press *per se*. It sought to hold the world, by force or persuasion, in awe of an idealized–Americanized holy grail of free speech and expression. The short shrift that these noumenal concepts got in the socialist camp did not help matters on that side of the Cold War either, and the razing of the Berlin Wall at the end of the 1980s had as much to do with the allure of the free market world peddled by the media, and the consequent revolution of rising expectations, as the dogma-ridden leadership and bureaucracy of the Eastern Bloc.

Around the same time, Noam Chomsky and Edward Hermann were giving us a reality check of the US media by pointing to the collusion of the state and the media market in manufacturing consent, particularly in matters of foreign policy. They went on to reveal the selective and nationalistically self-serving nature of media evangelism of the Freedom House variety, which abets US arrogance, arbitrariness and intervention across the world – in the name of protecting imaginary and omnibus freedoms. The freedom charade continued as the US, as the sole superpower, with its head in the stratosphere, strode into the new globalized epoch. Even as they have marginalized Chomsky, arguably the tallest public intellectual alive in the country, as an uncomfortable albeit truthful nay-sayer, the mainstream media cannot help living up to his characterization of them as a collective aberration, reporting the world in their image of it rather than as it is. It is as if they would consensually will into existence an alternative reality and live by it. And if they kept at it long enough, perhaps the rest of the world would turn deferentially, even reverentially, to these shores with the aspirational chant, 'thy mediadom come'. That would be another triumph for US exceptionalism, which, incidentally, the Republicans have been touting this election season as a core American value that the Democrats have lost sight of.

But the knight-errant smugness is beginning to wear thin as the US finds that it is itself at the receiving end of some discomfiting media liberties. WikiLeaks is perhaps as embarrassing to the US for the disclosures of diplomatic faux pas and lethal covert operations, as for the gumption the man behind it all poses to that peculiarly American divine right theory of media championship. If the US administration hoped to make an example of Julian Assange – having put away its own soldier and whistle-blower, Bradley Manning, for what could be a long, long spell in jail – they were almost there, with the British courts ruling that Assange must be deported to Sweden, where he is wanted for questioning in a case of sexual misconduct. From Sweden he would be extradited to the US to face prosecution under a slew of US laws, including possibly the Espionage Act. Or so went the plot, as suspected by Assange and as speculated in the media. That in itself would have been, and could still be, if Assange's fears of a witch-hunt against him are not unfounded – an extra-extraordinary rendition of the type WikiLeaks helped bring to shocked public notice.

But the script went awry when Ecuador inserted itself, as a US spokesperson inelegantly described it, into the picture and offered Assange asylum in its embassy in London. The disquiet over this development and the ensuing standoff with the British police takes the form of two constant caveats which qualify their reportage in much of the US media: remember that Assange is possibly a rapist–fugitive from justice; and don't forget that the socialist President of Ecuador, Rafael Correa, has a sullied record when it comes to media freedom.

The devastating public-interest impact and implications of WikiLeaks do not, in any way, become extenuating factors for Assange in the cases against him of possible rape or molestation or non-consensual sex involving two women in Sweden. He must answer for himself and face the legal consequences, if any. At the same time, to seek to flag this grand inquisitor of imperialist power play, this supra – even if maverick – journalist as a byword for sex crime instead, in daily news notice, comes across as pathetically below the belt. Select newspapers which made roaring headlines week after week from the tranches of cables he provided them, and which continue to cite wikileaked information in sundry news contexts, seem to have, for reasons not fully clear, all but forsaken him.

Assange's stated fears about what is in store for him if he travels to Sweden may well be a convenient ploy to evade punishment under the law of that land. The one sure way to find out would be to guarantee that should he go to Sweden, he would not be repatriated onward to the US. But oddly, neither Sweden nor the US is willing to assure him this. The US, which, everyone knows, holds the key to this tangle, pretends to look the other way.

The mandatory prefix 'socialist' to Rafael Correa's name (for that matter, to any known name of that political persuasion) fixes him and sets him apart as the other. To boot, or true to type for a socialist, he harasses the media in Ecuador, where he has shut down nineteen radio stations and a television channel; whips up popular passion against what he considers excesses of journalism; and has won a high-stake libel suit against a columnist, Emilio Palacio, whom he then pardoned, and who now lives in Miami and seeks political asylum in the US. Correa's side of the story, which suggests bringing to heel a section of the media under corporate control, and the historical context of media-instigated coups in Latin America by Miami-based dissidents of the type that briefly displaced Hugo Chavez in Venezuela in 2002, is not a part of this narrative. Be that as it may, and without cutting Correa any slack for his attitude to the media in his country, how this takes anything away from his bold move to offer Assange asylum, even if only to cock a snook at the west, is never made clear but left hanging in the air, as a vague and sinister insinuation.

Foreign affairs coverage in the average US mainstream media now seems as much about manufacturing dissent as manufacturing consent. Apart from the Assange imbroglio – and Syria, which of course is the new happening place – two other hobby-horses of the season are Iran and Egypt, which keep popping out of their assigned slots. That Iran was able to successfully host the summit meeting of the Non-Aligned Movement (NAM) received frowns all round, and was seen as some kind of an upset victory for Tehran. The tenor of the reporting leading up to the event and the incremental editorializing ratcheted up dissent and dissuasion. Egyptian President Mohamed Morsy must boycott the summit; his visit to China was bad enough. UN Secretary-General Ban Ki-moon must not go, unless he uses the trip to tell off Mahmoud Ahmadinejad & Co. to their faces. It was difficult to tell whether it was the Washington administration or the American free press speaking, and whether US-led sanctions against Iran extended to its fourth estate.

As it became clear that both Morsy and Ban Ki-moon would attend, there was even a note of sour grapes – coming from a columnist of no less a stature than Thomas Friedman. 'By the way,' he asked in his *New York Times* column titled 'Morsi's Wrong Turn', 'what is the Non-Aligned Movement anymore?', and went on to cite a foreign policy specialist at Johns Hopkins University echoing the same doubt: 'Non aligned against what and between whom? . . . There is no communist bloc today. The main division in the world is between democratic and undemocratic countries.' So you generally got the drift. It did not matter that the 120 countries which participated, the biggest group in the 193-member UN General Assembly, thought otherwise.

Morsy redeemed himself somewhat in the eyes of this coercive press by attacking Syrian President Bashar al-Assad in his speech, and Ban Ki-moon salvaged his reputation by talking tough on the Iranian nuclear programme. But the orchestration of consent and dissent, like alternating flux and reflux, continues to inform coverage of nuclear weapons-capable Israel's victimhood vis-à-vis Iran's (peaceful, says Iran – can't be, say its detractors) nuclear agenda. Not all of this is driven by the Zionist lobby or the state–media nexus. There is a genuine journalistic crisis of a *weltanschauung* mismatch, which shows up as biased or predisposed coverage. The fairest-minded reporting can look skewed when it is stuck in a paradigm warp.

The case for perspectival flexibility to engage more equitably with the rest of the world apart, there are prickly issues cropping up at home that become, in the persisting war-on-terror climate, systemic in nature and test the limits of the vaunted freedoms of the First Amendment. On the heels of Bradley Manning, whose virtual heroic presence in the WikiLeaks saga must worry the Pentagon no end, came another soldier, Matt Bissonette, who broke ranks with his alternative account of the raid at Abbottabad by the Navy SEALS team, of which he was a member, and the killing of Osama bin Laden. Threatening noises from the Defence Department did not deter him or his publishers from releasing *No Easy Day* under the pseudonym Mark Owen.

The realm of the social media, too, has come under pressure. Twitter has been repeatedly ordered by the courts to hand over to the Justice Department data of posts by WikiLeaks supporters and Occupy Wall Street protesters. The company itself blotted its copybook when it took to task a British journalist working for it, for his tweets criticizing the coverage of the Olympics by NBC, Twitter's corporate partner for the event. Earlier, Yahoo had handed over information that compromised a Chinese dissident and journalist, in 2002 and 2005 respectively, and led to their convictions. In this altered context, the touchiness in the US administration and the US press about media freedoms abroad appears a bit far-fetched and holier-than-thou. Some of that dissonance between media speak and practice was apparent when the US reacted to the recent Indian clampdown on social media to contain rumour-mongering feeding into an ethnic strife. The State Department spokeswoman, Victoria Nuland's observation – 'as the Indian government seeks to preserve security, we are urging them also to take into account the importance of freedom of expression in the online world' – could, as pertinently and gratuitously (with just 'US' replacing 'India'), be a message from the Indian Foreign Office to Washington.

First published in *Frontline*, 5 October 2012.

Clash of Exceptionalisms

The idea of the clash of civilizations trotted out by Bernard Lewis and creatively expanded by Samuel Huntington may find itself in the bin of discredited maverick theories, but there certainly seems to have emerged a surreal stand-off between two brands of exceptionalism. On the one side is the no-holds-barred, over-the-top variety of US liberalism that finds freewheeling – even cartwheeling – expression in all kinds of speech, including hate speech, in the western media; on the other, the touch-me-not prudish zealousness of Islamists who respond with Pavlovian predictability to taunting depictions of the Prophet by rogue elements in the liberalist hemisphere. Both seem to hold their credo and creed, respectively, dearer than the human lives lost in this grudge match.

The posture of profound helplessness with which the political leadership in the United States reacts to the chain of events let loose by the fourteen-minute trailer, *Innocence of Muslims*, is funny when it is not pathetic. It is a rarefied piece of casuistry and proceeds something like this: we find the film abominable and would like to do something about it, but then our hands are tied because anyone here has the right to say anything about anything and anybody with the immunity provided by our First Amendment. But try – with the same malevolence of the filmmaker or the mischief of a neophyte testing this paradisiacal liberalist freedom – saying bomb or terrorist or boo aloud in an airplane or the subway or any public place, and the chances are you will be promptly buried under a tonnage of Homeland Security. The First Amendment does not help you either to argue against the occasional gunman who creeps out of the woodwork and empties a cartridge on you in a movie theatre in Colorado, or a gurudwara in Wisconsin, or a busy street in the heart of Manhattan, or a university anywhere in the country – because there is another amendment, the Second, at work here, which makes the right to the gun another exceptionalist premise that no number of such killings and warnings about a rampant gun culture has been able to undo. This is the price of US liberalism.

On its part, political Islam could, in the interest of its own credibility, have been more politic in its reaction to the scurrilous footage. It is astounding that this piece of inert cretinous kitsch should generate any traction, let alone ignite the kind of passion that somehow ultimately seems to redound to its perpetrators' advantage in the way things have panned out. It would be clear to anyone who saw the stuff on YouTube that there is not even the pretence of a filmic effort here. The trailer – and reports suggest there may well be no film beyond it – was meant to be a red rag, period. The only response to this wanton offer to be insulted, in the first instance, should have been to pass. There is probably a lot more such execrable stuff floating around in cyberspace, those who put them there driven by a pathological *schadenfreude* that defies reasoning and humaneness. To notice it, to pay it any attention, is bad enough; to take offence and take off on a short fuse is to hand its purveyors smug victory.

The problem is compounded by Islam's circumscription vis-à-vis the representational function of the liberal media. Pictorial depiction or representation of the Prophet is anathema to the faith, and interpretation beyond or outside the parameters set by orthodoxy frowned upon. The Quranic text is a constant and its hermeneutics largely confined to refinement of the prescribed canon. The Biblical text, on the other hand, lends itself to wider and wilder interpretations and artistic liberties. As early as the third century CE, the Alexamenos Graffito inscribed on a wall of the Palatine Palace in Rome, discovered in 1885 and now housed in the Palatine Antiquarian Museum, was lampooning the Crucifixion by showing a human figure with a donkey's head on the cross. The Gospels according to Mathew, John, Luke and Mark have been continually second-guessed by ecclesiastical and lay scholarship, and, at a fictional remove, by novelists like Nikos Kazantzakis (*The Last Temptation of Christ*) and Dan Brown (*The Da Vinci Code*), and filmmakers like Pier Paolo Pasolini (*The Gospel According to St Matthew*), Martin Scorsese (who filmed the Kazantzakis novel) and Mel Gibson (*The Passion of the Christ*). Indeed, the plot of *The Da Vinci Code*, suggesting that Jesus may have been married to Mary Magdalene, has just stepped out of the novel and film into historical discourse, with Dr Karen King of Harvard University producing a fourth-century papyrus fragment in Coptic script alluding to Jesus having a wife. The jury is out on the authenticity of what Dr King fancifully calls Gospel of Jesus' Wife, but it is only the latest bid to determine his marital status and relationship with Mary – a project which apparently dates back to the so-called Gnostic Gospels of early Christianity.

Such academic or creative mediations in the narrative of Prophet Muhammad would, however, be considered blasphemous, and invite a seething backlash. The threshold of tolerance for heterodoxy in Islam has diminished over time, as Muslim writers in the twentieth century were to find out. The Egyptian scholar Taha Hussein's study in 1926 suggesting that what was considered Jahiliya or pre-Islamic poetry may actually have been the work of Muslims providing vignettes of Arab life after the advent of Islam, and not in the dark ages before, raised a furore and cost him his job at Cairo University. The Egyptian Nobel laureate Naguib Mahfouz's allegoric *Children of Gebelawi* was attacked for its miscegenation of the Judaic, Christian and Islamic prophets, and portrayal of the Prophet Muhammad by proxy. The work was banned on its publication in 1958 and the author narrowly survived a bid on his life by two assailants in 1994. The Iranian publisher, parliamentarian and polemicist Ali Dashti was, after the Islamic revolution of 1979, considered an apostate for his work *Twenty Three Years: A Study of the Prophetic Career of Mohammad*, which challenged the miracles associated with Prophet Muhammad, and although Ayatollah Khomeini did not issue a *fatwa* against him like he did against Salman Rushdie for *The Satanic Verses*, his death in 1984 is shrouded in mystery.

Paradoxically, the Quran or the *Hadith* do not specifically proscribe blasphemy (it is left to the *shariah* to handle this), whereas the Bible does; and it constituted criminal libel in British common law since the seventeenth century. But by the end of the nineteenth century, and notably with Lord Coleridge's landmark observation in *Regina vs. Ramsay and Foote* (1883) that mere denial of the truth of Christianity is not enough to constitute the offence of blasphemy, and that if the decencies of controversy are observed even the fundamentals of religion may be attacked without the writer being guilty of blasphemy, it had become a dead letter – long before it was formally abolished in 2008.

In the US, the precedence of First Amendment rights over censorship to tackle blasphemy or sacrilege was settled in the Supreme Court in *Joseph Burstyn, Inc. vs. Wilson* (1952), against revocation of the licence to exhibit Roberto Rossellini's short film, *The Miracle*. The film is a loaded parable about a retarded rustic woman (essayed by Anna Magnani) being plied with alcohol and seduced by a tramp whom she fantasizes to be St Joseph (played by Federico Fellini); when she finds herself pregnant she imagines it to be an immaculate conception, and is reviled and hounded by the villagers until she finds epiphanic release with the birth of her child in a church on the hill. A tortuous course that saw brushes with the licensing authority, Church-inspired picketing at the screening theatre and denial of relief by the trial court led the case to the Supreme Court, where the unanimous decision was in the film's favour. Justice Tom Clarke made the significant observation that it is not the business of government to suppress real or imagined attacks upon a particular religious doctrine, whether they appear in publications, speeches or motion pictures. The verdict at once made the plea of blasphemy or sacrilege untenable against First Amendment rights, and freed the motion picture from censorship by the state, society and the industry itself (filmmakers began to bypass the Production Code of the Motion Picture Association, so that it became irrelevant and defunct by the mid-1960s). The blasphemy bogey now finds little purchase in the US media sensibility.

Meanwhile, in his new work, *Joseph Anton: A Memoir*, a literary rendition of his years under the shadow of Khomeini's *fatwa*, a combative Salman Rushdie has upped the ante on the subject by identifying with the writers of the French Enlightenment who deliberately used blasphemy as a weapon, refusing to accept the power of the Church to set limiting points on thought. That, as we know in hindsight, cuts both ways, as the man who exemplified the libertarian spirit of the times and is often cited for his 'don't agree with what you have to say, but will defend to the death your right to say it' stand, also turned out to be a trenchant anti-Semite. Unless Rushdie, like those licentiously experimenting with the US First Amendment today, sees Voltaire venting his spleen on the Jews as primarily proof of his freedom of thought and speech.

Here and now, however, the boot is on the other foot. Subway stations in the city of New York are soon to have billboards with the exhortation: 'In any war between the civilized man and the savage, support the civilized man. Support Israel. Defeat Jihad.' A District Judge, invoking (guess what?) First Amendment rights, ruled against the New York Metropolitan Transit Authority's initial decision not to allow the advertisement commissioned by an ultra-conservative woman who runs an outfit called 'Stop Islamization of America', and who will 'not sacrifice my freedom so as not to offend savages'. Profiling, baiting and bashing Islam has, more so after September 11, become a stereotypical preoccupation in the western media, with even Hollywood weighing in with its Islamic typecasts. The Prophet Muhammad cartoons in the Danish paper *Jyllands Posten* in 2005, which led to over a hundred deaths, and this puerile movie trailer now are but periodic spikes in the graph.

For all their vaunted unalloyed commitment to freedom of expression, when it looks like their markets or trade may take a beating because of it, western governments, and media in tow, have been known to quickly temporize. When, in 1980, the ITV channel in the United Kingdom telecast *Death of a Princess*, a docudrama made by a British filmmaker about the execution in Jeddah of a 19-year-old girl of the Saudi royal family and her commoner lover, the Saudi government pulled out all stops to see it suppressed. The UK's Ambassador to Riyadh was sent back, trade sanctions were threatened, the British press was asking why a film should be allowed to put the market in harm's way, and London was soon scrambling to see that the film did not get any further play in the UK. In the US there was a media ad blitz by ExxonMobil against the film, and urging the Public Broadcasting Service (PBS) channel to reconsider its decision to show it, the State Department asked the channel to consider Saudi sensitivity; when it was eventually aired on PBS (some cities did not show it), the telecast was followed by an hour-long discussion that looked like an explanatory disclaimer.

The latest entrant in the fray is a strange French anarcho-libertine weekly, *Charlie Hebdo*, which has just lit its freedom torch from the raging fire following the infamous trailer with another series of cartoons on Prophet Muhammad. The French authorities naturally cannot but allow its publication, and will not allow street protests against it or the offending filmstrip. As comic relief in this hopeless situation, *Charlie Hebdo* protests the decision not to allow the protests – because that too, you see, is against the freedom of expression.

First published in *Frontline*, 19 October 2012.

The 'ism' in Journalism

So why is the free press contra-indicative in socialism? That may be begging the question because what is commonly understood to be the free press is, in the socialist scheme, the bourgeois press on the other side of the class divide, which is not free of the dictates of the market, the whims of advertising and the caprice of the capital that drives it. The free press of the socialist imagination is more liberating than liberalist, in which, as Lenin put it, 'all opinions of all citizens must be freely published'. An evolved socialized press would have its own printing presses, newsprint and advertising, all equitably provided by the state, and it would be a touchstone of the post-revolutionary order.

In the realpolitik of the socialist project, however, the press did not quite proceed beyond the transitional 'propagandist, agitator and organizer' function that Lenin set for it in the waging of war communism. In the ensuing nomenclatural order of the Soviet Union and Eastern Europe, a lead newspaper or news agency (like *Pravda* and Tass) set the agenda and corralled the news to be purveyed on a given day, subserving the interests of the state and the party. It was a command performance that lulled the political leadership into self-approbation even if the intended readership did not necessarily buy into it. Amartya Sen has drawn attention to the damning effects of such information blight and to why democracies, because the free press sounds an early warning alarm the moment the symptoms appear, are able to keep man-made famines at bay, whereas the socialist media and bureaucracy are so mutually parasitic that they either cannot or will not see the signs of a gathering storm until it is too late.

This vestigial media mentality will, one would imagine, be demolished as it runs headlong into a blindingly high-visibility, high-velocity information society. But then, it is as diehard as it is anachronistic. Russia *sans* socialism, and buttressed by the right to information guaranteed by the Constitution of 1993 and the specific Law on the Mass Media before that (1991), is not a better or safer place for journalists. An elaborate state apparatus dealing with the media continues to work overtime to withhold rather than provide information, and to cut journalists off from the corridors of power. On the other hand, contemporary socialist parties in, and aspiring to, power in different parts of the world, with innovative pro-people programmes that contest the overweening power of neoliberalism and finance capital, continue to be somewhat reticent in their appreciation of the merits of independent journalism. This, then, becomes their Achilles' heel which their capitalist detractors target with some success.

The Indian left too seems at a juncture where it needs to recalibrate and extend its inner-party democracy to give its media organs – print and television – better and freer play, so that they become an authoritative, credible source of information not only for their readers and viewers, but also for party functionaries at various levels and for the lay, plural press. In West Bengal, the party media got it very wrong in the recent Assembly elections, which the Left Front lost after an uninterrupted thirty-four-year run in power. The bullishness of this media up until all votes were cast was understandable enough as a probable strategy not to affect the morale of those yet to cast their ballots. But to persist in the prediction of a clear win constituency by constituency, even when counting was well under way and when the rest of the media were saying just the opposite, seemed to be creating an illusion of a self-fulfilling prophecy which of course came crashing down once the results were in. Nor was any of this dissemblance. A vicious cycle of hopeful rather than realistic feedback from party cells at the grassroots level, funnelled through the media and back into the party organization and ranks of the party faithful, seemed to have spiralled into the false build-up and expectation. An independent and critically distanced investigation by the media of the party, or media friendly to the party, could perhaps have cut this loop and helped them save face even if not the election.

Kerala has recently been through a tumultuous phase, with some flashpoints, in the interface between the left – particularly the leading party, the Communist Party of India (Marxist) – and the dominant Malayalam media. The State Secretary of the party has been in combative mode against what he sees as a campaign unleashed by a media 'syndicate' to discredit the left, with echoes of the so-called liberation struggle (*Vimochana Samaram*) of 1958–59 against the first-ever elected communist ministry of E.M.S. Namboodiripad, in which the bourgeois press was complicit. In this effort, however, the party has not been able to leverage its own media either to counter such tendentious coverage, or to effectively publicize the substantial achievements of the ministry and government it led in the state between 2006 and 2011.

While socialist journalism in the information age cannot obviously take after the corporate media in what it sets out to do, it needs to emerge confidently from behind the apron-strings of the party into the public sphere, to make a difference. This means stepping out of the backyard of the party – out of a tentative, self-conscious, censorious mindset – and striking a swathe through the media clutter. Indeed this, at its best, is a return to Marx, whose celebration of journalism and journalistic freedoms is as categorical as it is fervent. Both as editor of the *Sudenten Zeitung* and the *Neue Sudenten Zeitung* in Prussia in the 1840s, and later as a London-based correspondent of the *New York Tribune* through the 1850s, apart from his contribution to many other journals, Marx exemplified journalistic praxis in his conceptual exploration of the freedoms of expression and their deployment in his incisive columns and multipart articles on developments across the world. It was through journalism that he earned a living, his remuneration per column (he wrote over 350 for the *Tribune* alone through the decade of 1850–60) being five pounds, the highest paid by the paper to any contributor. As one of his biographers, Francis Wheen, notes in his foreword to the compilation *Dispatches for the New York Tribune: Selected Journalism of Karl Marx*: 'Even if he had done nothing else Marx would deserve to be remembered as one of the great nineteenth century journalists.'

Marx's ruminations on the freedom of the press are a philosophical *tour de force* which endows journalism with its intrinsic higher purpose and distinctive rationale. The immediate context was censorship by the Prussian state, against which he inveighed with passion and logic in article after article in the *Sudenten Zeitung* in 1842 – although in vain, because he had to shut down the paper and flee to France the following year. But a holistic theory of the press and its destiny to be free was already taking shape beyond the polemical contestation of the censorship provisions in the German Rhineland, and it was further forged when he returned to Cologne in 1848 as editor of the *Neue Sudenten Zeitung*.

As part of his insightful study, *Communication is Freedom: Karl Marx on Press Freedom and Censorship*, the late media scholar Hanno Hardt, who taught at the Universities of Iowa and Ljubljana, renders into English the strains of thought developed by Marx during his two editorial stints in Germany. They read like a string of prescient aphorisms. The press, for Marx, implies freedom *ipso facto*, for 'it is a realization of human freedom. Where there is a press, there is also press freedom.' There is a passionate personal investment in that freedom: 'one must have loved freedom of the press like beauty to be able to defend it. I feel that the existence of whatever I really love is necessary and needed, and without it my own being is not fulfilled, satisfied, nor complete.'

Marx's case for the freedom of the press is unqualified and absolute. 'The free press', he says, 'remains good even when its products are bad, because these products are deviations from the nature of the free press.' On the other hand, 'the censored press remains bad even when its products are good, because these products are only good insofar as they represent the free press within the censored press, and insofar as it is not in their character to be products of a censored press'. Thus censorship is a no-no because it goes against the natural grain of the press. It becomes the business of laws governing the press to keep the state of freedom intact. In a clinching, morally imbued comparison, Marx argues that censorship, even if it is the law, cannot be legal, in the same spirit that slavery even as law is illegal. Censorship, in fact, defeats the very public purpose it sets out to serve: 'Since people must consider uncensored publications as lawless, they will get used to considering lawlessness as free, freedom as lawless, and lawfulness as unfreedom. Thus censorship kills the public spirit.'

Marx anticipates, by well over a century and a half, a variation of the Amartya Sen theme mentioned earlier, of the free press serving an early-warning function. In a regime of press censorship, notes Marx, the government 'hears only its own voice, knows that it hears only its own voice and is yet fixed on the delusion to hear the voice of the people and demands from the people to fall for the trick'.

There may be, as Hanno Hardt and other scholars have pointed out, a breeziness of nineteenth-century liberalism in some of Marx's early take on freedom of the press; more so in his omnibus formulation that 'freedom remains freedom, whether it expresses itself in printer's ink, a parcel of land, consciousness, or in a political meeting'. But we find, at the same time, a clear distinction being sought to be drawn between the freedom of the market and the free press. Marx is clear that 'the first freedom of the press is not to be a business . . . when the press exists as a business it is not an interest of writers, but of printers and booksellers'. He posits the clear alternative of a people's press (*Volkspresse*) against the bourgeois press. Marx's humanistic and non-alienating embrace of, and prescription for, journalism is a far cry from its dismal reified construct in subsequent socialist practice.

That aberration and failure to realize a free press which enriches, and is enriched by, socialism must partly explain why this aspect of the man, as media thinker and practitioner par excellence, is marginalized in the corpus of Marxist historiography. Partly again, it is a victim of the Althusserian epistemological demarcation between the early and the later Marx, with 1845 as the dividing line. This partition of Marxist intellectual patrimony is, however, being increasingly challenged as, among other things, arbitrarily privileging his determinism over his humanism. In any case Marx's journalistic persona and preoccupation reach across the divide, and well into the 1860s. His articles for *New York Tribune* mirrored, both methodologically and substantively, his and Engels' work on *The Communist Manifesto* and large tracts of *Capital*, although stylistically they are seen as more of a piece with *The Eighteenth Brumaire of Louis Bonaparte*.

Today, more than ever before, the representational and make-believe powers of the formal media are game-changing – propping up fatuous financial markets against the real economy, fixing and finetuning market sentiment, and reducing readers and viewers into ersatz consumers. The potential and promise of socialism against the neoliberal order needs an agency which can evoke the alternative in freshly minted terms that capture the popular imagination. Online chatterati or twitterati, or a listless social media can at best supplement, not substitute, this grand task. If old camp shibboleths are shed, the free press and journalism which are essentially and ultimately pro-people, and which have been rendered passé in the business-of-the-media model now obtaining, could be the harbingers of this transformation.

First published in *Frontline*, 2 November 2012.

Digital Capitalism

The television screen turns into a static charge of salt-and-pepper hiss. If you have the patience to linger to find out why without instantly switching to another channel, you will eventually learn that this is what is in store for you if you are living in one of the four metros; if you are served by cable, not DTH (direct-to-home); and if you do not put in place that digital set-top box by the end of October 2012. It is a portentous public interest advertisement which serves notice on an analogue media era and prepares to usher in the digital-only realm of television-viewing.

It is part of building the momentum, in the wake of the Cable Television Networks (Regulation) Amendment Act of 2011, towards a total changeover to digital distribution via cable in four stages: the four metros by 31 October 2012; cities with a population of over a million by 31 March 2013; all other urban centres by the end of September 2014; and the rest of the country by the end of the calendar year 2014. The conversion is both a legal and a technological imperative. Digitize or perish is the writing on the wall. You're damned if you don't.

It is not as self-evident, though, that you're not damned if you do. The democratic logic of digitization is better, cheaper and more equitable access and choice for the consumer. The analogue hierarchy of a clutch of channels on prime band that register effulgent clarity in picture and sound, followed by a longish tail of poor and poorer cousins on the less and lesser bands with inferior, even indifferent visual and audio quality is, in the digital mode, replaced by a qualitative constant across the board where the look and feel of each channel directly reflect the production input and values of its content, and there is no distribution diffusion. That would be one obvious change, and would itself certainly make the difference between night and day for those yet stuck with analogue signals.

But the investments required for the digital rollout and spread, the high-end consumerist appetites and values they privilege, and the sheer scale of the operation put the business of digital cable networking out of the league and reach of the small- or medium-scale entrepreneur. This new regime in the media sector, as much as the policy and the law that propel it, is made to order for digital capitalism.

The fat cats of the business have already begun to parse the law to suit their rapacity, but are couching it in terms of the best interests of the consumer.

The path to digitization is paved with their good intentions. A recent conclave on 'Media and Entertainment Business' organized by the Federation of Indian Chambers of Commerce and Industry (FICCI) in Chennai revealed, to mix metaphors, their itchy palms in velvet gloves. In a panel discussion on opportunities in the digitized era, the participants, who were among the major stakeholders from the content and distribution side of the industry, seemed in no doubt that the *raison d'être* of digitization was consolidation and vertical integration of their businesses. There was a queer money-minded nostalgia for the business advantages of the analogue market being left behind, even as they scrambled to take over the digital El Dorado of the future. They would, if they could, have the best of both worlds – analogue and digital.

And so, while they are agreed that digitization would enable upscaled quality, they are even more agreed that consumers must be prepared to pay more for it; and we naively thought digital meant lower costs. The revenue model in digital cable networks is typically subscription-driven, so that advertisements do not hog and clutter airtime. But there is a clear reluctance to part with advertisement revenues, and the upshot may well be that even as we pay more we will continue to be subject to long stretches of commercials interrupting programmes (as the witticism goes, a programme on television is what happens between advertisements).

Then there is the question of carriage fees, which acquires critical importance in a situation where, more than ever before, how to get to be seen is the despair of every new television channel. Thanks to digitization, the bandwidth required for one analogue transponder or channel is compressed to spin off five or six new ones, making the transponder the least – from the most – expensive component in the outlay for a new channel. But with so many channels (there are over 600 on air now and as many or more awaiting licences) jostling one another for distribution, and with no norms or rules in place, the big multi-service operators (MSOs), like their DTH counterparts, have been charging exorbitant and whimsical carriage fees, skewing the field strongly in favour of the big media corporations which can cough up such amounts, with hefty additional premiums for prime placements. Those who cannot afford this are left out in the cold, and there are so many instances of new channels having to repeatedly delay their launch because of this acute distribution squeeze that the whole process seems ridiculously weighed against the small and medium players.

All this is, ostensibly, set to change in the digital milieu because the carriage capacity expands manifold to ensure an outlet for each licensed channel and on the same band as every other. And yet neither channel nor MSO seems willing to give up the carriage fee idea unless the regulatory authority, the Telecom Regulatory Authority of India (TRAI), or the nodal Information and Broadcasting Ministry, specifically prohibits it in the new dispensation. Even then, or so went the thinking on the FICCI panel, there could be a showcasing fee to, say, place a channel next to a popular one, or a price to become part of a special bouquet of upmarket channels – thus in effect re-hierarchizing the digital realm. The big league channels, faced with the prospect of losing their costly but exclusive premium positions in the analogue order, may also be perfectly happy to go along with, and pay what it takes for, this discriminatory tweaking of the new system, to procure their higher-visibility slots afresh in the pecking order.

If content is king, goes the well-worn saying in the industry, distribution must be god. Digitization is not about to upset that order. If the growing concentration of distributive power in the hands of a monopolistic cartel of MSOs was already a problem, this kind of digitization will further marginalize and imperil the independent local cable operator (LCO), the local self-employed entrepreneur who provides and services last-mile connectivity. The innate democratizing and devolutionary urge of digital technology, which could have been harnessed by the government to set up tens of thousands of such neighbourhood cable operators under pan-regional umbrella MSOs, is stood on its head in this top–down imposition of a corporate model prescribed and defined by big capital. The reigning media oligopoly – not the consumer, not the last-mile operator – becomes the biggest beneficiary of TRAI's digitization initiative.

A counter-initiative in Kerala tells us it could be different. Over 2,300 independent cable operators here, banded as an association and claiming as much as 45 per cent share of the nearly 50 lakh TV households in the state, have formed themselves into a public limited company, Kerala Communicators Cable Limited (KCCL), to take on the function of a professional MSO platform and meet their digitization deadline of September 2014. The confederation has leased signal carriage capacity on the optic fibre lines of the Indian Railways and the Kerala State Electricity Board (KSEB) so that it has reach through the length of the state. It is befitting that this is happening in Kerala, where the first statewide cable TV network in the country, using the electricity poles across the state under an agreement with the KSEB and with an elaborate system of franchisees as the local cable operators, was set up as far back as 1992.

An alternative model where the state undertakes the responsibility for laying and managing the cable and satellite (C&S) network, becoming in effect the MSO, is the government-run Arasu Cable TV enterprise in Tamil Nadu, which, as this article goes to press, is racing against time to meet the deadline of 31 October 2012 to have digital set-top boxes installed in all its subscriber households in Chennai. The company, with 58 lakh (and counting) subscribers in the state and over 2,000 LCOs under its aegis, has announced a base fee of Rs 70 for a package of 100 free-to-air (as against pay) channels. Now that looks more like the legitimate economics of digitization at work, at the consumer end. But the credibility, not to mention sustainability, of this public interest venture is tied to the fluctuating fortunes of the polarized party politics in the state, particularly because one of the two main parties which alternate in power has strong family links with the biggest media player in the state.

These two examples illustrate, at least in their potential or intent, the possibility of a different organization, economics and social architecture of digitization in cable TV networking that is local operator-centric; more attuned to the cultural appetite and price sensitivity of the end user; is not appropriated by the distant big corporation; and is bottom–up in its approach. This is what the government and TRAI should have set out to enable, instead of making this historic juncture of a standards conversion and a sea-change in technology, with such far-reaching social implications, an occasion for a business bonanza.

The sagacity with which the renowned media and cultural theorist Raymond Williams underscores this policy-choice aspect, even though he was engaging with it in the 1980s when digitization was not as much a fact of life, is remarkable. The moment of any new technology, he writes in 'Culture and Technology',

> is a moment of choice. Within existing social and economic conditions, the new systems will be installed as forms of distribution without any real thought of corresponding forms of production. New cable or cable-and-satellite television will rely heavily on old entertainment stocks and a few cheap services. New information systems will be dominated by financial institutions, mail-order marketers, travel agencies and general advertisers. These kinds of content, predictable from the lines of force of the economic system, will be seen as the whole or necessary content of advanced electronic entertainment and information. More seriously, they will come to define such entertainment and information, and to form practical and self-fulfilling expectations. Yet there are readily available alternative uses. New cable and cable-satellite television systems, and new teletext and cable-signal systems, could be wholly developed within public ownership, not for some old or new kind of monopoly provider, but as common-carrier systems which would be available, by lease and contract, to a wide range of producing and providing bodies.

In a situation where cross-media holdings have not been barred and where monopolies straddling print, television, FM radio, and the nascent but rapidly growing internet have become a *fait accompli*, competition between cable and DTH, too, is for a good part notional because the bigger players own and operate both businesses. This, and digital standardization and consolidation across platforms, make for a consumer who, to borrow freely from Henry Ford, can have any service at any price he wants as long as it is what the provider provides. If the consumer is at the mercy of the service provider, the state too seems to be at the mercy of the firm, taking its cues for a policy framework for the digital media market from the very industry that will exploit it. Else, wide discussion and debate in the public sphere, distinct from the charades in TV studios, should have preceded such a significant transition. Here was an opening, an opportunity, for the state to give meaning and substance to the Supreme Court judgment of 1995 that airwaves – as in radio spectrum – are public property. In the absence of the political will to make them so, they will increasingly serve private ends.

First published in *Frontline*, 16 November 2012.

Stings, Ratings and Shootings

'Don't shoot the messenger.' With this firm admonition, television news anchors routinely nip questioning of journalistic practice in the bud. It has got a little more difficult for them to carry conviction with that tack, however, after a corporate house actually went ahead and shot a couple of messengers – with a hidden camera. And it is not a pretty sight. The footage shows two editors of the media group Zee TV bargaining with a representative of Jindal Steel and Power Ltd for an advertisement deal of Rs 100 crores, spread equally over four or five years, to spike adverse stories on the business group. The editors, for their part, claim that they were playing along as they were sought to be bribed and that this was all part of their investigation into Jindal Steel in the coal blocks allocation scam. Implausible as the spin seems, at least on the strength of what transpires on the released video, it may well gain credence in the obfuscatory sequel to the exposé. Also, one can always count on public memory being short. After all, the worthies caught cosying up to big business in the Radia tapes are cheerily back to business (read journalism) as usual on the tube.

Close on the heels of this reverse sting comes the news of a reverse sterilization campaign by the government, seeking to undo the forcible vasectomy of female Maoist cadres by their leadership, to enable them to marry and bear children and eschew the violent path ever after. It is tempting to wonder whether the reverse sting could serve a similar reverse social-engineering role, by bringing to heel, rehabilitating where possible, rogue elements running amok in the media. Where digitization and miniaturization give you cameras with inbuilt microphones masquerading as shirt buttons, tie clips, pens, wristwatches, finger rings, spectacle frames, briefcases, belt buckles and what not, tit-for-tat stings should be easy enough, whether by or against corporations, the government, the bureaucracy, political parties, the media, civil society, NGOs and affected individuals. Of these, the government alone can only be stung and must not sting, or at least not be caught stinging, unless it wants a Watergate-like scandal on its hands. All in all, this could well be a more exciting and self-correcting, not to mention entertaining, proxy for the external regulator that Justice Markandey Katju keeps harping on. It would be an extension of 24x7, 360-degree reality TV into the social media delivered on computers, hand-held electronic tablets, mobile devices and what-have-you. Surely worth a thought?

Meanwhile, another weird thought crops up. How much of the advertising spend on the news media goes towards publicizing goods and services, and how much towards keeping things from being made public? Where the advertiser, as we all along suspected and now know, is paying for both, we as viewers are obviously being shortchanged, in terms of our right to information from or our voyeuristic expectations of the media, or both. Imagine the spice and sleaze and scam we are being done out of by secret, underhand deals of the kind the Jindal sting exposed. Imagine the opportunity cost.

If that seems like stretching things a bit even for television news, which is given to stretch as a figure of speech, it is precisely such reverse or twisted logic with which the celebrated French sociologist Pierre Bourdieu deconstructs news in its contemporary phase of interaction between print and TV, in his slim but incisive book, *On Television and Journalism*. Published towards the end of the 1990s and drawing mainly on his impressions and experience of the French news media, Bourdieu's analysis is nevertheless so spot on that it is as relevant and universally so today, as it was then. The performance of our own TV news channels almost uncannily illustrates his thesis. Take, for instance, Bourdieu's point about the invisible forms of censorship on TV, among them the peculiar but common one of hiding by showing:

> . . . it can hide things by showing something other than what would be shown if television did what it's supposed to do, provide information. Or by showing what has to be shown, but in such a way that it isn't really shown, or is turned into something insignificant; or by constructing it in such a way that it takes on a meaning that has nothing at all to do with reality.

In a situation where television is the dominant medium and the time on it is so dear, 'when you use up precious time to say banal things, to the extent that they cover up precious things, these banalities become in fact very important'.

Viewed in this light, the live newsroom has become a theatre of the flippant on Indian television. There are hardly any pre-packaged stories – which have the advantage of being better thought out, informed, rounded, diverse, information-packed and more complete (even for an evolving story) – feeding into the news programme any more. What we get instead in the live, as-is-where-is roll-out are, for the most part, reporters and correspondents who, apart from not being very articulate, add little to a story by their vacuous and half-baked views. They depend largely on the bluff and bluster of their anchor in the studio to give them a semblance of substance, and to give what they together fetch up: the appearance of a big happening. The same stock set of 'experts' hopping from studio to studio makes the whole affair both fairly incestuous and homogenous, leading to what Bourdieu calls 'circular circulation of information', 'a game of mirrors' which 'produces a formidable effect of mental closure'.

Another paradox with a similar circumscribing effect, that Bourdieu puts his finger on, is how the fear of missing a story rather than an original search for one leads to consensual herd behaviour in coverage. When the editor of a TV channel (or newspaper, for that matter) observes in a review meeting that we missed the story, all he means is that another channel (or paper) had a story his did not carry. If a channel, therefore, is not to miss a story, it must ensure that it covers all the major stories other channels do. Reporters across channels who are in touch and compare notes with one another, then, flock to the same set of stories. In the process, sameness rather than difference, barring the occasional scoop, is incentivized; the variety and choice that pluralism offers are forfeited in this mock competition.

The single most important arbiter of the television industry's fortunes, the ratings system, also seems the product of a backflip logic. Bourdieu points to the larger social malaise of a ratings mindset, which conditions us to choose the books we read, the music we listen to or the films we see, from the bestseller, star-rated, short and long or countdown lists generated for such cultural products. Apart from the subjectivity of the critics who pick and hierarchize them, the process of the listing is obtuse and, one suspects, subject to a variety of pressures. There are two kinds of problems here. One, idealized by the poet (Thomas Gray in 'Elegy Written in a Country Churchyard') where possibly, surely:

> Full many a gem of purest ray serene,
> The dark unfathomed caves of ocean bear:
> Full many a flower is born to blush unseen,
> And waste its sweetness on the desert air

– and we may never get to know of their existence as we stay fixated on the one or the other list. The second and perhaps more important concern is the surrender of culture to the dictates of the market via the register of popular demand. The market mediation of the popular, exercised by the ratings phenomenon, strikes at the very root of art and culture as autonomous, even contrarian fields of activity. Hardly fifty or sixty years ago, as Bourdieu recalls, market success was seen as suspect for truly artistic endeavour, and the biggest advances in literature and culture – as much as in science, mathematics or philosophy – were made against the grain of the popular. All that has changed as anything now cannot but seek its place under the overarching sway of the market.

The market model for the media sector is premised even more crucially on a formal ratings system which determines the advertisement revenues accruing to a newspaper or broadcaster; and, with a few exceptions of regional Indian-language papers, which post healthier subscription returns, advertising continues to account for three-fourths or more of their revenues.

Bourdieu looks beyond at the implications of the ratings–advertising axis for the practice of journalism in the media:

> like in the political and economic fields, and much more than the scientific, artistic, literary, or juridical fields, the journalistic field is permanently subject to trial by media, whether directly, through advertisers, or indirectly, through audience rating. . . . Furthermore, journalists are no doubt all the more inclined to adopt audience rating standards in the production process (keep it simple, keep it short) or when evaluating products or even producers (that's just made for TV, this will go over really well), to the extent that those who better represent these standards occupy higher positions (as network heads or editors-in-chief) in news media more directly dependent on the market (that is, commercial television as opposed to Public Broadcasting Service [PBS]). Conversely, younger and less established journalists are more likely to invoke the principles and values of the profession against the more realistic or more cynical, stipulations of their elders.

The tyranny of ratings is particularly acute in the Indian television industry, with channels literally drawing their sustenance from the Television Rating Points (TRPs) that viewership measurement agencies such as Television Audience Measurement (TAM) bestow on them. Unscientific, distorted ratings with skewed and disproportionately small sample-sizes or, worse, corruptly slanted to favour the one over the other, wreak havoc on a channel's fortunes. The unscientific methodology and unrepresentative scope of this exercise in India has been a talking point in the industry for some time now. But matters came to a head recently with the NDTV group filing a $1.3 billion suit against TAM India and its parent company, Nielson, in a court in the United States.

On the other hand, a faulty ratings system also becomes a convenient alibi for a channel that finds itself losing out in the competition for reasons that may be of its own making, including perhaps the poor or waning appeal of its programmes. In what is essentially an endogenous market arrangement among the channel, the rating agency and the advertiser, and where there is no external mandatory requirement or legal stipulation for advertising budgets to be allocated to channels on the basis of their ratings, how, or how far, can a channel bring a rating agency to account except perhaps on grounds of invidious or discriminatory treatment, or malpractice? It is in fact surprising that the industry has lived with what it considers a flawed or foul rating system, a virtual monopoly to boot, for so long, and not put in place an alternative, perhaps under the joint aegis of broadcasters and advertisers as has been discussed off and on. But then, the players who notch up good TRPs in the current system may not want any change. And who is to blame them in an industry not marked by a level playing field in the first instance, and where strong entry barriers protect the turf for the reigning media czars?

It is too much to expect that the media can, with some magical will, heave themselves out of the ratings' cauldron, especially when the rest of society has become so ratings prone. After all even the financial reputation of nation-states seems at the mercy of rating agencies such as Standard and Poors (S&P) who can, for instance (with the flick of a figure, so to speak), reduce India to junk status. The bottom line is that the ratings-culture is here to stay as a market imposition on the political framework of democracy, which at the same time detracts from the representative and inclusive nature of democracy. It has the media by the throat, and controls the expressions and discourses that emerge.

First published in *Frontline*, 30 November 2012.

Net Worth

For some time now, free expression on the net and freedom of the press have both been up for revalorization. That they are, and the manner in which they are, may not augur well for democracy in both its deliberative and institutionalized aspects. The regulatory urge seems to tilt over into setting limits to un-freedom rather than to move towards evolving a code of reasonable restraints on the freedoms guaranteed in the Fundamental Rights chapter of the Constitution. In fact the caveat of reasonable restraint is of late evoked far too often to be of comfort to the clause of freedom itself that it seeks to qualify. It is as if the norm of freedom of expression the Constitution envisages is no longer as desirable or viable as it was in less troubled times.

In what seems a residual colonial mindset, the news media profession in India was avidly tracking the Leveson inquiry into the working of the British press, following disclosures of the intrusive unethical practices of *News International* of the Murdoch stable, as if its outcome has inescapable implications for us. The report and its recommendation are being seized by the pro-external-regulation camp to buttress its case, although Lord Justice Leveson himself combined his heavy-handed diagnosis of an errant press with a light-touch cure that stopped short of statutory regulation. Paradoxically, it would seem, at least from the public pronouncements, that both in the United Kingdom and in India, the state is more wary of a regime of control of the press than sections of the fourth estate or civil society. Prime Minister David Cameron had almost preempted the Leveson report by offering to implement it only if it was 'not bonkers'.

Press Council of India Chairman Markandey Katju's tirade against what he sees as an irresponsible media, and his harsh prescription of stopping government advertisements to and suspension of the licence of such media, are in stark contrast to the sanguine commitment of Prime Minister Manmohan Singh on National Press Day in November, to 'complete independence of the media from external control'. Indeed Justice Katju had earlier dismissed 'self-regulation' by the press as an oxymoron. Interestingly, Union Telecommunications Minister Kapil Sibal, in the run-up to the World Conference on International Telecommunications (WCIT) convened by the International Telecommunication Union (ITU) in Dubai in December 2012, has called all talk of 'internet governance' an oxymoron. All this may well be only public posturing, as against real intent, by the state and the stakeholders in the media respectively; or it may point to a deeper cronyism marking the relationship between the state and the monopolistic corporate media. In any case, it seems to upend the notion that the state and the media are mutually adversarial. Media under state protection is surely as odd and irreconcilable as media under state control. Protection of the rule of law is all that the media must seek and merit, not state patronage.

The track record of the agency of the state is, of course, another matter. Nudged and ham-handed police action against a cartoon posted online by a professor on a maverick politician like Mamata Banerjee, or a tweet by a small entrepreneur on a parvenu politician like Karti Chidambaram, or a Facebook post and endorsement respectively by two young women on Mumbai being brought to a halt on the death of Bal Thackeray that lumpen Shiv Sainiks could not lump, are indicative of the growing intolerant and anti-social approach to free speech on digital social media. It is a farcical situation where much the same or more can be said and written in the formal print or electronic news media with impunity, because it ostensibly has the pedigree and stamp of professional journalism.

Cyberspace and social media, which should be the equivalent of the public square where people meet and exchange views, are instead becoming the more prohibited zones for freedom of expression. The by now infamous clause 66A of the Information Technology (IT) Act would be a joke if it did not have such dire consequences for the common man, who can all too easily and unwittingly fall foul of it. Omnibus in its scope and arbitrary in its definition and applicability, the clause makes the digital mediascape a minefield that the citizen must tread warily on. Even as the Supreme Court examines, on a public interest litigation (PIL) filed by an aspiring law student, Shreya Singhal, whether the clause is *ultra vires* of the Constitution, and irrespective of its decision, there is little doubt that keeping it on the statute book poses a summary threat to any netizen.

Surveillance of trolling is impracticable enough given the globalized and complicated architecture of the net, which does not lend itself to the cultural or political demands of individual nation-states – and can prove particularly impossible during surges of rambunctious cyberactivism. That, one would imagine, may be a bugbear for the totalitarian state, but would enhance the cause of a universalized democracy as a fitting counterpart of a globalized economy. From the anti-WTO (World Trade Organization) Seattle protests of 1999, through numerous cyber agitations, down to the domino effect of the Arab Spring or 'colour' revolutions in countries emerging from the former Soviet Union or the Occupy Wall Street movement in the United States and Europe, not to mention the myriad economic, ecological, social and cultural struggles working as local pressure points, digital communication technologies both engender and are constitutive of a pulsating popular dynamic that is supranational and universalizing in its thrust. Sooner or later, the nation-state was bound to take exception to this alternative virtual realm of freewheeling expression, cocking a snook at the established political order and social hierarchy.

Cyberspace, then, is no longer seen as the virtual expression of the Habermasian public sphere where people can congregate to express their opinion forthrightly irrespective of caste, creed or class – in other words, with the assurance and equality of anonymity of identity. It is construed, instead, as a potential hotbed of disaffection or anarchism that needs constant patrolling, and where identities of the participants or players must be disclosed. Habermas also alerted us to the transition from the liberal public sphere, a legacy of the Enlightenment and the American and French Revolutions, to one that is driven by a media market run by giant corporations, where public opinion is no longer the product of rational debate and discussion but manufactured by publicity stunts and the brainwashing of advertising, so that 'publicity loses it critical function in favour of a staged display; even arguments are transmuted into symbols to which again one cannot respond by arguing but only by identifying with them'. The space that should have been autonomous, de-hierarchized, universal, inclusive, subject to only the normal rule of law and not subordinated to special legal dispensations is thus caught in the double bind of hawk-eyed surveillance by the state and the grasping ways of the market.

Draconian provisions like clause 66A of the IT Act regress to the jurisprudence of early eighteenth-century England when even truth was no defence against libel – in fact the greater the truth, the greater the libel – and it was considered seditious libel if a citizen spoke up, or mustered opinion, against the state. As Chief Justice of England, John Holt, put it in 1704: 'If men should not be called to account for possessing the people with an ill opinion of the government, no government can subsist; for it is very necessary for every government that the people should have a good opinion of it.'

Goodwill, fraternization and amity among people, or between the people and the state, as legal imperative or command performance is, in this day and age, just that much more absurd and naive. And yet the government has been hyperactive in its effort to tame the net. Between January and June 2011, Google reports that Indian authorities sought removal of as many as 358 items from the net, of which it estimates that 255 were for 'government criticism', 39 because they were ostensibly defamatory and 8 for hate speech. The government has also borne down on hundreds of Facebook and Twitter accounts, and a few months back, looked like actively consorting with the one parliamentary democracy in Central Asia, Kyrgyzstan, to lobby for an agency to monitor the net. Last October the Indian delegate, after a rather long and gratuitous prelude that seemed more like a protestation of the government's commitment to a totally free and plural internet regime, initiated a proposal in the 66th session of the United Nations General Assembly to set up a Committee for Internet Related Policies (CIRP) to bring it under the oversight of a 50-nation body. The move earned the ire of multiple stakeholders at home who were not consulted, and the government too seems to have subsequently quietly distanced itself from this effort.

The real, if unstated, agenda behind the 193-nation Dubai conference seems a trial of strength between ITU (International Telecommunication Union) and ICANN (Internet Corporation for Assigned Names and Numbers) for greater say in matters related to the future of the net. As part of the process of Americanization that the liberalization and globalization of the 1990s meant, the functions of a multilateral institution such as the ITU, which traditionally allocated radio spectrum and satellite orbits and oversaw the information and telecommunications order, had been suborned by ICANN, under the purview of the US Department of Commerce, much like UNESCO had been rendered redundant by the WTO. The ITU has been showing some signs of wresting the initiative back at Dubai, but may well be forced on the back foot by the dissembling rhetoric of freedom of expression that the US-led lobby and proponents of ICANN are resorting to. Already media reports tend to project the ITU as indulgent to the pro-regulation position of countries like China and Russia, and ITU Secretary-General Hamadoun Touré's concern that the kind of lax regulation that brought about the crises in the financial and banking sectors should not be allowed to recur in telecommunications will find ready ominous readings.

The case for free speech on the net is not, *ipso facto*, for direct democracy or populism. There can of course be too much of a good thing, and there are different views on whether unmediated expression adds up to anything. Eugene Volokh sees intrinsic value in the 'cheap speech' the new communication technology promotes, making it 'easier for all ideas, whether backed by rich or poor, to participate in the marketplace. Even if many individuals still cannot afford to counter speak effectively, there will be many more organizations able to speak out on all sides of an issue.' Others, like Cass Sustein, argue that the internet tends to make users choose information that reinforces their predisposed views by filtering out opposing points of view and, in the process, perpetuates their own corners of prejudice in cyberspace. There is then the question of whether, as Alexander Meiklejohn posed it even in the mid-twentieth century, 'everyone shall speak' or 'everything worth saying shall be said'. Or just celebrate being there, as a Hansard Society report on blogging underscores: 'To blog is to declare your presence; to disclose to the world that you exist and what it's like to be you; to affirm that your thoughts are at least as worth hearing as anyone else's; to emerge from the spectating audience as a player and maker of meanings.' It is such a potpourri of ideas and types that vivifies the net and the interactive social spaces eked out by digital technologies of communication. To seek to regulate the traffic there may end up in the creation of one-way streets of information flow.

First published in *Frontline*, 28 December 2012.

Portrayals of Rape

She boarded a bus in Munirka to return home to Dwarka, southwest of Delhi, after an evening show of *Life of Pi*. What the six men on it did to her on that ride, on the one hand, is unspeakably horrific, and on the other, cannot be told brutally enough. The searing rawness of her hyperreal ordeal does not lend itself to allegory as a form of artistic cushioning which Yann Martel deploys in recounting the savagery that the young boy Pi of his fable (on which Ang Lee's film is based) witnesses, adrift on the ocean after the shipwreck – and which she saw on the screen before all too real savagery, with nothing imaginary about it, struck her. The best we are able to do to summon up the will to contemplate this macabre act is to resort to medicalese in order to anaesthetize our minds against the things done to her body.

The gruesome manner of it instantly made this rape more than a statistic. Through the thirteen days that the life of the twenty-three-year-old woman hung in the balance, along with the anger and indignation that hit the streets of Delhi and other cities and towns, and beyond the incredibly callous comments by politicians of the right, left and centre, was a sense of stark helplessness, a desperate search for meaning. It was easier to say what this act was not than to find a description that could fit its execrable extent. A television anchor called it beastly – unfairly to animals which do not, except in horror movies of mutant creatures, act with anything like perverse cruelty of this kind. Rape and gang-rape seem to have become insufficient, reductive terms, partly because they do not capture the complex cruelty of the physical and psychological violence and violation inflicted, and partly because they continued to take place with almost commonplace frequency in the same city and other parts of the country during the same period that the popular media and mind space were suffused by a fog of grief alongside ritual expressions and demonstrations of blame and atonement.

There were intimations of what some blogs call a 'Tunisian moment' in the street remonstrations. That prospect apparently proved too irresistible for some TV channels, which took to working the crowd. Prodding, often rhetorical questions only amplified, instead of interrogating, the clamour for rapists to be hanged, or at least castrated. There was mediated consensus on the need for fast-track courts, but, it would seem, with a hanging judge at the end of the track. Some respondents were for even quicker, summary dispensation of justice like spot-lynching or bobbitization or dismemberment Saudi style. One young man wanted the Delhi rapists to be put through prolonged pain and suffering, commensurate with what they inflicted on the woman, before they were killed. All this was part of both the studio discussions and the field *vox pop*-cum-dipstick surveys meant to convey the popular mood. Given that mood, no one, wisely, offered the routine homily that the law will take its course. Given that mood, there may have been tacit approval rather than opposition if the rapists had been killed in a police 'encounter' – like the cab driver in Coimbatore, a couple of years back, accused of killing two sibling children after raping the girl.

There can be no quarrel with television studio hosts and anchors, often doubling as editors of their channels, plunging headlong into a public cause, and, as in this case, forcing the issue in terms of a rethinking and recasting of the legal process and apparatus, to ensure that there is certainty of justice without undue delay. They undoubtedly also played an admirable role in keeping the issue live on their screens and alive in the public mind, so that the government and authorities could not look the other way. But the fixated approach to the story as one of crime and punishment, of law and order, made for a sense of cultural and social distancing, ignoring or being in denial of the question as to why there are so many rapists in our midst in the first place; even going by the reported cases, which must be a gross underestimation, a rape is perpetrated at least every half an hour somewhere in the country. A question like that hardly gets any play in the language game of contemporary television where, for a good part, hortatory declamations pass for anchoring and shouting matches pretend to be panel discussions. Anxiety and angst ruled the studio floor as much as the street, and the effect, in sum, was of a collective baying for blood. Indeed it is a moot point whether the coverage of the street was to that extent a misrepresentation because the protest was one of quiet and dignified pain for the most part, which should have made for more restrained, more reflective television.

There were truly moving, edifying moments too. In one studio discussion, a gang-rape survivor who had cast anonymity aside spoke with unblinking fortitude about the traumatic experience she was put through when just fifteen years old. Her example held up the hypocrisy of social acceptability to ridicule. She was clear that if anyone should be ashamed and be hiding away, it should be the rapist, whereas our moral and social conditioning pushed the survivor into a state of absent presence.

Sexual power and violence against women is coded into our popular culture and media as much as into our social relations. What Sarah Projansky says about the United States in her influential work, *Watching Rape: Film and Television in Post-Feminist Culture*, would be as applicable in our context:

> Representations of sexual violence pervade our social lives, occupying both public (e.g. movie theatres) and intimate (e.g. living rooms) spaces and defining gendered

> . . . social relations. Whether this ubiquity naturalizes depictions of rape for us so that we hardly notice them, draws our attention to them so that we feel overwhelmed by their presence, or places us somewhere in between along this continuum of awareness, it is impossible to avoid encountering representation of rape often in our daily lives.

Indian mainstream cinema is replete with such violence, and rape is routinely used as a device of both suspense and erotic titillation; as yet another component that engages rather than enrages. The brinkmanship of filmmakers in dodging the censor and having their salacious say by sexual innuendo in film songs and the so-called 'item numbers' is staggering. Even more dangerously, filmic versions of repressive social mores tend to sanitize and legitimize gender subjugation, and weave them seamlessly into modern life. The *katta panchayats* of Tamil cinema and television serials, for example, come across as quaint rural institutions enjoying diehard local loyalty, whose guardians are powerful but benign men who protect the life, limb and property of all under their care and keep the affairs of the community on sylvan even keel. In reality, however, much like their *khap* counterparts in the north, these are ruthless extra-legal bodies which enforce their writ on those living under their watch in supersession of their constitutional and legal rights, and perpetuate systematic caste and gender discrimination and oppression.

Sexual subjugation of the woman is so much second nature to our culture that it is, except where self-consciously challenged or resisted, the given in our media representations. At the same time it is a closet trait, not apotheosized by art like in the west. Rape, for instance, is a running thread in Greek mythology in which Zeus is, as Eva Keuls (author of *The Reign of the Phallus*) calls him, 'the master rapist'. She has this anecdote about a visitor to Athens curious to know why people there often use the expression 'By Zeus!' being told: 'Because so many of us are.' In Greek and Roman Renaissance art, like Poussin's *Rape of the Sabine Women* or Titian's *Rape of Europa*, the rape imagery is not so much gruesome as heroic and celebratory.

Social, legal, cultural and representational responses to sexual exploitation of and violence against women are clearly disparate and contextual. The challenge lies in unifying them to upend the archetype of patriarchy. As Susan Brownmiller noted in her seminal work of the 1970s, *Against our Will: Men, Women and Rape*, 'man's discovery that his genitalia would serve as a weapon to generate fear must rank as one of the most important discoveries in prehistoric times, along with the use of fire and the first crude axe'. There are differences, too, in intellectual representations of the violence intrinsic in rape. Brownmiller held that rape is an act of violence, not sex – a view not shared by subsequent intellectual feminists and post-feminists.

Michel Foucault raised a hornet's nest when he reflected along similar lines in a roundtable discussion in 1977 (quoted by Ann Cahill in 'Foucault, Rape and the Construction of the Feminine Body', in the Winter 2000 issue of *Hypatia*), seeking to divest rape of its sexual element for purposes of legal punishment:

> [I]n any case sexuality can in no circumstances be the object of punishment. And when one punishes rape one should be punishing physical violence and nothing but that. And to say that it is nothing more than an act of aggression: that there is no difference in principle between sticking one's fist into someone's face or one's penis into their sex. . . . There are problems if we are to say that rape is more serious than a punch in the face, because what we are saying amounts to this: sexuality as such in the body has a preponderant place, the sexual organ isn't like a hand, hair or a nose. It therefore has to be protected, surrounded, invested in any case with legislation that isn't that pertaining to the rest of the body. . . . It isn't a matter of sexuality, it's the physical violence that would be punished, without bringing in the fact that sexuality was involved.

Apart from the speciousness of the argument, especially in its analogy of forcible sexual penetration and a punch in the face, it seeks to wish away the fact that rape is also constitutive of the construct of vulnerable feminineness. As Cahill, disagreeing with Foucault, points out, 'insofar as the threat of rape is ineluctably, although not determinedly, associated with the development of feminine bodily comportment, rape itself holds a host of bodily and sexually specific meanings'.

Meanings of womanhood and articulations of a woman's body continue to be contested and renegotiated at the cusp of a globalized consumerist culture and a post-feminist assertiveness. They are counterintuitive in terms of the common understanding of the male gaze. The runaway success of *Fifty Shades of Grey* and other novels in the 'Fifty' series by E.L. James, which walk the thin line between sadomasochistic sex and pornography, coupled with the fact that their author and the overwhelming majority of their readers are women over thirty years of age, suggests a new leveraging of sexuality that is hedonistic without guilt. The commodification of the female body, it seems, is countered by its self-fetishization. 'Advertising', as Sarah Projansky points out, 'contributes to this version of post-feminism, celebrating women's "equality" and their access to "choice" (feminism), while marketing commodities that call for and support constant body maintenance (femininity)'.

In this new consciousness, the tease is taken out of Marshall McLuhan's pun that 'advertising is an environmental striptease for a world of abundance'. In the brave new world of explicit expression, embedded messages may have diminishing returns, and we may no longer need to worry about what Wilson Bryan Key (in his book *Subliminal Seduction*) calls 'the compulsion of the admen to dunk all their products in sex by erogenising every contour of every bottle or cigarette'.

Published in *Frontline*, 25 January 2013.

On 'Mediacracy' and Intellectuals

It may not be farfetched to speak in terms of a new 'mediacracy' riding the airwaves. The movers and shakers perched on prime-time television news shows seem, with growing vociferation, to be setting the gold standard of a new order of discourse where assumptions and decisions made before the show began are earnestly discussed during it, to give it the appearance of democratic debate. The effect is of something at once perfunctory and passionate, often of inanities discussed with profundity. At a time when journalism is wading into the social media and diluting its own identity and agency, we have this emerging spectacle of a praetorian club engaged in defending the notion of a 'nation' against the state. Functionaries of the state, at least the credulous ones who fall for it, are hauled up before its nightly durbar and asked to explain to the nation, no less, the sins of omission and commission levelled, then and there, against them. 'Tell the nation on this [or that] channel', 'the nation wants to know', 'the nation will not wait' – are some of the grandiloquent goads that drive the sound bites.

This conflation of the nation and the channel is at its bellicose acutest when something happens along the border with Pakistan. There is a recurring pattern of Track Two diplomacy between the two countries being brought to naught by the news media on either side second-guessing, blow by blow, the efforts at rapprochement, so that the diplomatic corps and the political class take one step forward and, the moment the media swings into the act, two steps back, lest it be projected as a sell-out. If only the media could wage peace with as deadly effect as it mongers war! Whether the media are themselves being played by one or the other section of the establishment – in the instant case to pave the way for higher defence allocation in the Union budget that comes up before Parliament in February – also cannot be dismissed as just conspiracy theory.

It does not, however, require the prospect of war for the channel to masquerade as the nation. The war-like emergency conjured up in daily domestic affairs demands that all and sundry be routinely called to account before the channel as nation. Politicians, lawyers, NGOs, public relations types, ex-bureaucrats, actors and socialites, who have become coopted fixtures in this charade, flit – in the space of the same half or one hour – from show to show, so that there is no escaping them even when you switch channels. This is television's known proclivity to give you 'more of the same' carried to a new level, where you get more of the same faces saying more of the same things on channels which seem different from one another only because the logos are. If any of them, or more likely an enthusiastic newcomer, strays from the script or challenges the assumptions of the debate, she is quickly put in her place – the place being one of the frames of the multiple-spilt screen where she is left to languish through the rest of the show without another chance to speak, and for all viewers and no doubt 'the nation' to see. Why anyone would, again and again, volunteer for such shabby treatment is beyond comprehension. That apart, the whole effect is mentally saturating and intellectually stultifying.

It falls upon the intellectuals in society to combat and counter such distortion of discourse. But there can be serious confusion when the 'mediacrat' himself pretends to be or passes off as the socially engaged intellectual. He easily fits the description of Antonio Gramsci's 'organic', as against the traditional, intellectual. Edward Said, in his *Representations of the Intellectual*, says: 'Today, everyone who works in any field connected either with the production or distribution of knowledge is an intellectual in Gramsci's sense', and this includes 'the advertising or public relations expert, who devises techniques for winning a detergent or airline company a larger share of the market . . . someone who in a democratic society tries to gain the consent of potential customers, win approval, marshal consumer and voter opinion.' 'Gramsci believed', Said goes on,

> that organic intellectuals are actively involved in society, that is, they constantly struggle to change minds and expand markets; unlike teachers and priests, who seem more or less to remain in place, doing the same kind of work year in year out, organic intellectuals are always on the move, on the make.

Said's own position is a step away and more carefully honed. The intellectual he envisions both includes and exceeds what the media (and mediacrats) do, and yet enjoys autonomy of agency and action. The intellectual, in his definition, is

> an individual endowed with a faculty for representing, embodying, articulating a message, a view, an attitude, philosophy or opinion to, as well as for, a public.
>
> And this role has an edge to it, and cannot be played without a sense of being someone whose place it is publicly to raise embarrassing questions, to confront orthodoxy and dogma (rather than to produce them), to be someone who cannot easily be co-opted by governments or corporations, and whose *raison d'être* is to represent all those people and issues that are routinely forgotten or swept under the rug.

For Said,

> in the end it is the intellectual as a representative figure that matters – someone who visibly represents a standpoint of some kind, and someone who makes articulate representations to his or her public despite all sorts of barriers . . . intellectuals are

individuals with a vocation for the art of representing, whether that is talking, writing, teaching, appearing on television.

At the same time, and even as he distances himself from the construct of the intellectual as an ivory-tower recluse and seems to concur with Michel Foucault that we are in the age where the 'specific' intellectual has replaced the universal intellectual (like Jean-Paul Sartre), Said is clear that the thrust innate in intellectualism to universalize counters narrow nationalism. He points out that 'great intellectuals like Rabindranath Tagore in India and José Marti of Cuba were exemplary in this regard, never abating their criticism because of nationalism even though they remained nationalists themselves'. Intellectuals (like the 'mediacracy', one might argue) have their audience and constituency. 'The issue is whether that audience is there to be satisfied, and hence a client to be kept happy, or whether it is there to be challenged, and hence stirred into outright opposition or mobilized into greater democratic participation in society.'

In Gramsci and Said there is hope yet for the media and mediacracy to intellectual pretension or aspiration. It may yet be possible to coopt the media into their definition and scheme of intellectual practice. But Noam Chomsky, Jacques Derrida and Pierre Bourdieu see it as a danger the other way round. In their view, the chances are that the media will coopt and compromise intellectualism. The media do this in various subtle ways. They use intellectual consultation as the imprimatur to publicize and propagate narrow political agendas. As Chomsky puts it (in an interview given to James Peck):

> The media . . . can turn to academic experts to provide the perspective that is required by the centres of power, and the university system is sufficiently obedient to external power so that appropriate experts will generally be available to lend the prestige of scholarship to the narrow range of opinion permitted broad expression.

Derrida being caustic about 'the scholarly claims of newspapers that do not have the means to accommodate scholarship and do not want to acquire them' may have something to do with his own row with *The New York Review of Books* over what he thought was an inept translation of, and interpretative spin given to, a work of his published in the magazine. But he zeroes in on the serious connotations of confusing simplistic with simple language in the media:

> One must teach the reader . . . that the difficulty of discourse is not a sin – nor is it the effect of obscurantism or irrationalism. And that it is often the contrary that is true: obscurantism can invade a language of communication that is seemingly direct, simple, straightforward. (Interview, 'The Work of Intellectuals and the Press')

Derrida and Bourdieu see the media as a snare to trap intellectualism. Succumbing to the wiles of the media, for Derrida, would be tantamount to a betrayal of intellectual integrity. He warns academics against what he calls the 'temptation of the media'. 'What I mean by this', he explains,

> is not the normal desire to address a wider public, because there can be in that desire an authentically democratic and legitimate political concern. On the contrary, I call temptation of the media the compulsion to misuse the privilege of public declaration in a social space that extends far beyond the normal circuits of intellectual discussion. Such misuse constitutes a breach of confidence, an abuse of authority – in a word, an abuse of power.

Strong words these, and an unequivocal indictment of academia flirting with the media. Bourdieu is equally categorical about the corruptive role of the media on intellectuals and warns of the loss of 'specific capital' in such engagement. Again, there is a sense of betrayal by those who seek media exposure over peer recognition; they constitute the 'Trojan horse' through which the laws of the market which govern the media sector are brought into the academic field. Bourdieu deprecates intellectuals hankering after the media as nothing short of pathetic: 'Journalists often take great satisfaction in noting how eagerly academics rush into the arms of the media, soliciting book reviews and begging for invitations to talk shows, all the while protesting against the oblivion to which they are relegated' (in *On Television and Journalism*).

The intellectual response in our context to our information media may not have been articulated in such forthright and fastidious terms, but our best thinkers and intellectuals too, happily, are not available on tap on our television screens. Instead of the diverse and original insights they may have brought to the burning issues of our times, what we get on the tube is role-play to fit the assigned parts in predetermined narratives by those who constitute the new mediacracy, a kind of home-grown, hybrid B-team of discussants who are apparently experts at talking the talk. The really informed discussions, meanwhile, take place outside the TV studios, in different forums in the public sphere. This was true of the gang rape of the 23-year-old woman in Delhi, to which the dominant TV response was to work up the lynch mob mentality. This is true of the reaction to the provocation along the Line of Control (LoC) with Pakistan which, all too predictably, is cast on the lines of 'war is patriotism; peace, cowardice'.

In Shakespeare's *Julius Caesar*, when his impassioned oration to avenge the assassination of Caesar has the mob instantly going berserk, Mark Antony savours the moment with what must have been a mix of malice and glee: 'Let it work: mischief thou art afoot, / Take thou what course thou wilt.' One cannot help wondering whether some of our TV anchors feel much the same way when, after a nightly show of heady demagoguery, they say unto themselves – a good job well done.

First published in *Frontline*, Vol. 30, Issue 02, 26 January–8 February 2013.

Art and Aura

In the strict technical sense, Walter Benjamin was no doubt right. Photography and film dissipated the aura around an original work of art. The burden of his seminal essay, 'The Work of Art in the Age of Mechanical Reproduction', was that the technology of replication in photography, which produced copies indistinguishable from the original, and the added facet of movement in film removed the pristine mystique and inaccessibility associated with a painting or a sculpture *in situ* in a cloistered gallery or studio. Benjamin saw this 'emancipation of object from aura' as progressing to a new and modern phase of artistic expression and experience. But aura, it appears, has defied Benjaminian determinism and stuck around well into the digital age. It has demonstrated tenacious 'stickiness' (to use the advertising lingo). The art market valorizes it as no other factor in a work of art – so that the greater its aura, the costlier the art. A painting or sculpture which is immutable and seen as having its aura intact fetches a price far above mutable and replicable, even if artistic, photography or film.

Thus, when the National Gallery in London, hitherto a preserve of auratic art like painting, opened its doors to photography and had an exhibition dedicated to the camera image titled 'Seduced by Art: Photography Past and Present', it was flagged by critics as something of a revolution – except that it was, for the most part, photography approximating to the imagery and idiom of painting. Reviews suggest that some of the work comprised time-consuming singular registrations using the good old camera obscura, apparently in defiance of modern digital photography's click-a-dozen technology. It is a throwback to the daguerreotype photographs of the nineteenth century, which, as Benjamin described in his 'A Small History of Photography',

> were iodized silver plates exposed in the camera obscura, which had to be turned this way and that until, in the proper light, a pale grey image could be discerned. They were one of a kind; in 1839 a plate cost an average of 25 gold francs. They were not infrequently kept in a case, like jewellery. In the hands of many a painter, though, they became a technical adjunct.

The process of this photography was akin to that of painting in that the subject had to spend hours posing in front of the camera obscura because the low light sensitivity of the plate necessitated long exposure. A balustrade, a pedestal, or an oval table was a recurring prop in a photographed portrait because it helped the person being captured stay still. As Benjamin points out, by 1840, portraiture, which until then was the provenance of painters, had become that of photography, and the painters specializing in this area were becoming photographers.

In the mid-nineteenth century, photography as a more faithful medium of *mimesis* than painting was a cause for both celebration and despair. If the Belgian artist Antoine Wiertz was waxing eloquent in 1855 about the daguerreotype as the machine which 'daily amazes the mind and startles the eye', and was destined to become 'the brush, the palette, the colours, the craft, the experience, the patience, the dexterity, the sureness of touch, the atmosphere, the lustre, the exemplar, the perfection, the very essence of painting', Charles Baudelaire was, by 1857, lamenting that 'in these sorry days a new industry has risen that has done not a little to strengthen the asinine belief that art is and can be nothing other than the accurate reflection of nature'.

This cusp of painting and photography was for Benjamin a retrospective vantage-point to predict the emerging superiority and excitement of the medium and technique of the photograph over those of paint and brush on canvas. There is almost a post-art aesthetic in his enthusiasm for photography; he sees it as 'something new and strange' that 'goes beyond testimony to the photographer's art, something that cannot be silenced, that fills you with an unruly desire to know . . . is still real and will never consent to be wholly absorbed in *art*'. Benjamin was already anticipating one of two key intrinsic elements of a photograph later described by Roland Barthes in his *Camera Lucida* (1980), namely, the *punctum*, which Barthes characterizes as that which 'rises from the scene, shoots out of it like an arrow and pierces me'. (The other element, *studium*, has to do with the denotative and deductive aspects of the work.) Compare how succinctly Benjamin, even in 1931, captures this sense of the *punctum*:

> No matter how artful the photographer, no matter how carefully posed his subject, the beholder feels an irresistible urge to search such a picture for the tiny spark of contingency, of the Here and Now, with which reality has so to speak seared the subject, to find the inconspicuous spot where in the immediacy of that long forgotten moment the future subsists so eloquently that we, looking back, may rediscover it. For it is another nature that speaks to the camera than to the eye: other in the sense that a space informed by human consciousness gives way to a space informed by the unconscious.

We know what a person walking is. But what happens when a person steps out? 'It is through photography,' he concludes, 'with its devices of slow motion and enlargement . . . that we first discover the existence of this optical unconscious, just as we discover the instinctual unconscious through psychoanalysis.'

With all that build-up of the promise of the materiality and intuitive energy of photography, coupled with its replicability, crushing the aura of art underfoot, the fact that it has not really happened, that it is still the aura that really goes under the hammer when a painting or sculpture is auctioned by Christie's or Sotheby's at mind-boggling prices, points to the supervening role of the dictates of the market, where exchange value is tied to scarcity and the unique aura of the artist, as much as of the art, is brand-leveraged.

Even as auratic art traverses a range of formal styles, including impressionism, pointillism, fauvism, expressionism, symbolism, cubism and abstraction, it occasionally comes in touch with, and leaves its mark on, the practice of photography, film and video, and even, as Todd Gitlin points out, on typography. What Gitlin calls the 'aesthetics of blur', for instance, is inspired by impressionism and expressed in terms of stop-framing, shutter motion and out-of-focus shots in photography and videography, as a 'visual style . . . to convey the instant of motion, the instant in motion, recorded as if the artist's hand were in motion'.

The sense of the instantaneous and the simultaneous is accentuated into a new consciousness with digital technology and digitized art. Any vestigial attachment of art to aura is rendered void in the discrete, decentred, digital phrasings that are creatively scattered expressions of impermanence. Such a sensibility of the *outré* is now being celebrated with abandon in the Kochi-Muziris Biennale in Kerala, housed in Dutch-period structures – shells of former warehouses, godowns and bungalows – that provide a stark, hoary context of contrast to the electronic pixels that configure and reconfigure our idea of art.

There is a memory of a hot, shadeless, saturating summer afternoon in a surreal landscape replete with shards of burnt and deceptively unfaded pottery. That is from a visit, many years back, to the remains of the Indus Valley civilization in Harappa, a few hours' drive south of Lahore in Pakistan. Vivan Sundaram's installation, *Black Gold*, at the Kochi Biennale is in two sections. The pottery and terracotta fragments from the Pattanam excavation site near Kodungalloor (about an hour's drive from Kochi and a part of the swathe of land comprising the historic Muziris port) disarranged across a floor-space evoke with mute eloquence a civilization that flourished on these shores over a vast span from 1000 BC to the tenth century AD, and that interacted and traded with West Asia, southern Africa, Mesopotamia, Greece and the Roman empire. It ignites a flashback to the Harappan site in the manner of a profound recall that A.K. Ramanujan (in *Uncollected Poems and Prose*) describes in terms of the connection between memory and cognition in the Indian philosophical system: 'to recognize anything, one must remember having seen the object before, and remember a few features of it – these features trigger the memory of the whole object, or with the direct perception help us reconstitute it – literally re-member it.'

To re-member the broken pieces of pottery is to reconstitute, in the mind, the ancient civilizations to which they belonged. History resides in, and has to be salvaged, shard by shard, from such monochromatic tedium of brown and grey. As a counter to that proposition, an abstraction of that materiality, the other part of Sundaram's installation is rendered as a mutating digital video-floor which fragments and layers and washes over a plethora of forms and colours – rocks, bricks, fossils and other excavational evocations – becoming a metaphor for transience and constant replacement.

Displacement by water, the theme of Ranbir Kaleka's multiscreen video-wall titled *House of Opaque Water*, is narrativized as displaced and segregated visual anecdotes that come together in the mind as a powerful indictment of a development paradigm. Nalini Malani's *In Search of Vanished Blood*, about the hounding and dismemberment of the female persona, is again a fragmented, stoic video-telling that is left to coalesce in the mind of the viewer and stays there long afterwards. There are many more such digital offerings at the Biennale that suggest the tentativeness of experimentation, but each – in its own scatter-and-gather manner – works. They are not only video productions but bricolage sculptures, pointillist graphics, and atomized forms and configurations in painting and photography.

Digital dispersion marks much of the work at the show. Whether this was a conscious element of 'the cosmopolitan spirit' its intrepid curators, Bose Krishnamachari and Riyas Komu, brought to their selection is not clear. But the dominant and recurring experience of the moment of exposure – visual, aural and, in one instance, tactile – to the work on display is of disjuncture and multiplicity. There is not a fighting chance for any 'aura' to form, let alone hover over any of this creation. The work of art does not as much draw you centripe-tally into it, as function like a centrifuge to scatter your attention in different directions or to its various components. The discrete elements assemble and cohere not in the body of the work itself, but in the process of their assimilation by the beholder. It is in the same process that one becomes alive to the difference between the 'visual' and the 'image': a series of visuals and sounds crystallize in the mind of the one contemplating them to constitute the image – or, more comprehensively, what Jacques Rancière in *The Future of the Image* calls the 'sentence-image'.

The tenor of the works on show at the Biennale points to beginnings and strivings, to struggles and uncertainties in a new digital articulation. In them there is an artistic sensibility at work in which it would seem that, to invoke Rancière again, 'all the common terms of measurement that opinions and histories lived on have been abolished in favour of a great chaotic juxtaposition, a great indifferent mélange of significations and materialities'. In a situation where auratic art commands the attention of the market and art galleries, they must have been created, assembled and installed against tremendous odds. Odds as tremendous as those faced by the Biennale team led by Bose and Riyas as, despite being starved of promised funding by the state government and let down by established peer and senior artists, it put up this mammoth, trail-blazing show.

First published in *Frontline*, 8 March 2013.

Cross-Media Currents

For some time now, rearguard action legitimizing *faits accomplis* has been passing for state initiative in framing legislation in the Indian media sector. What has come to be has come to be, seems the rationalization; let's see how to let it be, or give it a cosmetic tweak without ruffling too many feathers. Given the high stakes involved, this approach would almost appear complicitous, if we did not also know from tiresome experience that the state and the bureaucracy are just congenitally late and lazy in such matters.

So, more than two decades after cable and satellite TV came, saw and conquered; after much of the turf there is to be occupied has been occupied, indiscriminately; and a monopoly media regime is entrenched, fully and firmly, the government comes alive to the peril that rampant cross-media ownership poses to democracy and the citizen's right to information. Technological convergence has engendered media conglomerates that combine print, television, radio and the internet, and businesses that exceed these categories – like DTH (Direct-to-Home), HITS (Headend in the Sky), the yet incipient podcasting and IPTV (Internet Protocol Television) – and push applications across delivery platforms to 2G, 3G and 4G devices, electronic tablets, and so on. They draw on finite radio spectrum so that there is also implicitly an overlap of the purviews of the Ministries of Information and Broadcasting (I&B) and Telecommunications, in their management. The business logic and opportunity of such vertical integration have led to the emergence of big corporate entities straddling many of these businesses.

It took until mid-2008 for the I&B Ministry to take cognizance of the situation and seek the opinion of the Telecom Regulatory Authority of India (TRAI) on how to tackle it. The following year TRAI made a number of recommendations aimed at curtailing monopolistic growth, and at ensuring pluralism and diversity in the sector. The I&B Ministry then commissioned a study the same year by the Administrative Staff College of India (ASCI), which went into the state and extent of cross-media holdings in the industry, the international experience in this matter, the need for caps on vertical holdings, and for transparency and public disclosure of ownership and holding patterns in the media sector.

Three years later, in May 2012, the I&B Ministry again sought TRAI's expertise to evolve a comprehensive approach to balancing the technological and business logic of vertical integration and cross-media holdings, with the need for pluralism and diversity, and the need to protect the citizen's right to credible choice and competitive pricing of the media he consumes. TRAI has – after updating the ASCI data on 54 companies invested across print, broadcasting and new media, with further information on them provided by twenty Registrars of Companies, and domain information about market share and extent of cross-holdings of media companies from the I&B Ministry and the Registrar of Newspapers of India – come up with a 'Consultation Paper on Issues relating to Media Ownership', which is posted on its website (www.trai.gov.in) for comments by stakeholders, including the public concerned.

The paper recognizes the growth potential of the entertainment and media industry in India as the best in the world, with industry estimates projecting a compounded annual growth rate (CAGR) of 17 per cent for the five-year period between 2011 and 2016. China with a projection of 14 per cent, Russia with 12 per cent and Brazil with 11 per cent over the same period come second, third and fourth, respectively, in this survey of the top fifteen nations in the field, making the BRIC formation (comprising Brazil, Russia, India and China) the rising media constellation of this decade. The potential in India is underscored by the further fact that the average per capita annual spend on media and entertainment in 2011 was only US$ 6.6, as against $65 in Brazil and $22 in China.

The Confederation of Indian Industry (CII) and Price Waterhouse Cooper India's 'India Entertainment and Media Outlook 2012' cited in the paper projects that the combined advertisement and subscription revenue from the sector, which was Rs 68,500 crore in 2010 and rose by 17.52 per cent to Rs 80,500 crore in 2011, is slated to reach Rs 1,76,400 crore by 2016.. Of this, broadcasting shows the biggest gain. Television grew from Rs 29,400 crore in 2010 to Rs 34,000 crore in 2011, a year-on-year growth of 15.7 per cent, and is expected to touch Rs 67,400 crore by 2016, registering a CAGR of 14.7 per cent from 2012 to 2016. The corresponding figures for radio are Rs 1,300 crore for 2010 and Rs 1,400 crore for 2011, a 10.8 per cent rise over the year, and Rs 3,000 crore for 2016, representing a CAGR of 16.7 per cent over the same four-year period. Print posted a relatively modest revenue growth of 7.2 per cent between 2010 (Rs 17,800 crore) and 2011 (Rs 19,000 crore), but, bucking the international trend of steep decline, is set to accelerate ahead to touch a revenue of Rs 29,600 crore in 2016, with a CAGR of 9.2 per cent over 2012–16. The other media – a miscellany of internet, gaming, music and out-of-home (OOH) media – account for the rest.

But it has been a warped growth because the financial benefits accrue to a few pockets, and there is no evidence of a commensurate social or intellectual dividend reaped by the public at large. A consultation paper, understandably, cannot be a position paper; but a clearly stated political will is what is missing both in it and in the situation it seeks to discuss. The core and crucial issue in the media sector is that the pattern and trajectory of growth has systematically eliminated or marginalized the small and medium player in favour of the big corporation. Entry barriers that are operational against the small or medium entrepreneur are as much a function of monopolistic exertions in the market as are disabling rules and prohibitive fees prescribed by the government for the new entrant of relatively modest means. In October 2011, for example, the net worth requirement of an applicant seeking to launch a general information or entertainment channel was raised from Rs 1.5 crore to Rs 5 crore, and, in the case of a news channel, even more sharply, from Rs 3 crore to Rs 20 crore. Interestingly, the net worth stipulation for an additional channel by one already up and running was only Rs 2.5 crore for the general entertainment category and Rs 5 crore for news.

This was a blow to the notion of diversity. It was made out that the move was meant to keep non-serious players out and to place a reasonable limitation on the number of applicants. These are valid considerations, especially given that 848 channels had been licensed until December last year and about 650 of them are operational, including 350 news channels. But the profusion of channels has not meant democratic difference and variety. And privileging existing channels by making it cheaper for them, than for a fresh entrant, to get the licence for a new channel may at best lead to market specialization and segmentation catering to niche viewership constituencies – which, again, would be a mode of market optimization and not the same as diversity in the democratic sense.

The consultation paper's pious reference to democratic values of diversity and pluralism in advocating caps on the market size and cross-media holdings of media organizations seems more rhetorical flourish than an article of faith. There are also Freudian slips which confuse regulating the media market with controlling media behaviour and content, as, for instance, when it states:

> The inherent conflict of interest which arises from uncontrolled ownership in the media sector gives rise to manifestations such as (i) paid news (ii) corporate and political lobbying by popular television channels (iii) propagation of biased analysis and forecasts both in the political arena as well as in the corporate sector, (iv) irresponsible reporting to create sensationalism.

How or what any of these admittedly corrupt and unethical media practices has to do with the market reach of a media house, or its cross-holdings in the sector, is not clear.

The paper recapitulates the partial cross-holding restrictions in force, particularly in the licensing of FM radio; the extent of equity a broadcaster or DTH platform owner can hold (not more than 20 per cent) in a company providing HITS-based broadcasting and vice versa, whereas there is no such restriction between a cable TV operator and a HITS service provider; and a similar equity cap between any mobile TV service and a channel broadcaster, again not applicable between DTH and mobile TV, and so on. They seem, for the most part, measures to protect the specific markets for different parts of the industry from aggrandizement by the other parts, rather than to safeguard the interests of the end receiver or the public.

TRAI's belief that political and religious bodies, government ministries and departments, and urban and rural public-funded local bodies should not be allowed to own broadcasting channels or uplink stations would be unexceptionable but for the glaring example of Doordarshan, which, although behind the fig-leaf of the autonomous corporation Prasar Bharati, continues to be pretty much a broadcaster of, by and for the government. A conspicuous absence in the consultation paper is the interesting experience of Lok Sabha TV, which has charted a somewhat different and independent course (being under the Speaker of the House and not the government) of intelligent debate, discussion and docu-features, and oftentimes offers refuge to the weary channel surfer emotionally drained by the high-strung fare on private news channels.

One chapter in the paper skims over the key aspects of regulations in eight international markets, namely, United Kingdom, United States, Canada, France, Germany, Australia, South Africa and South Korea. These pertain to four broad restrictive aspects: of those ineligible to operate a media business; of the extent, in terms of percentage of market share, to which a publication, a TV channel or a radio station can dominate a given market; limitations on cross-media holdings; and conditions and caps on mergers and acquisitions. While how these countries have tackled these issues in their separate contexts is instructive, it is not clear whether the suggestion is to follow the one or the other example, or to arrive at an eclectic mix of the lot best suited to our purpose.

What emerges from the consultation paper is that the media in India first needs to be mapped thoroughly – and this may need some diligent investigative work – so that there is a clear picture of who owns what and, in some cases, who is a front for whom and how, or which big corporate is quietly bankrolling which media. The voluntary or even mandatory disclosures the paper makes frequent reference to are unlikely to reveal the real situation. A perspective informed by a sense of the political economy of the media in the country is necessary to frame an alternative media dispensation that is more inclusive, relevant, transformative and democratizing.

In the absence of this paradigm shift, it makes no difference, in the final analysis, whether concentration in a media market is measured by either of the empirical methods the paper proposes: C3 or HHI (Herfindahl–Hirschman Index). Nor does the quibble over whether 'entity' is a more appropriate appellation than 'company' in the media sector – as though just calling it an entity will help expose information the company is withholding. As for the suggested permutations and combinations towards arriving at the most foolproof, or least damaging, formula for keeping cross-media holdings in check, they tend to read like the riddle, or parable, of the boatman who has to ferry a lion, a bundle of grass and a goat across the river, and can only carry any two of them in each trip, and the lion cannot be left alone with the goat, nor the goat with the grass, lest the one eats the other. Both situations need some figuring out.

First published in *Frontline*, 22 March 2013.

Lend Me Your Ears

It was always, or so it was made out to be, a question of when, not if, private FM radio stations in India would be allowed to broadcast news. But then it has taken so long that one might be forgiven for asking, just when is when? Even as the government prepares for the third phase of auctions, later this year, for granting licences to private players, which will expand the independent FM radio market from the 86 cities now on air to another 227, it continues to demur and filibuster on this crucial issue. The halfway-house offer now is that the private FM stations can draw on – and only on, mind you – the news bulletins of All India Radio (AIR) for their own news, and – they are already doing this uninvited – throw in snippets of innocuous information like the weather, the traffic flow and pile-ups in the city at a given time, or some such locally useful disclosure, in their daily fare. The situation, to wit, presents itself as a ridiculous syllogism: no news was the good news on private FM; now it can use AIR news which, as many will argue, is no news or only the good news; so no news or only the good news is to be the news on private FM. Much like a little knowledge, in the matter of news, half a loaf can be worse than no bread.

Even more preposterous is the government's pop-psychological rationale for keeping independent news out of bounds for the FM licensee. Radio, seems the argument, unlike television or print, has a grassroots reach that includes sensitive, vulnerable, least-common-denominator minds which can be swayed this way and that by anything they hear on it, particularly on religious and caste issues. Besides the point that this assumption seems to be a variation of the Katju-ism that 90 per cent of Indians are idiots, it is an affront to the democratic credo of universal adult suffrage which places implicit faith in the capability of the people to choose their political condition. To deny them, on an easily accessible medium such as the radio, a broad spectrum of information to enable them to make considered choices, is to take away from the sanctity and right of that exercise of franchise.

If anything, the government should have from the outset made news and current affairs a compulsory component of programming on FM channels, so that they did not deteriorate into a regime of trivia talk and film songs administered *ad nauseam*. Imagine the saturating, lobotomizing effect of 245 private FM channels, and hundreds more to come after the third phase of licensing is complete, purveying film songs interspersed with the mindless chatter of radio jockeys (RJs) day in and day out.

What is worse, in the absence of news, you sometimes get a parody of news with RJs picking up tidbits of headlines that are current and incorporating them into their own flippant jargon to spruce up the show. In Chennai recently, one came across a channel running a *vox pop* between film songs on the very emotional issue of Indo–Sri Lankan relations, in the wake of the disclosures of gross human rights violations by the Sinhala army. It came across as a travesty of both the gravity of the situation and its treatment as a news story because the RJ was, no doubt so as not to fall foul of the no-news rule, trying to make it sound like part of his usual light-hearted, quotidian banter.

The case for including news on private radio channels is not *ipso facto* one against film music, which will continue to be the mainstay of this service – like a background score, at home or on the road, to our everyday urban lives. Indeed it is film music that saved radio from being slotted into a narrow, blighted cultural type in independent India. The first two Ministers of Information and Broadcasting, Sardar Vallabhbhai Patel until 1950 and then B.V. Keskar until 1962, sought to zealously protect AIR from '*tawaifi*' Muslim music. This, against the backdrop of a concerted move to cleanse AIR of Muslim and Urdu influence, led to the resignation of its first Director General, Ahmed Shah Bukhari.

The Urdu–Hindi question dated back to pre-partition times, and a committee set up by Bukhari to go into it in 1940 had come up with a syncretic lexicon by 1945; but this could not preempt separate broadcasts in Urdu and Hindi which in a sense anticipated, in its religio–lingual dimension, political partition. Keskar, who became Information and Broadcasting Minister in 1952, was bigoted against any Muslim influence on AIR, banning singers of the classical *gharana*s and even the harmonium from its studios. He pushed his puritanism to foolish limits when he banned film songs on AIR. Radio Ceylon moved into the vacuum and 'Binaca Geetmala', with the trademark voice of its iconic anchor Ameen Sayani, became an instant hit. AIR was forced to restore film music through its Vividh Bharati service in 1957 and, a decade later, when transistorization made radio pervasive, to launch commercial operations and accept advertisements.

Two brief strands in the history of radio broadcasting in India capture what the medium lost and what is missing in its cultural ethos to this day. One goes back to the beginning in the 1920s when J.C.W. Reith of the British Broadcasting Corporation (BBC), perhaps the father figure for all times of public service broadcasting, proposed a service for India, was initially rebuffed by Viceroy Lord Willingdon, but subsequently, in 1926, struck a deal with the British government of India to start the Indian Broadcasting Company (IBC). Interestingly, it was the same year that the BBC under Reith was testing the waters to see how far it could bring in all points of view, including that of the trade union and the opposition Labour Party, in its coverage of the general strike in Britain – a definitive moment for the principle of impartiality and the fairness doctrine in broadcasting.

The company became a public corporation the next year with daily broadcasts in Bombay and Calcutta. But the radio licence fees on which the service was dependent proved inadequate and the IBC folded up in 1930, and with it the possibility of a Reithian tradition continuing into the post-colonial present. The government took over the IBC and it became the IBS (Indian Broadcasting Service) under the Controller of Broadcasting, Lionel Fielden, and then, in 1935, was rechristened All India Radio. The Central News Organization, to which the Indian Information Service (IIS) which controls the news content and output of the organization today can perhaps trace its antecedence, was set up in 1927, and the tradition of a command performance was cast in stone.

The second strand comes at the later period of the independence struggle and the Quit India Movement of 1942, when a clandestine radio operation by a couple of students became a bugbear for both the colonial government and its official broadcaster. Usha Mehta and Babubhai Vithalbhai set up their enigmatically but, for their guerrilla mode, appropriately titled 'Voice of Freedom, speaking from somewhere in India' in an apartment in Walkeshwar Road in Bombay, and went on air on 13 August 1942 on the 42.34 metre band. They had to change their location every fortnight to evade detection and keep reinventing themselves as AIR jammed their signals. But they were able to keep at it and stay under the radar with two news bulletins, one in English in the morning and the other in Hindi in the evening, and transmit important news, including of the Chittagong bomb attack and the Jamshedpur strike.

Their first and foremost patron was Dr Ram Manohar Lohia who, once he had heard them on air, sought them out and provided them financial assistance. Content was prepared by Sucheta Kripalani and Aruna Asaf Ali, and talks were delivered by Lohia and Achyut Patwardhan. It was a dream run of about three months (until November 1942) before Usha Mehta was arrested and the operation had to be abandoned. The energy and nimbleness of this revolutionary broadcasting experiment did not, however, become an example of an alternative way forward for the medium even after independence, because of the preponderant, monolithic presence of AIR and its banyan tree-like spread beneath which nothing else could grow.

The Indian experience in this regard is in stark contrast to the vibrant and plural growth of the medium in the small neighbouring country of Nepal, where radio stations have proliferated like a cottage industry. The licensing of private FM stations has no doubt made a difference, but unlike in the television sector where private channels are independent of and have little to do with Doordarshan, there is still a strong sense of residual power over the radio dispensation in the country vesting with AIR, largely because it continues to monopolize news and current affairs.

There is little doubt that AIR, much like Doordarshan, will have to call the bluff of its nominal autonomy behind the façade of the Prasar Bharati Corporation, cease being a cat's paw of the government of the day, and reinvent itself as a genuine public service broadcaster with independent credentials, if it is to have any meaningful future. In fact, a catacomb of committees and expert groups under Sam Pitroda's supervision is currently going into the issue of how Prasar Bharati can be made truly free and creative. Given the track record of action on committee recommendations – and there have been at least three on this one – there is understandably more scepticism than hope on the outcome of the Pitroda exercise. But the objective conditions have changed and put pressure on the government to summon the political will to abnegate its control over Prasar Bharati and do what it takes to transform it into an innovative public broadcaster that can stand its ground against the commercial channels.

The historic Supreme Court judgment of 1995 in the case between the Cricket Association of Bengal and the Board of Control for Cricket in India versus the Union of India recognizes in even measure the right of the citizen to airwaves which, the court held, 'are a public property', and the responsibility of the public authority to control and regulate the use of airwaves in the public interest. This sets the legal basis for a public interest broadcast philosophy that is people- rather than market-centric and programme- rather than hierarchy-driven, and for a radical revamping and whittling down of the ossified and bureaucratized structure of AIR so that it becomes a creature of the public on the ground.

When the restrictions on private radio channels carrying news have been lifted and Prasar Bharati has become truly autonomous so that AIR is a public rather than a government broadcaster, there would be optimization of installed resources, in the fulsome sense of the term, in the radio sector. AIR would address the public sphere and the private FM channels their respective market constituencies. The two, of course, are not mutually exclusive and would overlap in good part, particularly in cities and urban agglomerations. The public broadcaster would have shed officialese in favour of a more people-friendly and relevant language rendered with restraint and dignity, and the private players would, imaginably and much like their television counterparts, be breathlessly sensationalist. The public broadcaster would of course eschew the stridency and hard-sell of the other. But it would not be a clinically distanced service provider with a take-it-or-leave-it attitude. It would be passionate and persuasive in winning the trust of its audience, to whom, and not to the political masters, it would owe its allegiance. In the process, the tenor of its discourse would have shifted from a magisterial 'listen to me' to an honest and earnest 'lend me your ears'.

First published in *Frontline*, 19 April 2013.

Melting the Pot

The melting pot may have ceased to be an apposite, or politically proper, metaphor for the integration of diverse immigrant communities into the way of life and the value system of the United States of America. The identities and particularities of the various strands that make up this demographic arabesque were, it was felt somewhere along the way, not to be submerged in the process of assimilation into a uniform cosmopolitan Americanism; they must retain and celebrate their individual characteristics. But in the systemic responses to threats and crises – and that includes that of the mainstream news media – these differences become loaded and coded with ethnic and colour stereotypes, allusions and insinuations.

It is not as if the media establishment is not aware of this intrinsic prejudice. To be fair to it, to the extent that one can be fair to prejudice, it shifts gear into a stretch of self-introspection and self-chastisement after it has jumped the gun and jumped to (wrong) conclusions each time. But it somehow cannot seem to help this reflex action, as the media scramble after the Boston bombings again sharply reminds us. CNN, Associated Press, *The Boston Globe*, *New York Post*, all got it wrong at one time or the other of the unfolding story, on one count or the other; as did, more egregiously, the social media sites Reddit and Twitter. After the dust has settled on the hunt for the bombers, we are left pondering the media goof-ups: CNN's baseless report of the arrest of a 'dark-skinned male'; the Rupert Murdoch-owned *New York Post*'s Saudi suspect who turned out, instead, to be a victim of the bombing in the Boston hospital; again, *New York Post*'s front page photo featuring two young men with bags whom, the story suggested, the Federal Bureau of Investigation (FBI) were searching for, but who turned out to be just two young men, a Moroccan high school student and his friend, with backpacks who had turned up to witness the Boston marathon; Reddit circulating the reckless hypothesis that a student of Brown University, Sunil Tripathi, who, to the imaginable concern of his family, had been missing for weeks, might be one of the suspects. Even those who goofed up must feel partially vindicated that their premise that there was an Islamic angle to the perpetrators of the crime turned out right, even if the skin colour kind of let them down.

It would seem that it was finally the FBI that did the honourable thing in the circumstances. Bedevilled by the media guesswork and hampered in its work by the parallel media hunt (including in large part the social media), the agency decided to release the pictures of the two real suspects, Tamerlan Tsarnaev and Dzokhar Tsarnaev, which it must have been keeping close to its chest earlier on for strategic reasons. That finally put an end to the media game of fishing for suspects.

There were other misleads the media kept harping on, like the robbery of a Seven-Eleven store by the duo, when in fact it was by someone else, and the freewheeling analyses of its implications: this meant that the perpetrators were amateurs, were not funded by any organization or terrorist group, and were probably self-radicalized individuals acting on their own, and so on. Some parts of this interpretation may have turned out to be right but (like the Islamic connection) only fortuitously, because they were, to begin with, based on false information. More serious was *New York Post*'s exclusive blunder that twelve people, not three, were killed in the blasts at the marathon.

Much of the media mess-up was no doubt because of the chase for exclusive tidbits within the developing story, about which Jon Stewart, the popular host of the television show *The Daily Show*, expostulated in colourful language: 'There was a very good reason why this was exclusive . . . it's exclusive because it was completely f---ing wrong. That's why it was exclusive.' There was also the occupational hazard of incremental coverage where, as Gideon Lichfield, the news editor of the digital news platform Quartz put it in his post-mortem of the Boston bombing coverage, 'all media are now competing in the same giant area for ever-smaller crumbs".

The tendency to make much of the part one has managed to grab at the risk of losing sight of the whole has become an intrinsic feature of the new journalism propelled by the pace and demands of live 24x7 television and the even more instant social media. At a recent workshop on television news in Kerala, the editor of a regional language channel provided a fascinating instance of how this bit-by-bit or byte-by-byte approach becomes irresistible, even if not best, practice in television reporting. A public figure says something unsavoury about another public figure. Journalistic ethics and norms would dictate that the response of the person so spoken about be included by way of balance, fair-mindedness or right of reply. But that would be one combined story and not lend itself to being ratcheted up in degrees. Worse, if the subject of the calumny is approached and convincingly refutes or repudiates the slur sought to be pinned on him/her, the story begins and ends there. So the ploy to stretch it out is to put out the allegation in one bulletin, the rejoinder of the affected party in the next, and join issue with them and/or both their supporters participating in the third, and so on.

Such piecemeal, in the name of blow-by-blow, coverage of the Boston bombings kept leading us up the garden path time and again. In the absence of solid facts, prejudicial theories and psychological punditry took over. A strange constant across channels was the eat–drink–smoke–make merry litmus test. If the suspect was given to partying, smoking tobacco (or better, pot) and drinking alcohol, he was seen as more socially integrated into American society (says something about that society) and that much less likely to be radicalized or to subscribe to a terrorism-prone creed – get it? The sweet, partying, wrestling, grass-smoking Dzokhar really had them flummoxed, and it took the dark religious hints of his Twitter posts for the theory to match the fact. In one hilarious psychoanalytic byte, which looked wise after the fact, there was this expert making meaning of the way the two suspects walk with their backpacks in the widely aired CCTV footage from the marathon site: the semi-casualness of the walk, was his conclusion, shows that they did it. In short, the fluff and the spin took up the bulk of the time and tended to reinforce, even if as a byproduct of the exercise, the religious profiling that goes with terrorism.

Some of the misinformation in the coverage of the Boston bombings may, as Murdoch professed in defence of the *New York Post*'s screw-up, have originated from the FBI, but reflects poorly on the media's application of due process in terms of verification. One of Noam Chomsky's five famous filters (that the mainstream media in the US are subject to as they go about 'manufacturing consent') was unthinkingly at work here – dependence on government information. Once the authorities had shut down Boston, and secured and sequestered the streets of Watertown which were the scene of the action, the media were by and large kept at bay and television switched to delayed telecast – unlike, one might add, in Mumbai in November 2008, when they had a run of the place and compromised the forensic investigation on the site of the crime, and when TV channels broadcast the evolving situation live, inviting the charge that they may have unwittingly aided the masterminds remote-controlling the attack. Real information on the Boston hunt for the suspects, after the initial scattershot coverage by the media, pretty much narrowed down to a flow regulated by the authorities.

The media discourse in the wake of the arrest of the surviving suspect suggests that these pressure-cooker bombings are being categorized and dealt as home-grown terrorism by the brothers acting on their own, without links to organizations within or outside the US. But their ethnicity, Chechens from Russia, and religion, Islam, give a different edge to the nature of the violence perpetrated by them. As studies – including a recent one by Angie Chuang and Robin Roemer ('The Immigrant Muslim American at the Boundary of Insider and Outsider: Representations of Faisal Shahzad as "Homegrown" Terrorist', published in the Spring 2013 issue of *Journalism & Mass Communication Quarterly*) – indicate, there are different yardsticks applied to mass violence of this nature, depending on whether it is committed by Muslim or non-Muslim naturalized US citizens/native-born Americans.

The authors, in their cited work, take up the example of another 'home-grown terrorist', this time of Pakistani origin, Faisal Shahzad, and his (failed) attempt to detonate a bomb on Times Square in New York City in May 2010. Much like Dzokhar in Boston, there was little that set him apart as a likely candidate for such a desperate act. It was the story of, as the headline in *The New York Times* put it, 'A suburban father who gave no warning signs'; in other words, of someone who had imbibed the values of US suburban life – jogging, barbecuing and pursuing the American dream. And yet, retrospectively, the coverage of his story hinged on his Islamic roots and tended, as Chuang and Roemer describe it, 'to tie motive to a trajectory from American to Muslim identity'.

No such religious or ethnic identity factor figured in the coverage of Adam Lanza shooting dead twenty children and six adults in the elementary school in Newton, Connecticut, last December. The discussions around that sordid deed were couched in medico-psychological terms. There was soul-searching and an attempt to understand why: Asperger syndrome, his being bullied when he was at school and so on. It did of course set off a frenzied debate afresh about gun control, but the killer and his deed were a recognizably, and pathologically, US aberration (one in a series of such mass killings), not an attack on the US state or society by an 'other'.

In another study ('Representations of Foreign versus [Asian] American Identity in a Mass-Shooting Case: Newspaper Coverage of the 2009 Binghamton Massacre', published in the *Journalism & Mass Communication Quarterly* of Summer 2012), Angie Chuang deals with a mass homicide like the one in the Newton school. Jiverly Wong, a 41-year-old man of Vietnamese origin, went on a shooting spree in April 2009, killing thirteen people including students and a teacher at the American Civic Association Immigration Centre in Binghamton, New York. He seems to have nurtured a complex about his poor English and a grouse against those who teased him about it. However, unlike Adam Lanza whose origin and ethnicity did not matter to the press, Wong's Vietnamese identity was always kept in focus; he was, Angie Chuang points out, regularly referred to as a Vietnamese immigrant even though he was a naturalized US citizen – another trail of ethnic name-calling that has persisted down to the present and is posed in terms of a 'yellow peril'.

The American dream turning sour, religious fundamentalism, inability to succeed in a demandingly competitive society and anger against official USA for its interventionism in different parts of the world do not seem to be recognized each for what it is, or are not seen as providing separate traction, as distinguishable motives for acts of violence, when it comes to certain immigrant groups that are traditionally viewed with suspicion or are more recently under the scanner. For a nation with nearly 50 million (legal and illegal) immigrants of diverse ethnic origins and religious persuasions, the broadbrush approach cuts both ways. It integrates and it alienates. A particularistic understanding of what drives the various denominations to a sense of belonging or to one of rejection seems a prerequisite for the different immigrant communities to cohere into a bond of nationhood.

First published in *Frontline*, 30 May 2013.

The US Media Muddle

A sampling of the news media in the United States over the past two weeks throws up a strange mix of real and surreal challenges to the freedom of the press in what is supposedly a mature media market. The surreal is right in your face – a self-anointed radio show host, Pete Santilli, who claims to be a 'recovering lifelong Reagan Republican who recently voted for Obama because I hoped for revolutionary change', but whom most media accounts place in the lunatic fringe on the right, went ballistic about former Secretary of State and First Lady Hillary Clinton, saying (hold your breath):

> I want to shoot her right in the vagina and I don't want her to die right away; I want her to feel the pain and I want to look her in the eyes and I want to say, on behalf of all Americans that you've killed, on behalf of the Navy SEALS, the families of Navy SEAL Team Six who were involved in the fake hunt down of this Osama, Osama bin Laden thing, that whole fake scenario, because these Navy SEALS know the truth, they killed them all. On behalf of all those people, I'm supporting our troops by saying we need to try, convict and shoot Hillary Clinton in the vagina.

Obama himself was not to be spared either: 'Barack Obama needs to be tried, convicted, and shot for crimes against the United States of America. . . . And if anybody has a problem with that, then you are an enemy of our state.'

It's the kind of rant that evokes the stand-off between individual libertinism of an extreme licentious kind and state-imposed order that Anthony Burgess's *A Clockwork Orange* (and Stanley Kubrick's film of it) explores but finds refuge, in the US context, behind the First Amendment. Indignant responses to this misbegotten mediaspeak included calls to interpret it as inciting violence to make it actionable. But as a piece of journalism *per se* it is, however uncivil and abhorrent, apparently beyond the reach of the law. Santilli clearly takes himself very seriously and is not averse to syndicating his show, now on his website, nationally, if only the AM or FM stations regulated by the Federal Communications Commission (FCC) can cope with his 'truth and honesty'.

From that surreal, postmodernist, predicament which the concept of freewheeling freedom of the press pretends to, and which sets up the First Amendment at some unassailable height, it is a nosedive into the real and substantive world of journalism where over a hundred journalists of the Associate

Press (AP) discover that their phone records have been secretly subpoenaed by the Justice Department as part of an investigation by the government into the source of the leak in an AP story of May 2012, about the CIA thwarting a plot by a satellite organization of Al-Qaeda in Yemen to bomb an airliner bound for the US. The move has been roundly criticized by the print, online and broadcast media. One discerns here what looks like the beginnings of a media-swell against the Obama administration's prosecutorial exertions against the time-honoured journalistic privilege of confidentiality of source.

'What, besides intimidation,' *The New York Times* demanded to know in its editorial of 15 May, 'is achieved by searching phone records of respected journalists?' It went on to dub the move 'a fishing expedition for sources and an effort to frighten off whistle-blowers'. In a letter of protest (signed by over 50 news media organizations) to the Attorney General, Eric Holder, the Reporters' Committee for Freedom of the Press said that 'the nation's news media were stunned' by the scope of the action which 'calls into question the very integrity of the Department of Justice policies towards the press', and demonstrates 'that a strong federal shield law is needed to protect reporters and their newsgathering materials in a court of law'.

President Obama straightaway conceded that a 'new media shield Bill' was in order but was hardly contrite about the action taken by the Justice Department because, as he saw it, given the 60,000 US troops in Afghanistan and US intelligence deployment around the world, 'part of my job is protecting what they do, while still accommodating for the need for the public to be informed'. CNN anchor and chief Washington correspondent Jake Tapper shot right back, saying, 'that's what every President says. Every President, whether it's Nixon with the Pentagon Papers or George W. Bush with the NSA wiretapping story, every President exerts "I am doing this to keep you safe."' Tapper was at pains to dissociate such encroachment into the freedom of the press in the name of national security from the bar of public opinion or approbation because 'it's not enough of an answer in and of itself. That's why there is congressional oversight of the executive branch. It's not enough just to say we're doing it to keep you safe, because the moment the American people cede that territory, then Presidents can do whatever they want.' Obama's is, according to him, 'a very aggressive administration when it comes to squashing freedom of the press'.

That is a reputation that is beginning to stick. There have already been six prosecutions of leaks under Eric Holder's Attorney Generalship, and a growing recourse to the Espionage Act of First World War vintage whose application to ferret out journalistic sources is, to begin with, a bit of a stretch. The balancing act attempted by the White House in pitting the need, as the President sees it, of 'the press to be able to be unfettered in its pursuit of investigative journalism' against that, on the other hand, 'for secret and classified information to remain secret and classified in order to protect our national security interests' has not cut much ice with the affected parties. The president and CEO of Associated Press, Gary Pruitt, has declared the seizure of the phone records of the news agency's reporters and editors 'unconstitutional', and warned that they would have a chilling effect on those wanting to share information with journalists. While he has not ruled out suing the Justice Department, media commentators seem agreed that the current legal and political climate does not hold out much hope for any aggressive assertion of journalistic rights.

The official mood of zero tolerance for intelligence leaks, which the same officialdom determines in its undisclosed wisdom to be sensitive or not, in effect erects a firewall, a 'national security' cordon, around journalistic practice, scaring off conscientious or morally outraged informants and putting the Whistleblower Protection Act of 1989 on the back burner. While this has been in the air for a while now – the state of emergency post-September 11 has not been called off or worn off – what is special about the latest development involving AP is that it contravenes the Justice Department's own guidelines issued thirty years back restricting the exercise of subpoenas of phone records of journalists – guidelines which had become a settled convention where, as the *New York Times* editorial put it, 'the media and the government have used a well-honed system to balance the government's need to pursue criminals or national security breaches with the media's constitutional right to inform the public'.

It doesn't help the press in this situation that it additionally has the onus of convincing the public that such abridgement, at one remove, of journalistic access will rebound on the nature of democracy itself; or of persuading the political class that it is dangerous to squeeze the channels of the fourth estate which, after all, provide and equip it with the material to formulate the public agenda and discourse at any given time. Security in peril is an alarm signifier before which all else must yield.

The mainstream influential media are also caught in a bind of their own making: where to draw the line on leaks. This in turn makes it difficult to rally support or consensus on where to draw the line on governmental action against leaks. A maximalist position would have been to question, or at least thoroughly discuss the pros and cons of, the incarceration and action against Bradley Manning, the source of WikiLeaks, who is a virtual looming presence in the current contention about leaks. But on Manning, the US media proved a pushover. And now, when it comes to sundry other leaks with a possible or debatable security angle, they find themselves ducking and dodging and crying foul as the establishment throws the book, and anything else it can find in its anti-disclosure arsenal, at them.

The action against AP is also historically significant. The news agency has a hoary lineage as an institution that was constitutive of the modern era of the fourth estate in the US. When, in May 1844, Samuel Morse sent the first telegraphic message over the wire experimentally strung between Washington and Baltimore, initiating the new technology of mass communication, the question uppermost in most minds was where the content to fill this newly created capacity would come from. It was a classic instance of networking preceding programming, which is how, as we know from Raymond Williams, mass media technology evolved and proliferated.

AP, set up in 1846, was a business response to that felt need, and provided a fillip to content generation as a wire service. It has the stature and gravitas to epitomize the fourth estate which plays a morally, if not constitutionally, sanctioned role in the scheme of checks and balances that underwrites the separation of powers in the US Constitution. To secretly and sweepingly search thousands of telephone conversations by over a hundred journalists of such a media institution is also to stigmatize it as a kind of Trojan horse concealing information, purportedly inimical to the nation, and its sources. To Gary Pruitt, the message from the government is clear: 'If you talk to the press, we're going to go after you' – the larger implication being that 'the people of the United States will only know what the government wants them to know, and that's not what the framers of the Constitution had in mind when they wrote the First Amendment'.

The takeaway from all this for India which has its share of media-baiting by the government, particularly social media through indiscriminate exercise of the infamous Article 66A of the Information Technology Act, is only too obvious, particularly because the US media has been the dominant professional and market model. As we are on the threshold of legislation (once Parliament gets to function, that is, and has the time to take it up) to protect whistle-blowers, the ongoing US experience must provide insights into what such a law can and cannot deliver or guarantee. But then there is a world of difference in what protection of a whistle-blower means in our two respective contexts. In the US, in the best of times – and these are not – it would mean a sense of immunity from prosecution for disclosure of private information in the public interest. In India, as over twenty tragic examples to date remind us, it perhaps still and primarily means protecting – if an Act can – the lives of those who dare to blow the whistle.

First published in *Frontline*, 27 June 2013.

Refractions off the PRISM

The problem is that you cannot pick up the phone and talk about it. Nor sign on to Facebook or Skype to vent your feelings about it. Because, as we always suspected but now know, some three-letter outfit out there – NSA, CIA, FBI – is tracking your call and your articulations (about anything really) on the social media; and colour-coding you, depending on where you live in the world, from a palette that shifts from safe green to dangerous red; and slotting you, depending on what you have to say, on a scale that imaginably ranges from 'friendly' to 'unfriendly' to possibly even 'dangerous'; and if you have been rashly discussing your plans to bomb the United States into extinction online or on the phone, naturally as downright 'terrorist'. If it makes you feel any better, you are the involuntary subject of humungous, innovative programmes dandily code-named PRISM and Boundless Informant that can pry into your life if you are as much as online. But maybe – and that's the hope which emboldens this essay – in this obsessive, sweeping, blanket electronic eavesdropping, what appears in good old print may just get by unnoticed.

The history of truth, said Nietzsche, is the history of the longest lasting falsehood. We seem to be living through that proposition in the Kafkaesque aftermath of the revelations by Edward Snowden about mass, indiscriminate snooping by the US secret service establishment, which cumulatively amounts to a universal violation of the human right to privacy. What we have at face value in Snowden is a morally outraged conscientious objector on the inside track of this spydom who cannot take the lies and deception any more, and blows the whistle on what he later characterizes as 'the largest programme of suspicion-less surveillance in human history'. All hell, predictably, breaks loose. Thus far there is, at least in some measure, a cause and effect relationship in the narrative.

What follows is a phase of disinformation and disorientation where your moral compass is magnetically deflected, and the meanings naturally associated with concepts and terms twisted and torn out to convey something entirely different, and sometimes just the opposite. So the Director of the US National Intelligence, James Clapper, brazens it out by telling NBC News that he was being 'most truthful or least untruthful' when he told the US Congress, in response to a specific question, that the National Security Agency (NSA) was not collecting data about millions of Americans; when in fact it was. For one given to such clever prevarication it should hardly be surprising that it is the disclosures made by Snowden that are 'reprehensible', not the secretive, intrusive, illegal large-scale quarrying of private communication by his agency, nor his lying about it under oath to the House. As Snowden, from his hideout in Hong Kong, described it in his Q&A session with the public in an online forum organized by *The Guardian*, 'James Clapper baldly lying to the public without repercussion is the evidence of a subverted democracy. The consent of the governed is not consent if it is not informed.'

US President Barack Obama's early reaction was cautiously benign: he was not, he suggested, averse to a debate in the public about the competing – at times mutually exclusive, he pointed out – demands of individual privacy and public security. Almost two weeks after the story broke, at the G8 summit in Northern Ireland, Obama seemed to suggest that he was stung into action by the disclosures to appoint an oversight board of independent US citizens, including 'fierce civil libertarians', as further check and balance on the collection and use of such metadata. But he has been ominously silent about what he thought of and what was in store for the one who sparked off the debate and the soul-searching, except to indicate that the Justice Department would initiate criminal proceedings against Snowden and move for his expatriation from Hong Kong – blotting out the whistleblower, as a variant, if you like, of shooting the messenger.

This peculiar tack of moral equivocation, that the Snowden revelations are important but no thanks to Snowden, seems to be adopted even by the influential mainstream press in the US, including *The Washington Post* (which, along with *The Guardian*, first published the exposé) and *The New York Times*, whose opinion writers (unlike, of course, those of *The Guardian*) had pretty harsh things to say about the whistleblower. Obama, meanwhile, put on a brave face at the meet of the G8 with what must have been uncomfortable knowledge that some of them now knew what he must have known all along, about the e-mails and phones of their leaders and those of the G20 being hacked in previous meetings. Earlier, in his first meeting back home in California with Chinese President Xi Jinping, Obama may also have had to abandon any idea of a show of indignation about cyber espionage by China, because by then Snowden had blown the lid off the systematic hacking for several years by the US of the computers of Chinese public officials, citizens and students.

If it is in the grain of the state to spy on its own people and the citizens of other countries in the name of real or imagined, in this case not necessarily either, danger to itself, multinational companies which handle the global personal communication of the people with one another, and who therefore are cast in a fiduciary role, are hardly expected to be collusive in this effort, especially in a system that celebrates an autonomous free market. Despite their protestations, the hint we have from Snowden is that the giant internet companies – Google,

Facebook, Yahoo, Skype and YouTube – made the data of their users, clients and consumers available to the secret service establishment, and cannot breathe a word about it. But then, such a nexus between giant digital corporations and the US state was both a political and market imperative.

In his recent book, *The Blind Giant: How to Survive in the Digital Age*, Nick Harkaway throws some light on how this comes to be. Citing the example of Google, he points out how

> the US considers Google a strategic asset. Google's Trust and Safety Manager is a former agent of the US Secret Service. This is not to suggest that Google would ever compromise its legal responsibilities to its customers, or that employees of the company would supply data to the government for which they should have to obtain court orders. Rather, it is to observe that while Google's public posture is of rakish defiance of authority – a posture that perhaps looks a bit odd now that the company is a global titan – it seems not implausible that where necessary and permissible, Google tries to be a helpful corporate citizen of the nation where it was born.

How corporate clout succumbs and plays second fiddle to the state as it goes after the whistleblower was amply demonstrated in the case of WikiLeaks, when MasterCard, Visa Europe, Western Union, PayPal and Bank of America severed all transactions with the website and Amazon removed it from its hosting service.

The credibility and reliability of the personal data of their users, acquired and compiled by digital corporations in the course of their business, are crucial to their leveraging their peculiar revenue model. As Harkaway points out about Facebook (and this would be as true of the others):

> [Mark] Zuckerberg's company has an immense paper value – investment firm General Atlantic put it as $65 million in March 2011 – and a large part of that is the notional value of all the customer information in the network. That information, properly analysed and deployed, could allow the kind of targeted selling companies are only able to dream about.

The value of that information is undermined to the extent that customers have different real and virtual (or social media) identities; and it is small wonder that Zuckerberg (speaking to David Kirkpatrick, who wrote *The Facebook Effect: The Inside Story of the Company that is Connecting the World*) characterizes recourse to such dual identity as lack of integrity.

Zeroing in on the identity of one who has been online by the electronic traces left behind, de-anonymizing the user, seems a matter of professional pride with these companies. As the CEO of Google, Eric Schmidt, boasted at the second Washington Ideas Forum 2010: 'With your permission, you give us more information about you, about your friends, and we can improve the quality of our searches. We don't need you to type at all. We know where you are. We know where you've been. We can more or less know what you're thinking about.' This is the hacker ethic, shorn of its rebel essence, in the hands of the corporation.

Advocates of the free software movement have, of course, been alive to the implications of concentrated digital monopolies. The founder of the Software Freedom Law Centre and Professor at Columbia University, Eben Moglen, in fact suggests that in the balance, the danger to freedom posed by the social media may outweigh their liberative potential:

> Everything we know about technology tells us that the current forms of social network communication, despite their enormous current value for politics, are also intensely dangerous to use. They are too centralized; they are too vulnerable to state retaliation and control. . . . It is not hard when everybody is just in one big database controlled by Mr Zuckerberg to decapitate a revolution by sending an order to Mr Zuckerberg that he cannot afford to refuse.

Moglen's counter-model of tens of thousands of encrypted servers inspired four students of the New York University to build an alternative decentralized social network they called 'Diaspora'. The project has had quick and dramatic initial success, and attracted a huge user following, but to endure, it may yet have to get around the ethical problem of how to monetize a social network without commercially exploiting the personal data and thereby betraying the implicit trust of its users.

Official India's reaction to the Snowden disclosure of the Boundless Informant data of March this year, which showed that 6.3 billion pieces of intelligence had been mined from computers in the country, placing it fifth in the hit list (the others being Iran, Pakistan, Jordan and Egypt, in that order), has been pathetically docile. After some initial half-hearted attempts to downplay the import of this level of interest in India, there has been a flurry of activity towards setting up a concerted cyber-security response mechanism in the form of the National Cyber Coordination Centre (NCCC). But it is not clear whether this is meant to counter or carry forward the agenda of the US National Security Agency in our cyber domain. It would be ironical, but entirely probable, that the Snowden exposé provides an excuse, a fillip and a boost to our own cyber sleuths to enlarge their scope and mandate, and bring what goes on online under more intense scrutiny.

Then there is the more troubling issue of the reluctance of the people at large to see such intrusion into their lives as an affront to their liberty because they are, at the same time, subject to the constant refrain of a terrorist threat round the corner. In his book *The Rule of Law*, published in 2010, the late Lord Chief Justice Thomas Bingham of the United Kingdom discusses how the shrill atmospherics of the war against terror beleaguers the rule of law. The tension of the times, he points out, is at a philosophical level: that between Cicero's position, '*Salus populi suprema est lex*' ('the safety of the people is the supreme law') and Benjamin Franklin's conviction that 'he who would put security before liberty deserves neither'. Bingham himself is with Benjamin Franklin because, he says, 'we cannot commend our society to others by departing from the fundamental standards which make it worthy of commendation'. Edward Snowden, too, cites Benjamin Franklin in support of his cause. Those who put security before liberty call him a traitor; for those who value liberty more he is a patriot.

First published in *Frontline*, 11 July 2013.

Envisioning a Fully Paid Digital Future

In the ethical minefield of sting journalism if you set out to establish that a subject, say, a low- or middle-level bureaucrat, is corrupt by piling him with offer upon offer of bribe until his resistance cracks and he succumbs to the temptation and you have captured the act with a hidden camera, you are resorting to entrapment by goading someone into a criminal act, someone ostensibly without criminal intent in the first instance. It may pass off as some kind of behavioural study inasmuch as it indicates how soon you can or how far it takes to reach the threshold of corruption (inherent?) in a human being, but it is bad journalism. It is sophistry to call this investigative journalism. It is a piece of eyeball-grabbing sensationalism and against the best practices in the profession.

Such unconscionable heavy-handedness, however, is market practice for some giant multinationals in the digital media business who enable their proprietary software to be fairly freely available on the net, deliberately don't crack down on cracked versions doing the rounds, and instead get after the end-user who may have downloaded and used it for free. True, there may be a law (of the land or cyberspace) – which the Free Software movement would in any case deny or defy – broken in the unlicensed use of the software, but when such infraction becomes the systematic basis of a marketing opportunity, even strategy, for the company to zero in on those who use their products and to penalize them for it by making them reluctant or unwilling customers, it seems more like compulsory draft than free market. The straightforward thing to do is to make the product unavailable unless paid for, like the paywall for digital content, rather than setting it up as a bait, and then for the company's marketing and compliance arms, interlocked, to be prowling on the net and pouncing on unsuspecting errant netizens to harass, pressurize and bully them into becoming paid subscribers.

This instance, perhaps more familiar to us in India, is not specifically mentioned in Silicon Valley preceptor and progenitor of the concept of Virtual Reality, Jaron Lanier's new but already influential book, *Who Owns the Future?* (released in May 2013), but it is of a piece with what he describes as the 'punishing network effect' of the big servers like Google, which he calls 'Siren Servers'. The 'captured populations' on these servers, says Lanier, 'think twice if they want to stop engaging with a Siren Server. In Silicon Valley-speak it is also called "stickiness". Players often can't take on the burden of escaping the thrall of a Siren Server once a punishing network effect is in place.' Regular users of a server like this have invested so much time and effort and money on it that the sheer prospect of having to reinvest all that all over again acts as a deterrent against shifting to another server. The dependence on Facebook is even more committing because a good part of the user's personality has gone on to it.

> Even if you capture every little thing you had uploaded, you can't save it in the context of interactions with other people. You have to lose a part of yourself to leave Facebook once you become an avid user. . . . Would you ever be willing to take the risk to sever a part of your own life's context in order to disengage from a Siren Server that ogles you?

One of the two big ideas Lanier proffers in this work is that even as these Siren Servers appropriate a part of us, eroding our privacy and garnering our personal details in the process, and trade that information to those who can use it to slot our consumerist appetites and proclivities into a business model, we who are the pivot of this transaction are paid nothing for it. The free services we are accustomed to enjoying online are not really free in that sense; they are premised on the value we offer in terms of our personal information. It would be a good idea, in fact necessary for long-term sustainability, for the major servers in the business to start paying the user for this data drawn from him. The user, in the very process of being one, monetizes himself. A new cyber equivalent of a social contract needs to be put in place, and the laws pertaining to copyright and intellectual property on the net modified, to factor in this huge hitherto missing dimension of, to pun, the exchange value of the user. This could substantially recast the economic model because, as Lanier recognizes, 'digital information is really just people in disguise'.

Lanier's book was published only shortly before Edward Snowden happened. In the light of Snowden's revelations, Lanier's proposition that the ordinary netizen has a right to remuneration for self-information acquires a whole new scale and currency. Lanier in fact posits this right as equal to that of the claim for payment for any creative work or software downloaded off the net. Himself a musician of some professional standing, he is aware of the plight of the performer whose work is mass-pirated on the net; but that is only one side of the coin because 'ordinary people are relentlessly spied on and not compensated for information taken from them. While I would like to see everyone eventually pay for music and the like, I would not ask for it until there is reciprocity.'

Post-Snowden, we suspect or know that the Siren Servers which are major corporations have been working in tandem with the secret service wings of the government in accumulating and parsing the data gathered from a vast sweeping programme of massive snooping. While Lanier is bullish about the 'revolutionary narrative . . . common in digital politics' pitting the 'quickness and sophistication of online social processes' like the Arab Spring and like upsurges 'against the sluggish, exclusive club of old-fashioned government or corporate power', he is not naïve either about the capabilities of the state in the digital age. He points out that a visit to

> a modern, digitally networked, national intelligence agency, such as the CIA/NSA/NRO complex in the United States . . . feels very much like a visit to the Googleplex or a major high tech finance venture. The same sorts of cheery recent PhDs from top schools cavort in an airy and playful environment with lots of glass and excellent coffee. Spymaster Siren Servers thrive in all countries by now. We tend to hear more about the excesses of foreign ones in China or even Britain, but the trend is universal.

Snowden must have been one of those not-so-cheery and not-recent-PhD types in the NSA contractors' fold. And Snowden's disclosure about the nudge-and-wink relationship between dominant Siren Servers and the US government must give Lanier pause in his implicit assumption that the US state and the digital corporations are on different sides of the fence. In fact he sounds almost dirigiste when he advocates that the principle of businesses having to pay for use of public airwaves be expanded to apply to all flow of information – and that would include the information tapped from citizens participating in the digital economy with or without their knowledge, because 'everyone is measured and tracked in the network age. So why not have government collect compensation for the use of that value in order to fund social welfare?'

The other major idea running through the book is that the digital economy must squarely be one of the middle class and not be allowed to be hijacked, as is happening, by a few multi-billionaire stars who render it 'like the old feudal or robber baron economies'. He seems to suggest that the star system with its 'winner takes all' mentality, given pop cultural expression in TV shows like *American Idol*, is a far cry from the ethos of the start-ups in garages in Silicon Valley by brilliant young entrepreneurs who

> announce that their goal is to change human culture globally and profoundly, within a few years. And that they aren't ready yet to worry about money, because acquiring a great fortune is a petty matter that will take care of itself. Furthermore, these bright little young bands succeed regularly. This is just Silicon Valley's version of normal.

Against the star system, which he believes is unsustainable, Lanier suggests the bell curve model of distribution where 'there is a bulge of average people and two tails of exceptional people, one high and one low'. This leavening, privileging and centre-planking of the middle class becomes essential because 'that is where customers come from. Neither a petro-fiefdom, a military dictatorship, nor a narco-state can support authentic internal market development, and neither does a winner-take-nearly-all network design.'

Jaron Lanier's discursive contemplation, *Who Owns the Future?*, would be scholarly if it were not, for a good part, zany. He claims not to be swayed by the fad of de-narrativization in the digital era; not to be caught between what the director of the *Matrix* film series, Lana Wachowski (describing her new project *Cloud Atlas*), called 'the future idea that everything is fragmented and the past idea that there is a beginning, middle and end'. But his ideas are as dense as they are eclectic and dispersed, almost at random, through his work.

His propositions and prescriptions seem at times at odds with one other. The mammoth digital corporations or Siren Servers, by only drawing saleable information from their middle-class customers and not recompensing them for it, may be eroding their own market base; a 'star' server like 'Google might eventually become an ouroboros, a snake eating its own tail, unless something changes. This would happen when so many goods and services become software-centric, and so much information is "free" that there is nothing left to advertise on Google that attracts actual money.' How this and the middle-class-dominant 'bell curve' model he espouses ties in with his vision, towards the end of the book, of a concentrated, cartelized digital media market, a 'confederacy' of a handful of the biggest Siren Servers who 'make log-ins interoperable', is not clear.

In his wishful scheme of things, the citizen, embodying the middle class, should be monetarily incentivized to become and remain a customer, and it is but inevitable if, in the process, the customer is divested of some of his democratic citizenship entitlements. His concept of empowerment seems to aim at parity of the man and the machine: currently, so seems the argument, the machines alone have unique identities like IP addresses; the people who interact with the machines should be given unique identities to bring the two on par.

Every now and then in the work, Lanier quixotically spars with an invisible ghost of Marx. Lest his countercultural persona and some of his unconventional ideas be misunderstood as coming from the ideological left (although there is no reason for any confusion – his celebration of capitalism is unequivocal), he goes to great lengths to put down Marxism, apropos nothing, even as he cannot help admitting that there is a Marx applicable to every situation. Sample this: 'Marx wanted something that most people, including me, don't want: a committee to make sure everyone gets what's best for them. Let's reject the Marxist ideal and instead consider the question of whether markets can be counted on to create middle classes as a matter of course.' Even we begin, after a while, to imagine with him the groans of his 'lefty' friends at his cuts and thrusts at poor Marx.

First published in *Frontline*, 8 August 2013.

Leveson's Lessons

We have been treated to the whys and wherefores of regulation in the Indian news media for some time now, and there is already quite a rhetorical heap of opinion, prescription and objection before us to negotiate. But if we imagined that all that accreted discourse was so much ground covered, at least in terms of an understanding of the situation, we imagined wrong. The refreshing thing about the bureaucracy waking up to a situation like this is that it really wakes up to it, starts on a clean slate, sets aside rather than cuts through the clutter of ideas before us, and begins by stating the obvious as if it just became obvious. Or, maybe it is a bureaucratic principle as well that understanding should not only be gleaned, but seen – step by step – to be gleaned.

So, we have just had the Telecom Regulatory Authority of India (TRAI) telling us that the problem is perhaps, one, the nefarious link between corporate ownership and editorial management, and two, cross-media holdings (where print, television and radio businesses have the same ownership). It is just a bit infuriating to hear this because we know, have known for long, that this is of course the problem; and it need not have come to this if the bureaucrats or their political masters had done something about it in time. We are now so far down that road, that undoing the news media mess in the country will take some doing, even if the political will is up to it.

Simultaneously, we have the Ministry of Information and Broadcasting, somewhat more circumspectly, asking a parliamentary panel to look at whether and how the report of the inquiry into the culture, practices and ethics of the press in the United Kingdom, and the regulatory recommendations thereof, by Lord Justice Brian Leveson may have a bearing on our condition.

Interestingly, the language of the two arms of the government looking into regulation of the news media varies and seems to speak to different target constituencies. TRAI seems to be addressing the media market and the need to protect consumers from monopolies controlling that market. The Information and Broadcasting Ministry sees it more in terms of ensuring the democratic right and choice of the citizenry and the community at large. The difference may be unwitting, but is a throwback to the sharp distinction sought to be drawn between the 'consumer' and the 'citizen' in the debate in the British Parliament on the draft bill of the Communication Act of 2003, which enabled and empowered the media regulator Ofcom (Office of Communication), whose remit covered telecommunications, broadcasting and post.

In their study titled 'Representing Citizens and Consumers in Media and Communication Regulation' (published in the May 2007 issue of *Annals of the American Academy of Political and Social Science*), Sonia Livingstone and Peter Lunt categorize the interests of the consumer and the citizen as separate from each other. The consumer's focus is on the 'economic', that of the citizen on the 'cultural'; the consumer is concerned about the 'networking' and allied 'services', the citizen's concern is programming 'content'. The consumer evokes the 'individual'; the citizen, the 'community'.

They elaborate this division in a further psycho-sociological checklist, which describes *inter alia*: (i) the interest of the consumer in terms of 'wants', that of the citizen in terms of 'needs'; (ii) the consumer as representing 'private benefit' and the citizen, 'public benefit'; (iii) the consumer's as being a 'language of choice', the citizen's a 'language of rights'; (iv) the focus of or for the consumer tending to be 'short term', that of or for the citizen, 'long term'; (v) regulation on behalf of the consumer becoming an action 'against a detriment' and that on behalf of the citizen, one in the 'public interest'; (vi) the consumer's interest, in the market model of the media, as likely to be 'rollback regulation', whereas 'continued regulation to correct market failure' may be what is in the citizen's interest.

These differences – some explicit, some nuanced – in the perception and the construct of the two terms informed the debate on the bill, and Clause 3(1) of the ensuing Communication Act 2003 reflected them when it stipulated: 'It shall be the principal duty of Ofcom, in carrying out their function; (a) to further the interests of *citizens* in relation to communications matters; and (b) to further the interests of *consumers* in relevant markets, where appropriate by promoting competition' (emphases added).

The regulatory body's mission statement, however, sought to integrate the two when it set out that 'Ofcom exists to further the interests of *citizen–consumers* through a regulatory regime which, where appropriate, encourages competition' (emphasis added). In actual practice, as Livingstone and Lunt point out, consumer and citizen were at times interchangeable, at times not. In short, Ofcom was born out of this confusion about whether and where a citizen or a consumer was at the receiving end.

In our context, we already see the beginnings of such a conceptual divergence in the approaches of TRAI and the Information and Broadcasting Ministry to media regulation. TRAI's stated objective of insulating the editorial charge of the news media from the vested interests of their corporate owners is no doubt the crying need of the hour. But what is overlooked in this approach is the equivalent of the publisher's rights which, though it is peculiar to print and may not apply to the broadcast media, were historically constitutive of the encompassing freedom of the press we speak about today.

In the advertisement-driven model of the press that came to stay even in the nineteenth century, that freedom was already being defined and defended in market terms, and the consumer–citizen divide was already apparent. Joseph Pulitzer's formulation that 'circulation means advertising, and advertising means money, and money means independence' was setting the tone for a democratic agency of the press via the market. Arguably, though, when push comes to shove, as it did in India during the Emergency of the mid-1970s, it is the publisher who bears the brunt of a concerted state action against the press and either capitulates or, like Ramnath Goenka, resists.

The decline of the publisher, even more precipitous than that of the editor, and the reduction of that position to a token nominee named in the print-line, on the one hand, and the conflation of the roles of the editor and the corporate CEO (chief executive officer), making the idea of editorial independence ridiculous and redundant, on the other, are a double whammy for the credibility of the Indian press.

When the Leveson report now enters the picture as a possible inspiration for a regulatory framework relevant to India, it is crucial to get the essence of it right and not to, like the Chairman of the Press Council of India, Justice Markandey Katju, tends to, overread it to create a case for a statutory body with rather summary powers including the leverage of licensing, or to oversee social engineering of the nature and course of news media content. The Leveson inquiry itself was a response to the exposé by *The Guardian* in 2011 that the Murdoch-owned *News of the World* had hacked the mobile phone of the 11-year-old British girl Milly Dowler when she was abducted (and murdered) nine years earlier.

This immediate provocation provided the impetus for a wider inquiry into the 'Culture, Practices and Ethics of the Press' including, as Lord Leveson put it in his report, 'recklessness in prioritizing sensational stories', 'covert surveillance, blagging and deception', and 'lack of respect for individual privacy and dignity'. In this task, Leveson sets himself clearly apart from and against the *News of the World* features editor Paul McMullan's ultra-libertarian view presented at the inquiry commission, that 'privacy is for paedos'.

What marks the Leveson report is that it balances the pathetic aspects of the performance of the British press, particularly the *News of the World* variety, with its gains and achievements and its putative role as a free agent of democracy, and provisions regulation with a light touch. While noting that 'large parts of the press had been engaged in a widespread trade in private and confidential information, apparently with little regard to public interest', and that these remain largely unknown because of the thick-as-thieves bonding in the profession, Lord Leveson is clear that 'this is not to suggest that the British press is somehow so devoid of merit that press freedom, hard won over 300 years ago, should be jeopardized or that the press should be delivered into the arms of the state'. He is against the government or parliament regulating the press, although the growth of monopoly news media calls for a fresh look at cross-media ownership and 'the necessary regulatory regime that will support plurality in the media'.

He accepts that it is in the nature of the press 'to be irreverent, unruly, opinionated'; that it has nevertheless done good work. 'But that does not mean', he cautions,

> that it is beyond challenge. Neither does it mean that the price of press freedom should be paid by those who suffer, unfairly and egregiously, at the hands of the press and have no sufficient mechanism for obtaining redress. There is no original profession, trade or industry in which the serious failings of the few are overlooked because of the good done by the many.

The moribund Press Complaints Commission (PCC), currently in the process of being replaced, which was effete and useless as a mechanism to address grievances against the press, adds a note of urgency to the Leveson mandate. Lord Leveson finds himself in agreement with the Prime Minister that the PCC is 'ineffective and lacking in rigour', and with the leader of the opposition that it is a 'toothless poodle' (they may as well have been talking about the Press Council of India).

The broad methodology adopted by Leveson, as evidenced in the report, is instructive. To begin with, he announced a set of criteria to arrive at a regulatory framework and sought opinion on it from a cross-section of the public. The criteria were meant to ensure that the proposed regulation is effective, credible and durable; that it will adhere to norms of fairness and objectivity; is independent and enforced with transparency and that there is compliance; has remedial or curative powers, and has funding to sustain it.

He was clear from the outset that it has to be self-regulation and reiterates this many times in the report: 'I should make it clear at the very outset that I consider that what is needed is a genuinely independent and effective system of self-regulation.' To this end, 'I have encouraged the industry to work together to find a mechanism for independent self-regulation that would work for them and would work for the public.' Again, he seeks a *via media* model 'for independent self-regulation that . . . would protect both the freedom of the press and freedom of speech along with the rights and interests of individuals; it should . . . command public confidence', and to do so it needs to be independent of both the state and the market. It is not only the people who need protection against excesses of the press; journalists themselves are susceptible to pressure and need what he calls a 'whistle blowing hotline' to function with integrity and true to their conscience.

He is at his gingerly best when it comes to the substantive aspect of how this prescription of self-regulation should be ensured and safeguarded. 'It is', he says, 'essential that there should be legislation to underpin the independent self-regulatory system and facilitate its recognition in legal processes', but hastens to add that such legislation will not establish anybody to regulate the press, nor give parliament or government any right to prevent newspapers publishing any material.

Lord Leveson knows that this is likely to be seen as 'the most controversial part of my recommendations', and is at pains to qualify it and to emphasize what it is not. It 'is not, and cannot be characterized as, statutory regulation of the press'. It is, on the other hand, 'independent regulation of the press organized by the press, with a statutory verification process to ensure that the required levels of independence and effectiveness are met by the system.'

The danger, though, is that a partial reading or heavy-handed interpretation of the Leveson prescription, which is really a nuanced take on regulation fine-tuned to the sensitivities of British society and which goes to greater lengths to warn against what regulation should not be than to say what it should be, could become a convenient tool in the hands of the government to clip the wings of the news media here in India.

First published in *Frontline*, 23 August 2013.

Retooling Journalists and Journalism

We do not really know what he meant, but he assures us that he meant well. Information and Broadcasting Minister Manish Tewari's rather vague suggestion that would-be journalists should undergo a common examination and obtain a licence to practise the profession may have been meant as a trial balloon, but tends to sound more like casing the joint before a bid to rob the fourth estate of some of its freedoms. To begin with, the sheer gumption of the idea sets it apart from normal democratic discourse. We would not, for example, be re-examining whether universal suffrage should continue to be the given in our form of representative government, although, if you put it up for discussion in the public sphere, there would be those who forcefully argue that an educational pre-qualification to exercise the ballot would make for a better democracy in a country with mass illiteracy like ours. The faith in every citizen as an eligible voter is a leap of democratic faith. So too, one would have hoped by now, is that in the principle of the freedom of the press.

It does not help that the inspiration for this gratuitous move to raise the standard of the press comes from the Chairman of the Press Council of India, Justice Markandey Katju, who has set up a committee to go into whether or what minimum qualifications might be set for a journalist. It does not help that the objective conditions, globally, in which journalism now operates allow the dominance of the intrusive surveillance state; that the super-state which boasts a Constitution guaranteeing unabridged freedom of the press goes after whistleblowers who put the media wise to its astounding violations – of the privacy of its own citizens, its allies and other countries; of human rights in Iraq and other US theatres of war or conflict – with a vengeance. All it takes, as we see in the case of Edward Snowden, is to arbitrarily dub the whistleblower a 'fugitive', to make it legitimate to hunt him down.

What is worse, it now emerges from a new instalment of the Snowden revelations that the giant media corporations, including Google, Yahoo, Microsoft and Facebook, which had appeared unwilling but helpless before the secretive legal requirement – imposed by the Foreign Intelligence Surveillance Court in the United States – to share their data about their customers with the National Security Agency (NSA), actually received millions of dollars from the intelligence outfit as recompense. They were no doubt making a monetary virtue of a security necessity. Some of these companies play a quasi-journalistic role – Google as news aggregator and Facebook as a social media complement of news – and make journalism to that extent vulnerable.

Another media conglomerate, Amazon, has not been mentioned in the redacted Snowden documents published thus far, but there has been some speculation of its involvement, partly fuelled by the tax breaks it is seen as getting in the US and the United Kingdom, and by Amazon Web Services' bid to provide cloud computing services to the Central Intelligence Agency (CIA). Amazon's founder, Jeff Bezos, taking over *The Washington Post* from the Graham family seems symptomatic of another kind of takeover – of the traditional publisher by the modern corporation.

We have our own variant of this trend in Reliance Industries, a corporate house widely seen as getting sweetheart deals from the government, making equity forays into TV18 and Eenadu groups. There are no doubt considerations of technological convergence and resultant vertical integration of business behind such acquisitions. But the nexus between the firm and the state is what makes the journalism in the business queasy. And yet it has been possible for many to see Bezos as a godsend because his deep pockets may help insulate journalism at *The Post* from the immediate pressures of the market, and foster more breathing and thinking space for journalists, making for better breadth and depth of coverage and analysis. The visible influence of Reliance on TV18, on the other hand, has been in terms of ruthless corporate and market efficiency, including a clinical reappraisal of its workforce requirement and retrenchment of hundreds of employees, including journalists. Indeed the media sector in our country seems to be moving into a parodic version of jobless growth, the joblessness accruing largely to the journalism part which once drove the business but is increasingly becoming an also-ran in the scramble for profit.

So it is bad enough for journalism as it is without Messrs Katju and Tewari lending a helping hand to suppress the independent, freewheeling, uncontainable spirit that distinguishes this calling, and seeking to convert it into some standardized and homogenized equivalent of a white-collar workforce meeting the expectations or requirements of what Manish Tewari calls 'stakeholders' (the government, he promised, while floating his exam-plus-licence idea, 'will not do anything that is not acceptable to stakeholders'). Because journalism, at its finest, is about and for those who may not be stakeholders in the market sense of the term, but have, at the same time, a lot at stake.

In the debates in the Constituent Assembly leading to the enshrining of freedom of speech and expression as a Fundamental Right in the Constitution, when the issue of stipulating specific separate rights for the press (as the First Amendment does in the US Constitution) came up, Dr B.R. Ambedkar held that the freedom of the press was implicit in the freedom of speech and expression as envisaged in Article 19(1) (a). The burden of his argument was that a separate coding of press rights would be a limitation on rather than an elaboration of the full entitlements of freedom of expression as guaranteed to every citizen of India. Courts in the country have also construed freedom of the press as inhering in the larger freedom of speech. The occupational freedom and right of expression of the journalist, then, is coequal with that of any citizen.

A disconcerting aspect of the recent readings of this Fundamental Right and freedom the press enjoys and shares with every citizen has been the repeated and undue emphasis placed on the 'reasonable restrictions' mentioned in Article 19(2), almost to the extent that the limitation proviso seems to get precedence over the empowerment clause. Apart from the grudging mindset it reveals, there is a spin on the clause (of reasonable restrictions) that makes it appear as some kind of a safeguard provided in the Constitution for the people against their press, whereas the burden of proof of reasonableness is in fact on those invoking the restrictions to hedge or restrict the freedom and right to speech and expression guaranteed by Article 19(1) (a). The Constitution specifies seven grounds for restrictions, namely, the interests of the sovereignty and the integrity of India, security of the state, friendly relations with foreign countries, public order, decency or morality, contempt of court, defamation and incitement to offence. It is the restrictions, the Constitution tells us, that must be reasonable, and not, as is sought to be commonly conveyed, that we, the people and the press should be preemptively reasonably restrained in the exercise of our constitutional and fundamental freedom of expression. There is a difference between the two.

The experience and legacy of journalism in India sets it clearly apart from the medical or the legal profession, to which it has of late been compared to buttress the case for introduction of a course of study or an exam or a licensing norm. Manish Tewari recognizes the heterogeneous nature of this vocation when he observes that economists and experts in international relations are today among the ranks of the journalists. Those who led the struggle for Indian independence were lawyers or journalists, and often both. Gandhiji's vast journalistic output – including in his *Satyagraha*, *Indian Opinion*, *Young India*, *Navajivan* and *Harijan* – seemed partly in the nature of testing his own evolving political philosophy. As he says in his autobiography,

> *Indian Opinion* in those days, like *Young India* and *Navajivan* today, was a mirror of part of my life. Week after week I poured out my soul in its columns, and expounded the principles and practice of Satyagraha as I understood it. . . . Satyagraha would probably have been impossible without *Indian Opinion*.

In this sense his journalism was constitutive, not the product or byproduct, of his political thinking.

The journalistic field needs to be kept open and open-ended. It does not matter that it is uneven. It must remain a site for contestation and questioning. With the formal news media segueing into the social media, the field opens up into a larger public sphere, and Gandhiji's mirror metaphor becomes all the more relevant. Journalism becomes less arcane, more quotidian, and of and by the people. We already see blogs of the local populace becoming a valuable source of first information and news where access for the formal media is limited or cut off, as in contexts of civil conflict or war (Iraq earlier, Syria or Egypt now), or natural disasters. We are seeing the categories of print, television, radio and online journalism merge into a common stream, and new demands being made on the journalist, in terms of the craft, to be multimedia-savvy, to multitask.

Journalism education may be a desirable but not a necessary precondition for a practitioner in the field – just as a film institute may be helpful but not necessary for a filmmaker, a course in a school of art for a painter or one in a design school for a graphic artist or designer, or a music school for someone taking to composing popular music or singing for films for a living. The parallels, if at all, must be drawn from these allied fields of communication rather than endogenous disciplines such as medicine or law.

In any case, it is curious that what was a debate about internal versus external regulation in the news media has suddenly somewhere flipped into a discussion on prescriptions about the norms of eligibility for a journalist. That all this comes at a time when mainstream journalism, despite its many drawbacks, shortcomings and excesses, is pounding away at the establishment, exposing, almost on a daily basis, scam after sleaze after scam, makes the agenda being subtly pushed in the name of reforming journalism rather suspect.

Official pronouncements, though, continue to profess a hands-off policy on the press. At the recent inauguration of the National Media Centre in New Delhi, the Prime Minister pointed out that the impact of changes in the media post-liberalization had not been studied and cautioned: 'A spirit of inquiry must not morph into a campaign of calumny. A witch-hunt is no substitute for investigative journalism. And personal prejudices must not replace public good.' But he seemed to put these aberrations down to the 'tussle between bottom lines and headlines', and said the government was committed to a 'free, pluralistic and independent media'.

He characterized the impact of liberalization on the media as a 'virtuous cycle', with the wider reach of the media creating newer markets to benefit both producers and consumers. But the virtuous cycle that made a difference for a good section of the news media, particularly private television channels, seems to have been stockmarket-boom-centric, as larger-than-real brands were quickly built up to raise money in the larger-than-real stockmarket. And when the market collapsed and recession set in to boot, the cycle turned vicious, with operating losses totting up and off-setting and undermining the bubble bonanza.

It is small wonder that the channels cannot subscribe to the advertising time limit of twelve minutes an hour set (in the interest of the viewer) by the Telecom Regulatory Authority of India (TRAI), and have sought the Information and

Broadcasting Minister's intercession to defer the implementation of the norm. So the viewer may, for some time yet, find it difficult to make out whether she is taking an advertising break from programming, or a programming break from advertising.

First published in *Frontline*, 20 September 2013.

Into the Digital, Oral Era

As we lurch into a future mediated by digital technology, we cannot but notice that the oral has returned with a bang and vies with the *written* to exemplify our communication and expression. It is not just that in this interactive, multimedia-enabled ambience, video, audio and text can combine seamlessly; that you can see what you hear what you read. Even what may be only written acquires an orality; a manner of 'oral writing' comes into force, somewhat as envisaged by Jacques Derrida as he rescued writing from subservience to speech, to which influential intellectual opinion had for long relegated it. The Derrida argument was set against the phonocentric western tradition of Socrates, Jean-Jacques Rousseau, Claude Lévi-Strauss and Ferdinand de Saussure that has privileged speech over writing.

The spoken versus the written debate goes way back to the Socratic dialogue of around 370 BC, as recorded by his pupil Plato. Socrates tells Phaedrus about the Egyptian god of invention, Theuth, waxing eloquent about his new creations – numbers, arithmetic, geometry, astronomy, letters – to the Egyptian king Thamus. The king responded with appropriate enthusiasm to each of these until the presentation came to letters. On Theuth's self-applause for his invention of letters as enabling writing, which in turn would, he claimed, aid memory, royalty gently rapped divinity on the knuckles and told him that it was not for the inventor to judge the usefulness or otherwise of his handiwork – it was for others to do so. The king went on to express his concern that writing, far from helping memory, would in fact make people less reliant on their memory, since they could now record, and afford to forget, what they otherwise had to remember. Himself a man of the spoken, never the written mode, Socrates was of course in full agreement with the king here. Writing, for him, was an illegitimate offspring of the original spoken word.

The origins of logocentrism were implicit in the Socratic parable of Theuth and Thamus. Speech came to be seen as superior to writing not only because it was anterior, but also because it was the originary act of language, writing being the derivative; and because speech implied *presence*, whereas writing implied *absence*. In his *Confessions*, Rousseau, in the eighteenth century, refers to writing as a means of absence: 'The decision that I have taken to write and hide myself is precisely the one that suits me. If I were present, people would never have known what I was worth.' However, writing is by no means a virtue in itself. It connotes 'destruction of presence and disease of speech'. It is clear to him that 'languages are made to be spoken' and that 'writing serves only as a supplement to speech' – supplement construed as an add-on to something that is already autonomously whole; thus, education becomes a supplement to nature which is otherwise whole, and masturbation a 'dangerous supplement' to wholesome sex.

Into the twentieth century, Saussure railed against the 'tyranny of writing' and against linguistic theory dealing with writing, declaring that 'the object of linguistic analysis is not defined by the combination of the written word and the spoken word: the spoken word alone constitutes the object'. Lévi-Strauss brought in the element of nostalgia for pre-literate cultures, suggesting that the practice of writing entailed a loss of innocence. More fiery opposition to the written word came from Dadaists like Tristan Tzara, who called for all books and libraries to be burnt so that a fresh oral era could begin. For the media guru Marshall McLuhan, the oral and the auditory had precedence over the visual, which, he recognized, became dominant with the emphasis placed on seeing during the Renaissance and on reading with the advent of the printing press.

Umberto Eco traces the origin of the spoken word in the western tradition to genesis, pointing out that creation itself arose

> through an act of speech; God spoke before all things and said 'Let there be light. . . .' He called light Day, darkness Night and the firmament Heavens. . . . We are not told in what language God (later) spoke to Adam . . . out of the ground God formed every beast of the field, every fowl of the air and brought them to Adam to see what he would call them.

Thus Adam, says Eco, may have been the first 'nomothete'; when he first sees Eve, he says: 'This is now bone of my bones and flesh of my flesh; she shall be called woman.'

Earlier, Walter Benjamin had described the essence of language as 'communication of mental meanings', the use of words for the purpose being only a part of the exercise. Thus, paradisiac language provided the perfect mental lexicon and was symbolized by the tree of knowledge. In this scheme, 'The Fall marks the birth of the human word' – the word becomes a byproduct of the loss of innocence.

Ancient Indian tradition, of course, was pre-eminently oral; and the languages of both the elite, Sanskrit, and of the masses, Prakrit, were ritually transmitted by word of mouth down the generations. The written form was disincentivized, considered infra dig, and seen as resorted to by those who did not have it in them to memorize and remember. There was a sophisticated approach to the spoken word, distinguishing it in terms of *dhvani* (word) and *sabda* (sound), and phonetic speech was considered superior to the non-phonetic. Writing was seen as polluting and ritualistically tabooed in certain contexts. The Vedic text *Aitareya Aranyaka* stipulates that 'a pupil should not recite the Veda after eating meat, seeing blood or a dead body, having intercourse, or engaging in writing'.

Well until the 1970s, historians considered the oral source and resource, drawing on a bank of memory, suspect categories for their study and research. Early in that decade, the socialist and social historian Paul Richard Thompson sought to cut through this mindset by setting up the British Oral History Society; in 1978 he published *The Voice of the Past: Oral History*, which not only treated the remembered life and experiences of the community as valid historical information, but also, in the process, was able to direct attention to silent and hidden or suppressed areas of history, like the condition of women or of the working class. Paul Thompson initiated a new approach to history which, as he described it,

> allows heroes not just from the leaders but from the unknown majority of the people. It brings history into, and out of, the community. It helps the less privileged, and especially the old, towards dignity and self-confidence. It makes for contact – and thence understanding – between social classes and between generations.

That characterization of oral history may well also fit the hubbub now obtaining in the new media online, which has an oral impulse both in terms of its freewheeling spokenness, and in its drawing on the opinions and experiences of a teeming cross-section of society. It is an oral multi-sited discourse that adapts to the technology which enables or 'pushes' it – whether on Twitter, Facebook, SMS, blog, or any of the many chat-and-interact fora in the digital social media. It is more than and beyond the formal mainstream news media, more than 'a nation talking to itself' as Arthur Miller described a good newspaper; it is more like a people discovering their social voice and themselves producing the information that sets the agenda for their lives, for their times. Variants of an autodidactic language suited to the requirements of the particular digital device or software quickly take hold and effect, and become accepted jargon for all participants in that space.

This is a continuous process, keeping pace with technological innovation on the one hand, and seeking to cope with technological obsolescence on the other. Indeed information has to be deconstructed to fit the new bill. Shunya Yoshimi, Professor of Cultural and Media Studies at Tokyo University, returns to the basic meaning of the term information, as 'the process of giving form to something' (cited in the recent work *New Media: The Key Concepts* by Nicholas Gane and David Beer). Physicist Hans von Baeyer (in his *Information: The New Language of Science*) elaborates on this idea of information, and says it is 'infusion of form on some previously unformed entity, just as de-, con-, trans-, and re-formation refer to the undoing, copying, changing and renewing of forms. Information refers to moulding or shaping a formless heap – imposing a form on to something'. Information, therefore, conclude Gane and Beer, is always *in-formation* on the new media. It is not surprising that the language of such information comprises a good proportion of neologisms, mostly with an oral inflection.

There is a frontline activity of mutating language and expression to match the emergent digital culture and technology of the new media. On the other hand, the written text and the writerly mode continue to exert a strong vestigial influence on television and cinema screens. At least in India, we have still not evolved a spoken tongue for television. News presentations, as much as dialogues of serials, on our television continue to be text-heavy and read, rather than spoken.

In our typical box-office cinema, punchy message-suffused stretches of stilted dialogue evoke the virtual looming presence of the written script. The oral and the aural, even in these modern media, have by and large been literary, even if vocalized, representations of the written word. At the same time, there are bursts of creative digital energy that are manifest as new-generation cinema, or showcased on the numerous sites and offerings online as text, sight and sound, which indicate a new confidence and assertiveness, and come across as first-person presentation rather than representation. These forces, various and uneven, are moreover moving rapidly from the margins to the centre.

First published in *Frontline*, 1 November 2013.

Codes and Tropes of Silence

It may be that, to borrow the words of Thomas Paine in *Common Sense*, 'a long habit of not thinking a thing wrong gives it a superficial appearance of being right.' Or, it may be a considered but unstated decision in which most news media are complicit. There is a sense of the fourth estate fraternity being bonded as thick as thieves and bound by a code of *omerta* about one another's failings, particularly in India. It may appear to be a matter of professional propriety or social grace for one newspaper or television channel not to comment adversely on the performance of another. But for a calling whose lodestar is the public interest, and where even not so legitimate means like the hidden recorder or camera or other intrusive methods of 'sting' journalism are absolved or pass muster in the name of the larger public good, this pretence of not noticing the sins of omission and commission in its own ranks smacks of hypocrisy. This is a type of self-regulation the news media can do without, because it is self-serving and goes against their vaunted cause of ensuring transparency, and informing and empowering society. It is not the making of a common cause; it is the masking of a common minimum programme whose sole purpose seems to be to protect themselves against, to get away with, their own ineptitude. In fact, often, commercial advertisements in the same media come across as more honest, as when a toothpaste or detergent brand debunks competing brands by portraying them as etiolated, drab and ineffective, and sets itself up as a class apart with a unique selling proposition. There is a forthrightness about that fiction, about that sales pitch.

Television news channels, on the other hand, routinely make a joke of the idea of 'Live and Exclusive' in their mutual one-upmanship. Surfing channels, you find the same bit of news or the same person speaking at the same time on more than one of them, sometimes on every one of them, with the legend 'Live' or 'Exclusive' boldly supered on the screen. Any child can of course see that what appears simultaneously on different channels can be neither 'live' nor 'exclusive' to any one of them.

The pack mentality of the media watchdogs, then, makes for a double whammy. It holds no one in the pack to account for excesses or lapses; when the media won't talk about their own faults, who or what else will, and how else will they be addressed? And, it drives them to make wrong or tall claims of exclusivity and instantaneity as each channel seeks to pip the other in the ratings game. The net result is that you begin to take the credibility of such media with a pinch of salt. On the other hand, it behooves a self-confident and conscientious news media to lay themselves open to criticism just as much as, and in the same spirit as, they criticize all and sundry around them. A regular print column or television slot dedicated to such intra-media appraisal and self-audit, to monitor how the media are acquitting themselves at the bar of public accountability, would surely be a part of best practices in the profession.

There is of course the risk that envy and meanness, and narrow business rivalry or misplaced notions about the role of the media in a democracy, rather than any sense of a larger moral or professional obligation to the public, may prompt such media-watch activism by the media themselves. But even when it is pernicious the result could be salutary, as the recent high-visibility spat between *The Guardian* and *Daily Mail* in the United Kingdom illustrates.

It began with a rather gratuitous, if predictably right-wing, attack in *Daily Mail* of the Labour leaders David and Ed Miliband's father and well-known Marxist, Ralph Miliband, in an article headlined 'The Man who hated Britain'. In the seething aftermath of its publication, when the *Mail* found itself under fire from various quarters, including *The Guardian* and, in what seemed to irk it more, the BBC, the paper opened a new front against *Guardian* with an editorial comment titled (much like that on the hatchet job on Ralph Milband) 'The paper that helps Britain's enemies'. The *Mail* seized on a comment by the new chief of MI5, the British spy agency, that publication by *The Guardian* of the Edward Snowden disclosures on indiscriminate and mass spying by the National Security Agency (NSA) in the US and its counterpart, the Government Communications Headquarters (GCHQ) in the UK, was like gifting terrorists the means 'to evade us and strike us at will'.

The editorial 'argued that a line needs to be drawn between the civil liberties we treasure and the interests of national security', and held that '*The Guardian*, with lethal irresponsibility, had crossed that line'. It sounded incredulous that *The Guardian*'s editor, Alan Rusbridger, could, despite the MI5 chief's warning, insist that he would continue to release the Snowden material and that he would make sure that nothing that imperilled lives would be published. 'But how in the name of sanity,' it expostulated, 'can he know. He is a journalist, not an expert on security.'

It went on to contrast *The Guardian* with even Ralph Miliband who, although 'he hated so much about this country that he wanted a workers' revolution to overturn everything from the monarchy to Parliament, property rights and the common law', 'never once' gave 'practical help to our enemies'; and, delivering the final punch, it asked, 'Isn't that a great deal more than can be said for *The Guardian*?'

The Guardian struck back, calling the *Mail* editorial 'a statement of anti-journalism: editors, it says, cannot be trusted. They must defer to the State'; and referred it to some thirty-two top-notch editors in the world for their opinion. Their responses, read together, could well be a manifesto for journalism in our troubled times. They eloquently weigh in for the rights of the free press over fears about national security; in fact, they forcefully argue that the less free the media, the less secure that state. These are views and voices wrought by conviction and experience, and constitute a bold guideline for the journalist at the receiving end of the machinations and obfuscations of the state.

'A public debate', says Jill Abramson, executive editor of *The New York Times*, in her response, 'about the proper perimeters for eavesdropping by intelligence agencies is healthy for the public and necessary.' Its former executive editor, Max Frankel, is even more explicit and scholarly:

> There is a superficial appeal in the argument that intelligence 'professionals' know better than editors what information must be suppressed, even if it has already escaped their control. Particularly at this time of terror, much of the public is impressed by that argument and so are American attorneys and judges, causing David Rudenstine of Cardozo Law School to name this the 'age of deference'. . . . Arrogant though it sounds, the fact is that experienced editors and correspondents who deal daily in the subject matter of 'national security' know better than most judges and prosecutors whether a given piece of information could seriously threaten lives or damage national defence.

The editor-in-chief of *Der Spiegel*, Wolfgang Buechner, notes that 'it is a classic approach for governments to attack media that have the courage to publish such stories with arguments that they threaten national security or that they are supporting an enemy of the state'. He goes on to point out that 'exposing the intensity with which intelligence agencies conduct surveillance on the Internet does not provide proof that such reporting in any way assists terrorists'.

The editorial director of *Le Monde*, Sylvie Kauffmann, sees it in terms of each to its own with a linking role for the media: 'The heads of intelligence services are entitled to voice their concern at the extent of the leaks, as ordinary citizens are entitled to ask what use is made, by whom and to what purpose, of private data collected from their daily life activities. Editors of media organizations are central to this debate.'

The director of the Spanish paper *El País*, Javier Moreno, finds it 'sad, baffling and dangerous . . . that attacks now come not only from governments but from other newspapers too'. 'Newspapers', he observes, 'have many duties. Having to protect governments and the powerful from embarrassing situations is not among them.'

The publisher of the German daily *Frankfurter Allgemeine Zeitung*, Frank Schirrmacher, sees the Snowden phenomenon as a 'milestone' marking the 'transition to a post-industrial society' that the German intellectual Hans Magnus

Enzensberger spoke about. The Snowden 'revelations are not only about secret services, but just as much about all the new social touch points of every citizen who is equipped with a smartphone and online access'. The editor-in-chief of the Italian newspaper *La Repubblica*, puts it in historical context:

> From the *Washington Post* with the Watergate case to *The New York Times* with the Pentagon Papers, the history of journalism is full of revelations that, according to the people in power, should have been kept secret, but later it has become clear that to publish them was a service to democracy, not a 'lethally irresponsible' act.

The executive editor of *The Washington Post*, Martin Baron, reminds us that 'a highly intrusive surveillance apparatus has been built without public knowledge and debate', and that 'there would have been no public debate had there been no disclosure'. The editor-in-chief of Norway's largest circulating daily *Aftenposten*, Hilde Haugsgjerd, states pithily: 'Truths are at times inconvenient, but inconvenient truths are at times of the highest importance.'

The editor-in-chief of the Swedish *Dagens Nyheter*, Peter Wolodarski, declares that 'the attacks against *The Guardian* by both the government and the representatives of the British press are unacceptable', while the former editor-in-chief of *The Hindu*, N. Ram, rubbishes as 'the worst kind of intellectual philistinism' the notion that 'editors of newspapers, not being experts on security matters, are unfit to make decisions on publishing confidential material and must leave the whole field of surveillance and security to the state to handle as it thinks fit, under an impenetrable veil of secrecy'.

The director of *Fairfax Media*, Garry Linnell, is biting in his sarcasm:

> Hell, let's not ask questions at all. Let's not scrutinize those with the power and ability to carry out widespread surveillance on their own citizens. Let's keep the public in the dark, rather than serving their right to know. And when the state acts unlawfully, let us look the other way. Then we will truly have the society our enemies wish upon us.

Editor after editor strikes, in this vein, a defiant tone against the aggrandizing role of the state in using the alibi of public safety and national security to justify secretive mass surveillance, and against the state's attempt to keep journalism's reach short of investigating the breaches it has made into the individual's right of privacy. Interestingly, that right, codified by Justices Louis Brandeis and Samuel Warren of the US Supreme Court in 1890 as the 'right to be left alone', was initially meant against the intrusions of what they called a 'too enterprising press, the photographer, or the possessor of any other modern device for recording or reproducing scenes or sounds'. The same press is now fighting for the people's right to be left alone by the state. Or rather, the press is, for good part, buttressing and carrying forward the act of defiance of the whistleblower.

The whistleblower as the supra-journalist is really personified in Snowden.

His understanding of and commitment to the core democratic values of individual freedom and privacy are not a whit less than that of the news media's high priests. Nor is his articulation of his faith in these values any less eloquent. Sample this from Snowden in his latest interview, in Moscow, with *The New York Times*:

> So long as there's broad support amongst a people it can be argued there's a level of legitimacy even to the most invasive or morally wrong programme, as it was an informed and willing decision. However programmes that are implemented in secret, out of public oversight, lack that legitimacy, and that's a problem. It also represents a dangerous normalization of 'governing in the dark', where decisions with enormous public impact occur without any public input.

The operative phrase here, 'governing in the dark', harks back to the eighteenth-century Benthamite concept of Panopticism which Michel Foucault analyses at length in his *Discipline and Punish: The Birth of the Prison*. Jeremy Bentham's 'Panopticon' proposes an architecture of perfect surveillance with a circular construction of rooms facing a central tower, from which all inmates would be observable day in and out. It was a construct, as Foucault interprets it, for a disciplined society in which power would be 'visible and unverifiable': 'Visible: the inmate will constantly have before his eyes the tall outline of the central tower from which he is spied upon. Unverifiable: the inmate must never know whether he is being looked at at any one moment; but he must be sure that he may always be so.'

'In order to be exercised,' Foucault elaborates,

> this power had to be given the instrument of permanent, exhaustive, omnipresent surveillance, capable of making all visible, as long as it could itself remain invisible. It had to be like a faceless gaze that transformed the whole social body into a field of perception: thousands of eyes posted everywhere, mobile attentions ever on the alert. . . . And this unceasing observation had to be accumulated in a series of reports and registers . . . a permanent account of individuals' behaviour.

This could as well be an account of the contemporary surveillance state. Except that the Benthamite model had a redeeming feature of accountability. For anyone could come to the 'central tower' and

> see with his own eyes how the schools, hospitals, factories, prisons function. . . . There is no risk, therefore, that the increase of power created by the panoptic machine may degenerate into tyranny; the disciplinary mechanism will be democratically controlled, since it will be constantly accessible 'to the great tribunal committee of the world'. This Panopticon, subtly arranged so that any observer may observe, at a glance, so many different individuals, also enables everyone to come and observe any of the observers. The seeing machine was once a sort of dark room

> into which individuals spied; it has become a transparent building in which the exercise of power may be supervised by society as a whole.

It is such public oversight that the current system of 'governing in the dark' dispenses with and the dark side of the state resists, by trying to keep the entire process of the blanket surveillance under wraps and beyond the reach of an enquiring media.

First published in *Frontline*, 15 November 2013.

Know Thy News

There is a peculiar effect familiar to us through the movies, of falling, and falling, in slow motion – motion slow enough to re-render your entire life in flashes of images, and even hint at what could have been. A new book on journalism evokes a somewhat similar sensation. At a time when at least the print part of the news media, at least in the west, is in free fall, and there is all-round despair about the future of journalism, Thomas Patterson's *Informing the News* recapitulates, in a series of swift discernments, the fatal flaws of the discipline and postulates how it ought to reinvent itself to continue to be relevant. The central revelation is that seeking knowledge and truth, rather than merely purveying fact and information, can make a world of difference, a paradigm change, to the practice of journalism, and resynchronize it to the demands of our contexts and times.

But then we had always assumed that fact rather than truth was the remit of journalism. Truth was evasive even for the most dogged historian and belonged, if at all, to the intuitive or epiphanic grasp of the poet. 'Poetry', as Plato put it, 'comes closer to vital truth than history.' That is, if we admit to truth being more than a chimera. In the Nietzschean way of the world, 'the history of truth is the history of the longest lasting falsehood'. Even Walter Lippmann, who along with Marshall McLuhan made the most meaning of the communication era initiated by the United States, and who is profusely quoted throughout Patterson's work, had warned that 'News and truth are not the same thing, and must be clearly distinguished.'

The truth Patterson grandly characterizes as 'the holy grail of journalism' is actually far removed from such epistemological concerns, and is a practical, limited exercise. It emerges, as he describes it, from the work in the late 1990s of the Committee of Concerned Journalists established in the US by Bill Kovach and Tom Rosenstiel (of *The Elements of Journalism* fame), which set about to try and arrest the perceived declining standards in journalism, and held wide-ranging discussions and public deliberations over two years to arrive at a 'Statement of Shared Principles' which adapted truth to journalism's purpose. '"Journalistic truth"', read the statement,

> is a process that begins with the professional discipline of assembling and verifying

> facts. Then journalists try to convey a fair and reliable account of their meaning, valid for now, subject to further investigation. Journalists should be as transparent as possible about sources and methods so audiences can make their own assessment of the information. Even in a world of expanding voices, accuracy is the foundation upon which everything else is built – context, interpretation, comment, criticism, analysis and debate. The truth, over time, emerges from this forum.

There may be a bit of the American versus the rest (particularly European) in this approach to a philosophical category like truth. It is not so much a universal, objective ideal to be striven for; it is rather a journalistic value constantly honed by, as Kovach and Rosenstiel put it, 'first stripping information of any misinformation, disinformation, or self-promoting bias and then letting the community react.' This is a construct of truth as a work in progress. It is not a function of facts alone, for as Patterson points out, 'a story can be accurate in its particulars – what was said, when and where it happened, who witnessed it, and so on – and yet falter as a whole. Even if the facts check out, a story would not be true for that reason alone.' He goes on to ask, by way of illustrating this point, whether American journalism has provided the US public a true indication of what the Islamic world thought of the US in the period after 11 September, or reflected the spike in anti-Americanism in parts of the Muslim world following the elimination of Osama bin Laden.

All this is only too obvious. Patterson's book is of little help in suggesting a way around journalism's dabble and babble with facts, a way to cut through the clutter of facts to arrive at the 'truth', even if as a modified or diminished idea tailored for journalism by the Committee of Concerned Journalists. If truth be told, we find ourselves concluding, journalism has really little to do with truth, and if we thought Patterson was about to change all that with this book, we were mistaken. Having put us on the scent of truth as something distinct from fact, he seems to then use the two terms interchangeably, so that we wonder what the fuss about mistaking fact for truth was, in the first place.

He interrogates somewhat more successfully the dubious role of objectivity in journalism. Historically, objective journalism came as a corrective to the rampant practice of yellow journalism at the turn of the twentieth century. The principle of insulating news from advertisement and opinion became a means of ensuring its objectivity. It meant going beyond one's subjectivity to seek out the other, opposing point of view. In actual practice, though, this often lapsed into a fetish for balance, and the book cites the senior literary journalist Joan Didion's characterization of such balance as 'a scrupulous passivity, an agreement to cover the story not as it is occurring, but as it is presented'. This led to a tame, play-safe, 'he said, she said' type of journalism. And yet a Carnegie Corporation Report of 2006 deplores that 'diminished objectivity' along with 'drive for profit' and 'spread of the "entertainment virus"' are driving the profession into decline.

Objectivity continues to be touted as a notional journalistic virtue, although in practice it becomes an exercise in what journalist James Fallows calls 'false equivalencies', or what is downright subjective masquerading as – and being legitimized as – objective.

Patterson seems to be on surer ground when he makes the case for 'knowledge' providing a new impetus and character to journalism. 'Journalism,' he notes, 'is not grounded in a systematic body of substantive knowledge that would protect its practitioners' autonomy and inform their judgment.' This is unlike other professions, such as medicine, law, the sciences and so on, where adequate domain knowledge is a prerequisite for practice. As a consequence,

> journalists are often in the thankless position of knowing less about the subject at hand than the newsmakers they are covering, a reversal of the typical situation, in which the professional practitioner is the more knowledgeable party. Only rarely do clients know more about the law than do their attorneys whereas newsmakers know more about the issue at hand than the journalists covering them. During the Persian Gulf War, journalists who visited the Pentagon press office were greeted with a sign that read, 'Welcome Temporary War Experts'.

That, on the face of it, would seem to make it an impossibly unequal relationship for the journalist who shifts from subject to subject, based not necessarily on his own subject expertise but on the subject's news value at a given time. As Patterson points out, 'Journalism is not a tidy discipline, nor are its subjects narrowly defined. It is one thing to explain the economy, which is difficult enough, and another thing to explain nearly the whole of public life.' But he is unclear about how exactly journalism out there can become more knowledgeable, except to throw broad hints at the vast resources offered up by the internet to the journalist much like to anyone else, including the citizen journalist.

Even here Patterson makes a distinction between 'the injection of knowledge into news stories' that the internet can help in, and the 'application of knowledge to reporting' which, he says (citing Cambridge University scientist W.I.B. Beveridge),

> enables the investigator to recognize things that would otherwise be misunderstood or go unnoticed. Knowledge can enable reporters to recognize whether they are on the right track with their explanations; whether they are keeping things in proportion; whether they are weighing plausible alternatives; whether they are avoiding attribution errors; whether they are fending off source fabrications; whether they are on target with their trend analyses and comparisons; and whether they are challenging their taken-for-granted assumptions.

As we continue to be in the dark about where and how the journalist acquires such knowledge, Patterson is convinced that 'the world of knowledge and the world of the newsroom are closer together today than ever before'. There is a sense of a departure from the well-worn understanding of the journalist as a hack, his work as inferior journalese and his intellectual ken as dilettantist.

In the later part of the book we realize that this knowledge-track Patterson paves for journalism begins in journalism school and not in the newsroom, and may not really easily accommodate the mid-career journalist already in the race, unless of course he is (as journalists often are) an autodidact on the job or a subject specialist who has chosen to become a hack. The J-school becomes the nodal agency, in Patterson's scheme (even if by default, because he does not point to any other as definitively), which can imbue journalism with the broad reflective knowledge that makes for greater depth of reporting, and generally for a more thinking and thought-encouraging professional practice.

Although, even at the turn of the last century, Joseph Pulitzer saw journalism as an intellectual profession and founded the Columbia School of Journalism to, in his words, 'elevate and educate in a practical way the . . . members of that profession, exactly as if it were the profession of law or medicine', the J-school has for long been the butt of ridicule, particularly among hard-nosed, self-made journalists. Patterson tells us about a cartoon commonly seen on the walls of newspaper offices through the first half of the twentieth century, which depicts an editor asking a candidate appearing for a job: 'And what, may I ask, is a school of journalism?' When, in 1935, Columbia University reduced the duration of its journalism programme from two years to one, the *New York Daily News* commented that it was a 'step in the right direction' and added gleefully that 'it was still a year too long'.

We have our own version of how the industry viewed university courses such as communications studies (which were supposed to prepare one for a career in journalism) in the anecdote, probably apocryphal, of a former editor of *The Hindu* assuring a job applicant proffering his communications degree certificate as proof of his capability, 'We won't hold it against you.' If the J-school with a curriculum focussed on journalism is relatively new in India and the earlier courses on communication had little to do with journalism, the pedagogic issue in American J-schools is whether and how to combine training in core skill sets, which makes one adept at handling the tools of journalism, with knowledge-induced education that broadens one's intellectual horizons.

We had first-hand experience of this academic tension between garnering knowledge in the broader sense and acquiring the specific journalistic skills when, at the turn of this century, three of us involved with setting up the Asian College of Journalism (ACJ) – senior editor and journalist N. Ram, economist and writer C.P. Chandrasekhar and I – visited, among others, the Columbia J-school and the Journalism Department at New York University (NYU), to learn about their respective programmes. The then Chair of the Journalism Department in NYU, Mitchell Stephens (who also figures fairly prominently in Patterson's book), told us about how his programme tended to give weightage and preference to the reflective knowledge aspect over skills-training. At Columbia, Dean Tom Goldstein spoke about his course being more hands-on and skills-driven. Both of them seemed to feel that their course content could have a bit more of the other – more training for skill sets in the case of NYU's journalism programme, and more in terms of education for knowledge enhancement in the case of the Columbia J-school. It was for us a timely input, so that when we designed the curriculum of the ACJ, we were able to keep the need for a judicious mix of the two in mind, and get it more or less right – way ahead, as it turns out, of many universities with journalism programmes in the west.

It was not until three or four years later that the need for a better infusion of the knowledge aspect into the journalism course at Columbia University was flagged by its president, Lee Bollinger, who set up a task force to look ahead at 'how journalism education in a great university can contribute to the process by which the media adapt to a new world'. The ensuing discussion and debate largely revolved around the skills-versus-knowledge axis, and was informed by Bollinger's realization that 'one of the most significant needs for journalists today is to have a high level of knowledge about the subject they are reporting and communicating'. The fact that well over a decade later, in his work published this year, Thomas Patterson continues to discuss the need for better integration of knowledge and skills in US journalism education indicates that the issue has not quite been settled.

What is surprising, however, is that the objective conditions today seem to be working against lowering of standards to the least common denominator, and actually favouring a qualitative improvement and sophistication as against quantitative mass-sell of journalism. Patterson cites a study correlating audience rating and news content by the Project for Excellence in Journalism spread over five years and covering 154 local TV stations in the US, which showed that the longer and more in-depth a story, the better the viewership rating; that newscasts with fewer but longer and well-treated stories were rated better than those with far more but shorter stories.

A more recent study this year by the same organization points to the higher economic brackets ceasing to watch or read news when there is a decline in quality. The market, it seems, churns and segments and remobilizes to resist and reverse the dumb-down-to-conquer rule.

So maybe, just maybe, we could, as cinematically as we began, end or break the fall by breaking out of it, to discover that it was after all a dream. A new journalism of knowledge hopefully awaits us somewhere in the future.

First published in *Frontline*, 13 December 2013.

The Rape Reality Check

Irrespective of what the law, when it has taken its course, may or may not do to him, what Tarun Tejpal did was downright despicable. His preemptive half-baked admission – a self-serving attempt at cover-up premised on the fatuous calculation that a show of contrition will fetch forgiveness and a quiet burial of the whole affair – does not, any more than evocations in his favour of his purported role in building the *Tehelka* brand and its trademark, if indiscriminate, sting and sting-type journalism, or his creative literary achievements, in any way diminish the moral enormity of his crime. He has, on the face of it, misused and abused his authority and power as an employer, cheated a friend, betrayed the trust of an unsuspecting and believing employee. His idea of 'recusing' himself from the editorship of his publication – for six whole months! – as penance for having attempted twice to force himself sexually on the woman to whom he was, more than a boss, a father figure, would be laughable were it not so pathetic.

Recuse – what a grandiose, self-important term of abnegation after such a lowly act. We normally hear the word used by and of judges who loftily opt out of a case for the reason that they know one of the parties to it or that there may be a conflict of interest. 'Lapse of judgment' and 'misreading of (the) situation' were among the other semantic proxies Tejpal thought up to give what would be, legally and with all the bullshit cut out, attempted rape, a more graceful construct. Such deployment of language to bail himself out of a fix of his own doing has been characteristic of the man in this case and, whether tutored or off her own bat, of his lieutenant Shoma Chaudhury, the managing editor of *Tehelka*, holding the fort, or should one say the beleaguered pass, for him against the media assault that followed – that is, before and until she realized the futility of her exertions and decided to put in her papers instead.

It took a while before Tejpal, perhaps, began to realize that he could not strut his way out of a situation like this. That it does not do to speak as if from another moral universe. That the ethical brinkmanship he brought to investigative journalism by making sting and honeytrap its stock-in-trade does not lend itself to personal professional relationships. He once explained away the use of sex workers to get army officers to boast, on hidden cameras, about corrupt arms deals as 'jumping the red light while chasing the murderer'. True, means such as these passed muster because they exposed sleaze and racketeering in public life and were seen as serving a larger public good, even if, in the process, intrusive hidden cameras became reductively synonymous with investigative journalism.

But this was a red light he should have heeded. He did not. He tried instead to reimagine, *post facto*, the signal as green, to reconfigure his act of sexual molestation as consensual sex. Shoma Chaudhury gave it credence by dropping hints of another version, and the duo followed this up with further innuendoes. Why was the woman continuing to party after her ordeal? Why did she get into the lift a second time with her molester? That she continued to attend to her work of looking after the partying VIPs at the 'Thinkfest' jamboree with all the dignity she could muster in the circumstances – which must have been as trying as it was admirable – now goes against her. All in all, the shamefulness of the offence was compounded by the shamelessness of the attempt to whitewash it by vilifying the victim. Another, equally reprehensible tack was to try and create a smokescreen of political conspiracy in the hope that an ensuing slugfest between the Bharatiya Janata Party and the Congress would distract attention from the 'Thinkfest' crime.

The media dived headlong into the story. There was good reason, in this instance, if the coverage looked like a trial. After all, the man who had started out on the promise of unleashing an alternative journalism had ended up tainting himself and, by extension and to an extent, the fair name of journalism itself. At the least, it was now apparent that women working in the news media were as prone to sexual exploitation as in any other profession or sector of the economy, but their plight hardly ever made it to the news because that would require proactive confessional reportage practice by the media of the media. The media fraternity reacted forcefully with righteous indignation at this vicarious slight by not cutting Tejpal any slack, even if old resentment, enmity or envy against the *Tehelka* brand of journalism or its progenitor may also have played a part in some of the stridency in the chorus of denunciation that followed. Even so, the fierceness of the onslaught, especially on television, and the bandwagon effect it generated may, at the margins, have evoked a counter-underdog ripple effect in Tejpal's favour.

This often happens on television these days, particularly when an anchor on a news channel hounds a subject with single-mindedness, brooks no oppositional voice, shouts down doubting Thomases, sidesteps all counsel of caution, and bears down on him in such unrelenting prosecutorial mode that the man at the receiving end, although we know him to be a thorough blackguard or villain, instead of being confirmed in our mind as one, actually begins to earn our unintended sympathy. It was good that Tejpal was arrested when he was. The media could not have kept it up much longer without beginning to become counterproductive. Already, reporters of channels who had rushed to Goa to cover the proceedings of Tejpal's anticipatory bail plea had been reduced to mouthing incoherent inanities because the hearing dragged on longer than they expected, and they had run out of things to say, but the channels would not take their eye off the ball. However you try to hype it up, the effect of a camera eye on a ball that is stationary for hours on end can be desperately wearying.

Then there was the matter of whether what is sauce for the social media is sauce for the mainstream news media. The full text of the victim's letter to the managing editor of *Tehelka*, Shoma Chaudhury, had already gone viral on the internet and the social media, and some newspapers too published it verbatim (what fidelity to source!) in all its graphic detail. It was as necessary for the victim to record such factual detail in her letter registering her complaint, as it was obligatory on the part of the media to respect its confidential nature and refrain from publicizing it.

Disclosing the contents of the letter was repugnant to the Sexual Harassment Act, 2013. Yet discussions in the formal media, again primarily on television, were informed by the disclosures circulating in the non-formal media. Television panellists assumed in one another, access to such information on the internet. It looked like they came equipped with information from cyber and social media to argue, among other things, against the same information being made public. That paradox apart, there were even reports of the victim's identity being disclosed in the social media. The judge hearing the arguments on the anticipatory bail application in Goa had to pull up the defence counsel for mentioning her name.

On the other hand, the incentive for a sustained news angle, to keep it alive in the public eye, to build up and keep the pressure for action on the system, may lie, much like the devil, in the detail – at least detail enough to drive the story beyond a simple allegation on the one part, and clinical refutation on the other. This operative need for detail is of course very different from the kind that feeds the prurient interest or voyeurism in sections of the public, and must not in any way tread on the dignity and sensitivity of the victim.

The 16 December 2012 rape case in Delhi became as defining as it did in part because of its shocking nature, its sheer sickening barbarity that challenged human imagination. Who or what process should decide the extent of detail available and allowable to the media, while reconciling a wholesome public interest with the need to protect the integrity and dignity of the victim, seems the crux of the issue. Where the victim herself is in a position to take that call, it becomes that much simpler. For the better part, though, victims of rape come from already disadvantaged and vulnerable backgrounds, and an agency becomes imperative in determining how much is legitimate for media consumption in the fair cause of the case, in a manner that is, at the same time, scrupulously fair to the victimized.

A grey area that emerges in the media discourse of the case is the role of another agency – that of the concerned woman's informed discretion and decision to seek and apply closure through means short of the criminal justice system in force. Such agency perhaps also implies a shift in emphasis from crime and punishment to crime and justice. But there seem legitimate doubts about the extent to which agency can second-guess the law of the land; about whether it can become a front for persuasion or pressure on the victim not to file a police complaint; or whether the internal committee or mechanism in an organization set up in compliance with the Vishaka guidelines of the Supreme Court will tend to play safe and prefer the automatic route of a police complaint, lest it be seen as found wanting in its response.

These and other related aspects of sexual crimes against women are likely to increasingly occupy media mind space as women step out of the stigmatized victim stereotype and, instead, stigmatize and shame the offender. Another case, relating to charges made by a former law intern against a former judge of the Supreme Court and currently chairman of the West Bengal Human Rights Commission, Justice A.K. Ganguly, is already on the boil. The media for its part needs to do better than to take up the refrain of rape for its sensationalist impact. They need to calibrate their response to allow for the sensitivities and nuances, the implications and precedents likely to be set as each case unfolds.

First published in *Frontline*, 27 December 2013.

A Potted History of National Television

Once upon a time, when it was still a good word, 'development' was Indian television's single most important agenda. An experiment in the 1970s, called the Satellite Instructional Television Experiment (SITE), had shown the way. The medium became the developmental message. Television screens warmed to the evangelical glow of this mission. They harped on the 20-point programme until it became second nature to bureaucrats and programmers as much in the media as in the government – whether it made any sense or difference to the people themselves did not seem to matter. Then, they introduced us to a young and modern and computer-savvy Prime Minister as he set out, post an aerial career that had kept him removed from the ground realities, to engage with earthy politics. Television cameras were dutifully at hand as he strode, retinue of ministers and officials in tow, into the heat and dust of villages, spreading his readymade brand of development. They recorded, with watchful eyes, every ribbon cut by every minister to inaugurate a scheme, site, road, bridge or building or anything that added to the development euphoria. It was all about ministers and their ministrations, of course, in the public cause. By the end of it, there was development coming out of television's and its viewers' ears, and the term became one of sufferance in the media.

Those, unlike now, were days of orderly television conduct, because those were times when television was owned solely by the government. There were clearly established procedures both on and off screen. In an interview the answer was normally longer than the question, which was a good thing. Sometimes, especially when ministers or VIPs were the guests, the answer was so long that there was no time for another question, or so final that there was no question of another question, or a question was framed to suit the answer they had come prepared with – which was not such a good thing because it looked like crony television (this was before the emergence of the crony capitalists whom the media picks on these days). Off and behind the screen, there were forms to be filled for everything. If a news producer got word that a fire had broken out somewhere, he proceeded to fill out a requisition form for the camera and the vehicle, and with some alacrity, lest the blaze died out before the unit arrived on the scene.

The young and modern Prime Minister also decided to mend some of television's set ways. Studiously avoiding taking sides on religion, for instance. He had by now become politically astute enough to realize that Hindus, the vast majority in the country, could not just be left at the mercy of the Bharatiya Janata Party (BJP). The Congress had to cultivate them as a religious denomination. He approached a well-known Bollywood producer and asked him to come up with a megaserial for television on the *Ramayana*. There were at least three hundred *Ramayana*s the producer could choose from. He did a cardboard cut-out fusion of the Valmiki narrative and Tulsidas's *Ramcharitmanas*. Some scholars say the Tulsidas version of the epic was influenced by the perceived threat of a Muslim invasion in the sixteenth century. Be that as it may, the airing of the serial was a masterstroke of galvanizing Hindu eyeballs for Indian television. The screen became an object of ritual religious worship when the serial was on.

Since the screen was owned by the state, its worship, it was hoped, would translate into support for the government, and therefore for the party that ran it. But the people were probably more discriminating and secular than that, and gave unto television the things that were of television and to the state the things that were of the state. With the telecast, though, an Indian epic had been converted into a Hindu epic. The persona of Rama had been converted into an aggressive and aggrandizing icon in battle mode, about to unleash the arrow from his bow. The older, familiar, pacific calendar-art image of a benevolent Rama standing with Sita and Lakshmana on either side, and Hanuman kneeling at his feet seeking his blessings, had become passé. The young and modern Prime Minister may have unwittingly set in motion more than a new television-mediated, homogenized, pan-national Hindu religious consciousness. He may have provided the momentum that set the wheels of the BJP *rath yatra*s churning, leading to the destruction of the Babri Masjid in Ayodhya.

Meanwhile, in the 1990s, unbeknownst to this television of and for the government, independent channels, enabled by new technology, were stealing a march over it. In the era of liberalization and globalization, and under not-so-young Prime Ministers of the Congress, the BJP and again the Congress, television was swinging from the one extreme of the state to the other extreme of the market. Like 'development' earlier, it was the turn of another word, 'subsidy', to become the butt of ridicule on air. A sanctimonious corporate ethic began to infect the screen, and television anchors began to lecture those in power on the need for market-friendly good governance. Good journalism, they say, is about talking truth to power. Television journalism was talking forcefully to power all right. Whether it was the truth was unclear. Politicians and bureaucrats continued to dominate the proceedings on the screen, but this time around they normally figured as scamsters or as defenders of corruption. Television was striking back and the political class was at the receiving end.

The initial response by and large of television, particularly the English channels, to the coalition governments at the centre since 1998 and the miscegenation in politics, with regional parties rubbing shoulders with national parties, was one of middle-class standoffishness. It tended to caricature Lalu Prasad Yadav and Mayawati as rustics, and be impatient for neater and more sophisticated categories and configurations on the national scene. Not that these and other regional satraps were innocents from the hinterland caught in the bewildering city glare of the media. But the fodder and Taj corridor scams seemed to get disproportionately higher coverage than the slicker misappropriation and malfeasance of urbane politicians.

In the aftermath of the terrorist attack on Mumbai in 2008, 'politics' joined 'subsidy' as a dirty word on television. The security lapses that led to the attack were placed squarely at the door of the political establishment. The candlelight vigils following the attack were as much in sympathy for the victims as in anger against politicians. The anti-political-class rhetoric on television fed into this inimical sentiment on the street. A good section of the urban middle class seemed to turn its back on politics. A series of scams unravelling and kept in the limelight on television did not help the respectability of politics and politicians. A non-political, even anti-political, middle-class mind space had been created, and was rapidly expanding. Anna Hazare and his cohorts waded into this space.

In its coverage of the Anna Hazare movement, non-governmental television established a relationship of continuum with the street. The studio became, as much as the street, a locus of direct democracy. It showcased an assortment that accommodated a range of persuasions and types, from strands of socialists to picaresque heroes like Baba Ramdev – and spoke like, more than for, them. Its agency was agent provocateur-ish. On the other hand, the leaders of established political parties treated the movement with disdain. The then Chief Minister of Delhi advised the leaders of the movement to move into politics, fight elections and win, and not dictate from the street, if they wanted to change the system. She must have been supremely confident that there was no chance of this happening.

But an influential section in the movement took her advice, stepped out of the Hazare line and reinvented itself as the Aam Aadmi Party. The party was born out of the movement. If there was a midwife, it was television. It was a motley group with a common maximum programme against corruption. There were no ideological underpinnings or other such theoretical liabilities that tend to cramp the style of political parties. From anti-politics, it adapted quickly to politics. It explained to itself and to others that (much as it might have misled us into thinking so) politics was not a dirty word. It was the politician who was dirty and had to be cleansed. It was protean and open-ended. It could speak the language of the moment. Corruption loomed so large and was so in your face that it needed little else to recommend it to the people. Television has not let it out of its sight for a moment since its birth. Indeed if it had not gone out there and won an election, one would think it was part of a reality TV show.

First published in *Frontline*, 7 February 2014.

Essays on

CINEMA

1979–2014

The New Cinema: How Real?

As the nascent new cinema in India comes into its own, it tends to revel in its rebel image. This reputation seems extravagant, however, for it is essentially a broad conglomerate of films, diffused and indeterminate both in its choice and handling of formal content, and in its societal context. It is premature to characterize this type, with its many disparate approaches, as a 'genre' or 'wave' with any common term of reference. As a phenomenon, it approximates to the French experience of the early 1960s, aptly summed up in the coinage *nouvelle vague*. Functionally, too, this trend seems a mimesis of that precedent, especially in its solipsist obsession with the individual.

A highly personalized account of the individual with an accent on his volitional or emotional response (as hero or protagonist) to his existential predicament is, perhaps, meaningful and reflective of life in the French context, but when transposed to the Indian milieu it becomes unreal, even a self-indulgence on the part of the filmmaker. It was no doubt this that prompted the use of the epithet 'narcissists' for filmmakers of this cadre at a seminar on cinema during the International Film Festival at Delhi last month [January 1979]. And indeed the charge is not entirely baseless.

While the new cinema in our country makes a conscious bid to ascertain that it is not redundant, and steers carefully clear of the path trodden by its starkly escapist and abstracted commercial counterpart, it does not seem so concerned about its social relevance. It is this that ultimately qualifies and limits its role as rebel, and circumscribes its viewing to minority, even exclusive, audiences. It is this erraticism, again, which makes the commercial film industry look askance at this development as a prodigal variant, still seeking its bearings.

The distortion in perspective is largely the extension of a process of imitation in literature and the plastic arts, where much that is considered 'avant-garde' or '*outré*' is inspired by the reigning trends in Europe. Europe, historically and politically, is a poor prototype to model our mass media after. The hangover of the Second World War continues to linger on in European expressiveness, and is reflected in the keen sense of introspection and particularistic philosophy of its films. They are anthropocentric in a highly individualistic manner. The French, Italian or German films shown at the recent Film Festival were, for the most part, such pinpointed, isolated briefs on the tensions of personal adjustment in an affluent society.

The Eastern Bloc too, despite (or in reaction to) Soviet influence, conforms to this pattern – though to a lesser degree. Hungarian, Polish or Czechoslovakian films are equally preoccupied with the World War, and devote a great deal of attention to the individual in society. The incisive study made into adolescence in many of these films leads one to reasonably surmise that the phase is itself symptomatic of contemporary European life.

The Polish director Krzysztof Zanussi, whose films are typical in this regard, explained to me at the Festival the features of this peculiar European *gestalt*. There is, he observed, in European films, 'great interest now in values of human life, in questioning our personal choices and in examining our options.' War consciousness, he explained, had 'made our arts more hermetic, in the sense that they became not accessible to other cultures.' Zanussi's own response to the War is intimate, unlike that of the younger generation to whom it has no such immediate connotation: 'I always feel that I am lucky to live. They [the younger generation] think this has been granted to them. . . . As a child, I was bombed. . . . My parents had a miraculous escape.' Thus his creativity becomes a very personal act, fostered by a sense of the mystique of life. He is impelled by the logic of his historical situation to seek to come to terms with his context; this is sought to be achieved in his films by the employment of an alter-ego who articulates an intensely private experience. 'I make films,' says Zanussi, 'because I must make them. It is my inner imperative. I must express myself and this justifies my existence.'

Zanussi typifies, at a superlative level, the temperament of the European continent, in its cautious and measured response to life, and its probing search for cultural identity. These traits appear conservative when contrasted with the US experience of crass philistinism and explosive violence – facts which, when captured on the screen, seem to be the stranger perverse facets of that society. As great a filmmaker as Polanski, also from Poland, was so fascinated by this 'id' in the American psyche that he forsook his native moderation to marvel at its disturbing features. Zanussi himself has had considerable exposure to the US as a filmmaker, but has ably resisted the 'culture shock.' He is drawn, rather, to the verve and vigour of the American people, and their incorrigible optimism. But his European mind is quick to recognize that this optimism 'on the other side of the coin means naiveté.'

The contextualism which shapes the different approaches to serious cinema in Europe and the US becomes all the more significant in India, the peculiar situation and circumstance of which demand separate evaluative criteria. In its socio-cultural configuration India is structurally akin to the European model, but unlike Europe, it has had no traumatic crises to engender a cohesive *gestalt*. The common denominators, poverty and social inequality, which have become the *cause célèbre* of new cinema in India, are in fact normative elements long-persistent in the country's historical and social continuum, and as such, fail to evoke a widespread response when depicted as startling new facts in the screen. The fallacy and futility of ascribing to cinema the role of emotional integrator of the nation in the macrocosmic sense are implicit in the logic of its situation; any such integration must be derivative of the endo-cultural movement that films from various parts of the country would generate. Utpal Dutt's assertion at the Film Festival seminar, that 'only by the intensely regional can we be truly national', must be seen in this light – not as a narrow, chauvinist claim but as a plea for grassroots realism in cinema.

Indeed the term 'national cinema' when applied to India is a misnomer, what is commonly referred to as 'national' being basically area-oriented. Shyam Benegal's Hindi films (*Ankur*, *Nishant*, *Manthan*, *Bhumika* and, now, *Junoon*), for instance, though construed as national in their use of Hindi as the spoken language, actually demarcate definite areas and their cultures. In his effort to universalize his thematic settings, Benegal seems to have imbued his films with an ambivalence and lack of specificity that make them glaze over the social reality at a given place and time. Thus Benegal acquires the status of a 'transitional' filmmaker, trying to syncretize the novel and the conventional, and his films become equalized between the specific and the general.

It is impossible to draw any organic relationship between such films and human life, and it is an intriguing ponderable how they act on what Kracauer calls 'the collective unconscious of the people'; whether they only reinforce, by their comparative credibility, the superficial values of commercial cinema, or help the viewers take a new and purposeful look at social reality. Given the fact that a film acts on the viewer at both the conscious and subliminal levels, the hope that this category of transitional cinema can help prepare the masses for a socially real new cinema seems farfetched.

Thus new cinema becomes, in its aspiration for nativity and its penchant for social reality, synonymous with regional cinema, and the responsibility to hold up the mirror that reflects a true image of society devolves on the regional filmmaker. The regional ambience of this cinema has not, however, *ipso facto* made for its social integration as art form or mass media. This estrangement from the masses is due as much to the prejudiced sensibility of the latter (brought up on a staple diet of commercial cinema), as to the dilettantism and urban bias of the filmmaker himself in his treatment of his subject.

As consummate a craftsman as Satyajit Ray has been accused of 'exploiting' Indian poverty in his films; of embellishing it with lyrical, romantic overtones which abstract its stark and sordid reality. While a Ray film is a marvel of technical finesse and aesthetic flow, it does not seek to provoke a questioning process, or engender thinking on its social content and context; thus, almost thirty years after it first showed the way, *Pather Panchali* continues to bear an exclusive stamp. Considering that Ray is himself influenced by Jean Renoir in his tentativeness and passion for nature, his reluctance to come to grips with social reality seems imbibed. This lapse, in turn, has persisted in the younger generation of filmmakers, most of whom are after all votaries of what one critic recently satirized as 'neo-Raylism' in films.

Mrinal Sen (at least until recently) typifies a contrary paradox. His avowed intent of using film as a 'political pamphlet', which can awaken the consciousness of the masses and trigger off their latent indignation against social exploitation, is miscast in not-so-simple and sometimes highly involved, formal style. His *Chorus* or *Calcutta 71* can hardly evoke mass empathy, and one cannot help feeling that this has something to do with what Goldmann calls the 'social genesis of aesthetic structures'. Sen's latest films, *Oka Oorie Katha* (Telugu) and *Parashuram* (Bengali), are more definitely on *terra firma* in this respect. But his dual approach to film as an aesthete and a propagandist has tended to make his work rhapsodic, unreasoned in its didacticism and impatient in its hortatory tone.

In the south, which is today the crucible of new cinema in the country, the emergence of a new crop of filmmakers has made for a shift in emphasis, the perspective itself undergoing little change. Films continue to deal with marginal situations. They are rarely 'transindividual' in a context where the collective or the multitude is the impinging social reality. They tend to be socially and culturally revivalist rather than progressivist; they observe the social scene with an exotic urbane sensitivity that circumvents the actual or the real. The different treatments of libido in Kerala, or caste in Karnataka, are as interesting as so many ways of flogging a dead horse.

In Kerala, where the difference between commercial and new cinema has been more subtle than in other states, personal sex and violence in all their sado-masochistic manifestations initially became the forte of new cinema. It took little time for this trend to degenerate into voyeurism (with oblique psychological references thrown in to bilk the censors) and today, Freud is the Moloch of a frenetic-paced Malayalam film industry (which, with 123 films in 1978, is only next to Hindi in output). Faced with this counterfeitism of a trend to plumb the depths of human psychology (perhaps initiated in the 1960s by P. Bhaskaran's *Iruttinde Aatmaavu*), new filmmakers in Kerala have turned to other less inflammable themes, which, by their reactionary nature, tend to be more isolated.

Aravindan, who was named best national director for his film *Kanchana Sita* last year, represents the newest element in this melting pot. *Kanchana Sita* was essentially an exercise in pure aesthetics, pre-logical and childlike in its awe of nature, its primitive setting and mythical symbols reflective of a craving for primeval innocence. Aravindan's latest work, *Thampu*, though still a peripheral subject, is interesting as a group study of the small circus that pitches its tents on the fringes of society and becomes the centre of attention at a place for a while, and, when interest wanes, quits to repeat its chore elsewhere. Here Aravindan does not dabble, but executes his work with an assurance and flourish that presume an intimate and firm grasp of his subject. The crux of the difference between the two films seems to be Aravindan's own relationship with them; while *Kanchana Sita* was inspired by a play by Sreekantan Nair which Aravindan had also produced for the stage, *Thampu* is reconstructed from his experience as a journalist when he had done a story on the lives of circus artistes. The film is also unique for its novel syntax which facilitates the smooth flow of its episodic content. However, in his forthcoming film *Kummatti*, a children's fantasy, Aravindan seems to be reverting to the supernatural.

The Kannada new cinema, which began with *Samskara*, has nurtured itself into a movement with a young and strong image. But its directional thrust has been revivalist, tending to look back rather than forward. Even with *Samskara* this cinema found in caste a social factor that had immense potential on the screen. But soon caste became a cliché, partly due to its overuse, and partly due to an attempted equanimity of approach which tried to simultaneously comprehend its malevolent and redeeming features, and thus became obscure. In its search for a way out of this stalemate, this cinema is yet to come up with viable alternatives. Girish Karnad's latest, *Ondanandu Kaladalli*, a competitive entry at the Film Festival and admittedly fashioned after Kurosawa's *Seven Samurai*, with a pit-a-pat narrative about martial clans in medieval Karnataka, can at best be a brief diversion from the serious business of cinema.

An earlier film that merits attention is Shivarama Karanth's *Chomana Dudi*, which uses the folk idiom in its native sense. The perception is total and true to life, and there is not the usual sensibility lag between the filmmaker and his audience at the receiving end. Though technically and aesthetically nowhere as sophisticated or brilliant as Ray, the film makes a searing impact because of its definite context; and though the reality it depicts may not be contemporary, it is patently relevant to our times. The film is tied down to the soil as inexorably as Chomana himself. This earthiness is hardly surprising in Karanth, who deplores that the camera alienates and cannot be used 'as a farmer uses his plough'.

In Tamil Nadu, new cinema is still in its infancy and there are more compromises than breakaway bids. It has evolved little beyond the stereotype set by K. Balachander, whose films invariably get bogged down in a surfeit of loud visual and vocal symbols. The legacy of the dramatic continues to be the axis around which even new cinema revolves. Of late Bharathi Raja has shown a more mature approach in incorporating a sense of the ordinary and the anti-climactic in his films, but he too has not extricated himself from the word–image conflict this cinema is undergoing.

The one film that is conceptually different is John Abraham's *Agraharathil Oru Kazhuthai*, which, however, has run into extraneous problems. As the title

('Donkey in a Brahman street') implies, the film can be and has been construed as communal and anti-brahman, and to this day has not found an outlet for exhibition in the state, although acclaimed elsewhere and especially by the foreign delegates at the recent Festival as a competent work of surrealism. If the surrealism in the film is emulative of the Spanish maestro of this form, Luis Bunuel, John's plight in having made this film is reminiscent, at a humbler level, of Griffith, who, despite his professions to the contrary, found that his film *Birth of a Nation* was popularly construed as anti-Negro in sentiment.

John's predicament seems to stem from a basic dichotomy in sensibilities. His use of the donkey in the film, as he explained to me, was as a beast of burden, as the humble animal which Christ himself rode, and not as a pejorative symbol against any community. Rather, the film is aimed at hypocrisy in social norms and behaviour. But here John's Christian sensibility seems not reconciled to the essential ethos of his situation, and the film and its maker are misunderstood.

While new cinema, by reason of its regional purview, defies broad generalizations, there is a commonness evident in its cultural leaning – characterized by a 'renascence', as distinct from a 'renaissance'. In what is considered a liberal democracy, it is surprising that there is no political cinema in the Latin American sense. Neither is this cinema heuristic like the young cinema in Africa, personified in directors like Ousmane Sembène (who headed the jury at the Seventh International Film Festival). Africa, however, has the advantage of starting on a *carte blanche* so that its indigenous cinema opens on a rebellious note (anti-colonialism and egalitarianism being its consuming interest there). This, then, affords the clue to why new cinema in India is what it is today; why it fails to 'move' in more than a metaphorical sense.

First published in *The Hindu*, 18 February 1979.

Box Office Culture

That there is more to a film than meets the eye is a more than a literal fact. Sociologists and psychologists have never ceased to be fascinated by the peculiar charismatic sway film (in its composite sense as mass media and art combined) exercises over the masses. However, while discussing threadbare the mechanics and manifestations of this interaction, they have never yet been able to lay their finger on the crux of the issue – the type and measure of impact film has on society, and vice versa. This, then, persists as a challenging enigma, setting film apart as a unique cultural category with inalienable social dimensions.

The sociological attributes of a film are best typified within the ambit of the box office culture. The Indian box office film – at the national level in Hindi cinema and in the various regional cinemas – is characterized by the jargonized stereotype, synthetic variations of the same theme, subserving a captive (though sizeable) audience. The target group is the urban middle and lower middle class, in whose uprooted and atomized lives this film acts as social cement. By the stilted simulation of the social milieu, this film affords its audience scope for 'substitute living'. The consumer durables and luxury items used by the hero in the film, his self-righteous or flashy lifestyle, his social mobility, simplistically portrayed in a rapid rags-to-riches progression, his emotional crises and their solutions, his class loyalties – all these are vicariously experienced by the audience. The wrong assumption that the box office film is purely escapist entertainment further reinforces the experience by proxy because the audience reacts to the film not with its intellectual or critical faculties, but at an emotional plane. The box office formula is designed to empathize with the audience at this level and no more.

Such a filmic experience, however, implies an utter dependence on the film, accentuated by the sheer physicality and size of the screen image, and the liturgical mood and setting of the cinema hall, where the viewer's identity is atrophied as one of the multitude. The frenzied, adulatory response by scores of avid film-goers to the opening title of an MGR film, for instance, takes on the proportions of a ritual. Such lively response is far removed from any concept of passivity of the film audience. The potency of the box office film is intimately bound up with the active response of its audience. A typical audience does not accept or reject a film *in toto*. There operates what Herbert Gans describes as 'selective perception', where the viewer picks and chooses – out of the fare offered to him – aspects that tend to strengthen his biases and blind spots, and determine his value judgments. Thus the social impact of a film would seem not so much what it offers as what the audience construes out of it.

While it is speculative to equate in a generalized way the palpable elements of a film with the conscious level of the audience and its implicit aspect with the subconscious, in many box office films it does seem to work out thus. MGR, for instance, though typecast as the champion of the downtrodden, is himself rarely originally from the class he wishes to emancipate – or as illiterate or 'uncultivated' as them. His act as social reformist is invariably one of voluntary condescension, a stooping low to conquer, rather than an economic or social imperative.

Endowed thus with an amorphous formal content, it is small wonder that the box office film – however trite or redundant – continues to hegemonize the loyalty of the film-going masses. However, whether repeated exposure reinforces this infantile fixation, or whether the law of diminishing returns gradually 'disorients' the viewer, is a moot point.

The manipulative potential of the box office is not consciously designed or purposed, but is systemic in a media which, however fatuous or superficial, after all holds the mirror up to society – past, present and future. In his book *From Caligari to Hitler*, S. Kracauer shows how films in Germany, prior, to the ascension of Hitler predicted the rise of fascist power.

Despite its vast reach and mesmeric influence on the masses, the box office has never been seriously viewed as a social functionary. Policy makers and its patrons themselves have tended to relegate it to the margins of their consciousness. Given its scope, it becomes necessary to recognize its true character behind the frivolous façade of a song-and-dance melodrama.

First published in *The Hindu*, 15 April 1979.

The Villain of the Piece

Should a commercial big-wig from the 'Bombay industry', as India's Hollywood is styled, contemplate an indigenous version of Shakespeare's *Macbeth*, his most agonizing doubt would not be copyright or the propriety of his enterprise – our film barons have never, as a rule, been averse to purloining from unacknowledged sources – but whether Macbeth is a hero or a villain. This ethical dilemma is a non-issue to Shakespeare himself; in his scheme the protagonist who moots the catharsis is central to the plot in an amoral capacity.

The classical Greek formula, which gives the west its hero type, lends itself poorly to India. Here it is compounded by a frame of mind that sees life as an eternal conflict of good and evil, of *dharma* and *adharma*. This becomes a recurrent theme in the Indian film which, while borrowing formal elements from the west, still has the epics as its archetypal reference. As a synthetic box office product, however, it concocts a peculiar amalgam, churning out, in the process, paradoxical character types. More interesting than the hero in such a hybrid version seems the screen villain.

The *raison d'être* of the villain in the film is manifest – he personifies evil in all its variations, a countervailing force set against the hero until the very denouement when, like the grand finale of a ritual, good triumphs over evil. The hero and villain as antipodal personalities are thus derivatives of representative characterizations in the ethico-moral perspective. And yet, in most films, the villain invariably emerges functionally anterior to the hero in the plot. It is paradoxically his role to make of the hero a hero.

The villain's crucial role in thematic progression is evident from the salient development the plot takes with his entry into the fray. After the preliminaries are over and the narrative is set on an even keel, the villain comes along to queer the pitch. It is he, significantly, who makes the gambit that calls for reprisal from the hero. The initiative at the outset is in his hands, and passes to the hero only in the ensuing trial of strength. If there is a crisis (as there always is) he is to precipitate, he is the catalyst of the catharsis. In the conventional western theme, he is indeed the protagonist rather than the antagonist; more hero than the hero.

If thus integrated into the plot, the villain is not (in the interest of the hero's credibility) to steal an edge over the hero, he has perforce to be suitably tarred and feathered. In the Indian film, this external characterization of the villain renders him a blatant anachronism. He sticks out like a sore thumb in its contemporary setting. A parodied version of the villain type in the theatre-dance forms of *Nautanki*, *Koothu* or *Kathakali*, he masquerades with grotesque facial contortions, crude and uncivil behaviour, and infantile mannerisms – all designed to evoke an emotive negative response from the unsuspecting audience. This incriminating physiognomy is further reinforced by the vices and perversions so arbitrarily foisted on his character – with no cause, rationale or redeeming feature to qualify them.

It is intriguing that despite (or because of) this distortion, audiences in India – especially the urban middle classes with the advantage of their anomie – have warmed up to the screen villain. His sado-masochism and his 'hubris' are mentally pared down, as they tend to identify their own human foibles and aberrations with him. The message and moral of the hero, at the other end of the scale, is too didactic to be instantly acceptable. His paradigmatic virtues (non-smoking, non-drinking, non-womanizing, ideal son, father, husband, friend) are equally arbitrarily imposed and less easily digestible to the average consumer.

Thus while increasingly the hero, in the conventional image, has to be kept alive as a conscious myth, the villain is more and more taken for granted in a matter-of-fact sense. This preference of types has made for a dual development in the Hindi and regional commercial cinema – a one-sided reversal of roles on the one hand, and the emergence of the gangster-hero on the other. Villains-turned-heroes (Shatrughan Sinha or Pran in Hindi; Rajnikanth in Tamil) have their own sizeable mass following. The bandit-hero, best exemplified by Amitabh Bachchan on the Hindi screen (*Deewar*, *Don*, *Muqaddar ka Sikandar*, *Great Gambler*), is a far cry from the moralizing, romantic, 'soft' hero, and approximates, rather, to the erstwhile villain.

Audiences, it would seem, have called the bluff and will no more glibly swallow an 'unreal' villain; he has become an affront to their cultivated sensibility. The credible villain, on the other hand, has gained instant mass rapport and approbation. We have the famous (or notorious) instance of Amjad Khan's memorable portrayal of Gabbar Singh in *Sholay*. The roles of the three stars in this film – Sanjeev Kumar, Amitabh Bachchan and Dharmendra – seem to acquire meaning and purpose only when brought to the touchstone of the ace-bandit, Gabbar Singh. In Tamil, we have Kamal Haasan in his anti-heroic role of a psychopath in *Sigappu Rojakkal*. Only, here, because there is the suggestion of a hero-turned-villain, care is taken to rationalize his behaviour by tracing it back to his early childhood and investing it with an extenuating socio-economic cause.

All this sophistication notwithstanding, the box office, at its best, continues to be in the grip of the polarity principle, isolating heroism and villainy as contrasting types, rather than seeing them in their mutuality as aspects of a whole.

First published in *The Hindu*, 22 April 1979.

Caste, Class and Harijans

The caste–class imbroglio, perplexing enough to the political theorist, can imaginably be far more confounding to the serious filmmaker – because he has to crystallize on the screen what he is not too clear about in his mind. Where, then, he is not evasive, he is circumspect, preferring an equivocal appraisal of caste and class as twin – rather than polar – concepts.

Too elusive in their mutuality to be stated explicitly, caste and class often become alibis of social exploitation as portrayed in films – unless the one aspect discountenances the other, as in a Mrinal Sen film which is manifestly a class indictment *à outrance*; even in *Mrigaya* (Hindi) and *Oka Oorie Katha* (Telugu), where caste moorings are inferable, Sen effectively softpedals the caste factor. Satyajit Ray's refusal to come to terms with these realities seems to have a lot to do with the lyrical, almost romantic quality of poverty in his films; a sense of abstraction inevitable when he chooses to transfix his gaze on the phenomenon of poverty without traversing the ground, however unsure, in between.

If circumventing the issue can be a lapse, taking it for granted can be obfuscating. In the gilt-and-tinsel formula Hindi film, caste is set in a dramatically feudal milieu and personified by the rapacious tyrant molesting his serf's womenfolk or ravaging his crop. 'Class', by the same standard, is a matter of self-abnegating heroism championing a lowly cause; the dehumanization of the oppressed as a facile and inarticulate mass renders them stunningly impotent *sans* the liberating hero who steps down from a higher class or caste.

This elitism seems to persist like an opinionated fallacy even in the more enlightened filmmakers. In Shyam Benegal's *Nishant*, ultimate revolt against the landlord by the villagers has to be led by the brahman priest. The hint of a caste-to-class shift has, ironically, to bear this orthodox imprimatur. Who raises the cudgel seems as significant here as why it is raised.

Kannada cinema in the south has, for some time now, made a fetish of caste, but without the class proponent, is reserved in its inferences. Renegade brahmanism (from *Samskara* to *Ghatashraddha*) is about the boldest it can get. The redeeming exception is Karanth's *Chomana Dudi* where caste was appositely brought to bear on class.

Malayalam cinema today, held in posthumous esteem for its 'socials' of the 1960s, seems to have left behind caste–class considerations in that decade, and is in the throes of an identity crisis. The handful of 'political' films seeking to cling on in this rat-race is itself an outcaste group with meagre resources or exhibition outlets.

The caste upswing of Tamil cinema (with the rise of Dravidian culture in and through films), unless transmuted into class terms (and there is little evidence of this), could be forced to forfeit its initial advantage, and fall back on linguistic and cultural parochialism.

Given its volatile nature, the caste–class conundrum holds out exciting possibilities to the brash filmmaker. But an exposé that gets straight to the heart of the matter can be revealing. *Harijan*, a Telugu film awaiting release, is a distinct departure in terms of such an expository style. The meiosis that underscores its every instant is as eloquent as it is terse. Down-to-earth without being trite, it maintains a linear course never once upset by drama or sentimentalism. Director Ravi seems almost defiantly to plod through his theme with an earthy equanimity so steadfast that one could dub him a philistine.

The Malas (Harijans) of this village in Krishna district in coastal Andhra are not pitted against the high-caste Kammas in a kind of exploiter–exploited relationship teetering on the brink of an outbreak. They are a subject ethnic subgroup kept in perpetual psychological subservience by the subtle mechanism of caste and class exploitation. There is a passive acceptance, as placid as the lake and as languid as the cud-chewing buffaloes in it. Into this is dropped, like a pebble, the righteous indignation of an educated Malla youth who returns to his village with a new social consciousness. However, time makes its convert, the ripples soon settle down, the ruffled surface is still again, and life resumes its unhurried pace.

One is sorely tempted to rebuke the director for his defeatism. Especially since the breakaway potential, identified in the leitmotif of the Mallas' ambidextrous martial stick-play, is not developed into a bid. Their ethnic fierceness and violence, the director seems to suggest, are in a century-old stupor and cannot be provoked by social indignities grating to our urbane sensibility. Accosted with the charge, Ravi's reply was instant: 'This is an age of defeatism.'

Madhu Ambat's camera, in close synchronization with the director's view-frames, gives the film its peculiar gestalt. Madhu adeptly translates the diminutive realism of this people and their surroundings to the screen without losing himself in the beauteous landscape. In the dusty field, the smoky hutments or the garnered tree trunk that has endured (the visual seems to tell us) as much as the lined face of the old man before it, one sees, after a long time, the really and typically rural on our screen, or indeed visual tectonics so ably subserving a theme.

When Shyam Benegal's *Ankur* brought him, towards its close, to an impasse, he had the boy pick up a stone and throw it at the landlord's house. The frame froze and turned red. Ravi also extricates himself by passing the buck to the younger generation. The Mala youth's brother, disillusioned and disgusted with him for his conformism, leaves him to tackle fish with his fishing rod and runs away to tackle (one would like to think) more challenging things in life.

First published in *The Hindu*, 13 May 1979.

On Aravindan and His Art

Four Films, Two Awards

A National Award can be as disconcerting as it is reassuring when it saddles the filmmaker with an unforeseen accountability to expectations, cramping his style and slotting his perspective. Happily, two consecutive awards as Best Director – the first for his *Kanchana Sita* and then again this year for his *Thampu* – have not shaken Aravindan's equanimity. He continues to look as stoically stolid as ever, and continues to be as sensitively aware, as resolutely (even selfishly) honest to himself, as when he made his first film, *Uttarayanam*.

All considered, Aravindan's work must find affirmation in some inner imperative. If awards are merely incidental, if audience apathy is a foregone conclusion, nothing else can matter. Except, of course, money. But Aravindan's qualms in this direction are set at rest by a producer who is willing to, and can afford to, write off such non-sellers as ample compensation for the vicarious pleasure derived. 'I am lucky in many ways', Aravindan modestly submits. 'There are many good films which do not get to be seen for obvious reasons.' The obvious reason being that a producer–distributor like Aravindan's is a rarity not all filmmakers can find.

But what luck cannot explain are his films – their increasingly assured style, their idiomatic expressiveness and the way they singularly relate to their author. Identifiably interpretative, they fall short of being purely personal because he draws as much from the milieu as from his mind. With treatment at such a premium, it is small wonder that his themes have been picked casually rather than selected consciously. A readymade script by Thikkodiyan led him to his first film, *Uttarayanam*.

What his producer had in mind when assigning him the task of making a screen version of C.N. Sreekantan Nair's *Kanchana Sita* was at best a mythological with a difference; what it turned out to be – a pantheistic and primeval exultation – was perhaps as much a surprise to him as to the audience, taken unawares; a surprise that no doubt turned pleasant when the film bagged the National Award.

Thampu as an idea began with a script by M.T. Vasudevan Nair on circus-folk. As a film it departed considerably from that script to narrate Aravindan's own earlier first-hand experiences with them as a reporter, and to fetch him, in close succession, his second award as Best Director.

Some such casual enough reason must have prompted Aravindan to make his children's feature, *Kummatti* – his deference, perhaps, to the International Year of the Child. But again, what has resulted is a delightful and delectable piece, for young and old alike.

The theme is simple enough: in a Pied Piper-like tale common in any village folklore, Kummatti is the mythical bogeyman children are scared of, or scare one another with. Aravindan takes the tale a step further. Kummatti does appear in a village. The initial awe and apprehension are soon replaced by friendliness and warmth. Kummatti becomes an aged playmate in their midst. And when it is time for him to leave, he gives them demonstration of his magical powers, turning the children into different animals for a while and then back again into children. All except a boy who, turned into a dog, wanders away from the field, loses his way and finally returns to find Kummatti gone and himself still a dog.

As Aravindan's fancy takes flight, he is careful to make it all plausible at one level. The fetishistic setting, where people still have abiding faith in rites and the powers of the exorcist, gives his story its subtle base. The circularity of the time continuum, brilliantly conveyed in the transition of the seasons, makes the crisis ephemeral, and yet poignantly real while it lasts. In all of this he is assisted by the elatingly beautiful camera work of Shaji, whose frames linger on in the heart long after the film is over. Shaji captures the panoramic landscape with a vision that lends it a three-dimensional effect. The tone and colour are crystal-pure, and in single shots there extends, as far as the eye can see, shades of green, chrome yellow, the still ponds reflecting the green, the brown and, beyond them, the blue mountains – their peaks veiled by translucent mist and soothing blue skies where one or a thousand birds fly.

The sound track, though with a logic of its own, does upset the technical repose of the visual. Harsh and flat in places, it is a rather odd combination of the symbolic, the impressionistic and the literal. One's auditory senses are, from the very outset, cued to bird-sounds even in scenes where birds are not visible, transporting one mentally into an open aviary. The impression, as the director himself explains, sets the unreal plane. So does a particular sequence of cacophony by crows serve as a symbolic contrast to the sylvan, more tuneful bird-sound pervading the film. But mingled with these are the realistic true-to-picture sounds (as of a buffalo lowing when someone happens to pass by it), which makes for confusion.

This and the editing, which in places conforms more to the cruder definition of 'cutting', are lapses which detract from the technical finesse – without, however, upsetting its overall syntax. And the pace, set after a few langourous scenes in the beginning, makes it absorbing as a visual narrative. The only other objection one can raise, if one is given to picking holes, is to observe that the film is revivalist in its thrust. An objection Aravindan sidetracks with the more interesting point that he used the folk idiom because 'a lot of action in folk can easily penetrate into children's minds'.

First published in *The Hindu*, 8 July 1979.

Mindscape in Twilight

The Indian Panorama entries at international film festivals in the country have become a qualitative index of serious cinema in the various languages: films that go on to vie with one another for the annual national and state awards. The section becomes significant also because it is the yardstick with which foreign critics and delegates measure contemporary Indian cinema. And they matter a lot to the filmmakers thrown into this elitist rat race because often films 'pooh-poohed' at home acquire a new respect on the rebound from a favourable notice in a foreign journal, or with an award or citation from a foreign film festival.

Accosted with this peculiar brand of 'xenomania', filmmakers are quick to point out how even Ray shot to fame only after Cannes recognized his *Pather Panchali*. What they fail to point out is that Ray was as successful at the box office, and not just with *Pather Panchali* – in fact the Panorama screening of his latest films, *Pikoo* and *Sadgati* at *Filmotsav '82* in Calcutta in January led to a near-riot; those who had stood overnight in queue and could not get tickets blockaded the entrance to the theatre and let no one in for over an hour. That public remonstrance, much as it inconvenienced pass- and ticket-holders, and set many of them cursing the agitation-prone Calcuttans under their breaths, was a demonstration of the demand for and faith in the much-maligned new cinema. It contrasts refreshingly, moreover, with the 'exclusively for festivals and awards' label most other Panorama films tout almost shamelessly.

But popular appeal or acceptance as the criterion can also be deceptive; because one would be left with no argument in this logic against the ravages of populist cinema. It can moreover be disconcerting to find what one holds as a film of great integrity and insight receiving short shrift from a lay audience as with G. Aravindan's *Pokkuveyil*. Public screenings of *Pokkuveyil* ('Twilight', Malayalam) both at Calcutta and in Kerala, have been more or less catastrophic. Judging from the reactions, the viewers tended to grow cold to the film if they had not warmed to it in the first few minutes; and for a theme that takes its own measured time to warm up, the reactive pattern can only be disastrous.

A more receptive and eager audience would find in *Pokkuveyil* a more fulfilling Aravindan. By his own admission, the film was in his mind all along. Even as he made *Kummatty* and *Esthappan*, he was trying to come to grips with the form it should take. The form it has taken is faithful to the man. It captures the essential genius of his art and exposes, at the same time, the relative poverty of his craft. But it is a scheme where craft itself, as a mechanism commandeering verisimilitude or surface realism, is given the go by. The unnatural pauses as two characters converse, or the hyped giggle of a girl in uncertain romance, or the lags and lapses in behavioural details may stick out like a sore thumb. But in the final analysis, they become as irrelevant to the deep structure of the film as a sore thumb itself to the soul of a man.

The film depicts not just Aravindan's depth as an artist but his deep-strike capability. If the viewer is willing to give it a chance, not distracted by peripheral inadequacies or the absence of the conventional narrative, it will register on the subconscious and demand attention. The visual and aural dynamics will in combination create a mood that percolates, as if by osmosis, to the viewer from the screen. Indeed, it is its subconscious resourcefulness that makes the film subliminally compelling. The intense account of a tremulous young man groping for direction in a psychological no-man's land unfolds in an impressionistic flow of mood-images. His futile attempts to relate to his immediate world (his aged and sick father who was a selfless political worker; his girlfriend who responds to his serious intentions with a dabbler's interest in his poetic sensitivity; the collegemate who is an ambitious basketball player; and the stolid extremist friend who tries to draw him out of his reserve) drive him to the precipice of sanity.

Balachandran Chullikkad, one of Kerala's most promising younger poets, is so thoroughly immersed in the role that the process of his internalizing his grotesquely impinging environment is almost palpable and excruciatingly physical. At the end of the film one wants to meet the real Chullikkad to reassure oneself that his personality is intact. The lyricism of the theme has a twist to it that takes away all the sugar and cream, and leaves behind a bated breath of longing rather than a sated appetite. The music track – a raga of pathos played out in *jugalbandi* by Hariprasad Chaurasia (*bansuri*) and Rajiv Taranath (*sarod*) – accentuates the sense of void the panoramic, yet controlled visuals evoke. Shaji's camera filters the scenic locales to arrive at the minimal budding colours of dawn and dusk (most of the outdoor footage was actually shot in twilight) so that, as one discerning viewer put it, 'the landscape becomes a mindscape' – the mindscape of a man drawn inexorably into dementia.

Pokkuveyil belongs to the inscrutable realms of pure cinema, even if there is a strong hint of Salvador Dali in the mutant red, or the surreal sense of 'edginess'. Significantly, most of Chullikkad's long drawn-out walks in the film are along edges – between water and land, the green of fields and the brown of earth, and, in time, between day and night. If a shot can summarize a film, there is one in *Pokkuveyil* where Chullikkad walks into a macabre-red twilight; into a time and space that is neither here nor there.

First published in *The Hindu*, 14 February 1982.

Aravindan's Art

Coming to grips with the oeuvre of a filmmaker like Aravindan can be tricky because his work does not lend itself to normative interpretation. It is not conscious cinema of a genre. It flits on the surface of organic society and life like a hovering ideatic impression. Indeed it suggests a passionate impressionist who is averse, even scared, to drop anchor. This wariness typifies, if at all, Aravindan's staple thematic concern, just as it determines the tentative, contemplative, formal style of his work. His films are like an observation in the margin space, on the eddies and cross-currents of mainstream society. An observation that does not necessarily study society critically or analytically, but is more a spontaneous response to aspects of his environment that impinge on his consciousness and sensibility. And a response, too, that is abstracted into the realm of the surreal and played out on the canvas of a pared-down, elemental nature. The cinema that emerges makes an overture to the senses. It surrenders to aesthetic spontaneity. There is an implicit disdain here for an overarching technique or craft. The pace is sedate and unhurried – it proceeds like an intense daydream. Tension between the image and the story, rather than any conflict of dramatic plot, is the chemistry of this celluloid. All of which does not detract from Aravindan's innate humanism. A humanism that seeks out the marginal man or a sub-group which is at odds with, and set apart from, the inexorable dynamics of the social context. This, in a sense, has been his abiding leitmotif.

The delectable cartoon series Aravindan ran for years in the Malayalam weekly *Mathrubhoomi*, before he took to filmmaking, had already set his quaint perspective. Titled 'Small People and a Big World', the anecdotal series, through the eyes of its non-participating and often nonplussed protagonist, stands a jargon-ridden, self-righteous world on its head. Again, this is not an effect achieved through sleight of sketchpen or overt caricature; rather, it is a natural byproduct of the everyday-life encounters of the transparently naive, ambivalent and diffident protagonist, Ramu.

It is not surprising, then, that Aravindan's first film, *Uttarayanam* ('Throne of Capricorn', 1974), is an extension of this small-man-in-a-big-world view. An unemployed young man, whose father had fought and died for national liberation and a new society which the son cannot comprehend or adjust to, is – like Ramu of the cartoons – the estranged protagonist who, from his vantage position of the outsider (as gratuitous scenes of his reading Camus' novelette of the same title jarringly remind us), acts as a sop to the hypocrisy and double standards of society. It is at best a vicarious indictment. The hero's feeble attempts to participate in the social rigmarole – whether in hitting the bottle with his zestful collegemate medical rep, or in the *ganja* session with a clone of a dropout who sings the same song each time in Yesudas's mellifluous voice – are doomed to fail. Nor is alcohol or opium an escape route for his more evolved personality.

On the other hand, he is not a victim sinned against by society either.

Indeed there is no such scheme of villainy in any of Aravindan's work. His is an amoral world; bribery, corruption, opportunism, narcissism – all are germane to it. Only the characters who mediate his artistic perception of it are not. This *marginalization* is the existentialist predicament thrown up by his films. Aravindan's finer moments of ellipsis lie in his transmuting that predicament. In *Uttarayanam*, the disconsolate youth goes through the paces of social contact – each of them a delightful cameo in itself – to seek solace finally in the warmth of a fire lit in some wilderness by an anonymous old woman. Her charming, naive, toothless smile lights up his face with spontaneous, childlike laughter. In a symbolic act of oneness with that pure moment, the youth throws the mask that is ripped off society's face into the flames. In that final imagery, the outsider is in harmony with his true self. His alienative experiences are brought to the touchstone of nature.

Almost as if elaborating on that image, Aravindan's second film, coming after a gap of three years, is an eclectic celebration of nature. *Kanchana Sita* (1977) is based on a version of the epic *Ramayana* according to which Sita's trial by fire (after she is rescued from Ravana) does not set at rest doubts about her chastity among Rama's subjects, and he is forced to abandon her. Slighted, grief-stricken and pregnant, Sita throws herself into the Ganga; and the river bears her twin sons, Lava and Kusa, to sage Valmiki, who brings them up. The narrative strand of the film itself is drawn from the sequel to that story, in which Rama's *aswamedha* sacrifice brings him face to face with his sons. In *Kanchana Sita*, Aravindan synthesizes into a consummate whole, his *marginality* principle and his anthropomorphic contemplation of nature. The roles of the epic heroes in the film are played by Rama Chenchu tribal people of Andhra Pradesh, who claim lineage to the mythological Rama. Sita is never actually seen in the film, but her virtual presence is compellingly evoked in the moods of the forest and the elements.

The anomie and rootlessness of marginal living become the striking metaphor of *Thampu* ('The Circus Tent', 1978), which deals with a roving, small-town circus of Kerala. Shot in black-and-white, in a direct documentary mode, the film gives sudden, fleeting insights into the lives of these itinerant entertainers. The filmmaker's effort – and its effect – is poetic and intuitive, rather than sociological; hence those moments of intimate empathy when characters, in deadpan close-up shots, talk directly to the viewer: who they are, where they once belonged, and how and why they joined the circus. When the circus pitches tent in a village, it is a welcome break for the local populace. But ringside is as close as one should get for the collective entertainment. Beyond that are atomised souls – the forlorn clown, the despondent acrobat, the slipping gymnast. Nor should they get their hopes up. Even as some of them begin to befriend or strike an emotive chord with some of the villagers, it is time to cut loose and shift camp to another village, another small town. The film itself does not venture to follow them onward. And how can it? Because theirs is a journey with no destination. And so it is as if the filmmaker hops on to the circus wagon as it moves into the village, and drops off as it leaves the place. In that slice of space and time, what can be attempted is a thumbnail sketch, not a full-blooded portrayal. Again that sense of ellipsis – that more has been concealed than revealed. But the thumbnail touches, now and again, a raw nerve – and then, those flashes of vital truth.

Then comes, ambling through the serene, undulating fields of northern Kerala, *Kummatti* (1979), the Pied Piper-like figment of Malabar's folklore. Here, and in the subsequent film, *Esthappan* (1980), Aravindan's formal content approximates to the magical realism of a García Márquez or an Italo Calvino. The bogeyman of grandmothers' tales materializes from nature one day, to mingle with and weave a spell of carefree abandon around the children of the village. He is not the evil spirit summoned to coax children into obedience, but a genial, if mysterious, companion who transports them into a world of fun and frolic. There are some anxious moments when a boy, transformed into a dog, gets lost; but all ends well and Kummatti melts back into nature. Again, typically, the ambience evoked is asocietal. The whole film happens on a plane of *distraction* from society – a heightened plateau of simple, sensual delight.

Esthappan, who walks in from the shimmering, quicksilver sea, is an even more elusive character. To the fisherfolk of the coastal Christian village, he is at once an eccentric simpleton, a possessed soothsayer and faith-healer, a satanic grave stealer. Esthappan embodies the enigma of the indeterminate individual whose inscrutable attributes are the stuff of which fables are made. He is, in this sense, the inverse image of Kummatti. While Kummatti already exists in the collective psyche of generations, Esthappan is the process of that transmutation; the making of the myth. The interesting coda, in which Esthappan is seen walking simultaneously in several places, seems a subtle allusion to the emerging legend of a godman.

Marginality and tremulous brinkmanship are made one with nature in the breathtaking aura of *Pokkuveyil* ('Twilight', 1981). Nature at twilight, captured in its bated tonality and lent a mood of the verge by Chaurasia's haunting flute notes, is the *terra incognita* of the human mind. Treading that slippery ground is the highly sensitive and introverted young protagonist, regressing irredeemably into a cocoon of alienation and insulation from society. It is, the director seems to suggest, a journey back to the source, to original innocence. The final shot shows the young man curled up in foetal position in his cell in a mental asylum.

If *Esthappan* and *Pokkuveyil* are, in a sense, about the indefinability of the human mind, *Chidambaram* (1985) is about its indestructibility, its amorphous nature. Aravindan here, for the first time, takes recourse to plot and dramatic progression. But at the end of it all, he makes a philosophical mockery of mortality. Death is sublimated into renewed life, a life of quietism and non-participation.

In the next work, *Oridathu* ('Once upon a Place', 1986), it is a bolder if uncharacteristic Aravindan who actually steps into a social milieu. Almost as if to confess that he is here himself seeking out his characters, he conjures up the situation of a village just being electrified. That simple act of technology literally sheds new light on the villagers and their mundane concerns. There is here an equivocal approach to technology – as a means of material betterment and a corrupting force. Its ominous potential is hinted at in the final scene, when a fireworks display during the temple festival takes on the apocalyptic vision of the mushroom cloud of an atomic burst. Such visual take-offs have often led to a reading of Aravindan as an anti-modernist. But this does injustice to the essential artistic totality and integrity of the man. Other readings that see him as an abstruse neophyte in the avant-garde school of filmmaking are equally off the mark and betray a predisposed cultural appetite. For, this is seminalist cinema; cinema that is in a sense aesthetically and culturally subversive; cinema that is not so much definitive art as ploughing its lonely furrow – as Dudley Andrew would call it – 'in the aura of art'.

Indeed Aravindan's latest film, *Marattam* ('Masquerade', 1989, made for Doordarshan), unfolds like a sensuous discourse on the phenomenology of art itself. In a *tour de force* of interpretative brinkmanship, he makes a mockery of cause–effect, subject–object dualisms. The artistic event – *Keechakavadham* (the killing of Keechaka) – breaks out of its formal Kathakali mould to become a tantalising murder mystery. Keechaka is actually killed, but is it the Kathakali personage or the actor who dons the role that is done to death? Why, and by whom? There are at least three constructs, three versions, each as convincing as the others. At the end of it all, was Keechaka killed in the first place? If these questions remain unanswered, already the process of unravelling the mystery has shifted subtly from a routine investigation to a metaphysical enquiry. After the relatively diffused phase of *Chidambaram* and *Oridathu*, *Marattam* comes like a reaffirmation that Aravindan's innate artistic vision remains as unfazed and uncompromising as ever.

First published in *Frontline*, 23 June 1989; reprinted in *Frontline*, 15 January 2010 , special issue to commemorate the fiftieth year of *Frontline*.

Thoughts on Aravindan

I am trying to define my relationship with Aravindan. It is not easy, because it was not friendship – or friendship alone. It was more than that. It was more in the nature of a 'bonding'. It was more internal than external, more implicit than explicit, more understood than stated. Whenever we met – whether in Kerala, Madras or Delhi – it was as if we were picking up the threads from where we left off last, and continuing a communion of silence rather than a communication with words. (In fact Aravindan is proof for me that you don't need spoken language for communication.) But a lot happened and changed in our minds and hearts at each meeting or session. He had a strange mystic quality that extended like an aura to engulf those who engaged with him and transformed them.

That does not mean that he was like an enlightened guru. Far from it – he was as human and casual and careless and opinionated and angry and sad as most of us. But through it all, there was this savant-like sense of another plane or dimension. Aravindan always reminded me of the Chinese saying about a man who slept and dreamt that he was a butterfly; then woke up to wonder whether he was a butterfly dreaming that he was a man. You could not quite place him except in this twilight zone. I am not surprised that *pokkuveyil* (twilight) became a theme of his film. That indeterminacy was his natural space and time.

Incidentally, the dream sequence in *Pokkuveyil* – where Balachandran Chullikad is chased by a squat bald man with a copper vessel full of boiling hot water – is actually my dream. It had been a recurring nightmare right from my early schooldays, through college and into my later adult life – until I mentioned it to Aravindan and he used it in the film. And, as he predicted, once I saw the film with my dream in it, it stopped occurring to me!

I have written at length about Aravindan's cinema in *The Hindu* and *Frontline*, and I do not want to repeat any of that here. I am actually not even sure I want to see his films again. Because I have internalized them so much that they vividly unfold in my imagination. And every time they do, I feel his virtual presence in them. I am not sure any screening can any more come close to that.

In fact I have been thinking a lot about Aravindan these days. I am fascinated by the idea that he was also the ultimate postmodernist. He once told me, in the early days of AIDS, that it was a fictional disease invented by the Church to deter non-conjugal sex, and promoted by the pharmaceutical corporates in order to sell their vaccines and medicines. This is of course only to be taken as literally as Jean Baudrillard maintaining that George Bush's Gulf War of 1991 happened only on television – in the sense that it was a made-for-TV war. Or, Kapil Sibal's mathematics that one lakh seventy six thousand crore rupees is actually equal to zero in the telecom spectrum scam. Were Aravindan alive today this 'Sibalism' would, I am sure, have been his Ramu cartoon strip on the subject.

First published in the *Commemorative Journal*, International Film Festival of Kerala, 2010; reprinted in *Frontline*, 15 January 2010, special issue to commemorate the fiftieth year of *Frontline*.

From the Fringes to the Centre

That the Khosla Committee report is simplistically reduced in the popular mind to an exoneration of the kiss on the screen neatly sums up the concept of censorship widely held in our society. The gravamen of the charge against the censors is that they relentlessly snip away an honest, uninhibited smooch, forcing the filmmaker to deviously circumvent 'cuts' with visuals far more suggestive and perverse in their impact. While it is admittedly difficult to draw a line or formulate a clear-cut policy that mediates between the right of expression of the filmmaker on the one hand, and the corruptive potential of a film on the other, there is a more definite case against the censors for their 'cut-to-rule' mentality – a clause by clause interpretation of the letter of the censor code, rather than an overall assessment of the film in its totality. A lapse that leads to such insufferable scenes as the hero sniffing and pecking his paramour at every inconceivable part of the anatomy, save the forbidden lips.

Thus, while to throw censorship overboard at this stage could mean a spate of yellow films, its retention as a mere statutory provision can have just about the same effect. The very concept and purview of censorship, then, need to be revalidated. In its deterrent capacity, it would of course reflect the constitutional provision (Article 19, Clause 11) for 'reasonable restriction in freedom of speech and expression'; but in a broader perspective, it would have to ensure the reasonableness of its role in the context of the total impact of the film. Which leads to a new complication. Fledged with such responsibility, the censor would change from an objector to a qualifier; he would find scope to make aesthetic and critical judgements on the film, which the filmmaker would not take kindly to. The problem is not period. As early as 1927, the Indian Cinematograph Committee recorded: 'We do not consider that it is either practical, nor justifiable, to make one man or one body of men, the arbiter of tastes of a whole population.'

In the immediate post-independence phase the censor was indeed a cultural commissar of sorts, tending to look askance at anything modernist or progressive on celluloid. True, he reflected the prevalent mood of the times, the revivalist fervour to hark back to the glory that was pre-British India or espouse traditional values. But he also preempted, simultaneously, the evolution of social realism in the media, or a tackling with verisimilitude of the contemporary social milieu. Censorship tended to be an adjunct of the system, in reinforcing set patterns of family and social relationships, and in dissuading non-conformist streams of creative expression. The concepts of patriotism to the land, dharma above all else, abiding faith in god, and unswerving obedience to elders or superiors, which are all too characteristic of the average box office film, even today, seem to have been firmly implanted in this period of intense cultural reconsolidation.

The censor then actually began to 'wield' the scissors. It was moreover futile to contest his strictures because it would be, in effect, challenging the entire system. The case of K.A. Abbas is an instance in point. Abbas's *A Tale of Four Cities* (a documentary) was severely mauled by the censors for its forthright depiction of the red-light business of Bombay, and its damaging contrast of the coexistence of poverty and affluence in the four metropolises. When Abbas decided to fight, it was a gruelling bout that dragged on year after year, taking his case meanwhile from the regional censor board to the revising board and on to the Supreme Court, where finally the verdict in his favour required him to make no cuts at all. But the documentary itself was never exhibited because the Films Division, with sole distributing rights for documentaries, refused to take it up.

The period of the Emergency, while delineating the censor in his most draconian light, is nevertheless not much to be made of, considering that it was an unnatural phase affecting as adversely all facets of free life and expression. However, the hypocrisy in the use of the code was particularly evident in the clearance given to a violence-torn film like *Sholay* by a Censor Board which was most finicky about excising even the most clichéd fisticuff in a run-of-the mill, imported American film. The latitude of the censors after the Emergency seems to have had a dual influence on the media. It has at once served as an incentive for the penchant for sex-centred movies on the one hand, and for bold new sweeps by filmmakers on the other. It no longer appears mandatory for the police (as the only legal force of law and order) to appropriate for themselves the task of punishing the errant hero or villain; they are not as often (and this is most gratifying) made to look ridiculous, arriving just moments after the action is over, when the hero has the villain trussed up and ready to be whisked away.

Social structures and values, hitherto taken for granted, are increasingly being questioned – and from the right end (the norm previously being to make a mockery of the process by having the hero, himself from royal background, spouting messages of social equality on behalf of his poor brethren). Even the role of the woman, consistently and incorrigibly stereotyped, seems to be devolving to something more individualistic and self-dependent. Evidence of such breakthroughs are still, no doubt, on the periphery, but now the margin, as never before, seems to be well-defined and one can, with reasonable expectation, wait for the process to move in from the fringes to the centre as a movement.

First published in *The Hindu*, 16 September 1979.

Pervasive Personal Touch

There are directors who so strive for craftsmanship that the effort shows. Situations and nodal points in the plot abound with a surfeit of 'directorial touches' one soon wearies of, because they serrate rather than smoothen out the sequential flow. Imagist and verbal symbolisms take off at a tangent so that a simple statement is made to look preposterously contrived. The short bursts of applause that greet such odd moments of self-indulgence by the director only confirm the suspicion that he is hogging the show – just as preponderantly as the star of yesteryear bulldozed his way through the entire footage of a film.

The director as superstar, a dream-come-true of the 1960s, can as easily become a nightmare today if the man in question is given to the enthusiasm and excesses of the neophyte in his treatment – like in *Nool Veli*, or *Thappu Thalangal*, or *Aval Oru Thodarkathai*, or *Manmatha Leelai*, or indeed most of K. Balachander's films. Balachander is today the single available instance of an influential, professional director in Tamil cinema who has made direction more than an art – a fetish. The personalization is so strong that to the mild and even-tempered sensibility, his film seems to scream out his presence every few minutes. In the course of a sitting, one is threatened with a host of incongruous visual similes and metaphors being rammed down one's throat.

The story line is indeed the least important factor; so low, it would seem, in his order of priorities, that he simply adapts it from earlier Indian or foreign films. *Nizhal Nijamagirathu* is a more frivolous version of an important Malayalam film, *Adimagal*; *Apoorva Raagangal* is *Forty Carats* in the vernacular; and now his latest, *Nool Veli*, is a potboiler rendition of the Malayalam *Aa Nimisham*. Not that Balachander has not been accused of plagiarism. But he is not abashed to admit to being a good copyist. Because, as he explained at a function a few months back, it requires aesthetic competence to copy a piece of art well. The reasoning was bad enough, but not as disconcerting as the sharp round of applause this candid self-exposure received.

The city culture with its cosmopolitan and bourgeois thrust has been the circumscribed milieu for almost all of Balachander's works. And yet, paradoxically, his approach has been not so much expository, in a manner that would help him grasp the essence and predicament of life in the city, as philosophical in terms of the inter-relationships between man and given social realities. The liberated woman, for instance, crops up again and again (*Aval Oru Thodarkathai*, *Nizhal Nijamagirathu*, *Nool Veli*), yet she is pitted not against male chauvinism but against the traditions and glory of idealized womanhood; and that in such a give-and-take stance, the director, it would seem, would fain have his 'prima donna' have the best of both worlds. This tendency to neutralize has prevented Balachander from making the strong assertions Bharathi Raja has shown himself capable of. His departure from set social mores has a comeback edge to them, unlike the rejection *à outrance* of Raja.

Balachander's sense of the dramatic must have been ingrained in him during his days as a playwright. This naturally explains the lack of the poetic quality that goes so well with celluloid. The conflict of egos and crass drama is really the crux of the difference between the stage and the screen. Film has its own native idiom, just as the theatre has a language most suited to its merits and limitations. And yet with Balachander, it would seem the differences did not exist. In *Nool Veli*, for instance, a character begins, at one juncture, to speak into the lens to tell the viewers what transpires during a period of transition. Highly dramatic, perhaps, but hardly cinematic. The technique itself has been put to more effective purpose in Aravindan's *Thampu*, where in a series of dramatic monologues characters look squarely into the lens and unfold their past history.

To the same source of the stage must be attributed Balachander's heavy dependence on dialogue. Witticisms, clever turns and twists of phrases and meaningless banter ('You want to know something about nothing? Nothing!' – *Nool Veli*) are yet the mainstay of the average Tamil stage, and when transposed to the media of film, present a dithyrambic verbal track that can at best win a few laughs or exultations, but is never integrated into the fabric of the plot. It is surely not true, as a Balachander film seems to make out, that people in this part of the country speak in crossword puzzles.

First published in *The Hindu*, 28 October 1979.

The Changed Course

Tamil cinema may not have arrived but it certainly has come a long way, especially since the monolithic phase of the 1960s and early 70s. When, for instance, it forsook its studio-bound tradition to get outdoors, the relief was writ large on its formal content. The decor-dominated and repressive structural parameters of the studio-set could not contain the expansive pressure of a new generation of filmmakers. Besides an intimate and realistic charting of the milieu, this moving out meant greater emphasis on spatial awareness.

The monomyth of the star-hero is being challenged with increasing vigour. The iconizing impulse that has consecrated a *Makkal Thilakam* or a *Nadigar Thilakam* may not yet be dying out, but is at an ebb. Not that this is the swansong of stardom. But second-generation film-goers seem to have called the bluff of an indiscriminate idealization of types, all striving uniformly to exemplify the same oversimplified notions of morals (repeatedly the same stark, mutually exclusive characterizations of good and bad), ethics (that of implicit obedience and loyalty of the petite wife to the domineering husband, of the prostrate serf to his feudal lord, of the modernist son to his old-worldly mother) or sacrosanct cultural traditions (*kudumba gauravam* or *khandaan ki izzat* that overwhelms the self-respect of the individual; a pervasive theistic awe of the gods in their heavens manipulating the fate of man).

The democratization of the star-image is no doubt temporizing of a sort by the filmmaker. Kamal Haasan as a homicidal psychopath in *Sigappu Rojakkal* or Rajnikanth as antagonist in *16 Vayathinile* is only representative of this updating of the image; in little else do they veer away from the career cycle of the star (lifestyle, remuneration, hegemonizing roles and sensationalism). The mass response to them is perhaps less characteristically populist than to MGR or Shivaji earlier. But they are stars no less, although a shift in audience tastes and sensibilities qualifies their characterizations.

Tamil cinema today, then, is not essentially star-determined to be a success. Indeed it seems increasingly impatient with the jargonized themes and stock portrayals of the anterior cinema. It tends, instead, to concentrate on vignettes of life and living in the village. Love here is less maudlin, passion underscored, faces more commonplace, language more native, situations less forced. There is even a suggestion of a determinism of the plot outside of (sometimes despite) the central character. In *Kizhakke Pogum Rail*, the social force that directs the destiny of the lovers seems inexorable to the end; the only escape being escape itself (the couple finally elope). In Mahendran's *Uthiri Pookkal*, in a brilliant *tour de force* of nemesis, the initiative devolves on the collective will of the village to act as arbiter of the hero-villain's fate.

The dogged hauteur of the central character in *Uthiri Pookkal* leads to dramatic hubris, but with a difference. It is not resolved, it is ended. When he is forced in the end into the river, it is a moot point whether or not the act constitutes murder. No one has laid a finger on him; he has simply been coerced into the torrents with the sure knowledge that he cannot swim. But what comes across is a sense of perverse martyrdom. 'I am sorry. I was the only bad man here. But now I have made so many of you bad', observes the unrepentant victim before his suicide perforce. He then beckons to his two children and touchingly advises them to be good, then deliberately walks into the river. There is a clamour by a few in the crowd, also initially indicters, forgetting all else, to save him. But they are held back. The current flowing swiftly by betrays no tell-tale sign of being an accomplice to the crime; it takes it in its stride.

Director Mahendran has struck a disturbing balance between the despicable 'id' of the main character on the one hand, and the culpability of the collective act on the other. The verisimilitude of the setting and the lifelike characters make the dilemma all the more real. No inexplicable force is invoked to explain the turn of events. We know all along that the hero-villain had it coming to him. Some of us hate him so, we are even looking forward to it. When retribution strikes, we see him as a victim (even though the director gives us no special reason to sympathize). We wonder why he was what he was. It is the closest to what we (in Tamil Nadu) have got to atheistic existentialism in cinema.

First published in *The Hindu*, 9 December 1979.

Low-key Festival

Last year the same time at Delhi it was festival to a fault – a star-spangled celebration with a high degree of bureaucratization (only to be expected in the capital) which tended to become unwieldy. *Filmotsav '80*, just concluded in Bangalore, by contrast, has been a low-key affair; so low-key in fact, that to call it a festival seems ambitious. This time it was a hasty, indiscriminate, miscellaneous collection of films which gave the impression that the Festival Directorate just brought over whatever it could lay hands on.

At his press conference at the outset of the festival, the Director, Mr Raina, had apologetically hinted at the economic constraints with which he has had to work. But there were identifiable lapses that have less to do with economy than efficiency. The issue of the subtitling of Satyajit Ray's films in the retrospective dedicated to him, for instance, was not something the foreign filmmakers and critics gathered in Bangalore were willing to dismiss as a trifle.

'No, it's not all right', protested the stalwart of Egyptian cinema, Yousef Chahine.

> It is a major scandal. I give myself the right to mention it to you in as violent a way as possible. Never again should a film of such an important man in film history be treated thus. He is a standard bearer of your country, like Mrinal Sen. So don't just let them go and spend 90 per cent of their time fighting to get a good copy or check whether the lab has subtitled their film. Somebody tells me we don't have the money for subtitling. This is crazy.

Reactions like this certainly do not redound to the credit of a Festival Directorate which, after all, is no 'ad hoc' body, and which had a full year since the last festival to attend to organizing this one.

Selection criteria for the Indian Panorama was another issue many at this festival were exercised about. Besides that films that are artistically almost banal, like *Ek Bar Phir* (Hindi) were included in this section, important recent regional films were left out on the plea that they were not submitted in time. There ensued a flurry of fringe activity with hectic private screenings of these 'late comers', well attended by foreign filmmakers, critics and distributors, while many of the Panorama previews ran to near-empty houses.

The selection procedure itself, it would seem, was tertiary in a manner that narrowed down the choice of the national committee set up for the purpose. The Malayalam entries, for instance, were made in such a rush that it is small wonder that significant films like Ravi's *Iniyam Marichittillatha Nammal* or Aravindan's latest, *Esthappan*, were overlooked. An official from the Directorate, as Mr P.R.S. Pillai, Chairman of the Kerala State Film Development Corporation, explained to us, arrived in Trivandrum one fine morning, called him on the phone and asked to be shown a list of films (a list he himself had made out) for entry to the Panorama section, and all this is in the course of a day.

The foreign entries covered such a broad spectrum that while variety was not lacking, it comprised a characterless medley. In terms of standards, there were very few films with that exploratory form and style of which the Madras *Filmotsav* in 1973 and (to a lesser extent) the Delhi festival last year had a good share. The graph, in this sense, shows a distinct plunge, and it would be simplistic to infer that general standards world over are on the wane.

Countries with formal experimentation as their forte hitherto, have now come up with rather pedestrian works. Many East European films, for example, were devoted to the problem of the working woman in a male-dominated society. For the most part these films went something like this: the working woman poised in a delicate relationship with her husband or family on the one hand, and the state on the other. A disgruntled critic summed up this type quite aptly: 'They are making films increasingly like they make tanks in East Europe nowadays.'

Latin American films were by far the best as a group. The continuous evaluation of form that steers clear, at the same time, of sterile artistry, was evident in many Cuban, Brazilian and Chilean films. But there were also those, linear and didactic in form, yet capable of making the viewer emotionally charged, which seem to indicate a reversal to the first principles of film as a heuristic and motivating tool.

The American and West European representation was as disparate – from Richard Kaplan's documentary approach, through Altman's and Fassbinder's personalized styles, to Scorsese's and Polanski's paced narratives.

At one of the innumerable token meetings that always punctuate these festivals, the chairman of the managing committee had hailed this by virtue of its modest scale and nature, as the festival of the small film. But at the end of it all one goes away with the feeling that it has been small in more than one sense.

First published in *The Hindu*, 23 January 1980.

New Trends in Indian Cinema

In any discussion of current trends in Indian cinema, the following lines of enquiry are important. How has the new cinema evolved, and what has been its impact on the Indian cinema as mass media or an art form? How can the films be categorized, and what is the ensuing role and motivation of the serious filmmaker? Does the 'new' Indian cinema tend to look back or forward? In the typology of films being created, what can be said about the regional as distinct from the all-India film, the commercial as distinct from the 'art' – and about the transitional category suspended between these two poles? Films have been used in many third world countries as political argument, but where does India stand in this respect? And what can be said about the role of the state in the evolution of the Indian film?

Sashi Kumar interviews, for *The Hindu*, some well-known filmmakers who gathered in Bangalore for the recent International Film Festival, to elicit responses to these questions. The filmmakers are:

G. Aravindan: Journalist and cartoonist-turned-filmmaker, he seeks to grasp in his art the enigmatic and the peripheral in life. Withdrawn and almost self-effacing as a man, Aravindan is noted for his keen cinematic perception evident even in his first film, *Uttarayanam* (Malayalam), which won a national award. His subsequent films, *Kanchana Sita* and *Thampu*, fetched him the President's award as best director successively. His fourth film, *Kummatti*, is a children's fantasy tale. In his latest, *Esthappan*, he reverts to the apocryphal set in a fishing community in Kerala.

Basu Bhattacharya: Entering the Bombay film industry directly after his studies in Calcutta, Basu Bhattacharya had his formative apprenticeship under Bimal Roy (whose daughter he later married). His first film, *Teesri Kasam*, won the President's gold medal in 1966. His other well-known films are *Uski Kahani*, *Anubhav* and *Aavishkar*. His latest, *Grihapravesh*, like most of his earlier films, deals with the man–woman relationship as the core unit of human society.

Gautam Ghosh: A young filmmaker, he brings to film a professedly didactic approach, which sets out to instruct and motivate. His documentary *Hungry Autumn* was received well by critics both at home and abroad. His first feature film, *Maa Bhoomi* (Telugu), is conceived in near-epic terms and deals with the Telangana struggle in Andhra Pradesh.

GIRISH KASARAVALLI: One of Kannada cinema's most promising prospects, Girish Kasaravalli bagged the President's gold medal for his very first film, *Ghattashraddha*, where he concentrates on highlighting defunct social mores which have ceased to have a logic in contemporary times. His latest creation, *Akramana*, features his wife as an artiste.

J. MAHENDRAN: One of the very few directors in Tamil who have departed from the box-office stereotype, J. Mahendran has made two memorable films: *Mullum Malarum* and *Uthirippookkal*. Keeping the viewer as his ultimate criterion, Mahendran is as contemptuous of the snob-valued art film as of the puerile entertainment afforded by the commercial cinema.

NACHIKET and JAYOO PATWARDHAN: A husband-and-wife architect team, the Patwardhans were financed by the FFC for their first film, *22nd June, 1897* (Marathi). Shot in 16 mm and blown up to 35 mm, the film deals with the martyrdom of the Chapekar brothers in the caste-ridden Hindu society of Pune in that period.

RAVINDRAN: Ravindran's emphasis on appropriate formal technique has made his maiden film, *Harijan* (Telugu), unique in its treatment of what he calls the 'class–caste syndrome' that characterizes this group in society. His subsequent film, *Iniyum Marichittillatha Nammal* (Malayalam), is a visual thesis of sorts, where through a fragmented narrative, he builds up the self-defeating case of the revolutionary gestures made by the enlightened middle classes. If the prevalent mood of his films is defeatist, Ravindran has valid reasons to let it be. 'This is an age of defeatism', he explains.

MRINAL SEN: Indisputably recognized (along with Satyajit Ray and Ritwik Ghatak) as a founder of the new cinema – which originated in Bengal – he is today its veteran exponent. Besides his well-known Bengali films, he has worked in Hindi and Telugu, the language never really posing a problem because (as he says) the language of poverty is the same everywhere. Ever aware that he must reach out to as wide an audience as possible, Sen yet continues to experiment with his form and content, but always steadfast to his stated sense of social commitment. His latest film, *Ekdin Pratidin* (Bengali), is a taut and incisive exposure of a typical middle-class feeling of inadequacy and insecurity.

Relevant extracts from separately conducted interviews with these filmmakers are presented here.

Evolution of New Cinema

How would you estimate the evolution of the new Indian cinema over the past two decades? Do you see this evolution as being shaped under the auspices of the state? How would you characterize this impact or influence, and to what extent does this determine the formal content, function and purpose of the Indian cinema as mass media or art form?

MRINAL SEN
Indian cinema as such started with diverse constraints operating at very many levels. Lack of awareness of the language of cinema and also a total lack of awareness of the socio-political scene in India are the two factors which thwarted the growth of our cinema. Before *Pather Panchali* was made – it was released in 1959, and that was possible because of the aggressive infiltration by outsiders headed by a man called Satyajit Ray – there were occasional flashes here and there, but no trend as such developed.

With *Pather Panchali*, for the first time, to my mind, an aesthetic of cinema was felt in India. Younger people appeared on the scene and more particularly in Calcutta, because Calcuttans felt it intensely. But all of them wanted to be mini-Satyajit Rays! Most of them did not take into account the fact that Satyajit Ray, even though he did not work under any director within the framework of the film industry in India, had been educating himself in cinema for long, long years. He was a lone student working within himself, as a viewer, as a reader and as a practitioner. And he used to write scripts just to educate himself.

Since filmmaking in India (like in any other country) has always been considered a money-fetching proposition, the financiers thought: 'Why not try out these young people who are more educated than those operating within the framework of the film industry, who are more serious, who are much less demanding and spend much less money?' So the financiers came forward and, in spite of themselves, backed these young belligerents. But they could not deliver the goods, because not all are Satyajit Rays, and not all films are *Pather Panchalis*. These financiers then withdrew financial support. The young belligerents too – some of them – became more careful and less courageous. That is why, again, a kind of compromise was made. The trend which could have been formed in a big way did not emerge.

You know, what you need for anything to be done is a kind of encouragement from outside, from other sources. Well the Government of India formed a commission, I believe in the early 1950s, which was followed by other commissions, and that is how the Film Finance Corporation (FFC) was built. But then the FFC made money available only to those who could guarantee a return of the money through mortgaging property or something else. So, for many reasons, the FFC could not be of much help. It was in 1968 that a friend of mine asked me to apply for a loan, and I was forced to make an application in spite of myself.

And that led to 'Bhuvan Shome'?
And that was *Bhuvan Shome*. The film was an accidental success – I mean commercially. This was perhaps the first time that government money was spent on an extremely low-budget film. I didn't have to produce any guarantee whatsoever. But when I went to the FFC office with a copy of the censor certificate – which clearly said that the film was 9,600 feet long – they were upset, because that

was in violation of the agreement entered into between one Mrinal Sen and the President of India! It was a 36-page agreement and at about page 30 there was a clause which said that the minimum length of the film should be 13,000 feet.

They asked me, 'Didn't you know that you had violated the agreement?' I said, 'No, I read only four pages', and I was convinced that very soon I would be sent to jail. They said, 'Until you make a 13,000 feet-long film we cannot accept it.' I said, 'I cannot add an inch.' So the matter was referred to Delhi, and at the ministerial level some amendment was made and the clause was withdrawn. So if *Bhuvan Shome* has done any good, it is the withdrawal of this clause. I tell you all this to show the stupid constraints that are put in the way. There are so many, and that was a new phase, a new chapter, for the FFC. They started encouraging good films.

So, in 1955 a trend started in Calcutta, and since then, for the last fifteen to twenty years, you see good films being made – in Bombay, south India and elsewhere. New people are coming up and the family is growing. But then, again, you see that there is not much of a dialogue among the new filmmakers. We suffer from what there is in the show business – as long as I am not your contender, you take a patronizing attitude; but the moment I become somebody, you look at me with a certain hostility.

You see this as something peculiar to India?
In a way, yes, because quite often we are seized with a sense of insecurity, almost of physical extinction. When I came here three years ago, I saw quite a number of south Indian films – films made in Kannada – and I was deeply impressed by the very healthy dialogue among the good filmmakers in Karnataka. So I wrote about it, I also started talking about it. But now I hear that this has also stopped. This is a curse of show business.

Well, the new cinema has been trying many subjects. They have been trying to use many forms, many styles, trying to communicate. You see, cinema, or any art medium, is a vehicle of communication. And if you fail to communicate, well, it is a failure as far as the viewer is concerned.

This implies that you don't agree with the view that art is expression first and communication only next; that communication is only incidental?
What expression? Expression of yourself? To whom? Is it a narcissistic complex or what? (*Laughs.*) Any filmmaker is primarily a social being. So, as a social being, he cannot but react to the situation around him. And he forms an attitude. If he feels like sharing his attitude with the people around him, the filmmaker has to express this through film. So I say, the fact remains that he wants to communicate. The expression is self-projection. Well, projecting for whom? For others, not for himself. And if anyone says that he makes films for himself and he doesn't care how other people react, I think it is a blatant lie. And it is

because of a sense of defeat that he takes to this kind of self-defence mechanism.

Now, over the past thirteen years, new filmmakers have come up and the greater ones are also reshaping themselves to make a new kind of cinema. They have put forward their aesthetic arguments and if this fails to communicate, it may be due to either of two reasons. It may be that the filmmaker has failed to communicate properly because of his lack of awareness of the medium or of the subject he is dealing with. It may also be that the audience has not been able to respond.

I think it was Ritwik Ghatak who said that it is not his films but the audiences who are flopping.
Well, I don't really know. In the initial stages, the moment I make a film and see the adverse reaction I come up with the same statement – that the audience has flopped! And then, when I retire within myself, I do a bit of soul-searching and try to find out where I have failed. So it is a continuous battle. You have to go on correcting your own conclusions and I would also invite the audience to correct themselves; to do a reappraisal of the film. It is very important for the filmmaker to know the spectators, and it is also important for the spectators to know the filmmakers. But we always find in India that the spectators do not want to budge an inch. The flexibility should be there on either side.

But don't you feel the urge at times to take on challenging new forms of artistic expression?
Yes, by all means.

Even if it means being less communicative?
Ah, there I come to a very important fact. Not that you can always communicate, but then it is, as I said before, a continuous battle and you go on discovering yourself. In order to be able to communicate more effectively you have to go on experimenting with your form. And as you go on experimenting with your form, perhaps, without your knowledge, you become a little self-indulgent. I am ready to grant this. Because, if not anything else, it at least breaks new ground.

I, for that matter, don't believe that there are some fixed norms for any art. The demands grow. In cinema, some artistic conventions are built, based on the physical properties of the tools, like lens, camera and so on. These physical properties are constant, but your inventiveness, your application of these physical properties, gives them a new dimension. And that is how artistic conventions change. To communicate more effectively you go on changing your vocabulary, you mould your vocabulary as you do in literature. And since cinema is, to a large extent, a technological performance, and since science and technology have been growing at a very rapid pace, the vocabulary is multiplying in cinema at a much more rapid pace than in any other art.

But in India, unfortunately, we are such a conformist country that we do not want to go beyond the experiences of our predecessors. And here, in a conformist country like India, we need to have a release of madness on the screen. Because this is how you can expand your area of operation. It is not necessary that you will always succeed in communicating. You may not succeed now, but there are others behind, standing in the queue, who will take it up and march again. In cinema, it is a continuous march, and a very rapid march, because of the fact that cinema is primarily a technological performance.

So I am not against such madness; I am not against self-indulgence if it is done without pretence, from an inner urge, like an artist. Not that the artist is always successful in using his brush or colours. Not that the poet is always successful in his use of words. In the same way, the sheer delight of making a film should be there, and a kind of abandon, a kind of verve, should be there. That, eventually, may lead you to expand your areas of operation and this is very important.

In your own career there seems to be a shift in style, almost a departure, from 'Calcutta 71' onwards – in the sense that you have chosen to be less subtle and more . . .
(*Laughing*) propagandist?

No, communicative.
No. I don't think I have been able to be that communicative. When I see that I have not been able to communicate to a larger audience, I feel like collapsing. And I have collapsed so many times in my life. I have been trying with many forms. I have been trying to educate myself in terms of content. For instance, many people, Indian and foreign, who have seen my latest film (*Ekdin Pratidin*) feel that here is a new Mrinal Sen emerging. They say it is very subtle, understated, but they felt emotionally charged. But I don't think I have shifted, I have been trying to be as faithful to myself as before. I think I have been able in many cases to do what I wanted to do – to disturb people. I don't believe that the film is a gun; that is just rhetoric. I would rather say that film is an instrument which will help you to use the gun properly.

Would you now modify what you told me once before, that film is ultimately a political pamphlet?
Well, it is a pamphlet. Did I tell you about this very interesting statement that even a lullaby is propaganda? Because a lullaby wants to put to sleep one who refuses to sleep.

Has the Left Front government in West Bengal come as a fillip to the new filmmaker?

Well, for the first time in West Bengal the government has been pursuing a very steady policy of encouraging good cinema. I was the first to be approached to make a film and I was given a very long rope. And I made a film on the pavement dwellers, *Parashuram*. But then, when you work within the framework of a certain party, you have to go by certain things which may not be reasonable. I have been having fights with the government. Desirable people are not always being given chances. Once when I frankly told this to the minister concerned, he said that he is not only a party card-holder but also a minister. He has to look to the interest of the economics of the film industry. But I feel like debating this point. Making good films and rescuing the industry from total collapse don't always negate each other.

Aravindan

In the present Indian context one cannot take film as a serious art form. It involves a lot of money. It should be technically and scientifically sophisticated, whereas we, in India, do things in a very primitive way. That is evident from the films which we see here. It is not a question of the filmmaker's capability. A lot of other restrictions and limitations are there.

You have not personally found it a problem to work within the given framework?
No. Not so far.

Because you don't proceed from a political standpoint?
That's a very interesting situation. My first film got a national award in the year of the silver jubilee of Indian independence. It was actually almost an indirect criticism of the situation. Frankly, I was very afraid that this may be really censored by these people. But I got the censor certificate and I got an award commemorating Indian independence too. So really I don't know. I can't make out head or tail of these things.

Basu Bhattacharya

No, it's not government-controlled at all. In certain states, these days, there is a little government patronization. But it is not government-controlled. You can almost say that the new cinema is anti-government cinema, anti-establishment cinema. And if you go to the mid-50s – that is the period I was contemplating joining films – there was a different kind of an awareness. This awareness is there now in a big way. It was there in a smaller way then, and this kind of cinema gave birth to filmmakers like Bimal Roy, Ray, Mrinal, Ritwik . . . all of them were there struggling to appear or arrive.

Going back to the evolution part of it, things started getting a little worse after the Second World War. The war not only killed lives, but also the culture of the people, and uncertainty became rampant in life. And cinema, which could have helped India in reconstructing the socio-political scene, failed – in spite of the fact that there had been many important films made during this period by important filmmakers. Say, now in the southern zone, so many films have been made and so many young filmmakers have come in. But the film that is effective is bad cinema. Aravindan has made a few films, but Aravindan's cinema is not dominating the Malayalam scene. That is the paradox.

RAVINDRAN

The major character of – and what appeals to me in – the new film movement is the trend of political consciousness with filmmakers like Mrinal Sen. I don't think the state apparatus has any direct control as such over these films. Surely, censorship places a lot of limitations. Maybe not on the political content of it, but when we make a film, we are very much conscious about what will be its fate with the censors. You cannot totally express what you want to.

J. MAHENDRAN

The new film movement is encouraging. It has given birth to a new group of filmmakers. But at the same time, most of the films by this new group are too abstract, for the sake of being different – like modern art. Only after it is explained, we understand what it is all about. It doesn't reach the common man. And they think this is itself their success. They think it a big thing that their films run for just a couple of weeks and are removed by the third week. They say the people are unable to understand them. They don't feel that they are also one among the people.

I don't think it helps to underestimate the people. Our Tanjore temple or Madurai temple must have been built so many years ago. The *Tirukkural* or *Kambaramayanam* or *Mahabharatam* must have been written so many thousands of years back. Only a society with a really developed mind and culture could have wrought these classic works. Tiruvalluvar all by himself could not have been the scholar he was. The whole society must have had this culture, this consciousness.

Art reflects society?

Definitely, definitely. So, the common man and the filmmaker are really one, they are not distanced. As far as I am concerned, I won't ever accept a product which does not reach the people as a good product. I don't say this because they have accepted my film. Tomorrow if they don't accept my film, I would think that there is something wrong with my film. Something they don't understand, something that is irrelevant to them, often goes by the name of new cinema.

I had seen Kasaravalli's *Ghattashraddha* (Kannada) and liked it immensely. There was some relationship between the viewer and the film. But recently I saw his *Akramana*. In it I could only see the gimmicks of a director. It becomes abstract because the director wants to project his intelligence. It was so vague I couldn't relish it. So I think a film must not be taken like that either. If in some way the film does not attract the audience, our effort has failed; the product is not good.

How would you see the change on the Tamil scene – say, over the past two decades?
There has somehow not been any great change here. Things have become a little better, that's all. At the audience level, there has come about a thorough change. But in the films themselves, the change is very slow. You see, it's like this. If there is only one tea-shop in a small village, the people have to drink tea only there – there's no choice. When a better tea-shop comes, they try it out and realize it is better. It's more or less the same case with our audience. But very few filmmakers here – only two or three – make a different kind of film.

And there are those who come with an approach that totally differentiates the common viewer and themselves. But they take the common man as their subject. They think, only if all the characters are morose, only if they speak unnaturally and slowly, it makes a new film. Different for the sake of being different. They try this and when one or two fail, they sit back. Basically, they don't observe their environment.

That's why I don't think the Film Institute as such can produce good filmmakers. A good filmmaker may emerge from there, that's a different point. It's not enough if they study acting or direction. They must study the society. Having seen a Fellini or a Bergman film at the Institute, they form some abstract notions and come to the field with a kind of preconception – a filmmaker should not be smart, he should have a beard, wear shoddy clothes – this is where their interest lies, more than in filmmaking. But a new crop of terrific artistes have come up in the new films. The people are ready to accept these kinds of films.

Does the state exert any influence?
As far as Tamil Nadu is concerned, the state influence – in terms of financial help – is hardly seen. In West Bengal, the government seems to be more involved in the filmmaking process.

You see, now the FFC selects scripts – I don't know on what basis they select them. Many have given scripts, most of them have been returned. There is no proper encouragement. But basically, I am not able to reconcile myself to the fact that the FFC goes through a script and grants the loan. You can never decide the final form of a film on the basis of the script. How can you? That too, a visual form like this.

What criteria would you suggest?
They have to see the finished product. Because you can never say whether the one who comes to them has the calibre to make a good film, or is just interested

and wanting to try, or even intending to exploit the FFC loan. Anyway, I don't think many scripts have been accepted from here, but I understand that in the north, in Bombay, this is happening. In the south, many lack knowledge of the FFC. Neither does the FFC publicize. The FFC had called me recently to discuss the possibility of a loan. But I said we have been trying to bring about a new kind of cinema here without the patronage of the FFC or the government. The producers have begun to believe me. So we don't really need government help or support. Only afterwards this comes – our problems with the government.

Take the problem of censorship, for example. Those who have nothing to do with the media are on the board. They quote the censor code and argue in a very childish manner. For example, they saw *Uthirippookkal* and praised it to the skies – so much so that I almost got embarrassed. And then they told me they were giving it an 'A' certificate. Their reason was that the central character was too crude. But he doesn't commit a rape or murder, doesn't use a filthy word. True, he's crude, he's meant to be that, and I'm glad that came across well. But how do these people decide that children will be corrupted by seeing him?

Suppose I make a film on the *Ramayana* tomorrow where Ravana is a character who carries away someone's wife. This is perhaps being taught in schools and colleges. And if I portray this, will they give me an 'A' certificate? Or if I depict Panchali of the *Mahabharata* with her five husbands? But to these arguments they have no reply. They ask me to go to the revising committee if I want.

So what happens is that even before I start a film, I am scared. Will they create problems about this script tomorrow? You see, these are practical problems. In Bangalore an 'A' certified film has to pay double tax. So the producer loses. Thus I am not able to keep my mind free of these problems when I think of a film. The government is to blame for this.

In other words, the government becomes more a hindrance than a help?
Yes. On the one hand they say, FFC loan, national award, etc., and on the other, there's censorship. The policy is not even. There are some parents who suddenly beat their children and then suddenly pamper them; such children develop a kind of nervousness towards their parents. We filmmakers are more or less in the same state. We don't know where the government encourages us, where it controls us. So mentally we are not free. They kill our interest. I think, even if they don't help, it's enough if they give us true freedom of expression. When we say freedom of expression they immediately construe it as sex or vulgarity. As if only these constitute free expression.

Gautam Ghosh

Even before *Pather Panchali* there were a lot of interesting films; there were filmmakers like Abbas who tried to make serious films. But with *Pather Panchali* what we got was the pure aesthetics of cinema. The efficiency was there, the sincerity was there, realism was there; but the aesthetic came with *Pather Panchali*. Bengal was in the forefront of the new cinema movement in the 1950s. But actually, only three directors – Satyajit Ray, Mrinal Sen and Ritwik Ghatak – could retain their sincerity and passion for good cinema for a long period.

There were other good films, but sporadically – some good filmmakers came, made one or two good films, and afterwards they compromised or collapsed. After this, new cinema again started in Bombay. Basically, the reason was this: Bombay had tremendous growth of an industry. We can say that it was actually capitalized, the only film industry that was capitalized in that period.

The FFC, particularly, had a great role to play at that time because it sponsored a lot of new films. The FTII (Film and Television Institute of India, Pune) also made its contribution, and really trained filmmakers came up in the industry. Since the Institute boys could see many foreign films, they were influenced by those films. But somehow, basically, that movement was a little empty as far as content was concerned. Most of these films struggled with a formal approach, the content was weak. Besides, there was no coordination among the filmmakers.

In Bengal, except for these three filmmakers, there has been a long gap during the past two decades. And then after that, again now in Bengal, I think a new generation is coming with good films. This is not only due to the film society movement, but also the political movement. The 1970s were politically turbulent years in Bengal, which had a lot of impact on the filmmakers. I think that's why a lot of filmmakers are giving serious thought to socially conscious films.

But the new cinema movement of the 1970s really started in south India, because a bunch of good films came together. I believe it started with *Samskara*. And then the south Indian states felt that they must produce, they must back good cinema. That kind of enlightenment led to state subsidy and financing.

As far as the central government was concerned, there were three factors – finance through FFC, the Institute, and then censorship. Naturally, to the filmmaker, there is always the fear whether he'll face the censor problem or not. But I think after *Garam Hawa* – *Garam Hawa* was first banned and then passed – there was a feeling that there was a more democratic approach to censorship. You know, if you follow the actual censor code, you can't make a film. So it's very interpretative.

Nachiket Patwardhan

The presence of the state is only seen in the fact that if it hadn't been for the state, some films would never have been made. Our film could not have been made if the FFC hadn't been there. Similarly, the movement in Karnataka is largely because of the subsidy. But in the content of the film, when you see the film, I don't think the presence of the state can be seen in it at all; what you see is a reflection of the society. I mean, even a film like *Muqaddar ka Sikander* reflects the world we live in.

But I think the basic concept of censorship is questionable – to give the right to a few people to determine for others. I don't think film should be singled out for special treatment (unlike printed matter or other art forms). I think, in a healthy society, even pornography has a positive role – as a safety valve. I think it would be better to have, apart from Universal and Adult, X, Y, Z categories. In our particular film (*22nd June 1897*) we didn't face this because it had no potential censorship problem.

Jayoo Patwardhan
I don't believe in censorship. Apart from that there are too many things coming in the way of breaking out of the old type and getting into the new cinema. Maybe because of the censor, maybe because of so many other things, we have a lot of inhibitions. We don't face censorship so much in Marathi. But I am sure in Bengal and Kerala, they must be having a lot of problems.

Girish Kasaravalli
I would estimate the evolution of Indian cinema over the past two decades as a reaction to the kind of films which existed then. At that time the filmmakers were using the media for the sake of entertainment. So the next generation started using the media with some purpose. They wanted to use it either as self-expression or to communicate to the masses. So they used it like this. It was only a reaction to the existing situation. The new generation of filmmakers wanted to react to the old tradition. It was a form of anti-tradition. This second generation's purpose was more towards interpreting reality than anything else. This is what I consider most important in them. Their treatment, their approach to the media was much different from the earlier one. They were taking a particular social problem and trying to analyse that problem from different angles, different viewpoints. I made *Ghattashraddha* where these traditions and rituals were being questioned; why were they founded? I have taken one particular issue which is no more valuable and which is not of any use to any particular society. So I was questioning that kind of ritual, that kind of tradition. What's their use?

The state doesn't have anything to do with filmmaking as such, except for one problem – that is censorship.

Film Categorization Role and Motive of Serious Filmmaker

Would you characterize film, in our given context, as predominantly a cultural, political or social category? On the basis of your priority, what is the ensuing role and motive of the serious filmmaker?

Mrinal Sen
I remember [Jean-Luc] Godard once did characterize two kinds of cinema:

political films and films made politically. Well, by political films you mean that you take an overtly political subject, where the characters are political, situations are political . . . any film which has something to do with society is a film made politically.

It is very difficult for me to draw a line between a social theme and a political theme. I have always tried to express myself in terms of human experiences. And, as I do this, I try to see how I can present the whole thing in an artistic form.

The serious filmmaker must consciously take a stance vis-à-vis the viewer? Must he formulate a stance?
I have always thought about it this way. I take up a subject only if I get inspired by it. And my business is to assess it, to examine the material on which I am working. The point is, then, to do justice to my own conscience. And when I feel that I have been eminently clear to myself, I feel that is how I will be able to communicate most effectively to my people.

And it is not the observed that I physically lift. But it is my observation which I project. Which means I have to project my attitude, which will be partisan.

ARAVINDAN
My feeling is that any art form, whether it is film or music or painting or literature, has no direct connotation whatsoever to the political or social reform movement. The impact in this sense is something which has to come later. As an example I can quote the Kerala Namboodiris. In the change of the political situation in Kerala they are the people who have suffered most – big landlords have overnight turned into paupers. But the way they have faced the situation is very interesting. They reacted in a peculiar manner. Instead of taking a gun or knife and revolting, they have taken this in a totally different episodical manner. There is not a single thief or murderer or (in common parlance) a bad person to be found in this Namboodiri community. And my feeling is that a person interested in good art form will be political and socially conscious.

So any art form – even if it is cinema – has nothing to do directly with the social or political struggle. But it contributes to the individual's psyche and personality.

A society without art, then, is more prone to violence and disruption than one which has a tradition of art?
I never say violence is bad. But a person who is interested in art will confront violence in a different manner, will be violent in a different manner.

What about your personal preference? Is its thrust cultural?
At my personal level, I entered film by accident. The first film I made was almost a political-oriented film, in the sense that it had a lot to do with the

1942 revolutionary movement for freedom. And that too, I won't say I initially wanted to make a film like that. The fact is I started that film on a script on the 1942 movement already written by a friend of mine who was very active in this movement. But instead of making a film on the movement as such, I projected it into the present context. I created a character who was a son of a martyr of the movement, and whose grandfather was a Gandhian. So I mainly dealt with the present youth in these circumstances – their reminiscences of the 1942 movement. People used to ask me why, after making a sort of political film in the first instance, I have gone back to mythology. But again, my second film, *Kanchana Sita* – based on a well-known play and taken from the *Uttararama Charitam*, the latter part of the *Ramayana* – I was not the one who selected it. My producer, who has made all my subsequent films, told me that he had this play with him and he would like to make a film with it. So, in all these cases, at least in the first two cases, I was not the one who selected the theme. But my primary concern was to make a cinematic version of whatever was given to me. In fact, in the third film, *Thampu*, I had all the freedom. As a journalist I had interviewed a lot of these circus people. I knew them intimately, and I thought I could do a film on them with sincere empathy.

My next film (*Kummatti*) – a children's film – was a fantasy. Then I had an idea of making a film on a person interested in classical music. I started on the script with a friend of mine, a psychiatrist, and found it was a very complex subject. I was requested by my producer to make a film in 1979 itself. Then I thought of the sort of strange people in every village who are always away from the main milieu and at the same time very active. I personally know a number of people in several villages of whom people say that they are 'erratic', or they have a deeper vision, or extrasensory perception and things like that. I have had my own relationship with many such people. So I said, why not make a film on a person who integrates all these characterizations of the people that I know. That's how I made my last film (*Esthappan*).

So what I am trying to arrive at is that in all these cases, my predominant concern was to make a film with all its cinematic characteristics.

Your films – and what you have just said appears to confirm this – are about the predicament of the small man or group on the fringes of society, rather than the average man in the mainstream of life. In your earlier career as a cartoonist too, your theme was the predicament of the small man. Your widely read Ramu cartoon series in Malayalam, for instance (called 'The small man and the big world')was about such a philosophical character. Are you not dealing with the exceptions, rather than the rule?

I am not very much with the political movement. I am not concerned with this aspect also. I am very much interested in individuals. Even if one person is wrong in a group, in a big situation or a big complex, I should stand with that individual. That is my primary concern always. The individual and his problems are more important than the non-human structure.

Have you found a development in your style?
After making these five films, I cannot say that I know the craft of filmmaking very well even now. But I have a lot of confidence. The freedom of the medium is with me now. I know that this, in one way, is not good. Only if there is striving can one make a good creation. If I am a painter, I must confront space. That confrontation and struggle must be there.

How would you rate a film which sets out with the limited objective of communicating a particular political message; a didactic film which concentrates less on cinematic values per se?
I rate such things only from the cinematic viewpoint. Because if you want to convey something political, film can be one of the mediums, that's all. You can always bring pamphlets and distribute them, or write on the wall, or use posters.

To you cinema is basically expression, rather than communication?
To me it is only expression, nothing else. Communication comes only later.

Basu Bhattacharya
Well, it could be all these primarily and it is not. Because in anything that is controlled by profit motive – and in a situation like India where only if you make profit you survive – sometimes you make profit monetarily, sometimes you make profit culturally. Many a time you will find that though X's films are not making any money, X is getting finance to make films. The reason being – either it is being exported and getting a little money, or that the film is earning a name for somebody else. You see, there are many people who can give money to Satyajit Ray or to Mrinal Sen, just because their association with Ray for a few lakhs of rupees will make them more famous.

So you think there is an exploitation of the filmmaker?
Oh, yes. It's not a question of what I think. I know definitely that many people have tried to make this kind of film only to get awards. At the same time I would say Mrinal might have been used like this by some businessmen, but that doesn't mean that Mrinal himself is not seriously trying to make socio-politically motivated films. But as I look at it, basically, Indian films always definitely had a social comment to make. That had been there even during the pre-Second World War and post-Second World War period. Then you had innocent films and socially relevant films; even some political films.

When you say 'innocent' film, is it the same as mindless entertainment?
Well, almost that. But the point is that if one is really designing innocent cinema, that is not mindless cinema. Mindless cinema is there today where the actions are designed in such a way that even a man with a mind cannot really keep his mind intact and see the film. Innocent films are a peculiar kind of innocent entertainers. Like the Wadia Brothers' films.

So, in your priority, film is more a social category?
You see, I don't really know. My situation is terrible. I come from middle-class stock and I feel that throughout the world the most neglected man is the middle-class man. Almost all sensitive people in the area of art and culture have come from middle-class stock. And most of them deny it; most of them reject everything that is middle class, including the existence of the middle class!

I feel that the agony of the middle class is not really understood by anybody. I feel that there is something wrong. You make films about classes you don't know – about the upper-class problem and lower-class problem, without really knowing them. Then you are representing, you are painting another kind of reality which really does not exist! And the reality that you do know, you are not talking about it. You are ashamed of it.

As far as I am concerned, as you've seen, almost all my films are man–woman relationship films. And I personally believe that this – man and woman put together – is the smallest unit of human society. This one-and-one-equals-one kind of thing, you know. And I try to portray that through my films.

Are you influenced by [Michelangelo] Antonioni in your recurrent theme of the man–woman relationship?
Not really. I would not say that I have seen many Antonioni films. But I am concerned about man and woman in a slightly different way. You will find that my films are set in realistic situations, but Antonioni films are very idealistic. I try to see the possibility of the *ideal* man in the *real* man, the man who is existing. From that point of view, my films are totally different.

Ravindran
I think it is the same thing; it is one. It cannot be divided.

But what is your motive in making a film?
Communication, surely. I like artistic films – well made, though less communicative. But when I personally make a film, I want to communicate. Because I think in our situation what we need at present is to teach, to educate, to propagate. That is very important in the kind of oppressed society in which we live. We cannot afford to be highly artistic. I am a journalist and filmmaking to me is

an extension of my career. Only, the film reaches a larger mass . . . (*laughing*) although in my case so far, it hasn't.

I have a certain ideology. I look at society from that point of view. I try to analyse society and 'try' to bring out these political values with emphasis. That is my attempt. Even when dealing with politics – many films have dealt with it as a cliché. Almost like any other film; like the MGR film – in the fight between vice and virtue, virtue wins and the people are happy that virtue has triumphed.

I think the new cinema should make a sociological analysis of the given situation. That's more important than making just a political film. You cannot simplify matters. It is not that simple. If it were that simple, our upsurges like the Telangana movement would have succeeded. A riot in a village, or caricaturing the landlord as a villain, will not solve the problem. The analysis must be there; the analysis will bring an awareness.

To me, film is a personal device to analyse a given situation. Like when I report as a journalist, I have my personal attitude but I don't interfere with the theme. But there is an attitude. My involvement as a filmmaker is seen in the attitude that my film exposes.

Well, although both your films are analytical in this sense, the reigning mood seems defeatist. Why?

Let me take *Harijan* (Telugu) first. There are innumerable films on Harijans. All these deal with the Harijan problem and end with a revolt by them – a revolt which is like a comfortable dream. And everybody leaves the theatre in a happy mood, that the oppression is revenged. I think that is not a positive approach. Maybe this approach is not defeatist, but it is not positive either. The Harijan problem – in the sociological sense – is that they fail to assert themselves. They are tradition-bound. The caste system and their social feudal relations keep them down. It is a peculiar caste–class syndrome. By stating it in my film, I wanted to convey an analysis which will make them aware of this state of being.

The same is the intention in my *Iniyum Marichittillatha Nammal* ('We who are not yet dead' – Malayalam). But it is a different kind of film. I wanted to do something different from other films. It is almost a confessional film for me. All of us have so many social or political ambitions, and yet we fail to do anything because of so many external pressures; because we get personally frustrated; because we are urban-educated people fighting away from the masses. I think we don't analyse ourselves. And only when we fall, we realize this. So, the defeatism or resignation of the characters is not negative. It has a positive effect because the film makes them aware that this is the situation you are in.

This film is not addressed to the masses. It is addressed to the particular classes portrayed in the film, to the urban-educated elite who are away from the mass struggles – the futility of their revolutionary gestures and their petit-bourgeois predicaments. And I am not accusing them. Because I am also a part of that class.

But you wouldn't go so far so as to offer solutions?
No, I don't think so. I may not be correct. It is the system. The system oppresses them. But when they abide by the bourgeois modality of the system, they cannot escape. They should get away from the existing bourgeois values.

But these are really systemic.
Yes, yes, that's why it becomes a reactionary statement, sometimes, when you say that you have to change the system first. But for changing the system also, you need this. That's why they say that finally, the bourgeoisie will not be very helpful in the revolutionary upsurge. It should come from the masses.

MAHENDRAN
As far as I am concerned, I don't like to make political films. I don't like to preach. If the people infer something from it, well and good. I look at films in a social light. When you listen to good music you feel physically and mentally happy; certain colours please you. These subconscious reactions regarding colours, sounds and so on take place even when you see a film. It affects the viewer without his being aware of it.

But one thing I keep in mind and try to introduce somewhere in the film. The end in *Uthirippookkal* is in a sense contrived. The director imposes himself in the scene where the people force the central character into the river, knowing he cannot swim. They could have killed him, like in *Nishant*. Why don't they? Because direct revolt is not in our blood. There may be injustice taking place before our eyes, at the government level, on the street, but we won't question!

Take the censors again. Have the filmmakers ever joined together to challenge the censors? Whenever they are individually affected, they say something, issue a press statement. But they won't raise their voice together.

So the quality of revolt is not there in our people. They lack self-confidence. I am always aware of this. I try to bring this indirectly somewhere in my film – this consciousness of revolt emerging, their raising their voice.

GAUTAM GHOSH
I feel as a medium, it is a language. I don't want to say that it is an art form. It's a language and with this language you can create, you can talk politics, you can make an educational, instructional film.

Is this language primarily political, economic or cultural?
Language is language. But with our language we can create literature, geography, many things. So cinema is a language. But basically all films are directly or indirectly political. Since my ideological understanding says that we are a

class-divided society, our culture is also on a class basis. So most films, directly or indirectly, will preach the ideology of a certain class.

But the average new Indian cinema seems so culturally oriented; it seems to bear a cultural stamp, unlike, say, Latin American cinema, which has more of a political orientation. . .

This depends on the situation. The basic economic or cultural situation is almost the same all over the third world. But in our country we don't have the kind of direct repression which Latin American cinema faced. Latin American cinema started with political cinema, because the whole cinema movement was part of the political movement there.

NACHIKET PATWARDHAN

Cultural. I think that is what it is. Film, or any other art, is a cultural form. What makes it culture is the process and the craft. The art of film comes first for a peculiar reason; because, if you put communication first, then the message which is being communicated and the audience which is going to receive it get priority in the process of making it.

Now, there are very few films which I have seen where the audience or the content has priority over the maker's vision and his preoccupation with his own views. Whether it is Pop or Op or art or commercial or sex or thriller or whatever. So even a commercially popular cinema is really the producer's idea of what the masses want.

GIRISH KASARAVALLI

Well, the filmmaker is using the film only from the social point of view. So far we haven't used film to carry a political message or anything, except for a few rare examples. The others are using film only to show the social aspects of a problem. And this was probably the impact of neorealism; the problem confronting man and the structure of society. How the structure of society affects the individual's abilities, and things like that.

Whenever we make film, we take a particular problem. And we should look at it from different angles and try to give our own solution to it. This can be done only if we are either directly experienced or if we analyse things in such a way as to bring some kind of awareness in the audience. And also a new approach. A commoner wouldn't have seen it from that angle. The responsibility of an artist is that he should try to find the root cause of the problem from different angles. Problems are not as simple as we think. They have different facets. The filmmaker must make the people understand the problem from all its different angles.

I am not saying that people have not been able to understand the problem. But they have seen it only from one particular angle. So the responsibility of the artist is that he should be able to find out all the different facets of the problem.

As far as new filmmakers are concerned, because of censorship and other problems. I don't think we are doing as much as we should do.

Looking Back or Forward?

The point has been repeatedly made that the so-called new Indian cinema has not really shaken out of the stupor that informs most of our art forms. It becomes, even where it deals with the contemporary human predicament, nostalgic and revivalist in its thrust – the casualty in the process being modernism. And this seems to have to do with both form and content. To what would you attribute this? Do you take cognizance of this in your work?

Mrinal Sen

This may be due to a long period of colonial rule. Without being disrespectful to tradition, I would like to say that we unnecessarily bring forward this factor of Indianness. We can clearly see that in these days of science and technology, we are living in a kind of what you may call bastard culture. I find it superb. You cannot escape it.

[*Sen here recalled how, when his son was six, the two of them set out one morning, and his son, enthused by the beautiful horizon, compared it to a 70-mm screen. Sen was thrilled, because his father or grandfather would instead, probably, have described the scene as Jatayu taking wings or with some such mythical reference.*]

I always take nostalgia with a pinch of salt. I am a little scared of it, because it quite often leads to a kind of sentimentalism which I have been trying to avoid all my life. Let us take the case of Ritwik Ghatak. He was a very fine filmmaker. He grew nostalgic about East Bengal and working from this nostalgia, he went in for a cinema and drew conclusions which – politically and socially – became almost reactionary. At times it sounds like Hindu revivalism.

Unintentionally, of course.

Very, very unintentionally. He was a very fine filmmaker, very warm, and his sense of visual was very exciting. But then you see, without his knowledge, this happens. So I am very conscious of this danger. And that is why I always have a big fight with social anthropologists who try to build a big case on rituals. Rituals are today just sport, nothing more than that. And quite often in the new cinema, whenever they have to take up a rural subject, they dwell on rituals quite a lot, making things very pretty, very beautiful, very exotic. It is almost like the Red Indians are being treated in the US, you know, the reservations and all that.

Aravindan

In a given political situation, for example, take the case of China or Vietnam, where even with all this imposed culture along with the revolutionary movement, it doesn't work out. For example, Mao Zedong was a very good poet and with the Confucian theory and philosophy and his poetry, he tried to effect the revolution; it required an artist to do that. The same was the case with Ho Chi Minh, he was also a poet. If it were a society where the people were really interested in all these things, instead of it being imposed, the situation would have been different.

But don't you think art has become purposeful and functional in China?
This art being made functional, or part of politics or part of propaganda – it may not work out. I come back to the Namboodiris of Kerala, people who are very interested in art. I think the first set of people who took up communism in Kerala were the Namboodiris. Such people will react to any political or social situation honestly.

Don't you see a conflict between the cherishing of traditional art on the one hand, and the demands of social change on the other?
I don't think so, because a person who is with the traditional art form will always be aware of the political situation, and he will react earnestly and sincerely. So, altogether, art – whether film or some other – makes a man better. That is, ultimately his reaction to a situation will be much more earnest, sincere and noble. So that is where the function of art comes.

Your 'Thampu' is contemporary in every sense. But 'Kanchana Sita', 'Kummatti' and 'Esthappan' have a mystical, almost apocryphal, quality about them. Don't you think this can become retrogressive in effect?
I don't think so. The ultimate thing is what comes out of the work. The ultimate style in any art form is to reach the stage of music. To me music means the abstract plane of the symphony, or classical Carnatic music. That ultimate form is very much a way for a filmmaker in India. There again, it's a question of finance.

Basu Bhattacharya
There's a point in this. But I would put it this way. Probably, when you say this, you have these films in mind – say, Ray's *Pather Panchali*, or Pattabhirama Reddy's *Samskara*, or Karanth's *Chomana Dudi* or Nagabharana's *Grahana*. They appear to you as being something from the past. But they are really not.

You see, this is another peculiar thing. Almost all of us have our roots in the villages and are living in cities. We think that the city is contemporary India and the village is the India of the past. But when you look at things properly, then you know that these films, though they appear to be from the past, are really not. They are around there in rural India.

But the filmmaker tends to look at rural India in an exotic light – you know, almost like a tourist.

Yes, this is the point. Whether rural India is being captured because the filmmaker wants to talk about it, or he is attracted to rural India because of its exotic quality and the foreign market for it. If one goes deep into it, one will probably find that this is true.

The real cinema of the country has to really take its birth in its own place. Its aesthetics and its appreciation must take place there. If your cinema is good because it has been accepted in Cannes, Berlin, or in Venice or Moscow, then I don't know what is the future. The good cinema of a country has to be primarily accepted, and appreciated, in that country first. I have seen so many foreigners coming here and picking up films for their festivals. I had occasion to talk to them and I enquired, on what basis do you choose? The point is they have certain ideas about the Indian scene, and when something confirms that, they like that. The India they want to see – they are looking for that India in us. If we are making films for them on this ground, do you know what we are doing? An educated Indian knows much more about Europe than Europeans know about India. And that's why our scope for misunderstanding is much less whereas their scope for misunderstanding is much more. India seems to be, to them, Taj Mahal and slums and tigers and elephants and beggars and kings, etc., etc. Suppose I think that Paris means Eiffel Tower and night clubs?

Or, take the instance of song-and-dance. It has been picked up by our bad filmmakers from our tradition and used in a very bad way. But a few filmmakers have used it very well. The operatic form – the *Nautanki* and *Jatra* styles – have been used by our filmmakers in a brilliant way. So it is very necessary to have a different kind of understanding – understanding without any motives. You know, today there is a lot of motivation about our cinema from outside India. They are culturally motivated, politically motivated, religiously motivated. They are not straightforward human motivations and that is why one has to be very alert.

RAVINDRAN

Yes, modernism is affected because when a work of art has to stress a particular value, it will have its effect on the total social response to it. If any work of art is to stress certain values in opposition to the existing values, this will have a political or social impact. A value assessment becomes important here.

When you want to bring back the feudal or classical values, it affects modern living and what is important to modern living. We had, in the last decade, a tendency to revive and reassess old films, Saigal's music and so on. But we cannot deny these either, because they were relevant and appreciated in their time. So I cannot really say that this has a negative effect on the contemporary political or social situation.

But my point is that in the very structuring of the film, say, in the framing of a shot, in the lighting – very often a soft, Victorian kind of lighting is used – this harking back is seen. And this seems to detract from the contemporaneity of what is presented.

Surely this makes the film less powerful, less communicative. For example, if I had made my film *Harijan* in colour and tried to bring out the beauty of the landscape, or if I had the girls made up, it would not have had the effect I wanted to communicate.

In *Iniyum Marichittillatha Nammal*, I wanted to make it very prosaic in form. It doesn't have the body of a narration. It has the body of an essay, an article – what we in Malayalam call a *prabandam*. I have underplayed the characters. I didn't trace them back to their sources or sharpen their characterization. They are there as political arguments.

Are you happy with the outcome?

I can't say. Always a work is a vision half-fulfilled.

MAHENDRAN

I have often thought about this and I once argued with Girish Karnad on this same point. The new Kannada filmmaker seems to think that villages, cows and brahmans make a new film. I think many of these filmmakers are city-bred, have been abroad, and so they are attracted to the villages.

You mean, they have a tourist's viewpoint?

That's the word. Yes. They look at it like a tourist. I'll give you an example from *Nishant*. In that film Shabana Azmi in the village washes her child's bottom and immediately reaches out for soap to clean her hand! Now this is not done. We know that even in the city a middle-class wife in the circumstance would just wipe her hand on her sari. I have been asked why I went to the village for my themes. But I had a good story set in the rural background.

GAUTAM GHOSH

Basically our attitude is very parochial in all aspects. We always, in the name of tradition, become nostalgic; we go back to the past. Although cinema is a mass medium it does not reach the masses as it should. I think it does not reach more than 30 per cent of our population. So although we produce the maximum number of films in the world, the exposure is not great or even, due to the distribution, etc. We must try to find a new language to communicate. If you analyse the Japanese cinema – Mizoguchi or Ozu – they have really discovered a Japanese form.

In your 'Maa Bhoomi' (Telugu) you use the conventional narrative form along with the documentary approach. This makes it look sincere, but loosely integrated in form.
I was very conscious about this. First, I thought of making this film in a totally non-narrative style. But then again I felt that unless we give a narrative which will go with our protagonist, it will be difficult for the masses to understand. And that's why I wanted to combine this fiction and documentary approach. Now when I see the film, I feel you are correct. It is a little disintegrated; that's the weakness of the film. I want to re-edit it. Because such a film is not my ego-trip. It's a film which should reach out; it should be perfected. It should be more refined.

Since you have interlaced fact and fiction, and as the viewer, as is well known, brings to film a kind of selective perception, do you envisage a possible impact where the fiction aspect overwhelms the fact?
No. I don't think so. The dialectical approach is always there. I believe this combination of fiction and fact will be interesting for people, as it is very simple and didactic. In any case, you have to attempt. This reminds me of a Chinese story of two mothers. One mother cautions her child against going to the big river as the child could drown. The other mother says: go and learn swimming there so that you won't drown. I feel that our films should be didactic and instructional. They should be simple in form and the narrative should be very clear.

You don't believe in pure cinema?
I like pure cinema; visual forms and all that. Excellent. But at the same time, you have to consider your situation. I feel that the Italian neorealistic style still has value and significance in our country.

JAYOO PATWARDHAN
Even if we can show realistically what is happening just now, that would be quite an achievement. There is this conflict: our own orientation takes us back to our culture, and what we are learning from the west is so fast that we can't really keep up with it.

To particularize, have you come across the criticism that your film ('22nd June 1897') on the Chapekar brothers is Hindu-revivalist?
NACHIKET PATWARDHAN
No we haven't, because it hasn't been screened anywhere else yet. What we have tried to show is that their (Chapekar brothers') religious fanaticism, which is shown by their pretending to be Muslims and trying to get out of the situation; their lying about the assassination until they are beaten into confession – these are fanatical religious ideas, but also the lack of bravery to actually face fire;

the weakness of a human being, to say that I didn't do anything, I am innocent. This, for any person who looks intelligently at the film, wouldn't seem anything to be proud of. Whereas if we had covered up these facts and only projected the religious element, that would have been disproportionately revivalist.

But you have construed them as martyrs . . .
We have tried to show that this is what is called martyrdom. But I think the whole issue came up after they were hanged. Political capital was made out of this.

So they were acting from communal motive?
The motivation of the Chapekars was based on caste feeling, on anger. After they were done away with, Tilak and other politicians made capital out of it. You know, you need a rallying cry for any movement. The Indian movement needed martyrs.

Haven't you been very interpretative in your social or historical analysis of the time?
I don't think the concept of India being one country from Kashmir to Kanyakumari was really there at that time. So the Chapekars' approach was communal, whereas Tilak's was not.

GIRISH KASARAVALLI
Right now, in our reaction to the old tradition, we may have gone into that kind of art form. Perhaps the reaction to this would be the right type. We are trying to find a new grammar, a new style of expression. Take Mani Kaul. He's trying to evolve a new language. Every language and every medium has its own different techniques. And cinema too has its own language. That is the cinematic language.

Film Types: Regional and National, Commercial and 'Art'

(a) With the growth of the new cinema in the country, there is taken for granted a dichotomy between the commercial cinema with its Hollywood heritage on the one hand, and the new, regional cinema on the other, with an uncertain cadre of transitional films hovering between the two.
(b) Does this transitional cinema present the possibility of making the masses gradually conscious of the more relevant cinema at the other end of the scale?

MRINAL SEN
Well, I don't think that's how you can strike a balance. You can't. Whether Truffaut practised it in his later films I don't know, but he once said that it is very important for us to organize a kind of planned violence on the audience. When I make a film I don't compromise with my understanding of the reality, however faulty it may be. Every time I make a film, I am inclined to believe that

this is my funeral film. But it is not impossible to continue to work on these lines. This kind of striking a balance is a very clever thing. Quite often you are liable to get into the wrong side.

What is true of cinema is also true of other arts. For instance, if you take literature, there are many works which are more popular than the more serious works. But it doesn't mean that popularity ensures aesthetic achievement. Never. In the same way, if the popularity of the cinema, if the communication is more, it doesn't mean that it is the right kind of cinema, or that it has communicated in the right manner. The point is to take up your subject – what you wish to communicate. And the popular cinema, does it wish to communicate anything at all?

In our country, for instance, we have a large number of bad films, and most of these bad films are made very unintelligently. There are very few bad films which are made intelligently, and these few can communicate to the people. So there we have to be very cautious, and we have also to take a lesson from such bad filmmakers.

At this point, I am ready to dispute the validity of a national cinema. I think that the concept of a national cinema should be examined and re-examined.

Is it an imposed concept?

To a large extent it is, and it is also due to a high degree of conformism. Now, for instance, there is nothing national in the use of camera or sound or in juxtaposing shots. You have heard about Ozu, considered to be very, very Japanese. He always has his camera on the ground, that is, the traditional sitting posture of the Japanese. But then, if I ask Ozu to take a shot of the Sanchi Stupa or Shravanabelagola, and if he places his camera on the ground, does it in any way look Japanese? You know, Kurosawa made the film *Dersu Uzala* in the Soviet Union with his own Japanese understanding of the medium. And it is called a Russian film because it captured Russian scenery, Russian physiognomy, Russian speech, food habits, etc., in a certain context. But then, this Russianism is just on the physical plane. Beyond this physical perception, he is what he is.

Pather Panchali was made by an Indian and it captured the Indian scene, but you feel as inspired as a New Yorker feels. So it has nothing to do with Indianness or non-Indianness. I remember I was so impressed by Polanski's *Knife in the Water* that I rushed to my home to bring my wife to see it again. I don't belong to Poland, nor does my wife. But even then, I could discover myself in the film. As we came out of the theatre, my wife and I, and as we looked at each other, perhaps we understood each other a little better. So you don't need to be a Polish citizen to understand this. It is universal.

When I came to Andhra Pradesh for my film (*Oka Oorie Katha*), in an alien atmosphere, in an alien climate, in the initial stages, because of the physical peculiarities, I had a sense of distance. But then, I made a frantic effort to be able to respect the circumstances in which my characters lived. The minute I am able to do that I find that it is very easy. It is my world. I never feel that I am an outsider. I am into it.

You are all along using the term 'national' not as against the 'regional'?
No, no, no.

I see your point about the universal appeal of film media, as something that makes you empathize across national barriers. And yet in Polanski's very case, his 'Knife in the Water', being truly Polish has, precisely for that reason, a peculiar edge over his later American, British or French films.
Well, I could not like his later films that much. It is true that you can communicate better when you are in your own area. Cultural closeness is very important. I feel quite at home when I have to work on the theme of poverty in Andhra Pradesh, in Maharashtra – being a Bengali myself – in Tamil Nadu or even in any part of Africa. But I feel like an outsider in a society crowded by such people. If I am asked to make a film on an industrialist in Bengal, maybe I will have to do a lot of spadework to educate myself.

So I feel culturally free in my world; that means the world of poverty and exploitation. That is why you see in most of the left literature in India, whenever they have tried to project the bourgeois society, they have failed. They go by a middle-class conception of morality. And that is why whenever they have to show an exploiter, they paint him black. The climactic scene shows the exploiter womanizing. This is purely middle class-ish. This is because of our ignorance of this culture. Womanizing, for instance, is only a secondary exploitation; the primary exploitation is economic and political.

Aravindan
My feeling is that it is not right to classify it into two simple watertight compartments like that. Again, we come back to the economics of it. Film is a medium not fit for a creative artist in India. It's simply a question of finance. A serious filmmaker has to get a rich person or run after all these government organizations – which is not required for a poet or a painter.

What about this talk of national cinema?
The national cinema makes no sense. What happens is if one makes a film in Hindi, it is seen as national. It is not like that. There is no truth in that. It is the regional milieu that is natural and universal.

But since you were talking about all films striving towards an abstract plane, is it necessary to have any definite topographical context at all?
It may not be necessary in that sense. But film has got an organic base. But

anything we, in common parlance, call regional is universal. I have had a lot of experiences of people and things, experiences which cannot be explained scientifically. I believe that what we have achieved through scientific progression so far is inadequate; it is only a point in history. There is much more than that. I believe in everything unscientific. I don't believe in scientific achievements as such, which are the criteria in many instances.

Basu Bhattacharya

There is the extremely commercial, and the extremely non-communicative cinema. The commercial cinema, designed commercially, is terrible cinema. There are many films which become commercial – they have been designed to communicate and they become successful. *Pather Panchali* was a very successful film even among the people.

But only after it got a Cannes award?

No. No. No. This is not true. This is a myth. I was there in Calcutta when *Pather Panchali* was released. I was a student. It did not run maybe the first two or three days; it picked up immediately. It swept the Calcutta audience off its feet. *Do Bigha Zamin* became successful, but it was not designed commercially, whereas *Madhumati* or *Chandralekha* were designed commercially and were successful films. That kind of designing is no more there. The present multistarrers are designed commercially, but they are designed with fear. That's why they are multistarrers.

I put it this way: there is one cinema which corrupts and that cinema is pampered by the common man. There is another cinema which confuses and that is pampered by the confused intellectuals. And there is yet another cinema which is very cleverly designed; that is partly commercial and partly art, of which they say: this is a good film because there is no song in it, no fight in it. It is not good for what it has in it. That is probably the cinema of the middle.

But I think there is a cinema which is above all this. That is the cinema of communication. If you see everything without any prejudice, then I think the motive of the man who has made it can be very easily detected in a film. There is a cinema existing through which that man is trying to communicate, and that man is important to me. And that cinema is above the art of commercial clichés.

When I see men like Karanth or Pattabhirama Reddy, I am absolutely convinced that they are trying to express themselves, not trying to impress the audience. The commercial man is trying to impress people. The so-called artistic fellow is also trying to impress somebody. And that's why I reject both of them.

Incidental to this, it has been observed that in our given context, a truly Indian film can only be regional, it cannot be national; that national cinema is just a pious aspiration. How would you fit the new Hindi cinema here?

I feel as a Hindi filmmaker, that Hindi is the real national cinema. You see, Ray's cinema is Bengali cinema and then international cinema. Aravindan's cinema is Malayalam cinema and then international cinema. It is not national cinema. It is very unfortunate that our regional films are not taken all over the country through dubbing or para-dubbing, or something of that sort. In certain areas it is being done; you will find regional cinema in Tamil or Telugu being dubbed in Hindi, and shown all over the country. But these films, unfortunately, are either mythological or sex films. Ray took so many years to bring his films to the south because it had to come via Europe.

This is tragic. This is where I feel another kind of awareness is necessary. There is a film society movement in this country. But again, they are all fond of seeing foreign films, giving only lip service to the local cinema movement. So it is very necessary that at least all the films that get national awards are immediately dubbed into the local languages, or at least in Hindi, or subtitled, and shown all over the country. Encouraging of good cinema is not just an award. It is the following up. Take me, for example. I, Basu Bhattacharya, was born in Bengal and have settled down in Bombay. I wear pants. I don't speak Bengali in Bombay, I mostly speak English. Now if you make a film genuinely on me, I am sure it has relevance all over India. If you look into it properly, you will find that the moment cinema started talking, it became regional. It's only because of the language. Silent cinema had been universal.

Doesn't the milieu create a problem? For example, when Shyam Benegal makes 'Ankur', it is the Andhra milieu and ethos, but put across in Hindi.
I don't think this is a problem. One gets used to it, like one has got used to wearing pants. Pants are no more European. You can assimilate, and India has a fantastic power of assimilation, because we are basically social human beings. We are basically lovers; we love everything – sometimes we love bad things too, and for a very long time.

Indian cinema has become characterless because of fear. Originally, Hindi films were made in Punjab, Bengal, Maharashtra. None of these are Hindi-speaking areas. And yet these films were made here. Even today, most of the Hindi filmmakers of consequence are not Hindi-speaking people; it is the desire to communicate with a bigger mass. But then, as soon as it was taken over by commerce, came the fear. And because of fear, Ashok Kumar, who is a Bengali, is called Ashok Kumar because he should not be known as a Bengali. Dilip Kumar is a Muslim. But he was scared to call himself Yusuf Khan; so he is Dilip Kumar. But that scare is no more. That's why today Sanjay Khan is Sanjay Khan, Feroz is Feroz Khan.

So I definitely believe – and I advocate – that a director, say, Aravindan should not only make Malayalam films; he should make Hindi films in Malayalam – where the appearance remains Malayalam and the characters speak some kind of Hindi which will be understood throughout the country. In the process, Malayalam culture will spread throughout the country.

Just a personal question. Being a Bengali – and Bengalis being intensely regional – you would probably be at greater ease with Bengali films.
Yes . . . definitely.

Then why do you opt to make films in Hindi?
Because I don't think the regional richness will survive if Hindi is not rich. Because Hindi is the central power. Hindi is reaching everywhere. Shakti Samanta and Prakash Mehra are known all over the country, but Satyajit Ray is not and Aravindan is not.

About two-thirds of Indian cinema is produced in the south today. And more than two-thirds of the south Indian films are bad, worse than Hindi films. Why? Because they have to survive, competing with bad Hindi cinema. That's why they have to be worse. Likewise, most of the Bengali cinema is worse than bad Hindi cinema. And this is why it is very necessary that there should be good Hindi cinema.

RAVINDRAN
All cinema wants to get its money back. Of course, the commercial cinema can be distinguished from the rest by its use of stars, etc. But I don't think it's right to say there is an art cinema and a commercial cinema. There is only good and bad cinema.

Why not use stars as a strategy to get a wider reach?
Because the stars will remain stars in my film. They won't be characters. The basic thing is this. When Prem Nazir acts in a film, the people see him as Prem Nazir, not as the character he is playing in the film. He is a kind of wish-fulfilment to them. Usually, I think when they say national cinema – as against regional cinema – they mean Hindi cinema. In that case there is a lot of distinction, because the regional cinema expresses a regional character. Even the commercial films of the different regions. Let us leave out the south Indian commercial films like Telugu, Kannada or Malayalam – because they are also going the way of the big-budgeted Hindi film. But regional films, as in Oriya or Assamese, definitely express regional character and regional values. Maybe these are not very artistic. But the regional stamp is there.

MAHENDRAN
I think there's even a fourth category. What would you say about an art film which becomes a commercial success? But I think these filmmakers would be

upset if their films ran. They would think: have we become so cheap? There's such a rush for our films. (*Laughs.*)

So I think the transitional type is better. We need not cheat ourselves making art films, nor need we cheat our audience making commercial films. There should be a better taste, but the film must reach the common man. There are filmmakers who take a vow that they won't have songs in their films. But then, the song is very much part of our culture. It's not necessary that you use the song only as a duet. There's nothing wrong in a song situation where the song comes naturally, in the course of the theme. Likewise, a street brawl or fight is very natural. It need not be a fight composed by a stunt director. But the art films avoid these. They become dull and dry.

As for the new film being regional, I don't think it has too much to do with language as such. When cinema itself is language, there is no need to think that only if one is a Tamilian, he is a Tamil actor and so on. We have in our films, artistes from various parts of India – Bangalore, Bombay, Uttar Pradesh, Kerala, Bihar, Gujarat, etc. So language is not a problem. But I don't have any fancy for making a film in any other language. In Tamil Nadu itself there are changes in the culture of the people, their temperament, the Tamil they speak, from district to district. There's a lot we don't know here itself. Then why go to a different state about whose culture we know nothing? The nativeness is very, very important for the new kind of cinema, perhaps not so important for a film like *Sholay*. So I think it is better if filmmakers restrict themselves to their own areas.

GAUTAM GHOSH

This concept of transitional cinema is very ambiguous. There will be a transitional period for any movement. But this kind of thinking is dangerous. Suppose these people make a film thinking: 'we will try to make ourselves popular'. What is the degree of the popularity?

It can become populist in the process?

Yes. In the process, yes. We still have to go with our film to a minority audience. This can't be helped, because throughout these decades people are habituated to this kind of cinema, and they think cinema is for entertainment, cinema is a circus. I am not basically interested in that kind of thing (transitional cinema). It is an eyewash just to support this commercial cinema. They say, if you make your film realistically, people don't understand. So why not incorporate your content in the usual form? But this is very dangerous.

New cinema has been identified with regional cinema. There is also the feeling that film should be national. How would you respond to this?

I feel that film should be national. But not in a sense of pure nationality. It should be based in your soil; it should reflect the problems of your own people. When I make a film in Bengal, I strongly feel for my own audience. That is national. There is no sense in saying that national integration should come through your film, or that some kind of national call should be there in your film. That is different.

You have made your first feature film ('Maa Bhoomi') in Telugu even though you are a Bengali . . .
Right. Right. That's a very interesting question. The obvious reason is that I got a producer there for the kind of film I wanted to make. But at first I didn't want to make this film because of the language; because of the people, whom I didn't know. But my producers argued that you are making a film on the Telangana movement, and if you make this film in Hindi or in your own language, it can't reach to the masses of Telangana. The prime motive was to reach the Telangana peasantry. So I travelled a lot, did a lot of research on the Telangana area and found that the basic problems are the same throughout the country.

Nachiket Patwardhan
I think it's difficult to describe a national character – can you?

Jayoo Patwardhan
Not in India. You can say, a Hungarian film. You can say, a Brazilian film. But you can't say, an Indian film.

Nachiket Patwardhan
Just as it is difficult to describe a national character, a national film becomes very difficult to make.

So it can only be regional?
I think so. Because there are very few greats of India that are anonymous culturally.

Which automatically puts the Hindi film at a disadvantage?
But Hindi is a regional language. Unfortunately, there aren't Hindi regional films. I think *Garam Hawa* is an excellent example.

Girish Kasaravalli
I don't have any faith in the transitional cinema at all. When you say transitional cinema, it's like sugarcoating the pill and taking it. But that is not going to help us in any way. Because only if we show them the harsh facets of reality, can they face the problem. So the artist becomes insincere, because he cannot project the problem in its true light. The advantage we have with the regional film is that we can really pinpoint the problem with reference to a smaller area, whereas

on a larger canvas the filmmaker makes compromises to appeal to everyone. In regional cinema, if one picks up a problem one can really tackle it very seriously. This is one advantage we have.

Political Films

Many third world countries, the Latin American countries, for instance, have used films as strong political arguments. Do you see the absence of such politicization in the most socially conscious of our films as a consequence of the censorship or our peculiar liberal-democratic tradition?

MRINAL SEN
This is primarily due to the fact that our filmmakers' awareness of politics, of sociology, is not adequate. Quite often they put the blame on censorship. But have they ever tried? When they can try, in spite of the censorship, the intimacy in the bedroom, why not this? Most of our films have suffered a lot of cuts because of their sex or violence. But when it comes to politicization, or putting forward arguments which may be found offensive by the censors, they never do so. Because of their lack of awareness, because of their lack of interest, because of their idea of involvement.

But then, again, the censor codes are very broad and become very interpretative. Let us take the code which says that the film must not offend the sensibility of any religion. *Samskara* was originally banned by the Madras Censor Board because it was considered anti-brahmanical. But was later certificated and released, without changing the censor code.

ARAVINDAN
Here again it's a question of finance.

But in our very conceptualization, we seem so much behind these countries. The cinematic sensibility itself is here not as developed.
There's one point here. The art of filmmaking came into India almost on par with other countries. It had perhaps just a four- or five-year gap. Naturally, it was a projection of what was being made outside. It was also a projection of the theatre in India. Cinema came to these other countries of the third world only later –there was at least a thirty to forty-year difference. So films made in many Latin American countries have a natural strength – the initial strength and capacity. We are only traditional filmmakers.

BASU BHATTACHARYA
It is not because of the state or censorship. I am sure if I want to make a definite political film, I will make it whatever happens. And there are such people; one

or two films of this kind have been made. But the point is that all our political leaders, our social leaders, our educational leaders, have been averse to cinema. Even today they have not accepted cinema as a medium which can change things.

You see in the socialist countries, cinema became a powerful medium only because Lenin one day just stood up and said: Here it is! Use this giant medium and reconstruct society and create the new man through this. And they did it. You see, it needs a Lenin, or a Gandhi or a Nehru, to pick it up. It has to be accepted by everybody. Can you imagine that Mahatma Gandhi did not know of Charlie Chaplin? Because he did not understand the medium. If he had understood, I am sure he would have been a filmmaker. Because he could have reached the common man much more easily.

Ravindran
In some countries, the national milieu is such that they have a particular taste. Latin American countries have undergone much greater oppression than we physically have – oppression which may have either tamed them or made them stronger. Moreover, technically they have much better facilities. They are closer to the sophisticated American industry.

Gautam Ghosh
We still don't have a nationwide solid class conflict. It is there; but it is hidden. Political cinema developed in Latin America because political parties were involved in filmmaking. But in our country, I think only one film was made by a political party; that is *Dharti ka Lal*, directly produced by IPTA long back in the 1940s.

You don't find the censors responsible for the absence of bold films in our country?
Yes, responsible indirectly, because we start with a preconceived notion. When we write a script, when we conceive a film which may create a problem with the censors, we feel that we can use some symbolism, or tone down our attitude. So this kind of compromise comes at the very outset.

But I was surprised that the censors should have let off your film so lightly. Especially the point where you depict the zamindar of Nizam's Hyderabad adapting himself to the new situation by switching overnight into unmistakably Congress garb!
The same thought struck me when I was conceiving the film and writing the script. But I decided to give it a try, because our Censor Board has limited experience of political cinema. Also because, at your point of departure, if you start with that kind of fear, it will be very compromising.

Mahendran
The main reason is the censors. Despite all this talk of lifting censorship, I am

sceptical. They won't let go of censorship. It's not our viewers; the ones with the poorest taste are our government leaders. There is no young blood there; no uniform policy, no guts.

Why, they give the best director award to someone and the best film award to someone else! Isn't this proof enough of their childishness? It's like saying this is the best suit and that is the best tailor. That's the way of satisfying everybody.

This has been happening in the national awards from the beginning. Or take the festival films. The kind of films they select. Why, when the whole country was wide awake – including your Ray, Mrinal Sen and Ritwik Ghatak – MGR takes a Bharat award for acting! Before our very eyes! After this, do you think we will have any respect left for national awards?

NACHIKET PATWARDHAN

This is primarily a problem of the whole national attitude. This is what we keep running into. I think we have not got independence; we have only got freedom. There's a big difference.

The totality of our problem is so vast and film constitutes only a part of it. And if you try to fight your way out, you can't remain outside the realm of politics. You see, you can live with a situation, and you know that you have the ability to break out of it. But unfortunately,we might all accept the situation so much that we will become incapable of doing anything about it.

GIRISH KASARAVALLI

I don't think filmmakers here have used films as strong political arguments. They haven't been able to do that because, as I said earlier, we are using film in the social context. One problem could be the strict censorship. They will even allow sex and violence, but not politics. So, what some of the politically inclined filmmakers do is they make it a fantasy type, putting the situation in a different context altogether. They are not facing the problem in the right space and right time; so the impact is lost.

I think they should be more lenient towards political films. Only then we can make better films. In other countries they can bravely criticize the existing situation, whereas we can't. Unless we broadly classify it as richer class and poor class. That way they accept it. The censors, as they are, are definitely not acceptable to anyone.

First published in *The Hindu*, 18 February 1980, in the newspaper's 'Outlook' series dedicated to in-depth analysis and lengthy exploration of each issue taken up.

Director's Alter-Ego

Pared down to its essentials, John Abraham's cinematic approach is a curious and typically erratic admixture of the solipsist, the solecist and the surrealist in him. The self-projection is egocentric – not in a megalomaniac manner but in that of a possessive artist. Sensationalism, then, seems hardly the intent when John announces, at press conferences, that to him his own films are the best ever, and he himself the greatest director. It takes a lot of reconciling to the streak of the absurd John invariably brings to bear on his films. Yet it is this that, while jarring on one's sensibility in one instance, fascinates with its *outré* dimension in another.

In his *Cheriyachande Kroora Krithyangal* ('The Cruel Deeds of Cheriyachan'), John has got together a rhapsodic narrative, insignificant by itself (even if the events portrayed are supposedly real, having taken place at a transitional period in Kerala's not-too-distant political history) but meaningful as an alibi for a confessional appraisal of the self.

The involuted, obsessive and compulsive fears that impel the main character (played by Adoor Bhasi) to his doom are articulated by the director by this semblance of a plot, surreal imagery and a tinge of Christian sarcasm (a weird parallel reference is made through captions to the crucifixion of Christ; and when Bhasi climbs the tall coconut tree from where he is to plummet down to his death, John calls it 'The Ascension').

Action and plot are incidental to this basic experiential expression. It therefore becomes futile to look for unity of action or structural logic. The gist of the story – a pathological dread of the police, as a hangover of colonial rule – is itself only a means, just as Adoor Bhasi himself is only the director's alter-ego, helping create a setting for this expression. The director and his film ultimately become indistinguishable, inseparable. The fears and hallucinations externalized by the director are internalized by the character in the film representing him; it is re-experience by proxy. It is this unity of inner purpose, rather than an attention to exterior detail or technical finesse, that sets the film apart from others.

For an out-and-out director's film, it is, paradoxically, the actor's performance that seems to clinch the effect. Adoor Bhasi, who has, if anything, been overexposed to Malayalam film-goers as the brash, tummy-shaking comedian whose wit borders (at times sickeningly) on the lewd, has stepped in for John with a total transformation of personality and style. The old, all-too-familiar Bhasi is hardly recognizable in this schizophrenic pull between the real and the unreal. His taut, withdrawn features convey fully the psychology of a disturbed mind, clammed up within his shell. It is impossible not to empathize with those eyes haunted by, and mirroring mutely yet eloquently, dark fears of the known and the unknown. It is a sheer living of a role no director, by himself, could have extracted from his actor.

With John's purpose and preference in placing a low priority on the technical aspects *per se*, it is small wonder that the film bears marks of hasty, haphazard craftsmanship. As proven a cameraman as Madhu Ambat (whose work in the Telugu film *Harijan* was so appropriate and to the point) has rested content with jerky panning and long-to-deep focusing, with a suggestion of soft focus here and there. It is difficult to decide whether the damage was done while shooting or editing, as in the instance of half-accomplished visual swerves. Yet, in certain well-choreographed long-takes, in the formal accentuation of the surreal tone achieved, among other modes, by snippet sequences in colour, or in the extra-visual treatment of the sound track – in all those the genius, however erratic, of John Abraham comes through; the genius of one rated by Ritwik Ghatak, years back, as one of the most promising (along with Kumar Shahani) among the country's new filmmakers.

First published in *The Hindu*, 16 March 1980.

FFC: Inadequate Institutional Status

Mood is the essence of the plot in *Lace Maker*, a French/Swiss/West German production, heralding a series under the Film Finance Corporation's (FFC) art circuit at the Kalaivanar Arangam in Madras. Here is a film not about people but about minds; minds, the director leaves us in no doubt, conditioned and determined by society. The intricate relationship between Pomme, a girl in her late teens working in a beauty parlour, and Françoise, a serious, sensitive college-going youth, develops to its inevitable parting of ways, impelled, it would seem, by some cruel inexorable logic. The director seems to be letting us in on a clue to the crisis when Pomme, intrigued by the word, asks Françoise what 'dialectic' means. He explains that it is the action of two opposing points of view. And yet, paradoxically, when the first flush of love is past and the promise has turned sour, the breach comes not as an issue forced but as a pent-up crisis. This sense of ellipsis vests the film with poignant pathos.

For the FFC itself, the art-circuit concept seems to be another measure to ascertain its own identity as a promoter of good cinema in the country. Sandwiched between a not-too-solicitous government on the one side, and the carping criticism of filmmakers who find the modalities of securing an FFC loan far too rigorous on the other, the FFC of late has been striking a no-one-understands-us note. The government, it points out, treats it on par with any other commercial importer of film – obliging it to pay the same customs duty, besides royalty, for the films bought. Faced with this dual aspect of its promotional function and its own survival as an independent organization, the FFC has perforce to reconcile itself to a rather ambivalent image.

It seeks to combine within itself the roles of a commercial distributor and a patron of good cinema. Entering distribution in 1976, the FFC now offers the commercial distributor a package deal – a new Indian non-commercial film with a foreign commercial film. *Gaman* and *Kasturi* have been negotiated for the south. More recently, the FFC has mooted a scheme to finance the construction of cinema halls, in collaboration with state governments or relevant corporations at the state level. The Kerala State Film Development Corporation (KSFDC) has already announced the construction of a chain of theatres in the state, and the Tamil Nadu Theatre Corporation (TNTC) is thinking on the same lines.

All this, while making the FFC more dynamic and comprehensive in its role as a sponsor of the new cinema, seems at the same time to diffuse its thrust in any one particular direction. If government apathy has thrown it into near competition with commercial interests in the industry, it would only follow that in its exercise to stay out of the red, its assistance to the new filmmaker becomes a marginal concern. What could otherwise be passing-the-buck becomes, in this case, a legitimate complaint of responsibility without commensurate resources.

Not that the government can be expected to subsidize, in any substantial manner, the experiments of our filmmakers. Economic imperatives and national priorities probably dictate otherwise. And yet, there is certainly a case for tax remissions, at least for films winning the national awards each year; surely the loans granted by the FFC, or at least the interest charged on them, could be written off or waived for award-winning films at the national or regional levels. The FFC itself could (if it can take on distribution, it can as well do this) produce the film it finances and have executive producers to keep the budget in check. Surely no filmmaker who takes recourse to an FFC loan has runaway profits in mind; it is the creative motive of the director rather than the profit motive of the producer that takes one to the FFC.

What is encouraging is that the FFC is aware of these possibilities, and has for some time now identified its tenuous relationship with the government as being responsible for its inadequate institutional status. The issue is ultimately tied up with the larger and long-standing need for a national film policy.

As Jagdish Parikh, Chairman of the FFC, observed at a symposium at the recent Bangalore film festival:

> The Indian film industry is the biggest in the world. . . . But it is also the most complex and most problem-ridden. . . . The major responsibility of, and challenge to the government, as I see it, is to bring about an organic goal congruence, among the economics, aesthetics and ethics of film-making on the one hand, and among the conflicting but interdependent functional interests of the industry – namely production, distribution and exhibition.

First published in *The Hindu*, 6 April 1980.

The Subtle Image of Sen

'This is a new Mrinal Sen emerging' – Sen himself sums up the initial critical reaction to his latest film, *Ekdin Pratidin* ('And Quiet Flows the Day'). 'But,' he adds, 'I don't think I have shifted from my position as a filmmaker. I have been trying to be as faithful to myself as before.'

At face value, there should be no inherent contradiction between the desire to communicate and the attempt at self-expression. And yet filmmakers have come to see the two as irreconcilable; if one is totally self-expressive one is not as efficiently communicative, and vice versa. Ultimately, of course, there is no such dichotomy between the two, as Sen realizes. He has often had the predicament of having to discover a well-meant film turning out to be not so communicative after all, in terms of its box-office performance. It would seem that his influence is restricted to those who have cultivated a taste for his filmic style and purpose. His *Oka Oorie Katha* (Telugu) was a reasonable success in Calcutta, although viewers in Andhra itself seem to have rejected the film.

So vital is form to the technological/aesthetic evolution of cinema that Sen is willing to grant even an amount of self-indulgence with form. Sen's career itself illustrates this priority. Beginning with more involved and compounded form (ending with *Calcutta 71*), Sen chose to scale down and simplify his structure so that in *Bhuvan Shome*, *Mrigaya*, *Oka Oorie Katha* and *Parashuram*, we have almost straight narratives, more akin to the conventional Indian style of storytelling. If motives must be imputed, Sen's purpose in this phase seems to have been that of the ideologue rather than that of a thoroughgoing aesthete. Not that he has ever been abashed by accusations of pamphleteering through his films. 'Even a lullaby is propaganda,' would be his stock repartee, 'because it wants to put to sleep one who doesn't want to sleep.'

There is perhaps the suggestion of a paradox in that one so committed in one's use of the media should be as exercised about filmic form as Sen is. Indeed, so fed up is he with the Indian disposition not to go beyond known experiences, that he speaks in terms of the necessity or 'a release of madness on the Indian screen'. But then, Sen himself has been evolving as an artist, and the emphasis seen on an aspect of form or message in any of his films must be placed in perspective on this scale of progression.

When we thus arrive at *Ekdin Pratidin*, what we see is not a new Sen emerging, but a veteran artist combining, with consummate assurance, form-as-structure and message-as-content in his work. From its choice to its conception and treatment, the film is subtle; far subtler, as many will point out, than Sen's recent films have been. But it is not the subtlety of temporized or euphemized sensitivity. It is a subtlety not soft but brittle, keeping in tense check the dense pressure of a rallying flood of dramatic possibilities.

Terse in form, the film is a gripping exposé of ambivalent middle-class values. Like a surgeon with his scalpel, Sen meticulously rips open the façade of middle-class propriety or prudery (call it what you like, he seems to say), to expose the malignant sense of insecurity gnawing away at the very vitals of this class. In a decrepit old building (built in the year of the Mutiny, 1857) in the sprawling, disarrayed metropolis of Calcutta, where the various tenant-families live perforce like a joint household, a young, unmarried working woman who supports the rest of her family does not turn up home after work one evening.

As the wait becomes unbearable, passions and frustrations, pent up for long, break out. The pensioned father, the stoical mother, the wasp-tongued but affectionate sister, the unemployed and constantly nagged brother and the younger schoolgoing one – all of them dependent in one way or the other on the sole earning member – react with mutual recriminations for what they assume to be her getaway bid from her tiresome responsibility, or worse, the possibility of a tragic fate (abduction, rape, death) overtaking her on her way back home. Added to this is the problem of keeping their apprehensions away from the only too sympathetic neighbours.

When the woman returns home, nothing untoward having happened to her, and accosts them with their basic lack of faith in her, the blame, so callously bandied about, turns inward. As the wearisome night passes and day dawns, the façade is perhaps back again. The tenants go about their morning chores, set to get through another day. But in the last shot of the coals being stocked in the quadrangular veranda, there is a hint that the shame of mistrust has not died down and will continue to torment their relations.

Sen's approach to his plot is amoral. His protagonists are what they are by virtue of their peculiar social circumstances. At one juncture – when the brother is scouring the city for his missing sister – Sen wrests his viewers away from the narrative briefly to treat them to statistics of the crime rate in Calcutta. So double-edged is his theme that if he did not make every moment potent, the whole film would have flopped somewhere in the early stages.

The splendidly in-character performance of each of his actors, no doubt, helped the building up of mood. But every frame reveals the director's sure hand. Everything said and shown is intrinsic and organic to the structure. There is no jarring, supervening message as in *Mrigaya* or *Oka Oorie Katha* or *Parashuram*. The film is a composite whole; its form and its message become inseparable, and so it is all the more effective.

The subtlety achieved has heightened, and not soft-pedalled, the impact. As Sen himself says: 'The whole thing is understated and through understatement I have been able to convey whatever I wanted to say, and they (viewers) felt emotionally very charged.' Not that such understating is not in danger of being misperceived as a toning down. 'I met a man', says Sen, 'who said it's a very very light film. Light, meaning it does not show much violence or much anger on the physical plane. . . . I told him, my English is bad; but your English is worse.' Not too courteous perhaps, but typical of Sen's impatience with intellectual responses to his films.

First published in *The Hindu*, 27 April 1980.

Surrealistic Horror, Sardonic Humour

It is easy to imagine Alfred Hitchcock – his face a disconcerting dead-pan – scheming away with perverse humour the gory details of his victims done to death, and dexterously manipulating the traumatic responses of his high-strung audience. The inner construct of a Hitchcock film, its externalized melodrama and its peculiar visual dynamics are all evolved from Hitchcock's own insight into the predispositions and psychological stance and cathartic potential of his predominantly average, middle-class audiences.

'Audiences', says Hitchcock, 'are strange. I know their reactions so well I don't have to go to the theatre any more. The emotional anxieties are pretty well standard. And they do not necessarily relate to right and wrong.' And neither does a Hitchcock film ever dabble in morals. The delineation of characters is never manichean in its purpose or thrust: people are what they are circumstantially and the circumstances themselves, it would seem, conspire to precipitate the action. There is an odd material determinism about a Hitchcock plot which, by its irrevocable and inexorable nature, becomes at once forbidding and compelling.

Critics have been reluctant to grant Hitchcock the credence of an original master. Manipulative plotting and slick, tense footage become only box-office stuff, having little to do with the evolution of a new genre. This scepticism is reflected in the fact that Hitchcock was nominated for but not awarded the Oscar thrice, despite his long sojourn since *Rebecca* (1939: produced by David Selznick of *Gone with the Wind* fame) in Hollywood.

His knighting by Queen Elizabeth seems almost a British reaction to the continents (America and Europe) side-stepping their great director. As early as 1949, Lindsay Anderson summed up this identity crisis of the British filmmaker personified in Hitchcock, thus:

> As, geographically. Britain is poised between continents, not quite Europe and very far from America, so from certain points of view the British cinema seems to hover between the opposite poles of France and Hollywood. Our directors and producers never – or rarely – have the courage to tackle, in an adult manner, the completely adult subject; yet they lack also the flair for popular showmanship that is characteristic of the American cinema.
>
> It is significant that the most widely celebrated of all British directors should be

> remarkable for just this quality. So much so indeed that, when his powers were at their prime, he emigrated to Hollywood: and today when he returns to work again in a British studio, he carries with him the pervasive aura of Hollywood success, and stays at the 'Savoy Hotel'.

That, however, may be an extreme British point of view, carried to the extent of being squeamish. Because, even at his most American Hitchcock could never really be un-British. The change in locales and the widening of the canvas notwithstanding, the craft was essentially British in style. Unlike Hollywood's elaborately grandiose productions, almost every Hitchcock film is informed by an economy of expression that becomes at once both a tactic and a technique – a tactic whereby once, with a few bold initial strokes, the viewers are shaken out of their complacence, fear and foreboding of things to come are firmly planted in their minds and begin to work themselves up to a heightened pitch of trepidation; a techninue in that, so developed, the screen images, moving in a paced, rythmic narrative, are not so much stupendously horrific as subtly suggestive or provocative, spurring the imagination in its frightful flight rather than confirming it on the screen.

Alienation is of little use to Hitchcock. His films are rooted in the mutuality of the viewer and the viewed; a Hitchcock film is primarily an emotive experience. Hitchcock himself offers the apt comparison: 'it's rather like taking them (audience) through the haunted house at the fairgrounds.' That his films are so immediacy-oriented did not really upset Hitchcock. He revelled in the dramatic and he was never ashamed to admit it. As he put it, 'I have too much conscience to make films that would please only me and the critics.'

But among the dramatic uses of plot on celluloid, Hitchcock's is perhaps about the best. His early experience with the silent film (he made ten silent films) helped him evolve a visual perspective that was unfailing in its impact. If, as is often said of him, Hitchcock had the film finished in his mind before it was actually shot (he took a whole year to script *North by Northwest*), the shots themselves were atomized so that sequences often acquired an expressionist rather than a merely narrative character. In his 'footnote to the film' Hitchcock wrote: 'What I like to do always is to photograph just the little bits of a scene that I really need for building up a visual sequence. I want to put my film together on the screen, not simply to photograph something that has been put together already in the form of a long piece of stage-acting.' As early a film as *The Lodger* (1927) opens with the close-up of a man's pale hand sliding down a bannister-rail.

In his very first sound film, *Blackmail* (1929), Hitchcock struck a novel note. The portrait of a laughing jester in the artist's studio in the film is used throughout as mute testimony to the strange goings-on in the street. In the last shot, however, when the portrait is carried away down the corridors of the police station, there is the echo of ironic laughter on the sound track. Or again, the shot where the chambermaid discovers the body in *The Thirty-nine Steps* and screams out in the screech of the train in the following shot as it emerges from a tunnel, may be stereotype even in a slick Hindi film today. But that was perhaps among the first such uses of sound as a track independent of or even more impactful than the visual. Almost the first attempt at an overlaid track speaking out aloud the thoughts of a character as he shaves was made in *The Murder*.

It has been commented that Hitchcock's 'best achievements have occurred when the counterpoint between reality and the abstract has been most disarming'. And, indeed, if Hitchcock must be classified, he is not so much realistic as surrealistic in his approach. Time and place are often suspended in favour of desired impressions. Cary Grant in the agarophobic backdrop of the prairies in *North by Northwest* and Anthony Perkins in the claustrophobic, gothic sets of *Psycho* are not as much characters we identify with, as personifications of aspects of our emotions.

And almost as if telling us that he himself does not believe in the stories he weaves for us, Hitchcock compounds horror at its worst with humour at its most sardonic. Audiences are only too familiar with his habit of making brief personal appearances in his films, almost as if he were making a mockery of it all.

First published in *The Hindu*, 1 June 1980.

Malayalam Cinema Today

The staunchest apologist would find it tiresome to stand by the kind of weird themes spewed out by the contemporary Malayalam cinema. The sheer physical output, averaging more than two new films each week (at over 130 a year), is bad enough, but having to cope with the spate of sex conundrums that have besieged the industry of late can be positively mind-boggling.

The cinema that had, in the late 1960s and early 70s, prided itself as having come of age with its socially realist approach, now presents a confused picture of libertine fetishes – almost as if a puritanical façade has been cast aside to reveal a gaping, gawkish, adolescent prurience. The distinctive Kerala ethos and native ambience have given way to half-baked psychological treatment of a variety of sexual urges and complexes which are passed off under the dubious classification of 'bold' themes.

Where this compulsive sex element could become objectionable, in a clever subterfuge that seems to remind one that evasion of the censor code is not the same as violation of it, it is woven into an appendage of a side plot which, even if scissored, would not affect the main course of the story. The sexual tangles themselves are contrived and overwrought: father marrying the son's harlot, lending a new incestuous edge to their triangular relationship (*Angadi*); husband fathering his wife's sister's child in one weak moment one rainy night (*Eden Thottam*); a gallant epic-type fivesome avenging feudal oppression and living, *à la* the *Mahabharata*, in communal polyandry (*Idimuzhakkam*); a brown-wigged hunter turning a peculiar combination of misogynist and compulsive womanizer ever since he returns home one night to find a stranger in his wife's bed (*Kavalmaadam*); a virgin-witch 'raped' of her demonic powers (*Kafka*).

What is worse, the social milieu itself is distorted to abet the escapist Freudian abstractions at hand. For all its slickness and pace, I.V. Sasi's *Angadi*, for instance, becomes highly retrograde for its flippant treatment of the vital aspect of its theme – class conflict, that is in the fore of Kerala's collective consciousness. In conventional, cultist terms, the collective momentum is individualized and lionized in the star (Jayan), whose physical endowments and role-play characteristics actually set him apart from the masses he seeks to represent. The absurdist finale is all too familiar. Wishy-washy romance calls a halt to a historically determined class conflict; the class hero falls in love with his capitalist enemy's daughter, the girl's father himself relenting his exploitative ways and turning over a new leaf! If the director is naive or presumptuous enough to try this on screen, the audiences themselves have been content to lap it all up: *Angadi* is reported to have broken all box-office records in Kerala.

The plight of Malayalam cinema today seems all the more deplorable in contrast to the Tamil scenario. Paradoxically, when a host of fresh filmmakers have made a dent on the monolith of stardom in Tamil, the director as superstar seems the undoing of the Malayalam cinema. Less star-centred than in previous years, it is more and more the director who calls the tune there today, as the one who makes or mars the story. That he has marred far more than he has made, is the peculiar tragedy of this phase in Kerala's celluloid history.

First published in *The Hindu*, 20 July 1980.

Peter Sellers: The Last Laugh

It will never be the same laugh again for millions of his fans and admirers the world over when they review, in the years ahead, his many facetious portrayals on the screen. Death would invest Peter Sellers' side-splitting verve with a subtle poignancy and the focus would shift from the orchestrated clowning to the Chaplinesque humaneness of his roles. What a writer for *The Guardian* observed way back in the 1960s becomes all the more significant in posthumous reference: 'He is . . . becoming funnier than ever – because, and not in spite of, the new humanity and pathos which he now achieves.'

Split personality, endemic to the actor's profession, must conceivably have been a far more complex problem with Sellers. Born into a family already in showbiz (1925), Sellers' early flair for mimicry developed into more obsessive and involving role-play, so that he soon acquired fame as 'the man of total anonymity and thousand voices'. Sellers was himself aware of the identity crisis ('As far as I'm aware, I have no personality of my own whatsoever'), and yet to each of his diverse roles he brought a seriousness of approach that belied the flippant nature of his themes. Like Sir Alec Guinness, Sellers gave the nuances of voice and accent primacy when broaching a role; but unlike Sir Alec, he relied a lot on his inspiration fired by a feel of the part. 'Alec', Sellers himself drew the difference, 'likes to work out just what he will do before he starts. I have to get into the part – feel it from inside.'

The man and the actor then telescoped into each other, and the headline-hitting personal life of Sellers, with its passionate romances, brisk divorces, jet-setting, outlandish tastes and interviews, fetish for cars and gadgets (he owned 150 cars in thirty years and rode a giant mechanical elephant), was devoured as eagerly by the public as his bluster-and-bungle characterization in forty-four-odd films and numerous TV shows.

Sellers himself seemed to find his real and make-believe worlds indistinguishable. Imagine calling up a programme director of the British Broadcasting Service (BBC) and impersonating voices of two BBC stars to recommend a young comedian, Peter Sellers. The gamble worked for its very brashness and Sellers clinched his first radio spot on *Show Time*. Teaming up with Spike Milligan and Harry Secombe, Sellers regaled British listeners with his mimic medley on the radio, *Goon Show* (1952) , which raised conservative eyebrows because it made a huge joke of British traits.

Already putting in cameo performances in films like *The Lady Killers*, *The Smallest Show on Earth* and *Tom Thumb*, his big-time debut came with *The Mouse that Roared* (1959) – in which he played a prime minister, a constable and a duchess in a small state which seeks a way out of its hopeless financial plight by provoking the United States into war with it, giving itself a chance to be overrun and rehabilitated. This obverse satire on imperialism gave US movie-goers a foretaste of his liberalist caricatures to come of the inscrutable workings of politics and big businesses: his delving into flippant details with hilarious consequences. If to the sombre cineaste his clownish mannerisms and contrived – though eminently laughable – predicaments at times appear kitsch, there have been occasions where his eccentricity impressed by its sheer range (Stanley Kubrick's *Lolita* and *Dr Strangelove*).

Though typecast in the popular mind as the all-too-familiar Indian doctor or the inept and muddling Inspector Clouseau of the *Pink Panther* series, Sellers' humour was at heart vibrantly and wildly surrealistic. His hectic-paced appearances since his first heart attack in 1964, almost as if he were racing against time, are not necessarily as memorable as they are instantly popular. A glimpse of the other Sellers, for instance, is available in an earlier 11-minute short film produced by him (*The Running, Jumping and Standing Still Film*, 1960), which opens with a girl scrubbing a field with soap and water; the film won the Golden Gate Award at the San Francisco Film Festival.

The conflict of images seemed not reconciled in Sellers himself. The man who had enthusiastically set out to 'ridicule without being ridiculous', to be 'serious without being solemn', was later to deplore: 'I writhe when I see myself on the screen. I mean, I look such an idiot.'

Published in *The Hindu*, 3 August 1980.

What Inhibits Indian Cinema

Hollywood really becomes a prototype to much of Indian cinema, past and present. While the system of big-studio, big-budget productions was faithfully imbibed in the 'industries' of Bombay and Madras, the more recent off-Hollywood (almost like the off-Broadway developments) departures find their echo in the jettisoning of the studio system, the devolution of functional power from producer to director, more democratized stardom and so on.

The seven American directors who figured in the recent festival of American films in the city share this quasi-independence of the system of Hollywood. While experimenting with their form and styles, they are yet keen on keeping abreast with the sensibility of their audiences rather than overtaking them. All the films – Francis Ford Coppola's *Finian's Rainbow*, Bogdanovich's *The Last Picture Show*, George Lucas's *American Graffiti*, Steven Spielberg's *The Sugarland Express*, Robert Altman's *Nashville*, Martin Scorsese's *Alice doesn't live here anymore* and Woody Allen's *Interiors* – share a sense of anarchism, of attempt and failure to come to terms with contemporary reality, an involuted structure that is saved from being self-centred by being piquantly (at times poignantly) anthropocentric.

The feeling of loss and uncertainty give the lie to the earlier phase of abrasive optimism – the culturally imperialist stance reflected in the classical western, or the dark *mise-en-scène* of the 40s and the 50s. Here, in contrast, is the consciousness of the late 60s and early 70s: an urge to revalorize, demythify, set images and roles. And yet it seems the iconoclasm of the unsure atheist, and it is small wonder that one participant in the seminar that followed the showings of films was prompted to diagnose the symptoms as a kind of schizophrenia over their own cultural background. 'The car is almost a totem for the American', observed another participant, referring of course to the fetish-image of the automobile ubiquitously present in all the seven films shown. Significantly, the car becomes a symbol for the rootless drifting; a prop that helps impress upon us the shifting, unsettled, insecure *mise-en-scène*.

Obversely, its counterpart in Indian film symbolism would be (as the same participant observed) an employer's address. The urge and search for security are common to both cultures. But paradoxically, while the American frustration is a 'look back in anger' from the affluence of the automobile, the TV, the fridge and so on, the Indian insecurity becomes in relative terms far more basic and primal: the desperate search for a job, for securing a livelihood. The images, then, that constitute the infrastructural milieu on even the new American screen are as different from those that dominate the serious Indian cinema, as the ethos and context of the first world cinema are different from that of the third world.

If the surface structure reveals such a diversity of types, the concerns of the two cinemas seem to converge at a deeper level. The new American cinema, as seen from these and other films, are better informed by a left–liberal principle than their predecessors. Take Robert Altman, for example. His productions represent class interests or ideological groupings. They are increasingly anarchic without being nihilistic, and almost any film carries the anti-establishment refrain. The phenomenon should be all the more true of Indian cinema because it is all the more necessary here to be questioning, challenging, repudiating set mores and status-quoist myths.

Our anti-establishment at its best perhaps has been the rash of anti-caste Kannada films (beginning with *Samskara*) or political films in Kerala (beginning with *Kabini Nadi Chuvannappol*), with the exception of Mrinal Sen's consistently political crusade against the system. It is difficult to attribute all the fault (for the failure of a 'genre' of new, relevant cinema becoming a movement) to censorship. After all the censor-free American cinema too was no overnight boon: American filmmakers must remember the McCarthyian drive against communism on the screen (in 1947, a House Committee on Un-American Activities, in a zealous inquisition, berated many famous filmmakers, who were promptly proscribed by the industry itself) or the ravages of the Hays Code. Even more recently, Coppola had to virtually take on the Pentagon to see his *Apocalypse Now* through.

Even less tenable seems the argument that if Kannada cinema has ceased dealing with caste, it is because the theme is stale. Surely, the thematic relevance of the new cinema is also societal. When caste outrages are almost a daily occurrence, the issue itself can hardly become obsolete even for the screen. What inhibits new cinema in India seems not so much the external constraints of finance or censorship, as the inability (or unwillingness) to innovate forms of expression that refurbish the issues present as impinging on our consciousness: the failure to come up with a fresh filmic unity of form and content that makes new perceptual demands on the viewers.

First published in *The Hindu*, 24 August 1980.

Beyond the Gangster Genre

Francis Ford Coppola's two-part *The Godfather* makes interesting viewing for many reasons. Violence, anarchism and belligerent exercise of power on the one hand, and protectiveness, obsessive kinship and hankering after peace on the other, form the twin aspects of Coppola's tightly controlled dialectic. It is this contradiction that gives the films their taut and tense structure. The films (Parts I and II) become antitype, indeed, transcending the familiar gangster genre.

We are drawn to a study of the immigrant Corleone family, its ascension to power in the New World's underworld, the constant fluctuations in the power equations it enters into against the other 'mafiosi' groups, and the strategy and fierceness of their internecine conflicts. We emerge from the experience not so much with a sense of awe or passive marvel at the bloody eventfulness of Coppola's work, as with a sense of empathy with the Corleone family itself (as the close of *The Godfather Part II* implies) at its point of breakdown. This breakdown, we are aware, is not the same as loss of power by the family; there is more a feeling of historical inevitability as we watch the family disintegrating in the face of US capitalism. The point has been made elsewhere by John Hess that 'Michael (Corleone) as America embodies a basic contradiction in capitalism between the luminous bourgeois ideals of peace, freedom, opportunity, love and community and the harsh, brutal realities of the irrational economic system which encourages these ideals and feeds off their unobtainability'.

At the sociological level, the family as the nucleus where the male members run their risk-fraught business in total exclusivity, without hindering (and unhindered by) the other members at domestic chores, becomes an anachronism in a context where the individual is increasingly becoming the nuclear social unit. That the Corleone family is never really reconciled to this to the very end is evident from the repeated infractions by members of the family (Fredo, in *Godfather II* is the last of them; we have earlier Vito Corleone's daughter who becomes a virtual dropout, and son-in-law Carlo who has to be harshly chastised by Sonny Corleone).

Any direct comparison between this familial aspect in *Godfather* and the Indian joint family ethos must appear overwrought. Yet, the crisis in *Godfather* (seen primarily as a crisis within the family) should be familiar to the average middle-class Indian film-goer by virtue of a remotely similar background – the joint family which has disintegrated. Mario Puzo's study of the family itself in his novels (on which the films are based) has, as has often been pointed out, been faithfully reproduced on the screen by Coppola. Indeed the film and the book become inseparably mutual: where the facility of the written word becomes inadequate, the film image takes over, just as the film throughout bears the stamp of the authority of the book.

But that is not saying anything less of Coppola. Because in his structuring of the work, especially in his arrangement and evolution of space, there is a distinctive perspective and method that at once makes each part self-sufficient and at the same time shows the director's consciousness extending from the screen space of *Part I*, even while he is at it, into *Part II* – and this, despite the fact that between the two parts Coppola had directed the entirely different theme of *The Conversation*.

Coppola's method in both parts is at once involvement and alienation. We are taken to the very heart of the Corleone family, their sanctum of power, but we are not allowed to participate in their strategy. The action itself, as a result, comes to us as a shock. Take the scene where Woltz's prize horse's head is left on his bed for him to wake up and find as a warning that the godfather will have his way. The method no doubt lends great dramatic punch to the violent scenes, which erupt so suddenly that one is kept perpetually alive to their volatile presence beneath the surface. The sudden shattering of glass by a would-be assassin's bullets in Michael Corleone's bedroom when he and his pregnant wife are there (in *Godfather II*) is all the more shocking because we find the enemy's reach getting uncomfortably close. It is a bolt from the blue, sensitized as we are to the affectionate bonds that hold the Corleone family together. But in their business of kill-or-be-killed, this should not be all that surprising.

The family becomes so central to the plot that little of the world they control is actually seen in either part of the film. The introversiveness is more pervasive in the first part than in the second. Brief street scenes, the meeting of the five families, the restaurant killing, the street where Sonny beats up Carlo and where the Don himself is shot at, are just snippets of the outside world coming almost as a fillip to the shadowy goings-on in the Corleone inner chamber. *The Godfather Part II*, in comparison, has a more liberal sprinkling of the real world – Havana on the eve of the revolution, the Senate hearings, the assassination at the airport (of Hyman Roth).

This expansiveness in spatial treatment is felt at other levels too. *Godfather II* has a more epic dimension, in keeping, it would seem, with the expansion of the Corleone network itself. At the juncture when success seems to be its own undoing, there is a going back to the roots to crosscheck one's bearings. The flashbacks in the film from Michael's point of view, along with the scene where Michael seeks his mother's advice when the irrevocable, inexorable nature of his business (which he seems to identify increasingly as his plight) is confirmed in his mind once more, really indicate the beginning of the end. The family has become a threat to itself. Fredo's vacillating and weak character has become dangerous enough to make it necessary to have him killed. Michael's wife has perforce to be estranged from him and their children. Mother dies. Michael Corleone is left at the end of it all to resort to a spate of fresh violence for stability and order, with himself in command again.

Published in *The Hindu*, 13 September 1980.

Paradox Facing the 'Art Circuit'

When the National Film Development Corporation (NFDC) early this year set out on its idea of the 'art circuit' (with the Lotus cinema in Bombay on 28 February and subsequently at the Kalaivanar Arangam in Madras), it was realistic enough not to expect any spectacular results. Neither, however, had it bargained for the less-than-lukewarm response to most of the films in the circuit. After the first flush of *The Lacemakers*, which had a 50-day run, fortunes nose-dived at the Kalaivanar Arangam (where these films are run as morning shows at two flat rates, cheaper by the waived entertainment tax), each film at the close of its week-long run netting less than a day's capacity collection of the theatre (approximately Rs 2,000). The figures are telling: *The Spiral* at week's close had collected a paltry Rs 400; *Merrygoround*, Rs 935; *Professor Hannibal*, Rs 947, *Death of a President*, Rs 1,200; *Baxter*, Rs 1,569; and *Dream of Passion*, Rs 1,800.

Even as these screenings to near-empty houses were worrying the NFDC and state government authorities (who share the publicity costs and profits equally), elsewhere in the city, NFDC-distributed films like *SHE* and *The Passage* were making comfortable winnings at the box office (*SHE*, in a five-week run in the dry, grossed Rs 1,20,000). Earlier, *The Bullet Train*, *Scorchy* and *Fear over the City* had recorded equally impressive gains. All of which leads to confusion about NFDC's role and stakes in the cause of good cinema.

The issue perhaps is not so much one of divided loyalty as of divided attention. Although not less than 50 per cent of NFDC's imports comprise art-circuit material, the pre-publicity and advertisement priority accorded to the two types would seem not so well balanced. A commercial film, no doubt, has inbuilt advantages in terms of ready availability of trailers, posters and so on. But one would expect the NFDC to give budgetary weightage to the films doing the art circuit and take extra effort in winning over the viewer to this cinema. If, instead, the film-goer himself is required to make that effort to attend a week-day, 11.30 am show of a film he hasn't the vaguest idea about, the chances are there will be few takers.

It is again surprising that with the supportive potential of the hundreds of film societies in the south, these films should yet go abegging for an audience. It has been said of Kerala that the hundred-odd film societies there alone suffice to make a modest-budgeted art film break even. If a go-getting effort is made to get these societies interested, and at the subsidized lending charge of Rs 250 per screening, there is no reason why they shouldn't respond enthusiastically.

All of this might generate more clientele without necessarily generating any profits. Because the art circuit by its nature, and until it becomes self-sufficient, cannot – must not – be after the profit motive of its commercial counterpart. It must then remain a subsidized periphery of our film development movement. The government attitude here, however, seems not too encouraging. 'We pay the same customs duty and import charges as any commercial company', said a spokesman of the NFDC, justifying the need to import commercial films to offset the losses suffered in the art-circuit experiment.

Considering that this means that the NFDC has to compete, on equal footing, with the eight US-controlled giants of the MPEAA (Motion Pictures Export Association of America) the government's attitude seems neither considerate nor considered. It thus not only pays but seems imperative for the NFDC in its present plight to be Janus-faced: promoting, on the one hand, the kind of cinema which, while it spins money at the box office, estranges the viewer from precisely that type of taste for cinema which the art circuit, on the other hand, hopes to instil in him.

The paradox is not easily resolved, enmeshed as it is in the question of economic viability. Weighed down as it is by these handicaps, criticism of the NFDC on this count would, at times, appear a shade too carping. 'Most of the criticisms, even within the industry, are either ill-informend or uninformed', lamented an NFDC official. One of the prime tasks before the newly constituted board of directors (under the Chairman, Mr D. V. S. Raju) would expectedly be to smoothe out these structural anomalies.

Meanwhile, and pending a policy decision, there is enough leeway even in its present set-up to rationalize its working. Some indicators do augur well. Plans are afoot for instance, to build a mini art cinema (with a capacity of about 450) in the Kalaivanar Arangam complex in Madras (the state government has reportedly agreed to give the requisite land); the Andhra Pradesh government has agreed to construct an art cinema in Hyderabad in collaboration with the NFDC; the West Bengal government is to hand over the Sisir Manch theatre in Calcutta to the NFDC; Delhi is likely to follow suit by making over the Shakuntalam Theatre in the exhibition complex to NFDC; in Bombay, in addition to Lotus, the NFDC is trying to procure the Akashvani auditorium; a mini cinema is also planned in Bangalore.

It has been the constant opinion of filmmakers and film buffs at film festivals and seminars that the new cinema in the country as well as the different cinema from abroad would go down well with our audiences if only they are exposed to them. 'Give them a chance and they'll make it', seems the refrain. The NFDC experience in Madras with the handful of films which have been shown so far on the art circuit seems rather disquieting as regards that assurance.

There are too many imponderables to hazard any one cause or reason. Maybe, the people are not really aware there is an art circuit on; maybe, Madras is not as ripe for such a movement as Bangalore or Kerala (this is very doubtful). Or maybe, a week per film is just not long enough. We have the classic instance of Ray's *Pather Panchali*, when it was first released in the 50s in Calcutta, playing to empty benches for the first few weeks – and then picking up to become a roaring success.

First published in *The Hindu*, 28 September 1980.

Complement to Conventional Cinema

Tucked away in a corner of Madras, the Institute of Film Technology, Adayar has, for too long now, remained an apology on the periphery of the south Indian film scene. What could have been a crucible of film culture (the Institute being the second of its kind in the country, after the one at Pune), defying the mores of a hard-boiled conventional cinema, has become an unconscious complement to that very cinema – supplying technical finesse and, in rare cases, aesthetic finish to its escapist fare.

Indeed the very *raison d'être* of the Institute, seen from an ideal standpoint, is sandwiched between the questions: is the student endowed to make a breakaway bid from the crass film culture that surrounds him, and, if so endowed, would he be found willing to make that choice. For either, it implicitly devolves upon the Institute itself to furnish both the know-how and the stance – something it doesn't even seem to have thought about.

In the absence of such an approach to film, on a firmly grounded perspective, the alumni of the Institute, essaying into the field with fresh styles in mind, are left to fend for themselves on a trial-and-error basis (what big-wigs in the industry choose to call learning the hard way). When *Aval Appadithan* or *Gramathu Adhyayam* is dismissed with scant respect by the average film-goer, pundits in the industry respond with a knowing 'I-told-you-so'. On the other hand, when a team, chastened by the experience of a mock-realist film like *Kudisai*, comes up with such half-baked stuff as *Oru Thalai Ragam*, the attitude is reversed to something like: 'If you can't lick them, join them.'

Increasingly, however, the acrimony between the industry and the Institute is becoming more notional than real. Almost as avidly as students of the Institute look up to the industry as the arena to graduate into from their cloistered three-year course, producers and directors have taken to film graduates for that slick touch to their work. (This is all the more evident in cinematography, which has almost totally gone outdoor, and colour, giving Institute products, among them Ashok Kumar and Nawaz in Tamil, an edge over the set-and-light-oriented cameramen.)

Indeed the Institute has come to have a label value and the students themselves are aware of this imprimatur of dignity their diploma invests them with. 'Any Institute student can fare better than the most experienced person in the industry', says G.M. Perumal, president of the Film Graduates' Association (an alumni association of the Institute), refuting the opinion that time makes a better technician than training. 'It's like saying', he illustrates, 'that a carpenter with twenty-five years experience is better than a qualified engineer.' The analogy may not be well thought out; maybe even in poor taste, considering the rather arbitrary value judgement involved in implying that carpentry is a lesser vocation than engineering. Be that as it may, what is interesting is that the craft of the filmmaker is set off against and above the art of the media.

Although the syllabus at the Madras Film Institute is patterned after that at Pune, this conceptual distinction between the art and craft aspects seems diffused and vague. While the alumni of the Institute, working in such diverse fields as television, All India Radio (AIR), Field Publicity, Indian Space Research Organization (ISRO), Department of Archaeology, as well as other private firms, bear testimony to the broad-based technical training imparted there, their diploma films made while at the Institute as well as their subsequent work outside show little grasp of the peculiar aesthetics and gestalt of film. The vocational thrust must naturally be expected to take its toll in terms of the orientation imbibed. The chances, then, are that once out of the Institute, they look for and find an entry into the industry on its own time-tested terms.

First published in *The Hindu*, 18 October 1980.

Should the Cinema Industry Be Regulated?

Even as south Indian films were, over the last decade, growing out of the studio system in approach, form and content, and becoming more intelligible both in terms of reach and accessibility to novice filmmakers, a freewheeling spurt in production was only to be expected. (Nearly 1,100 films are under production in south India, of which only 10 per cent of the films released are successful.) The reaction to them seems to have been snowballing until today, in the face of stalemate on several fronts. And using that as an excuse, there is talk of regulating the film industry.

The attitudes that comprise this backlash against the democratization of filmmaking are as diverse as they are vested. There is the self-righteous reaction of cartels like the South India Film Chamber of Commerce – indignant, as its president, Mr Kottarakara put it, that 'petty shopkeepers and domestic servants take to filmmaking'. 'Even for voting,' he compares, 'there is the minimum qualification that a person must be 18 and not mad. But for filmmaking, there is no such condition.' Pursuing his case for a system of licensing filmmaking, of regulating and standardizing output, he poses a queer idea of professional specialization: 'Why do only Udipi Raos do so well in the hotel business? Why don't Birlas, Tatas and Dalmias come into the film business?'

That reaction is shared, even if not for the same reasons, by the more enlightened crop of Institute-trained filmmakers. Besides a rather highbrow discontent at the film scene becoming a free-for-all, there is the more genuine lament of rising costs, despite the 'out-of-studio-and-set' trend. Stemming partly from an abrupt changeover from black-and-white to colour (about 300 black-and-white films in the south Indian languages are stalled with no buyers), and partly from rising raw stock costs, the cost factor becomes the major irritant to the independent low-budget filmmaker.

As if to snuff out what little initiative is left with the uncompromising filmmaker, the Tamil Nadu government brings to the whole question an attitude that almost disfavours the 'art' cinema as sterile and useless. At the recent State Information Ministers' conference in New Delhi, the Tamil Nadu Information Minister made known his government's patent distrust of such cinema in the context of waiving entertainment tax on award winners.

Given the vagaries of a system of decentralized state control of cinema, the recommendation of the National Film Policy Committee to include the subject in the concurrent list seems to make sense. And yet, offsetting this apparent advantage of a rationalization at the national level lies the danger of film being assigned the pious and subliminal role of a national integrator. That this is clearly the role which the decision-makers would ascribe to Indian cinema is evident from the numerous calls made time and again by ministers and officials to use the medium to emphasize the essential oneness of the nation.

Even if this were the *raison d'être* and function of cinema in this country, as the opinion seems to be well-entrenched, it doesn't work as simply or directly as that. Real cinema can only be, as has been often pointed out by most of our important new filmmakers, regional cinema. The specificity in ethos and the stylistics of nativity become really all-consuming to any film that must be true to the soil, in more than a mere chauvinistic sense.

While that would be a corollary problem, touching on the cultural identity of the cinema-to-be in India, the issue as of now that leads to this soul-searching is a fundamental economic phenomenon of too many films chasing too few theatres. Box office time, then, is at a premium as never before, and the handful of 'art' films, which in the normal course take a minimum warm-up period before audiences begin to realize there is something in them, are doomed to failure even before they are made: in most cases they are lifted even before a week's run is through.

Exercised as the governments (state and central) and film bodies are about the twin problem of distribution network and exhibition outlets, their response to date seems to be a queer mixture of over-reaction and sane stock-taking. Among the more acceptable proposals are mandatory cuts in the cost of production, maybe by restricting the number of song-and-dance sequences and thereby the total length of films. Working the other way round, there is the suggestion that the number of films to be produced in each language should be fixed at a fair proportion of theatres available in the area. This, by inference, would mean a regulation that would restrict filmmaking based on basic qualifications – surely an idea repugnant to the growth and the logic of that art.

First published in *The Hindu*, 23 November 1980.

A Look at Middle-Class Values

Normally the Indian Panorama section (appended to each international film festival in the country for the past few years) has a sequestered run, cut away from the mainstream of the festival as a kind of foreigners' zone. Indian critics and delegates choose to steer clear of this section in their rush to cram in as many foreign films as possible, just as logically as the visiting foreign delegates prefer a diet of Indian films – the logic in both instances being, 'We can always see them later.'

Only, things don't normally quite work out this way, at least for the Indian side. Festival over, many of these films return to their cans, to their long, often unrealized wait for distributors. A few lucky ones manage their way to festivals or TV networks abroad, or brief tenures at some enlightened box office or the other. Little is heard of the rest or their authors until, perhaps, the next festival the next year.

The scenario was, in this sense, a shade brighter at the Delhi festival in January (1981). There was a distinctive spurt of public interest in the Panorama films and many shows ran to packed houses. Part of that enthusiasm no doubt was evident among the organizers themselves, and there was the minister drawing the conclusion in his valedictory address that this 'speaks volumes about the enriched taste of our audience'. One wishes that this were so; but with one look at the films themselves, it becomes evident that they would have been as popular in any other context. In fact, quite a few of them have already done exceedingly well commercially (*Sankarabharanam*, *Lorry* and *Nizhalgal* from the south, for example).

The Indian Panorama this time, then, was a half-way house where the demands made on the audience in terms of intelligent cinematic perception were offset to a large extent by the very nature and type of the films chosen. It was a compromise that brought films that brought audiences. Little else can justify many of the films included in this section, and little else can explain the many films left out that ought to have been in.

The Golden Peacock and the ensuing prestige apart, Govind Nihalani's *Aakrosh* (Hindi) typifies this variety of watered-down cinema. The whole film unfolds like a pet idea Nihalani and Vijay Tendulkar (who is responsible for the story and the screenplay) seem to entertain about what is vitally precious to a tribal who is at a loose end in the social strata. Indeed Nihalani even has a ready piece of devious logic to explain it: 'A tribal has no possessions. What can he call his own except the people who are nearest to him. That's why rape is such a strong symbol of the total exploitation of our tribals.'

So we have a film hinging on rape as the single most significant factor in the exploitation of our tribals. This quantum leap from the primary cause (economic exploitation) to its secondary manifestation is at least partly justified, considering that the director here is only concerned with 'the attitude of the middle class towards their exploitation', and rape is certainly among the more sensational by-products of the stock middle-class response that sees the tribals as an enigmatic, ethnic group steeped in the pathos of history. What is, however, untenable and objectionable is that the director foists these middle-class values on the tribal himself, so that subjectivism yields to subterfuge.

When the film begins we are introduced to the vain attempts of a young lawyer, Bhasker (Naseeruddin Shah), to defend an adivasi, Lahanya (Om Puri), accused of murdering his wife. Lahanya, in the grip of a stony silence, refuses to cooperate. As Bhasker painstakingly reconstructs the case despite him, it turns out that the entire thing is a frame-up, that the real culprits are the local power combine. At its close we find Lahanya shaking out of his self-imposed stupor and, at the funeral pyre of his father, hacking his sister to death lest she too should suffer his wife's fate.

The narrative scale predictably lends itself to many engaging dramatic moments, among them the rape scene itself handled cleverly and differently (the camera is cut away from the action and contemplates Lavanya's frantic bid to break into the room where his wife is being molested; a sound track emotively surcharged with the cries of the victim heightens the violent impact). What is not clear at the end of it all, however, is what makes Lahanya's reaction in the circumstance (his long silence leading up to the final explosive fit of violence) typically or uniquely tribal. The paranoia that seizes him as he stands before his father's funeral pyre and propels him to deliver his sister from her impending fate with his own hands may be abnormal, but not aboriginal. The tribal milieu becomes a kind of façade, a cinematic prop that has little value other than as decor.

Lahanya's gloomy silence (the feeling is conveyed even at the outset that it forebodes no good) makes for good suspense, but does not quite evolve within the plot. If it is, as the director seems to suggest, the determined silence of a man who has taken charge of his destiny and is biding his time to play his hand, Lahanya's father's death and the funeral scene must appear contrived – almost as if the director was creating situations to carry the story forward to its finale. If, on the other hand, it is the silence of a spirit stubbed out by oppression, there is an ominous quality about it that needs explaining. Surely, the director cannot just give us a pathologically silent character and expect us not to ask why.

Drama and logic are clearly at odds with each other in Lahanya's (for that matter, most of the tribals') characterization, and Om Puri's splendid performance can only create empathy for the role, not explain it. Much of the fault seems to lie in the director's own equivocation, which in turn is projected on the screen. Thus, while Nihalani is reluctant to ideologize his standpoint (which, by his own admission, is typically middle class), he cannot resist introducing a young naxalite into the plot, shown organizing the tribals. The equivocation arises from the fact that like the lawyer Bhasker, the naxalite too is (by dress and demeanour) of middle-class origin, and yet the responses of the two to the tribal predicament vary radically. If within the strict confines of the plot, Bhasker's attitude is meant as typical middle-class ('I identify with Bhasker', says Nihalani), the naxalite becomes atypical – and yet a middle-class naxalite is hardly a rarity.

As sketchy is the adivasi-turned-public prosecutor, Dussaney, fighting Lahanya's case opposite Bhasker, who makes a fetish of the law and prefers to abide by it even when he knows that it is not just. In varying degrees, the entire spectrum of characters in *Aakrosh* seems imbued with middle-class values: the behavioural traits that come across are average middle-class (a flashback love scene between Lahanya and his wife rankles in the setting). While this becomes an asset in depicting the local power elite and their ruthless operations (a bold piece of indictment, that), it clearly jars in taking stock of the tribals.

First published in *The Hindu*, 8 February 1981.

Realization of an Ambitious Experiment

Akaler Sandhane

From the assured, consummate style of *Ekdin Pratidin* of 1979 to the less rounded-off, taking-the-plunge style of *Akaler Sandhane* ('In Search of Famine'; Bengali) of 1980 may seem a violent swing of the pendulum within the course of just a year. But it is by no means uncharacteristic of Mrinal Sen whose filmic career, at least since his *Chorus* in 1974, is marked by a diversity of approach that eludes definition. Since then, and through *Mrigaya* (1975) and *Oka Oorie Katha* (1977), an attempt to define Sen seems at once an attempt to confine his artistic fervour. His artistic vision does not plod along predictable lines, and he seems himself to consciously defy any attempt to slot him as a type. In fact he is quite explicit on the subject:

> I have tried to experiment with my medium and, in the process . . . I have at times exercised in indulgence and in madness. I have overdone things out of exuberance – out of the sheer pleasure of playing with one's tools, one's medium. . . . I am deeply convinced that these are no exercises in futility.

That tentativeness, that anarchy, spills over in a large measure to *Akaler Sandhane*. In the film one can almost see Sen reaching out backward in time to a situation about forty years back (the Bengal famine of 1943), and stretching it forward to the present and juxtaposing it with a contemporary setting in rural Bengal. The message is clear: poverty is never history. The filmic device he adopts to accomplish this is a film unit out in the village to recreate the scenario of the Bengal famine. Their makebelieve sequences and the living reality of their surroundings gradually coalesce, and the film that is being made becomes organic with the society it had merely set out to reflect. At this juncture the unit withdraws to its safe isolation in the city, but not before at least some members of the team have touched and felt the raw nerve of disguised poverty in the village.

Sen's two-pronged treatment of the subject evolves structurally, even if sketchily, into two levels – a surface structure and a deep structure. While much of the action is concentrated at the surface level (comprising the film unit at work), at vantage points along it the parallel undercurrent is plumbed, giving us brief yet devastating glimpses of that more basic facet. The film unit itself becomes a mediating agent, and the actors and the director shooting on the locale experience by proxy the hunger and famine both of their story and of their impinging reality. It serves too as a buffer zone that enables the audience to take a more detached and dispassionate look at the action.

In sheer terms of relating the viewer integrally to the plot and at the same time sufficiently alienating him from the action, Sen's *Akaler Sandhane* is a unique effort in Indian cinema. If the final impact is rather muted, it is the candid, qualified realization of an ambitious experiment. It is possible to point out that the film could do with a lot more attention to detail and more meticulous planning; that as it is, there is an impromptu, almost casual air about the whole thing. But that, again, is criticism the maverick in Sen would take in his stride.

Simhaasan

The first striking feature about Jabbar Patel's *Simhaasan* (Marathi) is that we find here a director poaching on the power preserves of politics with apparent immunity: the real or imaginary fear of censors seems not to have hounded him or cramped his forthright style. Of course, nowhere is his exposé of politicking in high places carried far enough for it to become an indictment. In a treatment that is diffused and disparate, Patel attempts to sum up the political process, with all its ruthless scheming and machinations, of a state ministry on the verge of collapse.

There is a simultaneity of point-of-view so that the effect seems to be of a number of characters (each of them vital components of the drama) moving abreast of our perception. While this approach precludes a focal thrust in any one direction and couples with it the risk of attention being spread thin on the array of characters at hand, it goes to Patel's credit that he does not let the matter get out of hand even if he hovers throughout on the superficial level.

We are introduced to what must be an ongoing phenomenon of ministry-making-and-keeping, midstream: the ruling and opposition factions are trading accusations in the State Assembly. An anonymous phone call to the Chief Minister warning him of a threat to his power from fifth columnists in his own ministry sparks off the crisis. From then on the *simhaasan* (throne) grows impalpably in emphasis as the central metaphor to which all ambitions converge. We are carried along the tide for a while until the crisis blows over and the Chief Minister reasserts his authority, and are then dropped off as abruptly as we were taken on.

The sense of temporal continuum that both precedes and follows the duration of the film helps place it in an identifiable contemporary context. As the profile of each minister is sketched, we instantly recall a real-life counterpart. The societal aspect that is infected by or infects this political plane becomes in effect a shady, sleazy edge of the plot, where smuggling, womanizing and the turpitude of incestuous relations are suggestive enough. No direct relationship is sought to be established between these and the power elite in question; often the responsibility devolves to a lesser functionary.

The film derives its dramatic construct from Vijay Tendulkar's screenplay, which for once does not appear out of place. The interplay of forces and characters in the power game warrants a degree of drama, and both Tendulkar and Patel have combined to see that it is well-contained. What emerges is a reasonably terse and matter-of-fact account which may lack depth and dimension, but which is not lacklustre either: a film which copes with the rather abundant material on hand without leaving loose bits and ends sticking out.

First published in *The Hindu*, 15 February 1981.

Panorama: Malayalam Pictures

The uncomfortable urge to disappear under the seat while a film is on was, for this writer, a new experience at the Indian Panorama viewings of two Malayalam films – K.G. George's *Kolangal* and V.R. Gopinath's *Greeshmam*. The films evoke a kind of irrepressible embarrassment at being caught in the public act of viewing something as preposterous and naive as this. At a more objective and critical level, they become an affront to the viewer's sensibility; more so because the directors are products of the Pune Film Institute, and George himself has been identified as one of the pioneers of the new cinema movement in Kerala. Indeed the two films reflect on the bonafides of that movement itself and seem to confirm the growing suspicion in the minds of many that it is a bogus phenomenon – 'the apotheosis of tedium', as one professor ponderously put it.

George's *Kolangal* seems all the more a fiasco because, given its definitive and intimate milieu – a small, introverted village across a river with an in-group structure – and that it is based on a well-known story by P.J. Antony (of *Nirmalyam* fame), it had the potential and raw material for a moving film. We have instead a cursory and rambling account of a stranger who sells balloons and playthings to children in the village, falls in love with a girl there but has, in the end, to forfeit her in the face of strong, almost ethnic opposition. In his effort to sketch a passive, self-effacing character, George comes up with a robot-like caricature (played by Venu Nagavalli) who talks and moves as if in a lethargic, mechanical stupor. One has not seen anything as dense and obtuse moving on the screen for a long time. The entire duration of the film seems one big lag in time, with frame compositions, camera movements and cuts that succeed in dissipating whatever intrinsic value the story has as a literary piece. It abounds with characters who are alternately stereotypes and forced types, the one blatantly banal and the other irritably pseudo-profound. Overall, it is irredeemably ersatz.

Freud-fixation is nothing new in Malayalam films. In the most commercial of them Freud becomes a convenient alibi to get away with all kinds of sexual fetishes and perversions. At least here there is the manifest purpose of netting good box-office results from a presumably sex-craved audience. V.R. Gopinath's psycho-sexual *Greeshmam*, to be fair to it, is not a sex-seller in this sense; but it is far worse for its pretensions of psychological self-righteousness. The director, who has also thought up the story, brings a dilettantish approach to psychology that is, to say the least, unnerving. A fertile (and, one suspects, perverse) imagination is no excuse to run amok in a field that fascinates us all by virtue of our sheer ignorance of it. At least not in the oracular, esoteric and intellectually impertinent style of Gopinath.

In an involved and overworked narrative that literally goes abegging for credibility, Gopinath attempts to get us interested in the mind of a young man (a psychology student) in love with an adolescent girl. Their own subjectivism and the circumstances that complicate their relationship have already got out of hand halfway through the film; the director then directly takes off into other states of consciousness, and when the film ends we find dream images conversing with physical being. All this would have been appropriately absurd if only it had not been riddled with weak psychological backing. As it is, the film is either false and pretentious, or too personal; what it does certainly is test the viewers' patience.

In such company, Aravindan's *Esthappan* must seem above reproach. But viewed in the context of his other recent films – notably *Thampu* and *Kummatti* – *Esthappan* leaves a lot to be desired. The aesthetic refinement that Aravindan, perhaps alone among the new Indian filmmakers, has achieved is evident through much of the film, except in an awkward and extended boating sequence, and at the very fag end where Esthappan is shown walking along as a legend, seen in many places at the same time. The ambivalence about the myth and reality of the character, Esthappan, is assuredly built up in the first portion of the film, and evolves into a conundrum that is both nonplussing and enigmatic. But in the latter portions, the balance is lost to sublimate the character into the realms of myth, and the theme becomes obscure.

True to character, Aravindan's concern here is again a marginal facet of our social consciousness – in this case, the subculture of godmen and faith-healers. Only, when he declares sides with the miraculous and the inexplicable, he leaves scope in the film for one to wish he had not done so. The essential purpose of the film is to point out to us the vagaries of our sense perception of life around us. The opening shot sets the tone: from a diffused and misty frame there crystallizes the figure of a man (Esthappan) walking on to the shore from the sea. The subjective–objective balance is lost towards the end and the narrative touches more and more on the apocryphal. And that, almost, is the film's undoing.

First published in *The Hindu*, 22 February 1981.

On Brechtian Lines

Seeing Ketan Mehta's *Bhavni Bhavai* (Gujarati) is more or less like seeing a puppet show. Quaint, folksy and stylized, the film narrates the *Bhavai* tale (and a decadent Gujarati folk drama), '*Achhootno Vesh*' ('Garb of the Untouchable'). Empathy is regulated throughout on Brechtian lines by the simple device of having a character relate the events in verse to a group of children and then taking us on to the story itself: how a lowly caste, whose members had to wear a broom as a tail trailing behind them so that their footprints were effaced and a mud-pot around their necks so that their spittle would not defile the earth, manages to wrest concessions from the king to do away with these.

Given this story and Mehta's apt choice of colours, locale and folk stylistics, the film would have been pleasant enough; but the imposed twist in the end and Brecht himself place it as something more than a children's film and less than an adult's. Mehta seems to play around with the alienative technique; from the look of it, he seems to have shot the core narrative (the *Bhavai* tale itself) at one stretch and interspersed it with the 'alienative' bits (Om Puri singing to a group of children) at points of time along it.

The final effect is one of a mechanical alternation between the alienated and the alienating; they are hardly integral to the plot. The meeting point between the two aspects apparently was meant to be the finale, when rejecting our narrator's end (which is the traditional end of the story) wherein the protagonist is sacrificed in return for the concessions on caste obligations, an alternative end is propounded – the menial caste rebels and is up in arms against the rulers. Logic and cinematic reasoning here give way to drama; that ideal climax is just too simplistically imposed and, tagged on as it is to the story, it fails to jell.

First published in *The Hindu*, 22 February 1981.

'I am always in the midst of the artistic process'

Coming to grips with Mani Kaul as a filmmaker, formidable enough when dealing with one who consciously and consistently defies the normative attributes of cinema, becomes all the more difficult if one leaves it to his films to speak for themselves – just four full-length features and as many documentaries in a span of twelve years seems sparse material to sum up the author, especially when one is certain that there is a lot more that is a lot different to follow. A total picture seems to emerge only when the professed views of the artist along with his art are taken into reckoning, even if Kaul himself distastefully refers to the tendency of the Indian filmmaker to be 'more articulate about than in his films'. Kaul has very considered views on what being articulate in and through his films means.

Mani Kaul: When somebody says – 'What do you want to say in your films?' – I usually have a simple answer: that I have nothing to say. And whenever a director tells me that he wants to say this in his films I think it is wrong, because what he has to say is truly what he is working with. As an artist, if you knew what you had to say, you would not be able to arrive at form.

To you, then, there is a lot of 'ad hocism' involved in filmmaking?
Yes, to a great extent. I'd like to quote a line from *A Grammar of the Film* by Raymond Spottiswoode, published in 1935, that 'the artist does more than what he knows'.

I hope that doesn't mean he over-reaches himself?
No. The extent of the repercussions of his work is unknown to him. Which means, he doesn't know exactly what kind of form he's arrived at. You often find this filmmaker, who is neither commercial nor perfectly artistic, telling you how he wants to make a film with social commitment. But that's not cinema. It is obligatory of me to push the medium in which I work to new horizons and new forms. You will find there are many films which are radical if you go by the token of the message, but the form is 1930s. Tformat beneath is 30s. So the message is really a parasite on that format. So even if it evokes a temporary hysteria I wouldn't consider that film political, because a more fundamental

description of what is political would be that which is able to transform nature. It must alter nature; even if I alter a tree and make a chair out of it, I think it is political enough. Even if you alter human nature it is political.

With your very first film, 'Uski Roti', you got the reputation of being a static filmmaker, in the sense that your frames, the action, even the characters are static. How do you react to this criticism?

I'll try to explain this. This is a general confusion that a certain medium ought to remain in its idiom alone. Suppose you are painting – you have the surface, the canvas, which is static. After you have applied the colours, the colour is static. So truly, because the idiom is space, which is static, a painting would not make sense unless the juxtaposition of colours or merging of colours, and division of masses, lines, creates movement. Or, take music. You have rhythm by marking points and having a symmetrical recurrence. But true rhythm which transgresses this temporal idiom creates not just this rhythmic beat, but also encompasses the blocks of silence between the beats. When I hear Palghat Mani Iyer on the *mridangam*, this is what I feel. I don't feel he is counting beats; he creates space, he solidifies space. So, unless you transgress the idiomatic quality of the medium in which you are working, you have no hope of becoming significant. The idiom must realize its contrary condition; there is no other way for a thing to become artistic.

Motion or movement is given to cinema. It's not something to achieve. To move a camera is nothing. When I see a lot of movement, a lot of noise in a film, when people get excited, I really see nothing happening. So it may be that when I began my career, in order to make a solid break with the tradition of lyrical neorealism, and also of the other commercial cinema, I took on a very extreme position as in *Uski Roti*. This extreme position will not be lessened, in the sense of my dedication to cinema. But if my camera begins to move or is speeded up, as in *Satah se Uthta Aadmi*, it will not be at the cost of stillness or silence, even in the midst of all this noise and people.

You have shown a marked preference for deserted milieus, for a sense of void. Is this a psychological extension of your personality or a matter of conscious style?

That's a difficult question, but I can say this much: that I have never been interested in the realistic genre. Because to be interested in the real is like turning it into an experience which is a simplification of the finer sense of life. For me, it must be either a violation of reality or a complete withdrawal from it. In both ways, I must form an oblique relation to life and not a parallel one.

One critic told me, 'We can understand one character in your film speaking slowly, but why all?' I replied that if I had one guy speaking slowly and the rest normally, that would be a very sentimental work. Why did Van Gogh paint all his trees crooked? Or El Greco paint everything long? Because it is no longer a question of presenting reality. It is a question of presenting the history of reality. So one has to have a vision, because from this history one is looking towards a certain point to which many people cannot relate at this moment; maybe the artist himself cannot relate, and that's why he feels alienated from himself. I am not surprised that most genuine artists suffer from neurosis.

Does this not reduce the artist's vision to a very subjective sense perception?
No. The forms of political and historical developments that have occurred cannot be presented in their naked sloganeering form. I see that normal relations between people are still feudal although as a society we are no longer feudal – in a family, in an office, you see feudal relations, and yet we are living in a society that is known as bourgeois or industrial. In terms of relations, then, why are we still lying? So it involves the entire social process. It's the total activity of a very humanized kind. And to reduce that to a mechanical understanding of, say, sloganeering or whipping up mass hysteria . . . this can be useful only for a political party, it's not good enough for art.

But then we have so many new filmmakers claiming all kinds of things. How is the viewer to know what to look for in a film?
That is difficult. The audience too has been conditioned to certain kinds of work. When I was at school I saw certain films. When I hear an old song today there is a feeling of nostalgia along with a total distaste for it. It is a strange feeling. But I am conscious of it. I realize then that a person who is not interested in analysing this kind of reaction will probably sink into it, suspend himself.

So I think this can be a kind of warning signal to tell them that they are losing themselves, that they are being reduced to receptacles. If they know this, it would be a warning. But then the problem is, if they know this they would not enjoy the film. So it's a vicious circle. I am really not in a position to tell them what to look for.

But any audience is conditioned in one way or another, isn't it?
Absolutely. Only, in the case of lower conditioning, the audience becomes supine. Whereas in a higher conditioning, your accumulated background prepares you to respond differently. It's like a musical instrument; if you pluck the strings after tuning it, it makes a beautiful sound. An audience is like that. The commercial cinema vitiates the audience. But only an audience can make a filmmaker possible.

I have practically no audience; even the elite get bored with my films, not to talk of the masses. So I make it for myself. And I have no qualms in saying this. Because I know that I am sufficiently impersonal. I am working with a discipline; my life is like research, I don't want to achieve anything. I am in the midst, and I shall remain in the midst; my films are incomplete, always. I have never produced an artistic object, but I am always in the midst of the artistic process. I am not interested in achieving an artistic object like Ray whose works are artistically more finished. My work is not, nor do I want it to be. I want to be in a state of strife – with myself, with the medium. This is very important to me.

Ray's stature too was no overnight phenomenon. It was built up over a period of time. I wonder whether you need to sound so defeatist.
Well, no. I got a report from Cannes, where my film has been accepted, that suddenly they have realized that Mani Kaul is very different from Ray – just as Ray is different from commercial cinema. I think after twelve years of my work this is quite a lot. I have tremendous regard for Ray. I have, in fact, maximum regard as a filmmaker only for Ray, because he is an honest filmmaker.

Now that you are working on a film on the Rajasthan desert for the German TV, and in the light of the reaction to 'Uski Roti' on TV, do you think it necessary to alter your craft for that medium?
The thing is simple. There is the *Chhaya Geet* (film songs) programme and the Sunday commercial film chunk which are watched by millions of viewers. Now, I would like to see TV schedule a programme by Bhimsen Joshi when *Chhaya Geet* is scheduled. I tell you, the TV centre will be blown up. So they have a programme called *Shastriya Sangeet* every third Monday, in which a sizeable number of people are interested. So they have to make such distinctions, and slotting my work (*Uski Roti*) into a time which was reserved for people who look for entertainment was like inflicting a kind of injury on them. I object to the fact that my film was shown in this category and time. They must have a different time for me; they can call it 'shastriya cinema', for all I care. So this is a problem not of communication but of transmission.

Communication doesn't exist by itself. There is always a certain kind of communication from a certain quarter, and there is also a certain audience meant for that communication. When a guy goes to a temple and to a prostitute, he doesn't communicate the same way; they would kill him. So in life, there are associations like this. The German TV, for instance, is giving me time in a category called 'experimental'. We know which audience will tune in for this. It should be regularized like this.

For the world's biggest film-producing country, India, it seems to me, approximates nowhere near many other developing countries – even repressed societies like in Latin America – in technical finesse or a distinctive stamp or ethos.
This has to do with the entire structure of our society and also our film industry. There is a kind of apathetic negligence – our labs are like *dhobi ghats*, there's so much dirt; people are throwing negatives down, handling them crudely . . . it is difficult to evoke interest in one's work. In the countries you are talking

about, the filmmakers have, historically, a greater sense of collective view. Here, everybody is in his own castle, living in one's own little world.

So there is no real new wave or movement in India?
No, nothing like that. Serious artistic cinema is determined by two factors, promotion by the NFDC and state protection. In the south, in Kerala and Karnataka, the state was initially interested, but now the interest has waned.

Do you find censorship a tangible problem? Or is it just a bogey, sometimes an excuse for a bad film? Does it operate in a preemptive manner so that you already obviate censorship at the planning stage itself?
I have not really landed into any problem with the censors except that in one of my documentaries (for the Films Division) on a historical sketch of women, the last portion showing women's labour in a lime factory was replaced by shots of women jumping from helicopters and commanding NCC battalions and at desks, to convey that women have progressed. I removed my name from that film and it doesn't carry any director's name. But there are many of my friends who deal with subjects of a more topical nature and face censorship, especially of a political kind.

Even many Latin American and Cuban films have been boldly critical of the prevalent system. Why not in our liberal democratic set-up?
I tell you, in India there is an extreme fear of the profane. Maybe we are too involved with emotions of what is sacred. We fear what is profane even if it is attractive. This terrible attachment to sacredness of things is peculiar to us. This, in fact, secretly results in a plethora of vulgarity and perversion.

First published in *The Hindu*, 1 March 1981.

Candid Opinion of a Director

Keeping a conversation going with director K.S. Sethumadhavan can be a trying affair. The questions always seem convoluted and in fact lose much of their searing, searching punch before his direct, simple, often monosyllabic response. Unless, of course, there is an opinion he likes to introduce into the discussion – as when he flays the entire subsidy scheme, or takes on the new filmmakers, or makes his plea for moral rectitude in films and filmmakers.

The man of few words then turns surprisingly voluble: 'Subsidy only helps some adventurists. If you are really interested in helping the film industry, construct more theatres, have subtitling equipment instead of giving fifty thousand to the producer. In the *Newspaper Boy* or *Neelakkuyil* period there was no subsidy, and yet *Neelakkuyil* changed the entire trend of Malayalam cinema.' Or: 'On the directorial side Institute students follow the continental filmmakers. In their formative period they try to imitate even the personal habits of these directors . . . in their immorality or drunkenness.' Or again: 'Government is unnecessarily giving too much importance to films. I very strongly feel that filmmakers don't deserve this. . . . You see, they are ruining the morale of the younger generation. Let the government help the teachers, the police personnel and the armed forces instead, because they sacrifice a lot and are the most ignored people in our society, whereas these filmmakers teach and preach all false values and immoral things' – and then, quickly sensing the preening self-righteousness – 'I don't want to be a puritan but since we are a developing nation we have a certain moral responsibility. And for these irresponsible people government should not waste public money.'

Given these attitudes, it becomes easy to slot Sethumadhavan as among those votaries of the film industry who have never ceased to resent the 'upstarts' who took over filmmaking in Kerala in the late 1970s, edging out the 'masters' of the socials of the 60s. Indeed the film itself that occasions this brave airing of views, and marks as it were Sethumadhavan's emergence from a 'period of hibernation' (*Oppol*, which has bagged the Silver Lotus at the twenty-eighth National Film Awards), has on its credit-card two other names of that bygone filmic era: M.T. Vasudevan Nair (story) and P. Bhaskaran (lyrics).

It then becomes tempting to wonder whether with *Oppol* Sethumadhavan has made a comeback or (from the point of view of newer filmmakers) just arrived. These ponderables, however, seem immaterial to the man himself. To him, it is just another film in his typical style, and not necessarily his best. This candour and total lack of pretension has remained the one consistently endearing trait about his work. From his early films, like *Kannum Karalum*, *Amma* and *Manavatti* in the early 1960s, through such memorable ones as *Odayil Ninnu*, *Daaham*, *Yakshi*, *Adimagal*, *Vaazhve Maayam*, *Oru Penninde Katha*, *Kara Kaana Kadal* and *Anubhavangal Paalichagal*, and on to the more recent (and perhaps more jaded after actor Sathyan's death) films like *Pani Theeratha Veedu*, *Chattakkari*, *Ormakal Marikkumo* and *Kanyakumari* (discounting his two Tamil films, *Naalai Namade* and *Kalyana Oorvalam*), the style has remained more or less the same. There is an economy of expression, a strict structure and literary quality that are as true of the man as of his work. It is the work of a conscientious director, a martinet on the sets, who has done his homework and will not allow the tomfoolery of technical assistants or the whimsicalities of starlets to diffuse or detract from his mental preparedness for a shot. (This writer once had occasion to witness him firmly pull up an actress when she lapsed into a flippant mood, midway through a scene.)

Oppol belongs unmistakeably to that Sethumadhavan. His control over the film is evident not only in its set structure (the first half being explanatory and the latter half, a playing out of the factors evolved), but also in his handling of the child artiste (Master Aravind, who won the Best Child Actor award) and the casting of Balan K. Nair in the key, cathartic role of a tough, pioneering estate builder with a soft core (the role got Balan Nair the Best Actor award). The film opens on a shot of promise, deceptive as it soon turns out. Using masked figures on a stark meadow, the director evokes the primal and subconscious sense of insecurity of a boy brought up in the belief that his mother is his sister. Because the child himself is illegitimate, the appearance of deluding the village with this piece of fiction must be kept up, if only to get the girl married to any unsuspecting groom. The plot is compelling enough. And after the pleasantly disorienting opening shot we are back in the only too familiar regional ethos of rural Kerala.

In the rather loose-knit first half, the predicament itself, with its immediate psychological and societal ramifications, is explained with the introduction of Balan K. Nair as the groom – the army behind him and the promise of a little land well-tilled, a little wife well-willed before him – and the plot again takes off to a more engaging plane. From the social environment that stifles, it now lifts to the more liberating even if social environment of the highlands, where the new husband with wife sets out to tame and cultivate virgin land. It is a blow to his acquisitive and possessive nature that his wife (unlike his land, seems the rather uncomfortable analogy) is no virgin, and worse, already a mother. But if he is hardened enough to take offence, he is also seasoned enough to reconcile himself to the situation, and it is this gamut of moods that Balan K. Nair has handled so adeptly.

In the ultimate analysis, *Oppol* may not be anything to rave about. But it is nothing to be embarrassed about either, and that is saying a lot for a Malayalam film these days.

First published in *The Hindu*, 19 April 1981.

Challenge in Making Pictures for Children

The tall, well-built man with a tough, weathered face presents a picture of a retiring cowboy than a children's filmmaker until you get talking to him. The undercurrent of humour you know is there somewhere surfaces at the oddest moments and takes you unawares. His tired eyes light up and his furrowed face breaks into a crinkly smile as he recounts the exploits of Winnie-the-Pooh or the Muppets. There is no change, however, in the slow measured tone and slightly hoarse tenor of his speech – whether he is talking about his various films (*The Jungle Book*, screened at the International Neo-Youth film festival in Madras, *Aristocrats, Robin Hood, Rescuers* and *Sword in the Storm*, among others); or about his son Bruce who gave the young, endearing voice for the Indian boy Mowgli in *The Jungle Book*, and who went on to college and got interested in field biology – the next thing we know, he got out of college, took up river-rafting, grew a beard, went down to Guatemala on a boat trip and has now taken up cinematography. Or when he talks about Walt Disney himself, with whom he was closely associated for three decades.

Except that when talking about Walt Disney, Wolfgang Reitherman's slow, halting style seems tinged with nostalgia.

WOLFGANG REITHERMAN: Hell of a guy, direct – simple, Strong leader. Had a vision always – a vision that was large. A respected talent. Most of all, a showman and a genius for comedy entertainment for all kinds of people, and especially for family-oriented pictures that had good US roots in values, in character. He was probably his best audience. When he enjoyed something you could be sure that many people would.

And after him, have you stuck to his style at Walt Disney studios?
No question, you can never replace Walt Disney. But in many ways he rubbed off on us and we rubbed off on him. He was a great leader but he depended very much on 'a team effort' of contribution, which again was part of his genius. He knew how to use talent and creative contributions, you follow what I mean? He wasn't a dominating leader, although a strong one. So he developed a team and an organization that outlasted his life, which, I think, is a great credit to the man. He was not at all self-oriented in that respect.

There must surely be a difference in the approach, the technique, from the time you started out thirty years back and now. What are the major challenges?
In animation, which was basically at the root of Walt's creativity and which also had a spin-off in the two parks, Los Angeles and Disneyworld, the change is minimal. The drive, because of the nature of the medium, has been in the way we started it. Essentially, Walt was not arty in terms of art on the screen. He was an artist who portrayed human foibles through animals and so on, which in a way had a broad scope internationally. It was such a natural identity for the audience. I think we didn't change that very much, although there was a time, after Walt died, when there was a kind of feeling that possibly we've done enough great classics, and we could ride along on that great library that we have. But luckily, soon the studio realized that the animated feature or featurette was the strongest motion picture force they have, even commercially. So I think that art form – not only the Disney art form – the animated feature, has such great potential in colour and sound, imagination and movement and characterization. The medium is unique because of Walt's desire for perfection, and the necessity for believability in fantasy was very important. You don't believe in fantasy unless it has a believability on the screen, and he stressed strongly that it would be the characters that would make you relate to the screen and give the magic rapport. I would say that it is very alive and we have a whole new group of animators whom we trained over the past few years, and still have an ongoing programme of developing new animators – and I think that's all alive and well.

In animation itself, has the technique changed considerably? Have you come to the computer era, say, with computers programmed to animate sequences as you want them?
Real changes – no. We've tried computers and we've given them the extremes of action, but the computer has a tendency to be mechanical. So far, no. I still think that the art of animation is directly related to the talent, creativity and innovation of the animator who is an actor with a pencil. I'm not negative. I think a lot of computer animation is very exciting and startling. But it has to be used in the right places. I don't think, in terms of character and personality, it really will replace the handcrafted quality of animation. But I'd like to say that animation today is still, and always will be I think, personal creativity – and God bless it for that.

How many animators work on a film? How many worked on 'The Jungle Book'?
Oh, I would say in the neighbourhood of eighteen to twenty, may be twenty-four in a co-production. . .

And would you mind briefly telling me. . .
Yes, I do mind . . . (*then laughing*) no . . .

How do you go about it? Is it frame-to-frame drawing? How many drawings are made?
Yes, technically it's a frame-by-frame drawing and sometimes we shoot a drawing, when it's moving slowly, on two frames instead of one frame. It goes through two processes. One is the rough animation where the animator is striving to find a creative approach. He makes some drawings and he shoots them, and we put those together and revise and adjust; then we clean up those drawings, and then they are xeroxed and handpainted by girls. By the way, we have quite a few girl animators.

In 'The Jungle Book' there were some places where the animation was so lifelike, like the glint of sun-rays in the water. Animation must mean achieving this kind of subtle perfection in the setting and backdrop, besides the active humour of the story.
Yes, I think a good animator is constantly observing nature and the human scene and effects like water works – you don't animate every drop; it's an effect, it's an illusion. Though it's a fantasy, if you don't give the feeling of reality on the screen, you simply watch it rather than become involved in it. And this is what Walt was so great at; he wanted things to be very real as well as imaginative. I think some animation is quite imaginative and very good for what it does, but it won't sustain – and here I'd like to say that there is a great difference between holding the attention of an audience for an hour and a half as against a sixteen or twenty-minute short where you can make a statement which is a little bit philosophical. There have been quite a few animation features, none of which, in my view, really ring the bell because part of the time you're just watching.

Are you an animator yourself?
Used to be.

What exactly is the role of a director in an animation film as against a live-action film?
It's almost impossible – in my view it's not possible – to animate a featurette with a writer alone and say this is it. To me animation is so dependent on the visual, and not only the visual but the ability to develop a character, a character that's a personality. You can't really know quite where you are going in terms of execution until that character is developed; and then when he develops, he makes the picture! You drop the story almost, because when the characters bump and rub and love together or whatever it is, they will make your sequences. The other thing is that music and song are so important. Oh, I digress here, but I suppose that music and movement and colour are probably the greatest communicator, internationally, anywhere. It transcends language, it transcends a whole lot of things, because it deals with emotions. And then if you add characters to that it will play almost anywhere – I am talking about the animated feature – and

the emotions of colour and all those things are so important. It's one hell of a medium. You're forced to do that in animation because you cannot, the animator cannot, do what I call prop animation. In live action you light a cigarette, take a drink from here to there, things like that, and you talk about them.

Although I think that we do too much talking internationally – I've always tried to get away from that but you don't really, because unless a character really talks he doesn't become alive.

A word about the characters, and their characterization in 'The Jungle Book'. Even though the milieu suggests a tropical Indian forest and the names of the animals – Bagheera the panther, Baloo the bear and Shere Khan the tiger – are unmistakably Indian and we know it's based on Kipling's novel...
Kipling would have rolled over in his grave...

Yet the characterizations are definitely American – and it's interesting here that you were referring yourself to the American value roots of Disney productions; for instance, Baloo is more the archetypal American bear of the comics; Shere Khan seems a typical American caricature of the British with their uppish accent, even if to us, he is the villain of the piece, the man-eater could also be reminiscent of the British as colonizers. I don't know if this is what you had in mind, but does this Americanism become a cultural block or does it not matter at all?
Oh, I can only say this that internationally – of course Europe is our biggest international market, then South America, Japan and so on – I don't think we've begun to really tap the foreign market. But you know, we're not all that different from other people. The bear is a big, kind of dumb chap, but by god, he's got a heart of gold. Certainly, he's the kind of guy children fall in love with. There's a quality about American jazz and slang and some of our mannerisms which are crude, or whatever you want to say, but have a directness that communicates to all kinds of people. I have listened to *The Jungle Book* in Japanese and to me it's funny as hell but the voices are not nearly as strong – the timbre and so on. But they work for the Japanese and they work for the Spanish. And it's far better than a live action picture that's dubbed into a foreign language, and the lips don't quite match and so on. And so the answer is, I don't think so. I think Baloo registers with all kinds of people.

With the changing trends in humour – humour, especially in America, seems to have developed a mad or sardonic edge to it – how are Disney productions received in the United States today?
They do quite well generally. But I think there is a problem with young adults – and young adults supposedly, by figures, go from about thirteen, fifteen to the late twenties; that's when they go to film shows a lot – there is a tendency that they don't want to see a kids' picture. Generally, if you get them into the

cinemas, adults will always enjoy us because we don't really make pictures for kids. How can an adult make a picture for kids? We value the appeal of young characters that are in trouble and keep going; we value that. Now, in Europe, the adults have a much greater appreciation of the art of animation. I think you people have that too. So we do have trouble, but our world market makes up the big difference. There is a problem making pictures for the young adult audience and still keeping it a family-oriented film, and not offend the grandmother and the father and mother. I think it's something that's happening all over the world really. And I think the more television you get, the more you are bombarded with visual images and sound, the more jaded it gets. You begin to want something new. It's the human insatiability for the new and the unique, for what is in.

Do you work on the basis of feedback from the youth? And in the light of what you've just said about changing expectations, would you say your problem is the image you have evolved over the years – a respectable, conservative production company, telling the family a fireside story?
Yes. There's a strong tendency to analyse markets. I think if you confuse merchandising with showmanship, you're chasing an elusive star. I think there's a strong attempt to put more edge on a picture, to put a little more violence in it. And like everything else, it has to come and go. I'd say, if you see enough pornography it's going to look like old stuff to you after a while. So what's new? I think with young people, the more you say you shouldn't go, you shouldn't see something, the more they want to see. I don't think we'll ever go extremely one way or the other. I think the two parks, the one at Los Angeles and Disneyworld, perhaps indicate this. Walt had the wisdom to diversify and integrate. The parks, because they havé separate areas, can appeal to the whole gamut of the recreation market. There are things for the little kids, there are dances for the young people, the father and mother and grandmother can watch the people, the nostalgia of the setting and all that in a wholesome atmosphere. I think that was Walt's greatest thrust towards the end of his life, that really takes in the whole gamut.

Where does India figure – how far down the list – as a market?
(*Laughs*) I don't know. I think it's wise in one respect to let things grow. Walt never got involved in politics or great movements, because they come and go. And he was very wise and solid in his own psyche. Maybe he was his own best audience, but he pretty well knew that he was going to be enjoyed by a whole, whole lot of people. (*Lights in the room dim momentarily. 'Put another nickel in the slot', Wolfgang calls out, then continues.*) I think that the foreign market is very important now for the studio. As far as India goes, I really couldn't say but I would guess it's on the back burner. Why? I suppose, because there is not that much return for what you put in – we don't even have our own distribution system here. Eventually, though, the need to reach all people is going to

come through, and that will bring about a greater exchange with India, Africa, or any of the so-called third world. (*Then, almost fearing he's made a mistake*) Are you in the third world?

I've always been curious to know how you put yourself in a child's frame of mind: the attitude that gives the right childlike quality to the film without making it childish.
I did a series of three featurettes. *Winnie-the-Pooh*, which was written by an English writer who wrote kids' stories. It was very simple-minded, the play on words was very delightful and a little on the silly side, but again, the writer had the child's viewpoint of the whole thing and yet in an adult way. I never followed a book closer than I did in those and yet cinematically had to restate it a little bit. They were quite successful just the way they were; they were played first theatrically, then on the TV for several years. So there is an example of a writer capturing a child's point of view. *The Wizard of Oz* books have some of that again, written for children. It's difficult to make pictures for children without playing it down. Children sense it very quickly if someone is just talking like Mama and Papa to them. I think there's a real challenge in making pictures for children in that the adult has to find their point of view and then has to be very simple with it, which an adult is inherently not capable of.

First published in *The Hindu*, 6 December 1981.

To the Home of Stalwarts

Calcutta as the venue for *Filmotsav '82* seems to get many people, the organizers among others, queasy in the stomach. The city's reputation no doubt has a lot to do with this: tram-lines crisscross roads, people go on strikes and take out processions, they are intensely chauvinistic – it's surprising how much we know about Calcutta that goes against holding a fete like an international film festival there. As if to corroborate these fears, cinema employees strike work on the eve of the festival, infighting surfaces in the lower rungs of officialdom in the State Information Department, a Marxist rally is scheduled the day the festival is to open (3 January) and the fourth cricket test match will be on. Officials catalogue all these to prepare the intending viewers (delegates and critics) for the worst, but hasten to put on a reassuring, 'we-shall-overcome' smile.

For the very low expectancy generated itself, the festival could prove successful But, more significantly, it could be more meaningful because of – not in spite of – the deterrents cited. What Calcutta, consciously or unconsciously, is doing is to challenge the concept of an insulated and elitist film festival, where film buffs and filmmakers gather in a campus-like atmosphere and indulge in two weeks of self-centred activity.

The apologetic attitude with which Calcutta as venue is explained away is akin to that bourgeois squeamishness with which we hastily clear the drawing room and stuff clothes on when a visitor drops in home unexpectedly. Calcutta can, just as surely as Delhi or Bangalore or Madras can't, make a film festival organic to its environment, and reflect, if not in its content at least in its interaction with the public, the values of the place of its occurrence. It can offer that dynamic resilience which can, hopefully, draw the festival into the mainstream of its life and political process, rather than let it run its two-week routine course as a quaint, artificial carnival. Not that all this will happen. But it can, and in that possibility lies the excitement, and difference, of a film festival at Calcutta.

The bona fides of the city are excellent in another sense too, to play host to *Filmotsav '82*. This is really the crucible where the new regional cinema crystallized in the mid-1950s. It is the home of stalwarts like Satyajit Ray and Mrinal Sen, and a vibrant film society movement (with a staggering membership of some 17,000). It has a strong film industry going, and the festival would afford the technicians and artistes (who are not stars enough to be invited) a chance to see at the public screenings what their counterparts abroad are doing with and on celluloid. The scaling down of rates this time (the minimum rate being Rs 5 as against Rs 10 last year) would also make the exercise affordable.

Of course, ultimately what speaks for a film festival are the films themselves. Categorized into four sections, the fare is fairly representative both in terms of the countries and the types of films entered. The 75-odd foreign films in the Main section include works of such well-knowns as Zanussi (*Constans*) and Felix Falk (*The Change*) from Poland; Ousmane Sembane (*Ceddo*) from Senegal; Alain Tanner (*Light Years Away*) from Switzerland; Robert Altman (*The Perfect Couple*), Martin Scorsese (*Raging Bull*) and Alan Pakula (*Comes a Horseman*) from the US; Reinhard Hauff (*Slow Attack*) from West Germany; Istvan Szabo (*Mephisto*) from Hungary; Kaneto Shindo (*Strangling*) and Yoji Yamada (*The Yellow Handkerchief*) from Japan; Hector Babenco (*Pixote*) of Brazil; Michel Deville (*Voyage en Douce*) of France; and, to boot, Daniel Kamwa from the Cameroons with his *Pousse Pousse*.

The Indian Panorama section, with six Bengali films, four Malayalam, three Hindi, two Tamil, and one Marathi, Kannada, Manipuri and Telugu each, comprises a disparate choice, based as the selections are, at least partly, on state-wise representation. And yet there are at least five films that demand serious attention in this section: Aravindan's *Pokkuveyil* (Malayalam), Aparna Sen's much-celebrated *36 Chowringhee Lane* (English), Mrinal Sen's *Chaalchitra* (Bengali), Satyajit Ray's *Pikoo* and *Sadgati* (Bengali), and M.S. Sathyu's *Bara* (Kannada).

The Foreign Retrospective section is perhaps the highlight of the festival. It is again a fitting tribute to Calcutta that eleven films of that masterly experimenter of cinema, Godard, are to be screened there; fitting because of Godard's commitment in life and work to the ideology of the left. The prospect of six Jansco films in the same section is no less fascinating.

Coming to think of it, then, *Filmotsav '82* at Calcutta may not be low-key as it is made out to be. Makeshift theatres, not too plush and a city having fun irrespective of a film festival in its midst may not, in the final analysis, be as decisive as public interest, participation and the quality of the films themselves in making for an effective film festival.

First published in *The Hindu*, 3 January 1982.

Godard Retrospective

Jean-Luc Godard doesn't so much make cinema as assail it. As Susan Sontag points out, he is more a 'Destroyer' of cinema, his iconoclasm leading him to discard and even perversely contradict established grammar and principles. Sontag credits him with having achieved in cinema what Schoenberg achieved in music – by repudiating the tonal language prevailing around the first decade of the twentieth century when he took on the atonal mode, or what the Cubists accomplished by questioning the validity of realistic figuration and three-dimensional picture of space.

For all that, Godard is never uncinematic. Yes, he constantly pushes its margins outward, trespassing at times on what would seem to be territory alien to cinema. There is often a marked irreverence in his approach to the medium, its intrinsic mechanism, the instruments employed and its normative role as communicator. But it is the cynicism of the unrelenting critic who first set out to analyse, and then to synthesize cinema.

As a critic, Godard is forged by a dialectic that impels him to revalorize and question continually. His analysis of the cinematic medium hinges on the twin aspects of 'dialectics' and 'semiology' (in fact very early in his career, he had set out his motto: 'The sign forces us to see an object through its significance'). Cinema was to him more than a sum of its parts, and the parts themselves were configured in a constructivist scheme: concrete, anti-aesthetic and political. It was not, however, a cinema of limited means or straitjacketed ideology. Interestingly, when Andre Bazin, countering Eiensteinian montage, put forward his concept of *mise-en-scéne* (or the total setting, in this case emphasizing its aesthetics), Godard struck to the 'montage', but with his own updated redfinition. His montage subsumed *mise-en-scéne* and sought to reveal the psychological reality behind the plastic reality of the image. This synthesis of form is really, for Godard, all-embracing; it covers semantics, popular culture, the distortions of capitalism, syntax, American culture, estrangement (Camus-like), amateurism, anger, disgust (Sartre-like) and a host of other subjects.

Funnily enough, it was Chaplin who inspired Godard to make his third film in 1960 (the first being *Breathless* and the second, *Le Petit Soldat*). Chaplin's observation that tragedy is life in close-up and comedy life in long-shot, had Godard taking a shot at a 'comedy in close-up', which he envisaged as a 'tragi-comic' film. The result was *Une Femme est Une Femme* ('A woman is a woman'), a quasi-musical that comments tongue-in-cheek on lyrical love in the arena of cinema. The technology of the medium itself becomes an object of pun: we see an egg being flipped up from the pan, the character (Anna Karina) leaving to attend a phone call, and when she returns, the egg falls back into the pan. The lyricism was also at least partly real – Godard had just married Anna Karina and he must have had mixed feelings about love when he cast her in the film. However, it is the first film of Godard where words and epigrams appear on the screen. It was also the beginning of a period during which Anna Karina would influence his style, method and subject.

Anna Karina is again the woman with two wooers in Godard's *Bande à part*, shot in 1964. Godard has already evolved to greater audacity with his form. The credits give the filmmaker's name as Jean-Luc/cinema/Godard. The narrative takes the tones of the American gangster genre – crime for the sake of crime – as three students, Franz, Arthur and Odile, decide to rob a house. Their ennui and non-motivation are conveyed in a series of quirky situations. In one instance they decide, since they have nothing worthwhile to discuss, to observe a minute's silence, and Godard actually lifts the sound track off for close to a minute.

In a dance sequence in the film, Godard decides to probe their thoughts, and the narrator goes on to tell us that Odile is wondering if the two boys are thinking about her figure and Franz, whether the world is a dream or dream the world. Arthur, who dies towards the close of the film, actually goes through the motions at the very beginning when Franz shoots him in a mock show, mimicking the American gangster. That genre is evoked in strong, nostalgic terms, and its influence on Godard is seen as much in the film as in his words, 'as soon as you can make films you can no longer make films like the ones that made you want to make them'.

Tailpiece: A heartening aspect, and indeed one that confirms the opportuneness of a Godard Retrospective in a city like Calcutta, about these screenings is that they are invariably full. The public had bought up tickets for all of these films within a couple of hours of opening of issue, and the press and delegates can be seen rushing from earlier shows in different theatres to make sure they are not left out in the first-come-first-served allocation of the limited seats for Godard.

First published in *The Hindu*, 8 January 1982.

'Cinema 2000': Crystal Ball Gazing

The danger with futuristic projections is that they can become mythical just as easily as projections of the past. Fortunately, a strong note of levity kept the seminar on 'Cinema 2000' (organized in Calcutta at the Gorky Sadan as part of *Filmotsav' 82*) from lapsing into the realms of serious science fiction. But that levity was also its undoing, because it was overweening. It made too light of a subject whose purpose we recognize to be more than a laughing matter. Much of the blame for the collapse of this seminar no doubt goes to the subject itself.

In a country where even the industrial revolution has not meant anything to the rural majority, the information revolution the twentieth century seems to hold out can hardly be expected to provide dividends in the foreseeable future. And if cinema is to draw its source material from living reality, it hardly needs to worry about a changed AD 2000.

The only participant to recognize this as the basis of his approach was Mrinal Sen. At the very outset, Sen defined the limitations within which he and other filmmakers in the country worked. He was stating the obvious when he said that 'the pace of technology is very slow', and since cinema is 'largely a technological performance . . . I do not think any radical changes will take place in the next eighteen years.' With characteristic sarcasm he observed, 'You don't need the vision of H.G. Wells, Orwell, Arthur Clarke or Stanley Kubrick to see that most of our country will continue to remain unelectrified, or that the rich will continue to grow richer.' As a filmmaker, he would perhaps have to adjust to a change in degree, not in kind. 'I will', he illustratively summed up, 'make another film on pavement dwellers in the tube [since his *Parashuram* on the pavement dwellers in Calcutta, most of the city's main roads have been dug up for the gigantic metro system] and I will perhaps bring in a situation where the walls will collapse.'

The cartoonist R.K. Lakshman, who was apologetic about his presence and presumption in talking on a subject about which he knew nothing, nevertheless managed to win a few laughs for his characterization of the cinema of the future. The film industry was, he said, one of the ten biggest industries in the country. But the problem with it, and what set it apart from the others, was that it had aged. That sounded like an interesting opening, but Lakshman did not elaborate. One was left wondering whether he meant it seriously.

The scale he went on to attribute to the cinema in or around AD 2000 was as arbitrary, though certainly more humorous. Budgets of spectacular films (his talk was almost confined to them, as the avant-garde, in his opinion, was totally outside the comprehension of 'the common man') would, he envisaged, increase multifold. The whole business would grow so big that 'laws would be amended to suit producers applying for loans directly to the World Bank or the IMF'. He fantasized a state of things where the housewife would have to plan a year ahead to see a film – the cost of travel to the theatre and the ticket would be so prohibitive.

Amita Malik, the film critic, adopted the college debate tactic of projecting herself forward into a film festival taking place in the year AD 2020 and taking stock. After a number of puns about the new trends in that era (for example, 'Anglo-Saxon domination at festivals are a thing of the past'), she got round to the point that it would be an age of television. M. Bhaktavatsala (former president of the Film Federation of India and distributor), tended to agree with Amita Malik on that score. He even predicted that the theatre would disappear altogether. But there were two serious blocks to change in that direction: the fact that the Indian viewing habit is communal (meaning that TV cannot be relevantly all-pervasive and must reckon with cultural variants) and that the Indian bureaucracy never changed (on the contrary, government control of the media was getting stronger).

The only other Indian participant was Viswanathan from ISRO whose very detailed paper on the latest inventions and experiments in media technology was heard the longest and understood the least. It left everyone cold, if not a little worried about the possiblities with which this plethora of technology bristled. The foreign participants were more evaluative (even if, sometimes, value judgments were passed) of this technology. Dealing with the economics of the spectacular American cinema of the future, Joseph Belford (Vice-President of the American Motion Pictures Association) speculated that the 'bigger is better' idea would catch on. Films like *Jaws* and *Star Wars*, which were de-humanizing, would be the vogue. They would be big-budgeted but intelligent spectacles, he surmised. He mentioned two recent films, *Ragtime* (made at a cost of $20 million) and *Reds* ($33 million) as indicative of this trend where, among other things, 'stars do not rank as high as other ingredients'.

The three British viewpoints of the futurology of cinema covered three different aspects. John Barrington (broadcaster and filmmaker), dealing with film criticism, spoke at length on the necessity for it to have a forward thrust. 'A good critic is a man whose watch is five minutes ahead of other watches', he proposed. But he soon became overcautious and began to summon up visions of 2001 as 'the audio-visual Armageddon'.

In a passionate indictment of American neo-imperialism in the video revolution, he pointed out that most video-games children play are about war and violence. He warned, 'it is the profit motive from the manufacturers of software that will destroy us'.

Directing his attention specifically to a country like India, he cautioned that satellite or other technology had ideological slants, and 'you will go back into colonialism if you are not careful'. Even if his tone was at times hectoring, there was the underlying sincerity of a man who strongly felt what he said. But the fear of technology seemed overstated. There is a disturbing retrogressive edge to his summation that the 'glories of thousands of years of culture' could be destroyed 'through man's greed for invention and his inability to use it'.

Derek Malcolm (film critic for *The Guardian*) was dramatic but not convincing when he pronounced 'to hell with technology', and proceeded to put himself firmly on the side of substance and content, which, he said, would always remain the creative filmmaker's domain, whatever the demands of technology on him and his work. When the topic was later thrown open to the house, he admitted to this writer, however, that economic constraints do apply to and affect the filmmaker's work. How, then, could he rule out the role of technology in determining the formal aspects of a film and forcing the filmmaker to adapt himself to it, is the question – which, unfortunately, could not be settled for want of time.

Derek Malcolm also got into trouble for his use of the word Indianness to define what 'the outside world seeks in Indian films'. An Indian film critic took him up on that and went on to describe how this thing of 'Indianness' was overwrought and corresponded to the preoccupation of the anglicized middle-class filmmaker of the country. It was nothing to be looked for, he pointed out, but something to be taken for granted, just like the camel is taken for granted in the Koran by the fact that it is never once mentioned in that text although it was a ubiquitous animal in that culture.

Ken Wlaschin (Director of the National Film Theatre in London) let his vivid imagination take flight and, in a humorous flash-forward, painted another version of Amita Malik's film festival in 2000. The things he thought up were ingenious and perhaps remotely relevant to his part of the world, but left the Indian from here-and-now wondering what he was talking about. Delegates at this festival (of his dreams), he said, would all be in their respective rooms with large video screens on which could be seen, at the push of a button, any of the thousand films entered. Distributors all over the world would also be seen in these films in their drawing rooms via satellite – and so it went on. The only concrete comments he made were that large audiences would yield to small ones and finally to the solitary viewer (an understandable consequence of the predicted atomisation with the break up of the joint viewing system), and that censorship would be ineffective and cease to be.

One recognizes that a seminar is, by its very nature, a token exercise. But it should be able to at least throw up issues worth mulling over later. 'Cinema

2000' is hardly the subject for an Indian film festival. To a cinema which is yet to update itself to the present and which is still fighting to shed the distortions of a peculiar legacy, the visions 2000 evoke in others are too far away, even if the date itself is round the corner. For us, it would be wishful quantum leap.

First published in *The Hindu*, 13 January 1982.

Glare of Living Reality

It may perhaps be said against Godard that he is a filmmaker's filmmaker, that his references (and there are so many of them) are too scholastic and academic. But it cannot also be gainsaid that no filmmaker since the very inception of the media has done so much to make cinema so organic with life, demystifying it and rendering it a malleable tool, like the brush in a painter's hand or the pen in a writer's. Godard's experimentation again is not an academic, laboratory affair. His multiple approach gives the lie to a simple narrative replication of life. It seeks to rescue our cinematic interpretations of life from slotted types. All influences that touch our everyday lives are grist to his mill. All our preconceptions of the ethical and the moral are targets of his attack.

The significance of this attempt to re-evaluate and question is as valid today as it was more than twenty years back when he started out with *Breathless* (1960). Which is why a Godard film is never really dated in terms of its relevance. As expected, the Godard Retrospective is certainly the best part of the film festival in Calcutta. It will undoubtedly leave a most lasting impression on those who manage to sit through the screenings.

Managing to sit through, however, may not be that simple. Besides that Godard is heavy stuff and taxes the viewer's intelligence, the projections tend to test his patience. Dim lighting, soft focus every once in a while, and unclear subtitles make you want to scream. Quite a few in the theatre actually do, but either the projectionist insulated in his cubicle can't hear or can't do anything about it. And so the substandard projections continue. Hardly a tribute to a master, which is what a retrospective is made out to be all about.

Godard's *Une Femme Mariée*, continuing his cinematic examination of the woman as a cultural, sexual and social being, caused ripples in France when it was produced. The censors cleared the film only after he had changed the title from the original *La Femme Mariée* (or The Married Woman) to *Une Femme Mariée* (or A Married Woman), and cut some four minutes out of it. The change in name may seem like quibbling, but given Godard's attention to each letter and word and their significance, the censors were perhaps afraid that the 'general' being substituted for the 'particular' in this case could be tantamount to tainting the entire womanhood of France.

On the surface the film deals with Charlotte who is a wife with a happy family, but also carries on an affair on the side with an actor. Her secretiveness in her rendezvous with her lover is almost paranoid. She even changes cabs each time (this because her husband once had her followed by a private detective). Within this framework, Godard analyses not only Charlotte's thinking process and behaviour, but the gamut of external influence that work on and around her. His form is, again, free and unrestrained. We have poetry (of the Joycean stream-of-consciousness variety), discourses, monologues, interviews, graffiti on walls and advertisement slogans – all creating a growing consciousness of Charlotte's world. The film opens and closes with a bare hand (Charlotte's) on an empty white sheet. That simplicity of imagery is, in a way, maintained throughout. But the complexity of meanings, a complexity which draws us into a vortex, makes *Une Femme Mariée* a film more than about its eponymous heroine, Charlotte.

Godard's perception becomes even more detailed and extensive in two other films, made within five months of one another: *Alphaville* and *Pierrot le Fou*. In both, he is inspired by Jean Cocteau to 'put the commonplace in place.' In our ordinary actions and words, in the everyday objects we take for granted, lie meanings which have become defunct with long disuse. They must be reawakened and rejuvenated, not in an exotic light but in the searing glare of living reality. That Godard was provoked to this purpose by Cocteau is interesting. We have the poet-turned-filmmaker (Cocteau) leading the filmic poet (Godard).

The notable similarity or dissimilarity between *Alphaville* and *Pierrot le Fou* is that while the former concludes on an affirmative note, the latter closes in negation and death. Lemmy Caution in *Alphaville* is a spy who enters the futuristic, computerized night-world of Alphaville (almost the world of Orwell's *1984*), destroys its figurehead, Alpha-60, and rescues Natasha von Brown from its dark confines and manages to de-brainwash her. The plot is similar to Cocteau's *Orphée*, where Orpheus leads Eurydice from the netherworld. Only here we have instead a city of signs and sounds where words like 'love', 'conscience' and 'why?' are treason. Natasha is rescued from total desensitization and conformity to 'logic', and reintroduced to stirrings of love and conscience. As she drives out of Alphaville with Caution at the wheels in the end, she has recovered enough to haltingly stutter out those all-redeeming words, 'I love . . . you.'

Pierrot le Fou shows us Ferdinand (Jean-Paul Belmondo) and Marianne (Anna Karina) going south towards the open sea – an open world unlike Alphaville's dark closed confines. They have robbed and committed murder, and are on the run. The film is far more complicated in all that it seeks to evoke and comprehend. Godard himself is more 'auteuristic' (the total authorship of cinema by the director) here than before. Scribblings in his hand keep appearing at vantage-points to suggest this. It really sets a new substyle, where a sudden rush of images in one sequence alternate with slow, eased-out shots in another to create a visual dynamic that is peculiar.

Being Godard's first film in colour and cinemascope, the use of colour in

Pierrot le Fou is both organic and commentative. Primary colours are evoked in strong unnatural terms. We have masked shots in red, and blue and yellow, cropping up again and again. At the end, after the law has caught up with the lovers and Marianne is dead, Ferdinand paints his face in blue, wraps himself in red and yellow dynamite, and lights the fuse. A long shot shows a volcano-like explosion and the camera slowly pans to show the serene sea.

First published in *The Hindu*, 17 January 1982.

Consummate Artistry Again

Coming from Satyajit Ray, they perhaps pitch expectations farther than they could have hoped to reach, given the relative modest scale of the productions and the different media (TV) for which they were meant. But if the image and stature of the man as an artist are not to domineer and surrogate the art itself, Ray's *Pikoo* (Bengali) and *Sadgati* (Hindi) quite fulfil what they had set out to do. Left-handed efforts of a master, maybe, but no less significant because the left hand proves to be as good as the right – or almost.

The two films (or filmettes) have enough in common to make them the two parts of a diptych – a twin portrait of the artist as an ageing man. There is. in both, a preoccupation with mortality, an accent on human frailty, that suggests a different phase, a different state of mind in Ray's evolution. Not that death, weakness, age or youth are new elements in Ray; but the strength with which they were handled hitherto yields now to a less confident reckoning. There seems a faltering awareness of a reality behind and outside of cinema. The resultant tentativeness in treatment may suggest a Ray slightly out of character, but perhaps more personal and sincere than before. It is a style that is assured, without being reassuring.

Both films, again, seem like episodes set in a continuing theme that could well extend into many more parts. There is no sense of finality in the end; a new possibility opening up offers an alternative ending in a different direction, perhaps after a few more episodes. If, at the end of *Pikoo*, the boy's adulterous mother is left with a tormented conscience that could well change the deteriorating relationships in the family for the better, *Sadgati* closes with the untouchables having gone through another eye-opening experience of caste oppression. In their refusal to touch the corpse of their fellow-untouchable, Dukhi, there are the stirrings of a passive resistance.

The milieu in which the two films are set form two extremes of the social scale. *Pikoo* unfolds as the crisis of an affluent Bengali family where the husband and wife are on the verge of separation, the mother meanwhile carrying on an affair with another man who visits her at their house while her husband is away at work. The grandfather, a heart patient, knows all that is going on, but is bedridden and can do nothing about it. The couple's only son, Pikoo, has no inkling yet of the impending crisis, and romps around the house and garden spending a little time with his grandpa, some time with the servants, with his mother, his toys and the flowers. In his small and innocent world, things are still beautiful and wondrous. He doesn't know why the veins on his grandfather's hands stand out so; when mother's friend comes with a gift of crayons for him he is thrilled and sets out to do as his mother suggests – draw flowers like in the garden, in the same colours. The power of his innocence is contrasted with the helplessness of the grandfather, who has a stroke while the couple is making love in the bedroom and the boy is drawing his flowers in the garden, and can't reach out in time for the emergency bell at his side. He dies simply and suddenly. The clouds that had gathered in the skies outside slowly turn into rain. The first few drops smudge Pikoo's crayon flowers.

In the old man's death Ray touches fleetingly a moment of awkward truth. There is something absurd about his (the grandfather's) desperate bid to get succour, set against the fact of the couple's impassionate embrace in a room nearby. But Ray does not dwell on that weak, but all the more real, moment: he transmutes it the next instant into pathos, lyrical and cinematic, when he brings in rain to wash out our mixed responses at this point and replace them with more conventional emotions. Consummate artistry reasserts itself and an inadvertent glimpse of not-so-beautiful reality is covered up.

Death is again as sudden and absurd, and rain becomes the 'great sop' in *Sadgati* when, after chopping away relentlessly at a huge block of wood with a blunt axe (when the untouchable Dukhi comes to request the Brahmin priest Ghasiram to go to his house to finalise an auspicious date for his daughter's marriage, he is assigned a number of household chores before the Brahmin can consider his plea), Dukhi falls dead to the ground. It is again a forlorn and desperate death – a death that has little meaning and reason. Again, both the absurdity and the injustice of it is submerged in the downpour that follows. When Dukhi's family and friends, learning it was death due to overwork – and therefore tantamount to murder and a case for the police – refuse to remove the corpse, Ghasiram is at first nettled, but soon thinks up a way to get rid of the body without polluting himself. He has a rope tied to the ankle of the corpse and drags it across to where the birds feed on animal carcasses.

Already, parallels are being drawn between *Sadgati* and the goings-on in parts of the country. When the film gets to be shown on TV (it is produced by Doordarshan), then, it will enjoy a contemporaneity Ray may not have envisaged, and which may really be too hot and close in time for him.

First published in *The Hindu*, 21 February 1982.

Symbolic Motif of a Rat Trap

A vestigial feudal attitude unable to cope with or reconcile to the realities of a new society, and slipping slowly into paranoia, is Adoor Gopalakrishnan's theme in his latest (and third in over a decade) film, *Elippathayam* ('Rat Trap'). For over two hours Adoor doggedly keeps his material under tight control; and that by itself is no mean achievement for a work shot three-quarters indoors. Repressed colours, controlled lighting (cinematographer Ravi Varma extends his skill in black-and-white chiaroscuro lighting gracefully and as confidently into colour) and a sound track gone over, it would seem, inch by inch by the director, gives *Elippathayam* a cinematic finish that speaks volumes of the patience and care of its author, which is rare in the best of Indian cinema.

The Adoor we know from *Swayamvaram* and *Kodiyettam* is suggested in the craft, especially at points where he is meticulous to a fault (there is a strict grammar about the cuttings and compositions of static dialogue sequences that makes us unduly aware of 'style'); but the class and depth he touches here seem to unfold another dimension of the man, a dimension the two earlier films had not revealed to us. The way Adoor condenses space to arrive at his milieu of a decadent joint family of a brother (Unni) and three sisters (Janamma, Rajamma and Sridevi) caught in the echoes of the conflict of change and yet insulated physically from society at large, is reminiscent, to a degree, of Tomás Alea's *The Survivors*. There in a similar manner, attention is focused on a family and class displaced by the revolution in Cuba, and living out their borrowed time within their compound walls, trying to pretend that nothing has happened outside. At another level the film evokes K.R. Mohan's 'Aswathama' (Malayalam) where, in a like setting of a crumbling Namboodiri household, profounder questions of mortality and alienation are raised.

The social factors impinging on the miniscule world of Unni and his two younger sisters (the eldest, Janamma, is married and away at her husband's place) are neatly atomised and woven into the plot. There is the inferred fact of the breakdown of the Nair joint family and matrilineal system with Janamma, instigated by her husband, demanding her share of the property and in her son's relationship with Unni, there is the veiled resentment of the new parvenu class in Unni's derision for his manager's son who has come back from the Gulf with a lot of money. The loss of authority and prestige are eloquently summed up in at least three episodes: when the family can hear thieves stealing coconuts at night and does not have the courage to confront them; when Unni himself catches a boy red-handed stealing cashew fruit, but finds it difficult to assert himself before his (the boy's) mother's suggestive and seductive excuses; or, again, when a man on the street almost abuses Unni for shining the torch in his face at night.

Unni's self-centredness and self-indulgence, on the other hand, tilts the balance against any undue sympathy for him. He must have his oil bath and two- or three-course meal irrespective of his sister's health; he would rather not have his sisters married at all for fear of being left to fend for himself. The introversive edge to his nature asserts itself more and more as the film progresses until it becomes all-consuming and borders on a pathological fear of the outside world. In two brilliant sequences, Adoor captures the essential fastidiousness of the man: in one, we see him clipping his moustache in front of a mirror with overwrought care; and in the next, he sets out of the house for a marriage only to return because he does not know how to cross a pool of stagnant water without wetting his feet. The behavioural details in these and other similar instances have been worked out very adeptly by both the actor (Karamana) and the director.

Adoor has synthesized the word and the visual so that one complements the other. With less of a narrative to go by than in his earlier films, he is able to concentrate on the dual aspect of dialogue here as a ploy for characerization and as a commentative aside. When the youngest sister, Sridevi, for instance, excitedly announces that their new teacher at college was a film actor and wonders aloud whether an actor can become a teacher, it is at once a measure of her naïveté as one cut off from the mainstream of social trends, and of the penetrating impact of the popular mass culture of cinema even in these remote bastions of tradition. When Rajamma one morning steps out of the house into the courtyard and hearing the drone of a plane passing overhead, looks up and feels faint, there is the suggestion of both the coming of the jet age and her inability to face it.

Action and shots here are symbolic without the symbolism looming large and distracting us, as in *Swayamvaram*. The central symbolic motif of, first, rats caught in a trap, and then Rajamma when she is sick, and finally Unni himself, when he is rescued out of his self-imposed exile, being carried through a pathway to their death (in the case of the rats) and liberation (in the case of Rajamma and Unni), remains, to this writer at least, a conundrum. The shot is accompanied each time with cathartic music that seems to tell us in unmistakable tones to take note. But the point, unfortunately, is missed and continues to keep one guessing even weeks after the film is seen. But that perhaps is reason enough.

First published in *The Hindu*, 28 February 1982.

Wider Perceptions of Censorship

The backlash was only to be expected. When it turned out that the growing incidence in recent months of a new type of commercial cinema at the south Indian box office – at times pulp revolutionary, at others more intelligently purposive, but by and large politically and socially bold – was the result, not of fortuitous lapses by the censors but rather of a conscious shift in emphasis in the implementation of the censorship guidelines, it was only natural that those who stood to lose the most from this policy shift should cry wolf the hoarsest.

The initiative of protest, first taken by the Tamil Nadu government vis-a-vis *Thanneer Thanneer*, soon passed over to the Film Chamber and the Film Producers' Guild, and was taken up again, on the rebound, by the state government in its mediatory role in the latest boycott (the Madras Censors) threat made by the film producers' bodies. But it is not as if both have the same stakes in the controversy – while the government's intent clearly seems to be to nip the stirrings of a political cinema in the bud, the Film Chamber is exercised about a newfound discrimination and inquisitorial zeal in the censors in tackling the three broad areas of sex, violence and superstition in films coming up before the examining committees.

Yet the two are seen to act in concert against the Regional Censor Board, or, more specifically, the regional officer; and were it not for the genuineness of some of the Chamber's grievances, especially regarding the 'double standards' used in censoring foreign and Indian films, or dubbed-language versions of the same south Indian film, this concert could well be an unholy alliance between an establishment hypersensitive towards criticism and the 'sex-and-violence lobby' ever touchy about anything that tends to detract from the saleability of its films at the box office.

The issue really revolves, in the ultimate analysis, on the role of the censors in interpreting the guidelines. The latitude with which they are worded makes for little definitive precision. The first guideline, for instance, says that the

> objectives of film censorship will be to ensure that (a) the medium of film remains responsible and sensitive to the values and standards of society: (b) artistic expression and creative freedom are not unduly curbed, and (c) censorship is responsive to social change.

The second guideline stipulates the deterrent role of the censors in ensuring that anti-social activities and drinking are not glorified, that the 'modus operandi' of criminals are not shown, that 'human sensibilities are not offended by vulgarity, obscenity and depravity', that anything constituting contempt of court or affecting friendly relations with foreign countries is not allowed, and so on. The third guideline asks the Board to ensure that the film is judged in its entirety and in the context to which it relates: and the last says that if these criteria are fulfilled, the Board may grant a certificate to the film in the 'A' or 'U' category, as it deems fit.

If the guidelines *per se* leave a lot to the imagination of the interpreter, in practice the meanings have been narrowed down. 'The Central Board of Film Censors meets once in three months', says Mr K. G. Ramakrishnan, Regional Censor Officer.

> And we may have had, so far, about 90 meetings or so in the last thirty years. In these 90-odd meetings so many decisions have been taken which have become a body of law for us. So a kind of advance towards precision and definition has been made continuously, and it is not as though it's a very wide field and one can interpret it as one pleases. . . . The guidelines, put in general terms, have been annotated by the Central Board over a period of years, so that there is a body of instruction which is available, reducing the areas of arbitrariness, whimsicality and subjectivism.

Arbitrariness, whimsicality and subjectivism, however, are precisely what the Chamber alleges against the censors. 'With over 750 films being made every year and no plethora of original scripts, a number of producers are dubbing successful films in one language into another. But even the visuals and sound track so dubbed are being subject to fresh and further censorship.' In a memorandum on the subject, the Chamber cites the instances, among others, of *Jayamalini*, a Telugu-dubbed version of the Tamil film *Swargathil Thirappu Vizha*, where the examining committee ordered 19 cuts and the reviewing committee 72 cuts; and *Amak Yuvan*, a Hindi-dubbed version of the Malayalam film *Vayanadan Thampan*, which has been refused to certificate.

The rigour with which sex and violence is excised borders on the ridiculous, so much so that 'we do not know where the vulgarity creeps in; in the film, or in the minds of the panelists'. It is not the function of the Censor Board, or the censor officer, they argue, to improve the quality of films or the morality of society. Censorship is, by definition, a negative function and must remain so; it would be dangerous to give it a positive role.

Mr Ramakrishnan, while willing to concede that perhaps there could be a case for discrimination in effect, if not in intent, in the censorship of foreign films vis-a-vis Indian ones, absolves himself of responsibility. All foreign films are, he points out, being censored by the Bombay office. It would, he further concedes, be specious to argue, as has sometimes been argued, that these films could be justified in the light of the guideline that a film is to be assessed in its cultural context, or again, that since the exhibition of foreign films is by and large restricted to the cities, and they rarely ever percolate down to townships or villages, there could be a different yardstick to censor them.

However, between film and film within the purview of the Regional Censor Board at Madras, he maintains, there has been no discrimination. That there must have been a departure in the censorship pattern is evident from the note he sent to the advisory panel members, reminding them that 'the policy of the Censor Board is utmost liberalism in regard to valid social comment and the utmost severity in judgement in regard to sex, morbidity, obscenity, violence.'

> One thing I am clear about. I think there is no conflict between my view and the government's on this that women being shown as commodities, as no more than sex objects in a country where women really play a very big role in large areas of public life and where woman's emancipation, relatively, is at a higher stage than even some western European countries, is something we should go on discouraging. And here again it's not a question of sex. The Censor Board has never cut anything on grounds of sex. It's only on grounds of obscenity, vulgarity and depravity. We have allowed quite a few scenes where sex has been projected with sensitivity and beauty. One example I can give is *Muddamandaram*, where we allowed a lingering passionate teenagers' love scene without a single cut, even with a suggestion of nudity. You know, very often a nude woman is not vulgar, but a fully dressed woman with back swings and breast swings in a titillating manner is. It is that we are objecting to.

On violence too, he denies that the attitude of the censors has of late been pettifogging. There, perhaps, has been an attempt to distinguish between violence and violence, and to excise that violence which has, in his words, 'a multiplier effect on society'. 'What kind of violence is permissible is debatable', he elaborates.

> When a woman is cornered by a man who wants to assault her and the only weapon she finds is a dagger and she thrusts it in the man's beily and blood gushes out, we will not cut even a single shot. Or take *Uchakkattam*. The husband enters the room and finds his wife in bed with another man. He suddenly goes and bashes the man's head. Maybe blood will gush out, but we will allow it.

To prohibit the sleazy in terms of sex or violence without being squeamish about it is one thing; to try and arrive at an objective 'all-are-equal-in-the-eyes-of-the-censor' principle, quite another. Mr Ramakrishnan's privileging the former in the light of the near-impossibility of the latter may have much to do with the current controversy. Comparisons or precedents cited to substantiate discrimination hold little water technically or rationally. The same act of violence or rape could surely have different implications and connotations in different themes, plots or cultural contents. Again, as Mr Ramakrishnan himself puts it, 'You cannot cite precedents, because law overrides precedents. Traffic laws are being violated every day. But a person being arrested for violating traffic law can't say the previous violators haven't been arrested.'

Interpretative discretion by the censors, then, still looms large in several crucial areas – a double-edged prerogative that can be used progressively or retrogressively. That censorship is institutionally and functionally a negative phenomenon becomes debatable. Inasmuch as there is the potential to socially interpret images flitting on the screen; inasmuch as a residuary area of manoeuvrability does exist, it seems better to come to terms with it. Surely a censor body with a brittle and mechanistic attitude to the role of sex and violence and superstition in cinema can hardly be the arbiters of a liberal guideline, that films must be responsive to social change.

If curtailing the licence to portray sex and violence can upset a lobby of film-makers, attempts to censor on grounds of superstition can imaginably be far more dangerous. At its meeting in Madras in April 1981, the Central Board of Film Censors directed that all those who examined a film should ask themselves whether it propagated superstition as a cult or promoted supernatural intervention in a manner that would reward the believer and harm the non-believer, and if so, suggest appropriate cuts and, in extreme cases, refuse certification.

The directive obviously means to more than safeguard secularism. There is in it a hint of the scientific temper espoused increasingly recently. That this is, in every sense, high-strung tightrope-walking hardly needs emphasis. Mr Ramakrishnan himself has no delusion about it:

> It's not going to be easy to implement it. Let's see how it works. It is very dangerous ground. I always tell my advisory panel members: Never go to that stage where somebody will go up a soap box and say 'God is in danger', or that the Censor board is anti-God. Because once that emotion is out, who is going to bother whether there is any case for them or not?

The new line on superstition even seems a shade anomalous in a context where mythologicals with miracles galore are still box-office stuff. But then, we are assured, the accepted lore of the country is permissible. But the 'problem would arise', says Mr. Ramakrishnan,

> in terms of existing people or people who have existed only a few years ago. In fact, I was wondering, if a film came on Sai Baba, we may have a problem. . . . But it is a difficult area, and it would be stupid of the censors to come to a head-on collision.

He goes on to cite an instance of censorship to set the balance where superstition tends to override the scientific temper:

There was in the AVM film *Amma*, a person who says, 'If you go to that goddess and worship you will become all-right.' We permitted that. Then the next person says, 'I have tried all medicines. I was not cured. But I went to that goddess; I am cured.' I only said, 'Cut out "all medicines". I don't want to spread the belief that modern medicines can't cure. Certainly you can say that faith in God can cure, but to say that medicines can't cure is not proper.' I remember, in the old days, when smallpox vaccine was first introduced, there was a propaganda that Mahamayi will interfere, so don't take the vaccination.

The censors seem to emerge vindicated, not just by the rhetoric of a progressive policy, but by the fact of numerous films which have emerged unscathed by their scissors and have gone on to register reasonable successes at the box office. What's more, in most of these films there is no evidence of prudery or squeamishness that a straight approach to sex or violence would suggest. The problem then seems to emanate from a strong core of the conventional commercial filmmakers who are piqued that they are not being permitted to continue to dwell on the cliched modes of obscenity and violence that film after film has been taking its toll on the sensibilities of the average viewer. Alternatively, it seems a personal equation gone sour between the censor officer and a few vocal producers.

For a body that has customarily got, and deserved, only brickbats, a *Thanneer Thanneer* or *Sigappu Malli* or *Pattam Parakkattum* or *Ezhavathu Manithan* in Tamil, or a *Viplava Sangha* or *Maro Charitra* in Telugu, a *Bara* in Kannada, or an *Eenaadu* in Malayalam, seem so many bouquets, bearing testimony to a determination – as far as possible and against the toughest odds – to deliver the film-going masses from their drudgery, and give them entertainment that is not necessarily escapist.

The euphoria of the moment could, however, be deceptive. Even if the censors seem to have won in the first rounds, and even if the censor officer himself claims the Central Board's and ministry's unstinted support, other factors, paradoxically unleashed by this very same liberalization in censorship, could well play into the hands of the state government and the Film Chamber and allied bodies in effectively reverting the Board to its old role as guardian of the status-quoist cinema. Many of the new films – varying in their political and social stance from adventurism to tongue-in-cheekiness – could well precipitate a reaction resulting in a stricter clampdown of censorship. Also, optimistically, that need not happen if, as Mr Ramakrishnan himself put it, filmmakers realize that they are using a permitted medium: 'You use a permitted medium up to a point and then try to take it beyond that point, and never use a friendly officer (or a liberal Censor Board) to shortcircuit a social process.'

First published in *The Hindu*, 4 July 1982.

Swing between Lyricism and Didacticism

It is not a happy circumstance to have known a filmmaker, to share the views and values he holds dear, and yet to have to say that he is more articulate about his work than in his films. The dilemma presents itself as a ludicrous choice between the man and his work, the absurdity of it patent in the fact that, for the critic at least, the man (creator) exists only through and because of his work (creation). And yet it seems unfair – not to mention incomplete – to insulate the film from the known predilections of the filmmaker on the one hand, and on the other, to arrive at a critical appraisal based on purely personal factors – factors which fall outside and beyond the film *per se*.

The problem is compounded in a scheme of analysis where cinema is, primarily and ultimately, mass communication rather than (and more than) artistic self-expression. The litmus value-test for any process of mass communication, as Raymond Williams points out in his corrective to the classic Laswellian model, is the purpose of intent behind the exercise. (Laswell had summarized the communication process thus: 'Who says what, to whom, how and with what effect.' Williams adds the qualifying rider, 'for what purpose', to fill in the missing causative or motivating factor. *Communications*, 1962).

Alert, then, to this crucial aspect of the purpose with which a film is made, there arises the problem of identifying it on the screen and in cinematic terms. This seems easy enough in the case of the staple fare in the majority of our films where the profit motive is only all too obvious, but where, nevertheless, sex and violence and song and dance and moral rhetoric are integrated in a well-knit and neat construct. Caught in the fierce, unremitting competition for better box-office time (and returns), these films perforce vie with one another in attaining newer levels of technical finesse and ingenuity.

Their blatant commercialism, however, tends to leave unnoticed their more insidious role as perpetuators of certain social and cultural archetypes, of status-quoist symbols and images, so much so that entire generations of viewers are conditioned by the static set of values these films impart. At heart, this cinema is stolidly conservative, the token sorties into modernity – in the spoken colloquial style, dress or behavioural details, or the calculatedly anti-convention image of the odd protagonist – being but a surface phenomenon, a pretence of keeping abreast of the times. The virtues it champions are essentially old-world, the images it idealizes almost feudal. More than half a century of this cinema in our country has, if anything, only helped to lull the viewers into a tacit acceptance of its norms and values, so that the supine martyrdom of the good, or the servility and sexploitation of the woman, the iconizing impulse inspired by the hero, or hierarchic family and social relationships form the matrix of our cinematic experience. Our sensibilities are already predisposed to this cultural obsolescence, made more acceptable as it were by the technical attractiveness and innovativeness of these films. Taken in by their visual dynamics – by the action and pace and engrossing narrative – we are prone (as indeed we are meant to be) to overlook their ultimate ideological stance.

The seeming paradox, then, of an unchanging set of values being refurbished and reinterpreted *ad infinitum* by the dynamic variable of formal style turns out actually to be a well-worked-out mechanism that serves at once both the palpable profit motive and the ulterior ideological purpose of the majority cinema. The task of the minority cinema lies precisely in challenging the appropriation of the media for these ends, in trying to wean viewers away from the ethics and aesthetics of the other cinema. This requires not just a contrary motive or purpose, but a form suited to that motive or purpose: a form that is oppositional not just by being reactive to the other cinema, but by virtue of a philosophy and a structure in which the intent is well-integrated.

Without any such original impulse to sustain them, and operating by and large in a reactive manner, the new (minority) filmmakers in the country seem (after their first couple of films) to lapse into a new set of stereotypes. The pioneers become settlers, not because they have arrived but because they do not go on. With a few exceptions, this cinema swings violently from extreme lyricism at one end to extreme didacticism on the other; the one tending to become abstract (if not pretentious) in its celebration of visual beauty, and the other bordering on the philistine in conveying the message. More than two decades of this new cinema has only made it synonymous in popular perception with an extended sense of time (characters just walk on and on or laze around for minutes on end, much of their ennui actually spilling over into the viewers), actors who are robot-like in their expressiveness and movements, and difficult-to-relate departures from the narrative norms. All this is well by way of initation into a counter-culture of cinema, so that action and pace and narrative flow are deliberately retarded to question set preconceptions of their role in this media. But because these formal elements have not been inspired by a considered motive or, where they have, the motive has not been made aesthetically organic, the end-product is not even as consummate (as a piece of art or communication) as in the majority (commerical) cinema.

This failure to integrate the motive in this sense is seen, almost illustratively, in K. Hariharan's *Ezhavathu Manithan* (Tamil), although, paradoxically, this is apparently what he had set out to do. 'It was definitely experimental', says

Hariharan, explaining what is perceived as a difficult and often jarring mix of old and new forms.

> Many viewers have thought the film was too fragmented. There were a lot of cuts, a lot of movements, a dissection of all events, which distances a lot of people, because one is used to that typical theatrical structure where you see two people keep on talking till they finish their point. Now we were seen to be breaking the point, using lots of cuts, intercuts and camera movements. So that way it was analytical. It is the taking, the aspect of taking which might appear to be intellectual. But I think that's where we have to make a beginning in terms of initiating an audience . . . otherwise, in terms of communication, one is at most times very direct. Most of our comments are very direct attacks on political parties and personalities.

There are no doubt brilliant sequences in the film where Eisensteinian montage and the consequent alienation almost suggest a take-off in terms of form, but the next instant we witness a lyrical song-and-dance sequence with all the character and connotations we have learnt to ascribe to it in a hundred commercial films. If this random combination of the archetypal (and the songs and dances are not the only instance) and the novel (adapting Eisenstein's montage, for example) just doesn't jell, plain realism – and this writer, again, cannot ultimately see the film as more than realist in genre – is stretched in the effortlessness and spontaneity with which workers are unionized, strikes organized and the capitalist villains defeated.

'It would appear very simplistic that unions are formed like that,' concedes Hari,

> but that is why I used a certain amount of analytical approach. The image of ripping open the picture of Kali [when the protagonist is insulted on the factory floor by the owner's son who slaps him in front of the workers, he rips off a framed photo of Kali hanging on the wall, scribbles his protest on the cardboard behind, and organized resistance begins] is almost mythological. So at that level, it transcends the possibility of believing in it really. So I have not made it look real. So the very usage of forming a union like that by ripping open an image of Kali and through that managing to convey the force of Kali, the image of Kali, the emotion of Kali as destroyer, as the angry woman.

Besides the propriety of using Kali as the axial symbol in a film that seeks to get away from archetypes, to be alienatory in form, and to be modern and scientific in outlook, there is again the danger that in a milieu and setting that are real such attempts to employ the mythical even in a metaphoric sense could easily be misconstrued as subscribing to that myth itself.

Hari, of course, sees and interprets it differently. 'I would have loved to make a total myth. But you see, it is not possible, because cinema has not reached that kind of grammar. The grammar should be so developed that one can express a theme like a dancer expresses *mudra*!' The alienatory form of Eisenstein itself, he admits, is not pursued consistently but used to advantage here and there, because,

> I don't think it is suited to the Indian cultural ethos. The alienation in the Indian cultural ethos is totally implicit, in the sense that one can watch a Bharatanatyam dance and the same woman will do the role of Krishna, Yasodha and Radha, but the audience will still receive the emotion as the same. So they don't see it as different because in the form, the alienation is implicit.

Such cognizance of the Indian tradition and cultural ethos, besides being highly subjective and interpretative, is also speciously selective. The problem we are introduced to in the film, for instance, is industrial pollution, but most of the plot deals with the wage demands of the workers and their unionization.

> Industrial pollution was merely a catalytic mode, like in [Eisenstein's] *Potemkin* starvation was the main problem. But the film was not talking about starvation. It was talking about workers' movement, workers' unity and so on. You pick up a problem which will directly affect the life of a person you know, and then you discuss it further. So industrial pollution was only a take-off point to comment on other things.

But surely Hariharan, with his concern for the subsisting cultural ethos, should have suspected that death may not be all that crucial in this ethos. Indeed while death represents liberation, a rape, for instance, suggests living damnation and evinces far greater feelings of outrage and sympathy. Surely Hari must also know that it is in the name of the cultural ethos that the status and role of the woman is what it is in the average Indian film, the caste and class relationships are what they have been for years in our cinema.

The shortcomings of *Ezhavathu Manithan*, however, are not due to such complicated reasons. Indeed its failing is that none of these finer arguments are reflected in it at all. It is the failing of a well-motivated and by all accounts (except by proof of the pudding) adept director to be as articulate in his film, as he is about it.

First published in *The Hindu*, 8 August 1982.

International Film Festival in India at Crossroads

Bedevilled by a host of problems – some of them so tiresomely recurrent over the past few years that they seem by now almost endemic to international film festivals in India, and others peculiar to this festival – the Ninth International Film Festival opening here today could well hit a new low in performance and rating. Interest and expectation are at such a low ebb that the festival looks in danger of being bogged down in the cold and damp of a severe Delhi winter.

An apologetic Festival Directorate running round in circles this last minute in an effort to whip up some enthusiasm and salvage the show would have been a pathetic sight, were it not a shade too familiar by now. Indeed the regular festival-goer is almost innured to the ad-hocism and tokenism that has marked the running of these festivals these past few years. But it now suddenly seems to dawn on everyone that the apathy and flippancy have eroded the prestige of festivals here so much that their very future stands threatened.

Manila is what helped precipitate this realization. The growing apprehension – since last year when Manila entered the festival fray with Mrs Imelda Marcos, wife of the Philippine President, herself as promoter – that we would soon find ourselves hopelessly upstaged now seems a certainty. Coming as it does close on the heels of our festival, prospective entries have to choose between India and Manila, and they increasingly seem to prefer the latter. That the Marcos regime is characterized, in most of the liberal press, as 'fascist' has made no difference to this fact. Last year there was the mild stir caused by India's ace filmmaker Satyajit Ray's decision to chair the jury at the Manila festival. This year, in a move that is bound to rankle more and longer, Sir Richard Attenborough's *Gandhi* (in which, incidentally, the Indian government has a 33 per cent share besides a thematic stake) has overlooked the anticipation of critics and delegates at the Indian festival, and is being billed as the closing film at Manila.

Hard put to explain this anomaly at a press conference here yesterday, the Information and Broadcasting Secretary (and chairman of the festival management committee), Mr S.B. Lal, resorted to light banter. Perhaps the victims of fascism in Manila needed *Gandhi* more than we do now, was his diplomatic, if unconvincing answer. But then, again, it would be cussedness at one level to envy Manila its success. We here in India had the chance, while the going was good and there were no Manilas waiting to take over from where we defaulted, to invest our festivals with a third world character, to consolidate an ideological stance that would have made it difficult for the disparate demands of world cinema (in terms of acceptance) to wreck our show. Looking back, a naive pretence of third worldism and a credulous west-fixation seem to add up to our undoing. We are not important enough for some, we don't take their importance seriously, and festival after festival here has to go abegging for its fare.

Nothing illustrates this criss-cross of attitudes this year as dramatically as the search – Pirandello-like – for a jury. The initial list mooted a few months back bears little resemblance to the final panel arrived at. Not that the members empanelled now are any less illustrious, but it certainly makes them appear – and unfairly – so. In fact, even if it came about by sheer accident, the present panel is as balanced as it is competent. With the British critic and filmmaker Lindsay Anderson as chairman, it has Soviet actor and filmmaker Sergei Bondarchuk (of *War and Peace* and *Waterloo* fame) and Czech director Jiří Sequens (*Assassination, Chronicle of a Hot Summer*) from the East Bloc, journalist-turned-filmmaker Jean Delannoy (*Marie Antonette, Le Soleil des Voyou*) from France, the brilliant Cuban director Thomas Alea (*Death of a Bureaucrat, Memories of Underdevelopment, Survivors*), Lino Brocka from Philippines (*Stardom, Bona, Jaguar*), and Medoun Hondo from Mauritania (*Soleilo*) representing the third world and Adoor Gopalakrishnan (*Swayamvaram, Kodiyettam* and now the much-acclaimed *Elippathayam*) and Vaijayanthimala Bali (renowned danseuse and yesteryear film star) from India. Nothing to complain about there in terms of the bonafides of the jurors; what irks one is the Festival Directorate running after more fancy names only to be rewarded with a firm and polite 'no'.

Going through the list of films to be screened in the Competitive and Information sections of the festival, there are just about a handful one wouldn't really miss – among them Ben-Barka's *Amok* (the inaugural film), Lindsay Anderson's *Brittania Hospital*, Costa-Gavras' *Missing*, Ingmar Bergman's *From the Life of Marionettes*, Carl Reisz's *The French Lieutenant's Woman* and Humberto Solas' *Cecilia*. The known 'greats' being so restricted, one sets great store by those sudden surprises by relatively anonymous filmmakers that every once in while makes the viewers sit up and take notice. Unless a series of such coups wins over the audience assembled here for these screenings, it looks not just like defeat, but a rout at the end of it all. Going by the Calcutta experience last year, where a number of third world films one went to indifferently turned out instead to be aesthetically or emotionally compelling, this is still a plausible though unpredictable way out of total disaster.

In stark contrast to the strident public response the Calcutta festival got, however, there is yet little evidence of any such mass upsurge here in the capital. Although the statistics given out by the festival authorities assure us that season tickets have been sold out at many theatres, the cinemas themselves wear a rather desolate look. Which really takes one back to the old argument that film festivals in the country should be held only in states with a film industry base. The stock counter that Delhi has the requisite infrastructural facilities for stay and screenings seems not too relevant this year with Vigyan Bhavan not available for the festival (since the hall is being spruced up for the March Non-Aligned Meet) and all activity centred at and nearabouts the Asiad Village complex. Although the main theatre is impressive enough, it is doubtful whether it lends itself to film screenings.

The rather mediocre fare in the Indian Panorama sections suggests a low-key year for the new Indian cinema. Most of the known stalwarts are not represented, apparently because they had no entries to make this time. The Retrospective section, however, seems a better-organized affair, with collections from the father of the new Brazilian cinema, Glauber Rocha (who died in 1961), the veteran Sri Lankan filmmaker Lester James Peries ((who completes twenty-five years of filmmaking this year), Bondarchuk, Frederick Wiseman (US) and Claude Sautet (French).

From all indications, the international film festival in India seems to have arrived at the crossroads. The direction it will take will no doubt depend on the decisions its sponsors take now. Piecemeal efforts – like, for instance, the proposal to shift the dates to August from January and out of the shadow of Manila – may only give us a respite. A comprehensive approach that seeks to lend our festivals a distinctive identity and make eventually for an Indian international film fete on Indian terms (we are, after all, the biggest film-producing nation in the world) seems the lasting answer.

First published in *The Hindu*, 4 January 1983.

In Search of Gandhi

Richard Attenborough's *Gandhi* has made a big impact internationally, among film critics as well as viewers. The three differing assessments here seek to evaluate the strengths and weaknesses of the stupendous effort to project on the screen, the triumphs and struggle of Mahatma Gandhi.

The story of Gandhi is, of course, the story of a hero. In fact, it neatly fits Joseph Campbell's definitive configuration of the archetypal hero as one who undergoes the rites and stages of *separation*, *initiation* and *return*, in that order. 'A hero', Campbell elaborates in his *The Hero with a Thousand Faces*, 'ventures forth from the world of common day into a region of supernatural wonder; fabulous forces are there encountered and a decisive victory is won; the hero comes back from this mysterious adventure with the power to bestow boons on his fellowmen.' Prometheus or Jason or Buddha exemplifies this set formula. Gandhi updates it.

This would, imaginably, make the task of a director essaying a film on Gandhi easier – he already has on hand a compelling hero and a well laid-out plot line. But the relative contemporaneity of his subject throws up a complex set of peculiar problems. Distanced from us by a mere three-and-a-half decades, Gandhi is not yet – and cannot quite be cast as – a *monomyth*, like his predecessors in the limbo of history.

And yet the urge to canonize is strong. The generations now living already tend to see him in a more-than-mortal, sublimated light. Further, Gandhism, as an amorphous concept rather than as ideology, pervades the collective Indian psyche. 'Like a novelist', writes V.S. Naipaul in his *India: A Wounded Civilization*, 'who splits himself into his characters, unconsciously setting up the consonances that give his theme a closed intensity, the many-sided Gandhi permeates modern India.' The man and his message coalesce ('My life is my message', said Gandhi himself), and 'Gandhi' becomes at once metaphoric and metonymic in the popular mind – even if often it is much like the different parts of the elephant signifying different visions and versions of the beast to the blind.

Any attempted celluloid profile of Gandhi, then, is trammelled by this conditioning. Faced with such a demanding and elusive protagonist, Richard Attenborough resorts to an equivocal treatment. On the one hand he traces the life of Gandhi along the conventional heroic lines – his years of *separation* in

South Africa, the *initiation* after the train incident at Maritzburg and his subsequent *return* to India as the apostle of non-violence. On the other hand, and perhaps not to tread on the freewheeling 'Gandhian' susceptibilities in India, he pares him down to a kind of irreducible and essential minimum. What he is left with, unwittingly, is a simplistic and textbook Gandhi; a virtuous character straight out of a morality play.

It is a one-dimensional, neutral characterization, where Gandhi is always kept at a safe distance so that we can never get too close to him. There is hardly a single intimate moment in the film where the man's mind process or his conflicts or 'experiments' with truth are probed. Indeed, much of Gandhi's autobiography where the transformation of his self is so revelatory is of no use to Attenborough. We are introduced, instead, to the external Gandhi; we watch him metamorphosing from the fastidious, awkward young lawyer in South Africa to the home-spun-clad, homily-spouting 'Mahatma' of the freedom years.

With such a blinkered vision of Gandhi, Attenborough has to make up for the lack of depth with expanse. As more than fifty years of Gandhi's life are compressed into a naturalistic, episodic three-and-a-quarter-hour-long narrative, there is the uncomfortable feeling that Attenborough has bitten off far more than he can chew. Scenes collide into one another – a fresh one seems to start before the previous one has quite ended – and historic characters appear flitting around in Gandhi's orbit with the perfunctoriness of 'extras' rather than as significant cameo roles.

The personality of Gandhi too marks the strain. Given the extensive scenario, Attenborough just about has time to hustle his Gandhi through it all, so that his sudden switches from western dress to the Indian turbanned apparel and on to the celebrated loincloth seem quirky rather than the conscious forging of an identity. The greater casualty, however, in this rush is the humaneness that Attenborough was all along so determined to keep intact in his screen 'Mahatma'.

'Whatever you do, do not deify him', Nehru had cautioned Attenborough. But then Gandhi has always struck a precarious balance between the politician and the saint ('Men say I am a saint losing myself in politics. The fact is I am a politician trying my hardest to be a saint'); all it takes to make him a saint is to ignore or softpedal the practical, political side of the man, whereas to save him from sainthood is far tougher because it means a thorough bid to place him firmly on *terra firma*. There is naturally little scope in the film to pause and work out a determining milieu, to delineate the social and political backdrop against which Gandhi stood so tall. This failure to broadbase Gandhi, to see him as a product of his material context, gives the benefit of doubt to Gandhi the saint. Attenborough's account becomes, by default though not by design, hagiographic.

Attenborough's explanation that he has his sights fixed on Gandhi and not around him is well taken as the legitimate prerogative of a director who chooses to see what he wants to in his subject. But it deprives him and the viewers of a proper perspective to Gandhi. As a grandson of Gandhi succinctly put it to this reviewer, 'The argument that the film is about Gandhi and not about satyagraha or the freedom movement does not wash, because without these there is no Gandhi.' And so when audiences in the west (in India the reception to the film is still lukewarm) leave the theatres raving about *Gandhi*, it may mean no more than a brief diplomatic euphoria for India.

The subtlety of his skewed perspective does not, unfortunately, extend to Attenborough's lopsided priority in keeping certain characters and events in, and some others out of the film. Even going by his own guideline (set down in his *In Search of Gandhi*, a handbook to the film) 'to follow Gandhiji's' own life, and concentrate upon those events, circumstances and relationships which touched directly upon his existence, setting aside all others, no matter how momentous, which did not directly affect him, the absence of Rajaji, Tagore, Bose and Ambedkar, or of the entire Quit India phase, becomes a serious lapse.

Considering that all characters other than Gandhi and his immediate ashramite kin represent the attitudes prevalent at the time to Gandhi's role in the freedom struggle, and pitted as they are as checks and balances to one another, Attenborough might as well have preempted the charge that there is no south India in this independence movement by a reference – however brief – to Rajaji. As for Tagore, besides the fact that historically Gandhi had always sought him out as a touchstone of faith and confidence, the lyrical–romantic possibilities were immense, and a meeting of the two in the film could have added immeasurably to Gandhi's own stature.

Even taking the extreme view that Bose and Ambedkar were Gandhi's detractors, there was surely no harm in letting them have their say. If nothing else, they would at least have kept Jinnah company. As it is, Jinnah is the sole villain of the piece. Alyque Padamsee struts in the role with a fixed wily sneer that succeeds in making him look more wicked than the British or Godse. Balancing Jinnah's glowing malevolence is his co-religionist on the other side of the fence, Maulana Azad, who has no function in the film except perhaps as a sop to the Indian Muslims. Nehru and Patel, of course, are Gandhi's solicitous blue-eyed boys, although there is nothing of Nehru's blue-blooded elegance in Roshan Seth's two-bit facsimile. Saeed Jaffrey makes a very affable and jovial Patel, his manner and mien hardly presaging the iron man of later years.

One becomes doubly conscious of the illustrious omissions when the screen time and space that could have been saved for them is expended, instead, on a number of lesser known or relatively unimportant characters. There is the photographer of *Life* magazine, Margaret Bourke-White (Candice Bergen who plays the part, after a fifteen-year-long wait as Attenborough tells us, was actually a student of Bourke-White and handles her camera well); the American journalist Walker (played by Martin Sheen); Gandhi's German disciple from the South African days, Kallenbach; and, more acceptably, the Christian missionary, C.F. Andrews, in the earlier portion. The connotations Attenborough places on some of these extraneous roles quite escape us. He tells us, for instance, that the American reporter Walker is 'based on an amalgam of Louis Fischer, Vincent Sheean and William Shirer', although why and how this fits into his naturalistic scheme of things is not clear. They are neither intrinsic to the plot nor mediatory in an understanding of Gandhi by a non-Indian audience. They seem to have been grafted into the script in the hope that their presence would internationalize Gandhi.

The already sketchy characterization is made worse by Attenborough's inveterate predilection for the dramatic. His purpose, he tells us in his handbook, is 'to discover and then dramatize the spirit of this extraordinary man'. But as it transpires in the film, dense drama hinders any perceptive discovery. The situations are stagey and the dialogues stilted; and the idiom of cinema itself goes abegging. In putting words into the mouths of their various key characters, moreover, Attenborough and his screenplay writers (at different stages Gerald Hanley and Robert Bolt had worked on the script before Jack Briley took over) no doubt had to keep a tricky balance between the need to carry their story forward and the behavioural aspect on the one hand, and the historicity of the language on the other. They couldn't, for instance, attribute to Gandhi or Nehru or Patel or Jinnah, statements not actually made by them. And such statements as were actually made need not always get a lively conversation going. That this cramps the style of the filmmaker is evident from many of the 'wordy' scenes where the action is guillotined before a point is pursued to any exciting degree, or a debate developed to a rounding off. The film, then, settles down to a paradox – dramatic in form but not in spirit.

It is not just incidental that the best moments in the film are those where the spoken words are minimal. There are at least two such momentous scenes. When the ailing Kasturba quietly dies on Gandhi's lap in Yerwada jail, there is a poignant lull. The shot stays a while on the window frame, beyond which in the soft sunlight the branches sway lightly, with a soft breeze and the chirping of birds the only sounds that break the silence. The shot then shifts to Gandhi, his wife still on his lap, his face averted slightly from the camera so that a three-quarter profile favours it, his spectacles glinting in the light seeping into the room, the hint of an inconsolable tear behind them. Truly a moment of ineffable sadness and truth only film can capture in all its intensity.

Again, when Gandhi sets out from his ashram on his historic Dandi march, the compositions have a sense of choreography without artifice. As Gandhi walks between the rows of the inmates of the ashram respectfully standing by and bidding him farewell, and reaching the end of the line, launches, in one deft movement, into that characteristic purposive and brisk stride that even those years younger than him found difficult to keep pace with, the visual merges with the musical as an overture. It is a rare lyrical take-off from the generally plodding course of the film.

All this, of course, would have been quite impossible if Ben Kingsley himself had not got into stride as Gandhi so superbly and effortlessly. He brings to his role not only the consummate artistry of the professional actor, but a 'feel' that is more inspired than studied. The mantle of Gandhi rests lightly on him. The spontaneity of his sudden smile and puckish humour; the earnestness in his eyes and heart whether he is listening to the Congress leaders discussing the strategy for independence, or to the woeful tale of a poor old peasant from Champaran, or to the concerned young girl in the ashram who wants Gandhi to put a mud-pack on the sprained foot of a goat; the difficult puritanical streak of the self-expurgating ascetic or the frustrating stubbornness of the man on a fast who will not relent until his every demand is met – in all this Kingsley approximates very closely to the Gandhi we know from Louis Fischer, or Tendulkar, or his own autobiography.

The choice of Kingsley itself was, we learn from Attenborough's account, fortuitous. Both his and Nehru's earlier favourite for the role was Alec Guinness – partly because he alone, among the established actors, bore some resemblance to Gandhi, and partly because Nehru felt that 'the experience of a classical English actor trained in the theatre and accepting a totally naturalistic style of performance would be invaluable'. Kingsley has the added advantage of his relative anonymity and his half-Indian extraction, so that he doesn't have to fight any pre-set image of himself, and can go through the commonest gestures and motions – like the *pranam* and squatting at the spinning wheel – with naturalness rather than quaintness. How much Attenborough's concept of Gandhi must have cramped Kingsley's style is anybody's guess. But he does come up with a performance that is more than mere mimicry and, to an audience uninitiated to Gandhi, he would be a striking personification. Small wonder, then, that he is being mentioned (along with Dustin Hoffman for his *Tootsie*) for the Oscar.

The other significant character who maintains a virtual (more than flesh-and-blood) presence through the film is Gandhi's consort, Kasturba, played by Rohini Hattangadi. Her best scene – and the only one where she comes into her own – is at the community farm in South Africa, where she is asked by Gandhi to take her turn at raking and cleaning the latrines along with 'untouchables'. She refuses, Gandhi flies into a rage and almost throws her out. But age diffuses rather than mellows her character, so that we soon begin not to notice her discreet presence behind Gandhi. This is unfortunate because the screenplay intends her to be not only the faithful wife, washing clothes in the river, teaching Gandhi to spin or nursing him through his fasts, but also the key to quite a few things about her husband. But all this is clearly too much for the Kasturba of the film – and Rohini Hattangadi isn't much help either in the later phase – so that the relationship between husband and wife appears, ultimately, feudal. As if in comment, there is an entire scene in the film devoted to the philosophy of the Hindu marriage. On a platform by the lake Gandhi and Kasturba enact the marriage ritual for the American journalist, Walker. As they go round the imaginary sacred fire, tie the nuptial knot and take each vow of marriage with each step, one is perhaps required to infer that women's rights are a non-issue in the 'dharmic' view of things.

The British roles in the film are a shade better than the Indian, not because they are filled out any better but because experienced artistes handle them. Also, as characters not in the shadow of Gandhi but opposing him, they acquire a certain distinctiveness. This helps such veterans as John Gielgud (as Lord Irwin), Trevor Howard (Judge Broomfield), Edward Fox (General Dyer) and Athol Fugard (the South African playwright and actor playing General Smuts) come through unscathed, even though the director didn't make it any easier for them.

At the lesser level, however, Attenborough's differential treatment is rather disconcerting. The Indians almost always become a collective mass without clear-cut feelings or sensitivities. The huge crowds that adulate Gandhi, for instance, are faceless – in the absence of those invaluable candid-camera shots that pick out a few representative close-ups (of joy or grief or pain, as the case may be), the scenes themselves look grandly orchestrated. When, after partition, two huge columns of people displaced from the two new nations cross each other, we see them without really realizing the enormity of their plight. The insensitive Indian soldiers, in British uniform, as they fire on the crowds at Jalianwala Bagh or lathi-charge the salt satyagrahis are even more telling examples. The Britisher on the other hand, is an entity with a sensibility and conscience.

In the only instance of direct physical assault by a European of an Indian in the film, an officer clubs Gandhi down when, as a protest against the iniquitous pass law in South Africa, Gandhi attempts to burn a number of passes at a street-corner meeting. Gandhi takes blow after blow lying down, but continuing, all the while, to burn one pass after another. As the last pass is burnt the shot shows a confused and moved officer, his club raised but not able to bring it down again on the prostrate Gandhi. No such pang of conscience, however, troubles the Indian constables as they beat to pulp column after column of salt satyagrahis at the Dharasana saltworks, or the Gurkha and Nepali soldiers at Jalianwala Bagh who, under General Dyer's orders, spray round after round of bullets into the captive crowd before them. This disparity comes across not so much in these episodes themselves, as in the composition and structuring of shots. The ethics of Attenborough's aesthetics here becomes questionable.

Naturalism as a mode of expression imposes certain obligations on the artist. He must, for one, be a stickler for detail. Attenborough is clearly handicapped, with Gandhi's own autobiography as his primary source material, in painting the account of a man and his time in all its shades and colours. As Naipaul points out, Gandhi's account, whether of his years in England or South Africa or India, is introversive and pays scarce attention to the physical details of his environment. It then becomes clear why there are no Africans in Attenborough's South Africa (the scenes were actually shot off Bombay); there are none in Gandhi's record of Africa either.

There are other incongruities and factual lapses that for a film researched over two decades, cannot really be glossed over. The topography of Jalianwala Bagh in the film, for instance, is not consistent with the report of the Hunter Commission that probed into the massacre. It is 'a rectangular piece of unused ground', says the report, 'covered to some extent by building materials and hidden debris. . . . At the end at which General Dyer entered there is a raised ground on each side of the entrance.' Attenborough apparently took it for granted that the Bagh hadn't changed over the years, or he didn't care at all; because there is neither any suggestion of 'building material and debris', nor any raised ground where General Dyer, and his Gurkha and Baluchi soldiers, enter and take their positions.

The setting of the Dharasana saltworks too and the action there differ from the eyewitness account given by Webb Miller who was on the spot as a correspondent of United Press. In his *Witness to India*, Frank Moraes recalls his meeting Miraben at London as part of Gandhi's entourage to the Round Table Conference. Moraes, who had lunch with Miraben, writes that she 'wore khadi, her attire was Indian and her head shaven.' But the Miraben of the film (Geraldine James) has lovely flowing hair right through. Surely one of them – Attenborough or Moraes – must have been mistaken.

More seriously, the film tends to dispute Louis Fischer's graphic account of the moments before Gandhi's assassination. As Fischer describes the scene, Patel had come to see Gandhi; his last supper is brought in; as they talk Abha indicates that it is late for Gandhi's prayer meeting; 'I must tear myself away', says Gandhi to Patel and walks away. The film, however, literally substitutes Margaret Bourke-White (busily clicking away, as usual) for Patel; after a brief banter with her, Gandhi proceeds to his prayer rendezvous, even as Bourke-White stands wondering aloud why he looks so sad.

These may sound like carping criticism, but inasmuch as they do appear to distort the little facts and test the formalistic rules of naturalism, they need mention. They are no doubt too pettifogging to judge the film by. But they do tell us, along with the more salient reasons, why Attenborough's film fell short of Gandhi; why Attenborough, in search of his Gandhi, has not quite arrived.

First published in *The Hindu*, 27 February 1983.

Ugly Intruder in Serious Cinema

That even in what is meant to be a festival of serious cinema, proportion and perspective tend to be suspended when it comes to reacting to stars was the dismal moral of the inaugural function here last evening. A longwinded and boring ceremony caught up in the show-whirl of stardom, with rambling speeches – the chief guest. Raj Kapoor, made some fervent but unconnected declamations about the film fraternity being one family and the world being threatened by a nuclear holocaust – was hardly a fitting start for *Filmostav '84*. Festivals like this, one would think, should give the lie to the myth of stardom as something that stultifies the growth of true cinema. What one was offered at the very outset, instead, was a Bombay star parade on the dais, a sickening commoditization of glamour.

The aftertaste, however, lingered only long enough for a sinking feeling to take over as the inaugural film, Mrinal Sen's *Khandhar* ('Ruins', Bengali), unfolded on the screen. For those, and this writer is one, who rate Sen as one of the abiding hopes of the new film movement in the country, *Khandhar* seems a work he could have done without. Indeed, after his *Ekdin Pratidin* in 1979, Sen seems to have reached a plateau in his career. His *Akaler Sandhane* (1980) and *Kharij* (1982) were showing signs of anaemic weakness, a kind of atrophy so uncharacteristic of the man himself even today or of his earlier films (especially of the 1970s – *Interview, Calcutta 71, Padatik, Chorus, Oka Oorie Katha, Parashuram* and *Ekdin Pratidin*). With *Khandhar* he takes himself farther away from the style and genius that marked those memorable years.

There are echoes here of at least two earlier films: *Ekdin Pratidin* and *Akaler Sandhane*. But they are lost in the ruins which Sen makes his setting to tell us the story of three young men from the city who retreat here over a weekend, to be caught up in the emotional cross-currents generated by a blind, paralytic and widowed mother (played with poignant assurance by Gita Sen) and her daughter (Shabana Azmi) in a vestigial feudal household.

The dramatic crux of the plot lies in the pathetic irony that while the mother has all her mortal hopes fixed on the return of her daughter's betrothed, the girl herself knows he will never come. Enter Naseeruddin Shah, professional photographer and one of the city trio, to find himself mistaken by the mother for the awaited groom. City-bred insensitivity plays out its logical role, and we see Shah, at the end of it all and after a brief grapple with his conscience, back at his studio clicking away at a model for a sari ad. The values of civilization stand questioned before the mute yet plaintive plea of the photograph of a girl in the ruins, now a part of the photographer's memorabilia on his studio wall.

Sen could surely have wrapped up all this in a good half hour less than the two hours he took to tell it. And that would have helped in a tauter treatment of his material. As it is, there is a loose alternation of the denotative and the connotative that gets quite trying at times. The camera tends to get self-conscious as it lingers on the anamorphic details of the ruins. There are brilliant edit points which, however, lose out on intrinsic worth precisely because they are so clever.

In refreshing contrast to the crisis of resourcefulness that marks the new Indian cinema today (the Indian Panorama section here is illustrative – but more of that later), the young film movement of West Germany shows a process of continual renewal and progress. While Rainer Fassbinder's recent death will no doubt be felt on the contemporary film scene there – as it will in future international film festivals – the movement itself seems so well rooted that it continues to throw up filmmakers of doubtless calibre. Notable among them at this festival is the husband-and-wife team of Volker Schlöndorff and Margarete von Trotta. Schlöndorff's *Circle of Deceit* coming just a day behind Fassbinder's *Veronika Voss* reassures one about the vitality of German cinema.

Schlöndorff's milieu – arena would be more appropriate – is Beirut before the evacuation of the Palestinian fighters in 1982. A reporter of a Hamburg daily and his photographer are sent to the war-ravaged city. Although the factions involved in the fighting and the bombings, arson and bloodshed form a disturbing backdrop, they become, for the purpose of the film, only a foil to the journalist's strained relationship with his wife, of his suppressed and impotent anger at being able to report only the facts that disguise rather than reveal the starker truth of death and destruction. Bruno Ganz plays the role with such chastened restraint and inner conviction that his every moment of self-doubt, fear and anger gets across with devastating impact.

First published in *The Hindu*, 5 January 1984.

Metaphysics on Celluloid

Adi Sankaracharya

It was heartening to see a full house sitting right through the two-and-a-quarter hours of G.V. Iyer's *Adi Sankaracharya*, giving it patient viewing and a good hand at the end. For Iyer it was a plaudit well deserved, not so much for what he has accomplished in the film as for what he had taken on in trying to translate the difficult concept of Sankara's monism into celluloid – and that in Sanskrit. For the NFDC, the producers of the film, it seems a gambit that promises to pay off, especially in foreign markets where even as a basic reader on the precept of the Vedas and their interpretation by Sankara, it would find wide demand.

Iyer must also be credited with having kept an even head when it was so easy, dealing with a subject such as this, to become obscurantist on the one hand, or infantilely mythical on the other. If he is to be faulted for the hagiographic treatment of Sankara, he must also be commended for the abstract yet lucid treatment of the Advaita philosophy through the elemental symbols of nature. The use, and rather repetitively, of the sun, moon, earth, water, or fire could easily have become tiresome but for the refreshing photography by Iyer's cinematographer, Madhu Ambat.

The locales themselves, from Kanyakumari to the Himalayas as the film traces Sankara's life pilgrimage, are resplendently panoramic. Add to this a well-worked soundtrack resounding to the primal chants of Vedic hymns, and the viewer finds himself drawn into an ambience of eclectic pantheism where every stone and leaf breathe metaphysical meaning. Iyer, however, does not lead his sheep blindly on and chooses, incredible as it would seem, a dialectic rather than a lyrical mode in expounding the logic and substance of monism as perceived by Sankara.

Whatever the shortcomings of the film – and a carping estimate would discover many – one is thankful to Iyer for what he did not do through a film of this nature: he does not vest it with a proselytizing edge; he does not glorify to a fault the grandeur of Hinduism.

Imperative

Transport Sankara, with all his nonconformism and self-doubt and an urge for spiritual perfection into the modem age and the west, and we arrive at Zanussi's alter-ego (played by Robert Powell) in his film *Imperative* – the case of a mathematics professor who looks beyond the empirical facts of his environment and the conceptual horizons of his discipline, for a larger, more vital meaning to life. The film, as its protagonist, deals simultaneously with the sublime and the ridiculous. It seems about as profound in the end as posing great epistemological questions in terms of the chicken-or-egg conundrum. The crisis, in this case existential, is so personal and peculiar to the director that to the viewer it is mindboggling.

Cries and Whispers

It is again the soul and its deepest corners that are probed in Bergman's *Cries and Whispers* (Sweden). 'I've never been able', Bergman had stated, as far back as 1954 when he was yet on the threshold of serious filmmaking, 'to keep myself from believing that I'm in charge of so sensitive an instrument that it should be possible to use it to illuminate the human soul with an infinitely more penetrating light.' That belief has been fulfilling itself in film after film since, and reaches almost a point of consummation in this, his most intimate autobiographical and introspective work, produced in 1972.

The entire film rests on a figment of Bergman's imagination that the soul was like a room in red and its attributes, three women dressed in white. In the film inspired by this vision, the three women are sisters, one of whom is dying. It examines the inter-relationships of the sisters, each of whom, as Bergman admits, is fashioned to represent a dominant trait of his own mother. The allegory of a spiritual journey through pain, defeat and despair unfolds in the red-dominated and dimly-lit interiors of the countryside manor (a favourite Bergman haunt). The frayed emotions and keen soul-searching lead, through scene after scene emerging from and fading out into a red void, to a typical Bergmanesque denouement – a process of purification by self-torment and unsparing introspection to arrive at a level of awareness qualitatively different, if not better.

First published in *The Hindu*, 6 January 1984.

New Perspectives in British, American Cinema

There is a certain familiarity – part-historical, part-cultivated – with which Indian viewers approach the British or American cinema, that really works both ways for the films themselves. While on the one hand, a predisposition to the language and behavioural details (the middle-class city cinema in India has been miming this for years now) make empathy easier, on the other, this leads to a syndrome of slotted appetites.

Until the 1980s, when *Chariots of Fire* came as the first real fillip for British cinema, pulling it out of the groove in which it had stayed through the 70s, all that one got at festivals from England smacked of a ponderous Royal Shakespearean tradition. It was the homogenous British image, with a veneer of conscious civility, a wordy charade of images and ideas that hardly outlived their momentary flicker across the screen, which was sold and obligingly lapped up by anglophiles in all erstwhile colonies.

Chariots of Fire heralded a new crop of independent producers and directors in Britain with nothing of this hangover, so that today it is possible to speak in terms of a 'renaissance' of the British film. Much of this flowering, however, seems to take place on very native soil, especially in south Britain, hitherto infertile areas for the culture of film.

It is easily understandable why Bill Forsyth's *Local Hero* became such a *cause célèbre*, not just in Scotland but in all of Britain. The film is representative of the renewed idiom of this cinema. A simple idea, originated by producer David Puttman, of an American oil company sending its representative out into a Scottish coastal township to buy out the whole area for an installation, is worked up into a modern parable on economic exploitation and the hazards of consumerism.

At the surface is a discreet overlay of Scottish humour. The film does not take its audience for granted and for a British film, that is almost something new. It demands a kind of critical alertness which, in turn, proves rewarding. The viewer who does not actively respond to the film could easily be taking the wood for the trees, the spice and the light-heartedness at its face value. For, Forsyth's intention here is not just to win the laughs. 'People think', he said in a recent interview quoted in *Sound and Sight*, 'comedy is about making us laugh, and if there is nothing more to comedy than laugh, a lot of effort is going for nothing.'

Martin Scorsese's *King of Comedy* was another surprise, not because it was un- American (and there's no pun on McCarthy here) but because it was so un-Scorsese-like. The Scorsese of *Alice Doesn't Live Here Anymore*, *New York, New York*, *Taxi Driver* and *The Raging Bull* excels himself in this, his latest work. In retrospect, one can see that it was coming. Already in the closing scenes of *The Raging Bull*, Scorsese had alluded to the emptiness of success, especially show biz. But what one would not have anticipated is his method in *The King of Comedy.*

The swirling, moving camera of the early film seems now to come to rest. A sense of stasis pervades the taking of the shots. There is a reversal here to the old narrative of Hollywood with its omni-moral of social mobility (the aspiring man achieving success through perseverence in a dynamic American society). Only all the trimmings are cut away and we have the barest, minimalist plot taking us through the fortunes of a would-be talk-show performer (Peter Pupkin, played by Robert Deniro) hell-bent to get on to the tremendously popular Jerry Langford show (of Jerry Lewis himself). When, despite all his attempts, Jerry remains unrelenting, Pupkin kidnaps him and blackmails his way into the show to become, overnight, a success and a criminal.

Robert Deniro as Pupkin comes up with a performance that is as riveting as it is different from his roles in earlier Scorsese films – as La Motte in *Raging Bull*, Jimmy Doyle in *New York, New York* or Travis in *Taxi Driver*. The flamboyance of a man so bent on and sure of success, the nervous energy, the never-say-die cheer, all combine to fill out a character with whose cause the audience soon finds itself sympathizing avidly.

Even if the title may not suggest it, it's a world far removed from Scorsese's showcasey America in Dshima's *Merry Christmas, Mr. Lawrence*, a British–Japanese–New Zealand co-production. If war (Dshima's setting is the Second World War here) brutalizes, it also sensitizes, and the inter-relationships of British prisoners of war and their Japanese captors are dragged through the jagged ends of an emotional precipice in this sordid saga of intense love consumed in intense hate and vice versa. Based on a novel by Lawrence Van der Post, the film was a hot favourite for the Grand Prix at Cannes this time, but ended up getting nothing, possibly because the jurors, like many in the audience, found it tough to believe that homosexuals, unlike heterosexuals, can do one another such great harm and yet burn with such great passion for each other. Or so, the film would seem to suggest.

First published in *The Hindu*, 8 January 1984.

Bergman Props Up a Collapsing Festival

Only mid-way into this festival, and already a lot of people who came here specially for this are asking themselves what they are doing here. The dwindling interest is all too palpable. Delegates and critics walk into films already half-way through, to rise and leave a quarter-hour later. Press conferences are delayed for want of a quorum, and in the festival theatres open to the public, most seats go ahegging. But then the disinterest and disrespect (if any) seem mutual. Prints of many films are brought bearing the editor's graffiti – the crosses or circles with which the cutter marks the end of a shot or scene. Apparently, the participating country or filmmaker concerned has decided that for a festival in India, prints short of the final release print will do.

All this, however, is trivia against the more troubling fact that even the favourites have been a let-down. One is inclined to agree with Mrinal Sen's observation at his press conference today, that 'The masters are no longer making masterpieces.' But, like a solid exception to the rule, Ingmar Bergman props up this first half of the festival with another compelling work – what he has called his last film – *Fanny and Alexander*.

It is total surrender to the magnetic charm of the Bergman world – a world historically so isolated, and yet artistically so real and crucial – as he once again turns inward and back in time to his childhood memories. What takes the viewer unawares, however, is the way Bergman, in this film, transmutes his intrinsic theatricality, his Christian-humanist inheritance, into an experiential revel that transcends the characteristic intellectual–emotional introspection that marks his other films.

It would almost seem as if the man who was always searching for the causative in and of existence has now decided to shift focus on the effect – an approach that brings to the film a mood of abandon which closely approximates the style and essence of Fellini. For Bergman, it is a shift from the end to the beginning. The terminal sense of mortality and tremulous reaching out into the life after are replaced here by an affirmation of the intuitions and fantasies of the formative years. It is as if suddenly, at the peak of his genius, the truth of Eisenstein's statement dawns on him: 'The prologue is the eternity.'

The large-sized Ekdahl family with grandmother, children and grandchildren, set in the early twentieth century, becomes the miniscule, hermetic world of

Bergman perceived through the impressionable and highly imaginative eyes of the grandchildren, and sister and brother, Fanny and Alexander. When their father dies and mother remarries an austere bishop so full of hatred in his self-righteousness, it is – and that is the wierd part – the sparks generated in the innocent children that set off the flames that consume the 'man of God'.

Austrian cinema has a peculiar ethos that sets it quite apart from the European or East European type. Hannes Zell's *The Profiteers* narrates in an unhurried, yet never tedious manner, the story of two men who set out to racketeer themselves into money and fame, playing the factors operating in the flux of Austria–Hungary in the wake of the First World War and in the context of a rising labour consciousness.

It is a complex intertwine of loneliness, unreciprocated love, and tongue-in-check cheating – rather well deserved for the victims who go bankrupt when a project to which they have subscribed, floated by the enterprising duo to restore capitalism to power, goes kaput. As the credits fade in the end, the sound track becomes an animated chorus of the proletariat whose rising voice, as it suggests, history could not ignore. It also becomes an amusing epitaph to the punchline with which the protagonist in the film tries to sell his racket to the capitalists: 'I want my capital', he says, 'to work against that of Karl Marx.'

First published in *The Hindu*, 9 January 1984.

A Rendezvous with Reality

The resilience of the French cinema is remarkable. Whether Parisian or regional in its thrust, whether by a pioneer of the new wave of the mid-1950s or by a newer filmmaker surfacing more recently, French films are continuously evolving – both in terms of formal departures and in their awareness and response to the contemporary realities.

The generation of 'new wavers' (Truffaut, Bresson, Godard, Resnais, to name a few) do not become castaways in this age and time, but cope with vitality and skill with the changed situation. It may be tougher to detect the change in a filmmaker like Bresson with his brooding form and repressed aesthetics, than in a Truffaut with a style far more spontaneous and easygoing. The characteristic Truffaut traits are all faithfully present in his *Vivement Dimanche* – the moral realism, the work-and-love axis, the lyricism of Renoir, and the left-handed, humour-interspersed suspense of Hitchcock. But they are there ever so unconsciously, unseen, somewhere in the wings, as the simple and direct narrative of a real-estate owner finding himself suspected for the murder of his wife and her lover being helped out of the fix by his lovelorn secretary unfolds before us.

Ostensibly, the film would go against the Truffaut of the 50s who had sought to destroy the strangehold of Hollywood on French film-goers, and there is a section of critics in France that has not quite forgiven him for slipping into the commercial circuit. But *Vivement Dimanche*, if anything, is proof to the contrary. We see here the reification of the artist, his arrival to a point of simplicity and innocence that conceals, without meaning to, as much as it reveals. Truffaut here mocks the fallacy that wide acceptance *per se* makes a film inferior as a work of art.

The same briskness and quiet charm mark Eric Rohmer's *Pauline at the Beach* (France) with its Racinian plot of two women (one, Pauline, only an adolescent and three men (again one of them still in his teens) together at a beach resort, and falling head over heels in love with one another in a confused pattern that goes something like Pierre loves Marion who loves Henri who really prefers the loose Candy girl who, in turn, has taken quite a shine to Pierre. Pauline, who can see the parody of it all from the outside, returns from that beach rendezvous wiser and maturer in her perception of love. Well-structured and well-worded in the spoken parts, the only disconcerting thing about the film is the straight reduction of love into a just sex (at the risk of sounding squeamish, in many European films love seems just a matter of getting into bed), so that it becomes more a sex quartet than a love quandrangle.

The Festival Directorate's unexplained decision not to screen Warren Beatty's *Reds* is bad enough. As if to add insult, it was announced that a Finnish film with the telling title *Big Blonde* would be shown instead. But it didn't prove to be a 'red-or-blue' alternative after all. The explicit sex scenes notwithstanding, Veikko Kerttula's *Big Blonde* is a sincere, even desperate bid to find some substance and meaning worth holding on to in lives drained of love and hope. Kerttula imbues his characters with an emptiness and void that is disturbing. The dichotomized personality of an individual whose one aspect has exceeded the point of no return while the other side shows faint stirrings of rejuvenating love is displayed in all its stunning contradiction.

First published in *The Hindu*, 11 January 1984.

Crying Wolf against Video

George Orwell's *1984* seems to have been taken so seriously that when the year doesn't really show signs of living up to that scenario, there is almost a sense of being cheated. But if Orwell let us down, Toffler surely won't – and, in any case, *The Third Wave* is a better bet than Huxley's *Brave New World*. Media pundits went on in this strain, invoking apocalyptic visions of the electronic technology of the future, of a video age that would render all humans into programmed zombies. The topic of the seminar itself (organized by the Festival Directorate as part of *Filmotsav '84* in Bombay), 'Video, Cinema and Society', was given a one-track interpretation to read, at the end of it all, something like this: 'The drastic threat posed by the medium and idiom of video to cinema, human values, and society'. Of course, at no stage of the three sessions was that specious proposition ever borne out in terms of logic or reasoning. All argument was emotive, sometimes even paranoiac, and the closest anyone got to any realistic reckoning of the new culture of video was to lament that since we cannot wish it away, let us try to learn to cope with it.

The undercurrent of hostility to video was prompted, as one suspected all along and as was confirmed in the last session devoted to the issue of distribution and copyright, by 'the menace of video piracy', which, especially in a city like Bombay, hits the commercial film industry below the belt. However, while holding no brief for the video pirate (who really has no ethical or legal *locus standi*, and to tackle whom the government, as the Information and Broadcasting Minister emphasized in his inaugural speech, is contemplating immediate legislative action), from the point of view of good cinema or impact on society, commercial filmmaking and illegitimate video-copying as both operate today seem different more in degree than in kind. The one renders counterfeit and retrograde social values into celluloid, the other gives them the 'multiplier effect' through the tube.

Seen only, as the seminar tended to, from the 'cinema subverted by video' angle, the populist cinema and the parasitic video are pitted against one another in a private equation into which the cause of the new cinema and the real society it seeks to reflect does not enter. Which, of course, is not to say that the video has not affected cinema or society in more general terms. As the filmmaker Shyam Benegal pointed out in his preliminary remarks while chairing the first session on 'Technological Interaction', the growing prevalence of video tends to polarize (a phenomenon already obtaining in the west) filmmaking into the very grand, high-budget spectacle at one end, and the very small intelligent film at the other. That, in the balance, would prove beneficial to the 'parallel' or regional cinema in India, the vagaries of the box office being a disincentive to very high budgets.

Even where, and it was rare, the 'paperists' managed to liberate themselves from the mundane issue of video-film hawkers infringing copyright, the bias against this new mode and format of mass communication persisted. It was a film-centred and status-quoist assessment, in terms of this new technology. At least one paper in the second session on 'Impact on Life and Culture', by Fr. Rozano, Director of the Xavier Institute of Communications, Bombay, saw it as a runaway technology with a diabolic, scheming mind of its own. The Australian film critic John Hinde saw the home video set as a retail outlet (perhaps the collective setting of the cinema is the wholesale outlet) that dishes out more commoditized stars and more commercialized filmic values.

Even a filmmaker like Buddhadev Dasgupta, starting with the intelligent premise that there is ever a dialectic relationship between the nature of a medium, and its patrons and clients – which really set one hoping that something else was coming – went on to assail the video as a potential purveyor of vulgar mass culture, unlike cinema which would ever (he did not say why) be subject to social censorship.

Scant attention was given, too, to the overall television ecology of which the video boom becomes a part. Instead, it is television that by preparing the ethos for the video culture, heralded its advent and mushrooming growth in India – a fact none of the speakers could see or would acknowledge. A lack of this perspective, perhaps more than any other single factor, made the seminar a self-defeating exercise, with a distorted perception of the electronic video technology as something totalitarian rather than as something that pulls towards democratization so that filmmaking devolves increasingly to the small community or even home levels.

Amidst all the passion and panic of the occasion it was refreshing to see a coolheaded R.K. Narayan dismissing all alarmist questions directed at him (he did not present a paper) with a left hand. Nothing here to be so exercised about, he pointed out. As for piracy, he only finds it adding to the circulation of and proceeds from his work, and whatever video may do to cinema, it can't short-circuit or substitute the reading habit, for 'love of books will never disappear'. But the dissonant note was perhaps too much for the hall and a false fire alarm (set off by the heat of the TV lights) cruelly cut him short.

First published in *The Hindu*, 17 January 1984.

Godard: Annotation of Social Contradictions

The most striking thing about Godard – and forty-odd films later this has not jaded – is the guts of the man. His relationship to his film, and the simile is about as irreverent as Godard is to his audience, is that of a dog to its bone, now just contemplating it, then licking it, growling and baring its teeth, then attacking it as if detecting some resistance, and then again sitting by, smugly guarding it. Of course, society is no inanimate *objet d'art* – and Godard, more than any other filmmaker, is always so steeped in his immediate time and space – that it can be dealt thus. This leads to the contradictions that make him the *enfant terrible* of modern cinema; to the disturbing tentativeness of his work; to the film of ideas, observations and fears he is so obsessed with and so possessive about.

More than any other filmmaker, again, Godard remains as stubbornly uncompromising in his attitude to his viewers as when he started out. He does not invite them to share his point of view or even as much as empathize with what he has to say, but that they invariably do and are compelled to (his films at our festivals always draw a full house), is a measure of how much he represents them by proxy, of how vital his exposure of paradoxes and hypocrisy is to a society that, left to itself, would never tear the mask off its own face.

The supreme irony is that while we are drawn to him like to a Pied Piper who does his bit and does not get his due, he is himself rueful in that role. His films have not built up any definable cause or philosophy. If they are not socially affirmative, neither are they nihilistic or anarchic in content or purpose: a cinema of questioning without providing the answer, because there are many right answers. A Swiss Calvinist by upbringing and entomologist by training, Godard, at any given time (as in any given film), is deeply engaged in dissecting his society and showing it up for what it is, in conducting a near-inquisition of his times.

His latest work, *Prenom Carmen* (France), made – as the end-caption tells us – 'In Memoriam to Small Movies', carries the vigour and the form of film noir of the early Godard (*Breathless*); but at the same time, becomes a further departure from the format of the linguistic-determined cinema – a further probe into this art form as atomized image and sound, that cohere in our minds into ideas and feelings, that are startling in their novelty as they are in their incisiveness.

First published in *The Hindu*, 17 January 1984.

A Critical Look at the Anti-Heroine

Smita Patil has that silent screen-presence that is alluring without being obtrusive. In the assortment of stereotypes that constitutes the commercial cinema, she tends to be starkly delineated from the rest, as a sensitive and spontaneous artiste who can do without the rouge and the lipstick, and the mannerisms that go with them. But the cosmetics of the industry have a way of rubbing off on the most distinctive of characters and Smita Patil, unfortunately, is no exception. When the balance sheet is drawn, one wishes that her assurance in some roles in some films was matched by an assertiveness about the kind of roles and kind of films she should take on.

Even in the roles in her early Benegal films – *Nishant* and *Manthan* – there were the makings of what later set as the anti-heroine image. The dissidence in type came on strong in *Bhumika*, in which she personifies, with stunning effect, the dilemma and self-contradictions of an actress undecided between the searing glare of publicity and the stifling norms of conservative housewifery – an updated version of Nora of Ibsen's *Doll's House*.

While a subdued and quiet but strong style has become her forté, the real test of her creativity and innovativeness as an actress is her ability to give this basic characteristic a range: to impart those subtle nuances, add those extra inputs that keep her from going stale or becoming typecast even as a breakaway character. Without the histrionics or emotional flamboyance of some of the older thespians, or the strenuous striving of the new crop of low-brow glamour girls, she is able to play with equal conviction such varied roles as the village woman in *Manthan* (Shyam Benegal), *Aakrosh* (Govind Nihalani) or *Sadgati* (Satyajit Ray), the naive, giggly virgin-in-a-whorehouse in *Mandi* (Benegal), the sunny girl in a seamy slum (the bared back in the street-tap-side bathing scene, remember?) in *Chakra* (Rabindra Dharmaraj), the paranoiac 'other woman' in *Arth* (Mahesh Bhatt), and the conscience-stricken social worker in *Subah* (remake of the Marathi film *Umbartha* by Jabbar Patel).

Her approach and school of acting, while certainly making for more realist than escapist fare, do however face the problem of being neither here nor there. There is a structural theatrical element that easily goes unnoticed, but reinforces the value codes of the status-quoist cinema. Seen thus, the 'transitional cinema', which the Smita Patils and Shabana Azmis represent, does not at all fit into the truly avant-garde camp.

This structure and plot and role definition is no doubt the purview of the director rather than the actress. But the artiste must have a commitment too, at least to avoid the kind of credibility gaps created as when in between roles in *Sadgati* or *Subah*, Smita Patil chooses to become a gawky dancer in a film that celebrates old-world feudalism in a modern cardboard setting called *Ghungroo*, or a simplistic 'dread disease' specialist in *Dard ka Rishta* (another cliché in celluloid with cancer as a plot peg), or put out those very unmemorable performances in *Haadsa*, *Namak Halaal* and so on.

The new 'prima donnas' of the Hindi screen seem rebels with natural and innate limits, rather than rebels with a purpose.

First published in *Frontline*, 28 December 1984.

The Cut and Thrust of Eisenstein's Montage

In much the same manner as Che Guevara, uprooted from the cause of his struggle and the context of his death, has been suborned by market capitalism, to become fetishized commodity and iconized brand as an aspirational romantic rebel hero of our times, montage – a product of the first flush of the October Revolution – has been appropriated and vulgarized by commercial advertisement and publicity films and videos, over the decades, to serve precisely the opposite artistic and ideological purpose. In the space between what montage promised and what it has been reduced to, lies the story of the loss of a seminal concept of cinema.

The loss is felt even more acutely today because had montage matured to its fullness, and taken hold of cinematic imagination and method, the excesses of the present star system where the star holds singular sway over the plot, the economics and the box office fate of the film, where an obsequious viewership lays its sensibilities supine before these screen demi-gods, may not have come to be. Montage, then, is not all about cutting and a quick succession of shots as applied in breathless advertisement shorts or MTV imagery. It has the power to subvert the stardom of individuated heroics and position in its stead, or against it, a collective heroism that is more empowering and transformative. It has the potential to counter the prescriptive storyline with a constructive, non-linear narrative of dialectic progression that is as emotively compelling as it is intellectually stimulating. It has the striving to make cinema the synthesis of all arts. It is Hollywood, or Bollywood, stood on its head.

Although most discussions on montage tend to begin and end with Sergei Eisenstein and his *Battleship Potemkin*, the filmmaker and the film really exemplify a movement that was rather short-lived but intense in the exultant decade of the 1920s, following the Revolution. Cinema emerged as the vehicle of a new artistic consciousness, so that even by 1922 Lenin was telling Lunacharsky, 'of all the arts, for us the cinema was the most important'. Already the typical psychological dramas of pre-revolutionary Russian cinema were being jettisoned, and a new aesthetic was being conceived and put together by a process of collective authorship. It was a phase of rejection of the old and experimenting with the new.

True, the shortage economy of the war also provided a fillip to montage. Film raw stock was scarce and dear, and some filmmakers busied themselves with innovatively re-editing the old footage of pre-revolutionary cinema to make new sense of it. The scale of this operation was such that a separate 're-editing department' of the Moscow Film Committee came into being. Indeed, it was in an address to this department, in February 1919, that Vladimir Gardin heralded the concept of 'montage' as the quintessence of the new cinema. But the first clear demonstration of montage, based on Gardin's ideas, came with the 'Kuleshov Effect'.

Lev Kuleshov juxtaposed the same static close-up of Ivan Mozzukhin, a star of Tsarist cinema, with stock shots of a plate of soup, an old woman in a coffin and a child playing, respectively, and found the net result, in terms of construed meaning and emotive response, different in each version. In another experiment, *The Earth's Surface Created*, Kuleshov showed how splicing together disparate shots can achieve bold geographical shifts – characters walking up the Gogol Boulevard in Moscow in one shot appeared on the steps of the Capitol in Washington in the next. Shots, for Kuleshov, were building blocks which could be arranged any which way to convey or evoke different messages or effects each time. The viewer provided the connection and inferred a narrative. This was montage in its infancy – a product of pure editing. The camera hardly figured *a priori* in any of this.

But the idea grew beyond the cutting room and evolved in many directions. Different schools of filmmaking were soon contending with one another, and montage was deployed by them to serve quite different, often contradictory ends. There was a broad stand-off between Eisenstein, to whom montage was all about conflict and progression (or progression through conflict), and Pudovkin, who saw it as a means of linkage and transition. The montage-ists generally rejected the Stanislavsky school of method acting; and the Pudovkin group, which included Kuleshov and Vladimir Fogel among others, came up with a counter-'model' which entailed a clinical study of reflexes and automated acting. Both actor and storyline were suspect before the camera eye (or Kino-eye as he called it) of Dziga Vertov, whose *The Man with a Movie Camera* was the precursor of the *camera verité* style of the French New Wave of the 1960s.

It was in this ferment of avant-gardism that Eisenstein developed his own unique brand of montage as an eclectic and organic tool to design a new cinematic ethos and aesthetic. He drew from a variety of forms – like Japanese and Chinese poetry and ideograms, Kabuki theatre, Joycean stream of consciousness – and integrated them into a polyphonic effect that was at once intellectually stimulating and emotionally engaging. The part subsumed the whole, the instant moment contained the chronological scale. Shots were for association, not representation.

Eisenstein's insight into Japanese and Chinese culture enabled him to set his template of the montage on the model of the ideogram and haiku poetry. The associative principles were somewhat self-evident, as in:

Child + mouth = cry
Bird + mouth = sing
Dog + mouth = bark

Or, evoked through pithy haiku abstraction:

A lonely crow
On leafless bough
One autumn eve.

Or, in ideogrammic terms:

A lonely crow + leafless bough = autumn.

Montage, for Eisenstein, had a lot to do with biomechanics, but this did not by any means suggest a reificatory approach. As he himself notes, the distinctive twin traits of his *Battleship Potemkin* are the 'organic unity of its composition' and its 'pathos' – pathos described as being enabled to partake of a moment of historic culmination, or, in the context of *Potemkin*, 'feeling oneself part of the collective waging of a fight for a bright future'. And pathos, he says, 'cannot but fill us to the highest point with emotional sensation'.

The organic unity he held dear was, again, an evolved concept, drawn from Engels' definition of the organism as 'a higher unity'. It was not the mere sum of its parts but the product of its constituents. He cited Lenin to point out that 'the particular does not exist outside that relationship which leads to the general. The general exists only in the particular, through the particular.' He was fascinated by what he called the 'disintegrated acting' of Japanese Kabuki theatre. It opened up the possibility of dispersal of action, and of atomised time and space. He was acutely aware of the time element, not only in terms of rhythmic or metric cutting but in the creation and rendition of shots. Working up a frenetic multitrack pace with rapid cutting, Eisenstein could, it would seem, select and stare an aspect of the action into slowness. 'My attention', he realized early on in life, was 'fixed permanently on the second hand.' Pudovkin called Eisenstein's montage 'a close-up of time'.

The dialectical conflict that drove his material on screen was structured as a series of collisions, posed by camera angle and shot size, lighting, editing, contrapuntal sound track and music. Montage, for him, was about all of this. He likened it to the explosions in an internal combustion engine that propelled the vehicle forward. The disparate elements he dispersed across his scenario were, however, energized and calibrated to serve the meaning he sought to invest them with. They succumbed and subscribed to his unified vision. His text, in this sense, was not open-ended, polyvalent or polysemic, but determined and closed, as by a consummate *auteur*.

The first two of his Revolution trilogy, *Strike* (1924) and *Battleship Potemkin* (1925), bear the stamp of his full authorship. By the third, *October*, made to commemorate the tenth anniversary of the Revolution, he had begun to run into bureaucratic impatience and interference, and to compromise his style. He had to remove almost a third of the film to cleanse it of Trotsky and, paradoxically, of a speech by Lenin, because Stalin, who ordered the cut, felt that 'Lenin's liberalism is no longer valid today.' By the end of the 1920s formalism itself was under attack, with the 1928 All-Union Party Conference on cinema calling instead for a 'form which the millions can understand'. That was the beginning of the end of the search for an alternative cinematic idiom which the Revolution itself had unleashed. Montage was just about coming into its own as a viable instrument of a new revolutionary screen consciousness, when it became a casualty to political expediency and ideological compulsions of the moment.

But by then, what Charlie Chaplin called the greatest film ever made had been made. *Battleship Potemkin* was sheer sleight of montage. Unlike *Strike*, in which, by his own admission, some gimmicks of collage intruded on his montage, *Potemkin* was the fulsome realization of the device and its best expression in Eisenstein's uneven oeuvre. Evoking and celebrating the failed revolution of 1905, the film is cast not so much as a retelling as an investigation of events, in keeping with Marx's definition of the course of genuine investigation where 'not only the result but the road to it is also a part of truth. The investigation of truth must itself be true, true investigation is unfolded truth, the disjuncted members of which unite in the result.' It takes a non-linear, multitrack, simultaneous and multilayered approach to investigate these disjuncted members and bring them together.

The various elements and dimensions of montage come to a head in *Potemkin*'s Odessa steps sequence, which has become a part of film folklore. The perambulator of that scene has morphed into various versions in various genres and languages of cinema across the world. To get a feel of what elements of montage heighten emotion and how, we can do no better than listen in as Eisenstein describes the steps-sequence himself:

> First, there are *close-ups* of human figures rushing chaotically. Then, *long shots* of the same scene. The *chaotic movement* is next superseded by shots showing the feet of soldiers as they march rhythmically down the steps.
>
> Tempo increases. Rhythm accelerates.
>
> And then, as the *downward* movement reaches its culmination, the movement is suddenly reversed: instead of the headlong rush of the *crowd* down the steps we see a *solitary* figure of a mother carrying her dead son, *slowly* and *solemnly going* up the stairs. . . .
>
> The shot of the rushing crowd is suddenly followed by one showing a perambulator hurtling down the steps. This is more than just different tempos. This is a *leap in the method of representation* – from the abstract to the physical . . .
>
> *Close-ups* . . . give way to *long shots*. The *chaotic* rush (of the mass) is succeeded by the *rhythmic* march of soldiers. One aspect of movement (people running, falling, stumbling down the steps) gives way to another (rolling perambulator). *De-*

> *scent* gives place to *ascent*. *Many* volleys of *many* rifles give place to *one* shot from *one* of the battleship's guns.
>
> At each step there is a leap from one dimension to another, from one quality to another, until, finally, the change affects not one individual episode (the perambulator) but the whole of the method: the risen lions mark the point where the *narrative* turns into a *presentation through images*.

For the 1920s, montage was perhaps ahead of its time. Eisenstein's prescience strikes us from the vantage-point of the present, when we are at the cusp of a changeover from analogue modes of perception and representation to the *dispersed* sensibility of the digital technology. The modern TV screen typifies this shift as a site where montage and collage conflate all at once. The viewer is expected to, and does, multitask, taking in several elements and actions simultaneously – the talking heads, the intervening visuals, the text scrolls, the flash news, the sensex bar in a corner, the advertisement pop-ups and so on. Unilinear attentiveness and experience of the media are being replaced by non-linear grasp of the clutter. True, the average mainstream, star-strapped cinema, with its iconizing impulse, yet uses this digital possibility very superficially. But already with digital surround sound in cinema theatres, the sound track is an experience of *several-ness*. What montage might do to deconstruct the conventional rectangular screen we are riveted to, and similarly unbundle and disperse our viewing experience, is a fascinating thought.

First published in *The Hindu*, 22 November 2002; reprinted in *Frontline*, 21 December 2007.

IFFI 2004: Goan with the Wind

Having to put up with a decrepit film festival in Goa without putting Goa down is the problem. Nothing said, hereafter, should be construed as detracting from the sun and sea and sand and feni and fish curry and beautiful buildings and lovely people that Goa is for any visitor. Indeed Goa was at its carnivalesque best during the ten days of the International Film Festival of India (IFFI) held there earlier this month. The stretch from Dabolim airport to Panaji was festooned with festival buntings. Arches across the road and rectangular props with the festival motif on traffic islands en route welcomed you again and again to the celluloid fiesta. The street on which the twin festival screening complexes and the structures housing related festival activity were located had been cordoned off to local traffic, and looked like one of those boulevards for strollers you find in old European cities. Evenings transformed the street into riotous music and song, sung for the most part like the teenage-skirted Dimple Kapadia's Goan family of revellers in *Bobby*.

Outside the four-screen Inox multiplex where delegates hung around in between, and increasingly through, screenings, a never-ending succession of live bands belted out their high decibel numbers, as a variety of other performers – jugglers, monocyclists and ten-feet-plus-high guys on stilts – kept small groups around them amused. Stepping out of a rare disturbing film into this raucous partying, you instantly put any artistic mulling behind you and decide to let it be. It was Fellini de-screened – the carnival of his frame becoming the framework of the festival itself. This hypercontext seemed to have rubbed off as mild hysteria on a section of the audience, judging by the fit of giggling when a couple of cops, in a Hindi film in the Indian Panorama, were beating the protagonist into pulp.

If this was the scene outside, what was happening inside? Very little, unfortunately. The foreign fare, but for a handful of films including *The Motorcycle Diaries* and *Syrian Bride*, was dismal; and the Panorama section, supposed to showcase the best of creative Indian cinema of the year, found itself brushed aside by the high-pitched lobbying and publicity of the new brand of 'crossover' films from Bollywood. The long queue for the good old Amitabh starrer *Bombay to Goa* told it all – Bollywood, old and new, had come to Goa, and Goa was delightfully lapping it up. The new and the different, which one thought our international film festival would privilege, instead found themselves strangers lost in this scenario.

Waging the celebration from the front was Goa's young Chief Minister Manohar Parrikar, an affable impresario weaving through it all, releasing a publication, inaugurating a festival event, enquiring after his guests, helping form a line for a buffet. Having staked his claim to making Goa the permanent film-fest venue and hugely invested in that prospect, he was not about to be disheartened by Information and Broadcasting (I&B) Minister Jaipal Reddy's overly noncommittal response at the inaugural ceremony. From the look of it, he seemed to roll up his sleeves and enter the fray with redoubled vigour. And there was party after grand party to win over the festival gentry.

At least one such party hosted by the Chief Minister was on a bridge too far and perhaps went too far. It was held on all of a new bridge located so far and away that the invitation without transportation back-up was useless. Through the festival, as one took the designated buses and ferry services to the venues of screening, partying and other happenings that were often far apart, one had to remind oneself that Goa is not a city but a state (apart from being a state of mind, that is). Having, however, managed to get there on one's own, one found the bridge lit and done up like a dazzling movie set, and stand-up comedian Javed Jaffrey in his element with his familiar mimic act. The sound was so overbearing that you could either scream polite conversation to the person standing next to you, or save your throat and stare in dumbfounded awe. The mimicry was followed by a lady in a suspended-ring act by Daksha Seth's troupe which left you wondering why the big circus trapeze had gone out of fashion. Anyone (who drinks) needed a drink after that, and as you moved to the generous bar you bumped into the festival-people-friendly Chief Minister. You thanked him for the party and, partly because you didn't know what else to say, invited him to see your film in the Indian Panorama. Perhaps partly because he didn't know how to respond, he said he would try, but his problem was that he could not sit in one place for more than ten minutes.

But he did put in select appearances, among them for Bharat Bala's *Hari Om*, a rite of touristy passage through Rajasthan; and, true to his word, stayed for about ten minutes and left. Indeed, at another level, watching only a few minutes of a film seemed to be a ploy hit upon by a section of the delegates to cover as many films as possible, so much so that many screenings had a floating population moving in and out – making it exasperating for those who wanted to see an entire film undisturbed. Taking off from the festival one afternoon to see the exposition of St Francis Xavier and filing past the body preserved miraculously in a glass case over so many centuries, one couldn't help wondering whether new Indian cinema isn't already dead enough for mourners to file past a screen flickering with its desolate images. And whether it takes film festivals like this one to point it out to us.

Is Goa as a setting injurious to serious cinema? That would even be an unfair question because this festival only bared the foamy, celebratory face of the state. There is, no doubt, a cerebral Goa which should have engaged with the festival but couldn't, because of the way it was cast. The fun-and-frolic state of mind that Goa willy-nilly invokes, and which its government seemed to promote during this festival, would possibly be good tourist promotion, but bad for a rigorous and critical contemplation of newer forms of style and expression, of thematic departures, of artistic brinkmanship. These are attempted and achieved, for good part, by the *auteurs* of our time and in our country, with little means and a lot of pain and sacrifice. An international film festival, in most cases, is their only forum of expression and hope. To deny them this space and occasion of fulfilment would be to strike a body blow at the already beleagured, even if relatively young tradition of the different cinema in India – a tradition that is strongly nurtured in regional cinema.

A senior and internationally renowned filmmaker was miffed enough with the IFFI at Goa to lament that 'they will never accept the south'. That may be an invidious complaint because the cinema of the east or north or west – representing the regional, rather than Bollywood and derivatives of Bollywood – must feel the same way. But Goa has another chance, next year, to set at rest the doubts and concerns that have been raised this year about its commitment to serious cinema.

First published in December 2004.

Rahman and the Oscar

A.R. Rahman is our best bet yet for an Indian win at the Oscars (other than the honorary Oscar conferred on Satyajit Ray for lifetime achievement in 1992). And there is no reason why the same qualities that fetched him the Golden Globe should not find him holding the statuette at the 81st Academy Awards. But as the heave to get him there gathers momentum, it may be worth a pause to remind ourselves that the Oscars are not to Indian cinema what they are to Hollywood.

An Oscar nomination and win arguably belong to the best that Hollywood has to offer in terms of artistic merit. But shift location to India, and a rash of mismatches surfaces. It takes a quick-fix acculturation into a highbrow, Anglo-Saxon way of seeing for an Indian film to make Oscar-sense to the invited voting cabal of the Academy. The operative barrier is 'sensibility', and Bollywood and Kollywood are replete with pathetic instances of Oscar aspirants raring – and failing – to make it over and across the sensibility threshold. At least one heavy-weight worthy from each has had this persistent Oscar bug – like an itch for all to see – but has never quite made it over that threshold.

There is nothing obvious about the Oscar needing to be the holy grail quest, or test, of Indian cinema. It really speaks to another context and culture, and idiom and ethos. True, the top end of the Indian box office has for long now, coveted this as the ultimate prize. And the urge got worse with a process of globalization that somehow neatly slips into Americanization. As filmic themes and concerns moved metroward and into the multiplex cinema mould, the traditional 'B' and 'C' circuits of distribution were destroyed – and along with them, the target-specificity of the semi-urban and rural viewer. What is left has often been called the NRI cinema, which strives to share a seamless appetite with British or American audiences but remains an ethnically separate category from their perspective.

Of course, we are discussing the mainstream and the popular here, not the seriously profound or the experimental, which would take us to Cannes or Berlin or Venice or Locarno or Pusan. Even these Meccas of the best of world cinema have of late been coopted by the Hollywood brand and become more *de rigueur* than alternative, as the presence of Aishwarya Rai as jury member at the Cannes film festival in 2003 reminded us.

The makeover to meet the Hollywoodian sensibility entails a strange retrofit of the Indian stereotype. Song picturization, our unique and surreal contribution to the celluloid form, has to be dropped. The dialogue has to be couched in a language they would understand, not necessarily as we would speak it. The cultural markers and references must be instantly communicable or neutralized so that they don't hinder the narrative. In short, a lot we would consider 'given' in our cumulative cinematic experience needs to be reinvented and explained across the divide. And it doesn't help to notice that no such eagerness to be easily understood comes our way from there. We are expected to, and do, take the extra effort to crack the language and the codes, although even after several decades of a Hollywood diet, this writer must admit to finding it difficult to follow all of the dialogues in a typical American film.

But that seems to be the price to pay as the world's biggest, and most varied, cinema goes chasing after the world's richest, and more or less homogenized, cinema. It hit us monumentally way back in 1983 with Richard Attenborough's *Gandhi*. The film, no doubt, deserved each of the major eight Oscars it bagged that year (including for best picture, director and actor), limiting competition of the stature of Steven Spielberg's *ET* to just four wins in the sound and visual department. But all that India had to do with this achievement was to provide the eponymous subject of the biopic and money as co-producer. A western crew, westernized cast and mindset took care of the rest. It could not be otherwise, seemed the accepted assumption, if the film was to be in the reckoning for the Academy Awards.

But there was an uneasy sense that, in the process, something was being cannibalized somewhere. Six years later, not so charitable cine-buffs were talking about how Mira Nair had 'attenboroughed' Kamatipura, Mumbai's red-light district and her setting for her cast of real-life street children in *Salaam Bombay*. That film, which sought out the city's underbelly but didn't look like it belonged there, comes closest to being the precursor of *Slumdog Millionaire*. It made it as far as nomination to both the Golden Globe and the Oscars of 1989 in the Foreign Language category.

Slumdog Millionaire has its awkward share of conflict-of-sensibility moments. But in its hybrid wantonness, its unapologetic overture to formulaic Bollywood, its volatile mix of the childlike and aborted innocence, it seems more homegrown than most. Simon Beaufoy (screenplay) deftly herds disparate elements forward together as his 'moving finger writes, and having writ, moves on', perhaps just a shade too fast. Anthony Dod Mantle's supple camera follows, but even in the fleeting time he is allowed to dwell on his material, invests it with mood and meaning. The vibrant faces of slum children as they rummage through their lives with gusto rather than self-pity stay etched, vivid and stark in the mind, long after the plot has moved on.

Excellent casting by Loveleen Tandon gets selective play as some characters are less fleshed out than others; and the difference tells, as with the police officer, played by Irfan Khan, who seems to get left behind somewhere along the way. But British actor Dev Patel's understated and heart-warming performance as the protagonist Salim in the 'Kaun Banega Crorepati' hot seat sets aside any quibble about whether someone from India couldn't have handled the role instead. His delicate, at-a-loss look is a clinching counterfoil to the steely determination of one who knows what he knows, and wants. Anil Kapoor breezes through his role as the savvy TV-show host with panache.

But they are all ultimately, and efficiently, the handiwork of the director Danny Boyle, who adds a bit here and removes a bit there as he churns his cast and plot in the melting pot. The one strong independent element that, in separate but equal measure, adds to the feisty tone and tenor of the film is A.R. Rahman's musical score. We have known Rahman long enough to know not to expect him to repeat himself. Not only does he not, there is no obvious chunk of music in the main body of the film we can put to a typical Rahman test. As the background musical track segues into atonal musical effect and back into the strains of a tune, it provides, alternatingly, lilt and gravitas to the visual mood and action. One stretch alone lingers long enough to foot-tap to – a leisurely rap accompanying the young siblings on the train taking them away from their tormentors into the magical world of the Taj in Agra.

It is a score that elevates the film without drawing attention to itself. And if you are missing the Rahman you want in all this, it comes like an assertive coda at the end of the film with the catchy 'Jai ho'. Even if the credit titles rolling on that robust song and mass-dance sequence is a bit distracting, it is a fitting Bollywoodian finale for the film which might just make the cross-over breakthrough.

As for Rahman, an Oscar for his score in *Slumdog Millionaire* will certainly add to his lustre. But so much he has composed is already on par – and some, like in *Jodhaa Akbar*, even better – that without it he would not be any less sparkling. For the little maestro, the Oscars may be a defining moment but not a definitive reckoning of his musical genius.

First published in *The Hindu*, 21 January 2009.

Conversations in the Cacophony

In the course of a conversation between us, and before an audience attending the seventeenth International Film Festival of Kerala (IFFK) in Thiruvananthapuram, the accomplished, veteran Australian filmmaker Paul Cox wistfully recalled the distinctive cinematic sensibility of the 1980s, exemplified, in Malayalam, in Aravindan and John Abraham. We were discussing the deadweight of Hollywood bearing down on any independent idiom of the medium, and that much more acutely in the globalized realm. Hollywood, as Cox quaintly put it, sees its constituency as so many bums in so many seats, and not as persons with integrated psyches. Violation of gestalt marks the dominant Hollywood fare, typified at its worst for Cox by Quentin Tarantino, and his rending asunder – at the drop of a hat – the human body on the screen.

A Tarantino film is more unleashed than released, with critical clamour in hot pursuit; and his latest, just out, *Django Unchained*, is no exception. Its intent and content are set to frazzle and drain the mind, to atomise the senses and strew them, scattered and spent, before the big screen. Nothing could be further from this than the Coxian oeuvre and approach to filmmaking, where the screen persona's dignity and intactness are the given, and the viewer arrives at a sense of artistic repose. In this clash of tropes lies a dilemma of categorization. Cox is recognizably and assuredly of pure cinematic vintage, even if of the new wave and even as he embraces digital technology. There is nothing morally squeamish or self-limiting in his approach. His reaction to the controversy surrounding the ethics of filming, in real life, the birth of a child to an actress in a Malayalam film as footage for use in the same film, was telling: why would we object to the depiction of this beautiful process of creation if we can accept the destruction, blood and gore, and dismemberment and violation of the human body as the standard commercial cinematic fare?

Tarantino's is, at the margins, a post-cinematic aesthetic that wears the Hollywoodian narrative inside out, and samples an eclectic variety of sounds and sights with digital verve. He strikes a contrarian note in the languaging of his craft, not least in stretches of dialogues that dip at once into pop allusions and evoke a febrile cultural restlessness. The desultoriness of the words he puts into the mouths of his characters engaged with traumatizing visual sequences may be as non-significant or non-meaningful as the coincidence, pointed out in an elucidation of Carl Jung by Dr von Franz, of a man blowing his nose just as a plane crashes in front of him (as against Jungian synchronicity, which would be meaningful coincidence as, say, your ordering a blue dress and being delivered a black one instead, on the day a relative has died). The problem, though, is the dehumanization at work in his films, which is of a piece with the disembodiment that characterizes Hollywood, as cyborgs, robots and futuristic beings take over from thinking, feeling, emoting *Homo sapiens*.

That contemplative cinema dealing with the quotidian and the humane can surpass, and be more devastatingly enduring than the spectacular or speculative cinema invoking an apocalyptic present or a phantasmagoric future, was driven home by at least three profound works screened at the Thiruvananthapuram festival. All of them deal with the inertial phase of old age when terminality becomes a natural human condition. Paul Cox's *Innocence*, made in 2000, steps into the life of a woman in her late sixties, not unhappily married and with an adult son who is a doctor, just as she meets her old lover, a widower and retired musician with a grown-up daughter, after forty-five years and – there is nothing incredible about it the way it progresses in the film – they pick up the thread from where they left off to get blithely into a re-relationship. Cox lets the delicate situation, which lends itself to a mix of curiosity and anxiety, move carefully and incrementally forward, as if wary of upsetting the natural course it will take. Even as the director stays aloof, we find ourselves empathically imbricated in the very practical, at times intense conversations among wife, lover, husband, son and daughter, about what course the affair will take or how it will resolve itself.

Djamila Sahraoui's *Yema* (2012) explores the filial and the familial in a sequestered, parched Algerian milieu. The sixty-two-year-old director herself plays the eponymous mother, somewhat in the conscious manner of a Greek tragedienne, as she seeks to reconcile herself to the death of her soldier son, possibly at the hands of his mujahideen sibling. She finds herself becoming adoptive mother to the young rebel assigned to guard her as she works the earth and makes it yield vegetables and fruits. On the death of her dead son's wife, whom the living one had taken over, her infant child is brought to her care. Sparseness is the figure of speech; indeed there is little the mother says through it all, and her silence becomes more powerful and indicting as the stand-off with the son continues. There is no music track well until the end when the credits roll. More than the minimally articulated context, the film rides on the power of the unspoken word.

Austrian director Michael Haneke's French film *Amour*, which won the Palme d'Or at Cannes in 2012, is a hauntingly intimate study of an old couple, both retired music teachers, whose full and gracefully mellowed lives in each other's implicit company and in their common world of music are inexorably whittled down by a stroke she suffers, just like that, in the middle of a conversation with her husband, which leaves her right side paralysed and her mind lapsing into dementia. As conversation between them is replaced by indecipherable guttural sounds from her supine form that seem to alternately suggest pain and protest, the silent frustration, anguish and bewilderment of the caring and tending husband as he begins to slip down the slope of sanity himself is wrenching to watch. Jean-Louis Trintignant as the husband and Emmanuelle Riva as the wife are riveting every inch of the way, and stay alive in our memory, long after the film is over. Haneke, who once set out to teach the violent American film a lesson with even more antidotal violence in his *Funny Games* (1997), and whose other Palme d'Or winner, *The White Ribbon* (2009), and very first feature, *The Seventh Continent* (1989), are not very much more pacific, seems to seek asylum from the high-voltage mayhem he is both averse and accustomed to, in the quiet Parisian apartment of *Amour* where his two protagonists wind down their lives.

'Conversation' and 'asylum' are the key words which lead to a different impinging context where the facts appear so much stranger than fiction. With the European Court of Justice ruling that US Central Intelligence Agency (CIA) agents had themselves shackled, beaten and sodomized a German citizen, Khaled al-Masri, the continuing forced asylum of Julian Assange (the founder of WikiLeaks, which played a central role in bringing this terrible business of extraordinary renditions to public attention) in the Ecuadorian embassy in London since August 2012 is beginning to look like theatre of the absurd. The sex offence case against Assange pales into a blip before the charge of torture of an innocent man proven against the CIA in the European court. But the Agency will no doubt go scot-free, for who will bell the cat even when the pretence that it was the cat's paw that was independently at it all along has collapsed; and Assange will continue to be holed up in his refuge because he will not be given the minimum assurance he seeks, that he will not be delivered unto the United States and the likes of the CIA if he left the protection of the embassy for Sweden to face the charges against him. The moral indignity of the situation stares us in the face and taunts universal values of freedom. Meanwhile, undeterred by his circumstance, Assange, along with three of his colleagues, has published a 'conversation' that runs into a book of over 200 pages, and that would seem direly alarmist if it was not likely that we are living in times when, to quote Nietzsche, 'the history of truth is the history of the longest lasting lie'.

Titled *Cypherpunks: Freedom and the Future of the Internet*, its introduction is 'a call to cryptographic arms' to stop the world 'galloping into a new transnational dystopia' where the 'Internet, our greatest tool of emancipation, has been transformed into the most dangerous facilitator of totalitarianism we have ever seen' and become 'a threat to human civilization'. The conversation that follows features, besides Assange, his fellow-travellers: Jacob Applebaum, founder of Noisebridge in San Francisco and a member of the Berlin Chaos Computer Club; Andy Muller-Maguhn, a founder of the European Digital Rights; and Jeremy Zimmermann, founder of the citizen advocacy group La Quadrature du Net.

Myriad troubling bytes of information emerge from their conversation: the net is under total and totalitarian surveillance; the multinational media corporations which straddle the net, like Google, Twitter and Facebook, to whom 'we give up all our personal data', abet this intrusion of our privacy and appropriation of our identities so that they 'have essentially become privatized secret police'; instead of targeted surveillance, everything about everyone who has left an electronic trace is now recorded and archived for possible future use, and this is made possible because while the human population doubles every twenty-five years, surveillance capacity doubles every eighteen months; monitoring takes precedence over communication so that, as Assange puts it, 'a mobile phone is a tracking device that also makes calls'.

This panopticon on the net is sought to be legitimized by constantly raising the bogey of what Jacob Appelbaum calls 'the Four Horsemen of the Info-pocalypse: child pornography, terrorism, money laundering, war on some drugs'. Cryptography would be one sure way of dodging this dragnet on the net because codes can be made faster than they are cracked; but then international law is stacked against it because encryption technology cannot be exported under the Wassenaar Arrangement, whereas surveillance equipment can be sold internationally. The prospect, then, for freedom and privacy on the net is dismal, and only the 'high-tech rebel elite', assumedly the cypherpunks, can wrest freedom from this state of siege. It is, for a good part, a surreal conversation which envisions a stark and scary scenario laced with disgust for the media, which are seen as falling for the censorship routine through compliant redactions, and anticipatory impatience for those who might still be cynical about their doom theory of the net. The sense of hyperbole notwithstanding, what it certainly is not, is a quixotic tilting at windmills; it is obvious enough that the core concerns raised are real and urgent.

Although, in its very opening, Assange asserts that this publication is not a manifesto, it reminds one of the philosophical treatise, *The Society of the Spectacle*, by Guy Debord of the Situationist International (SI) movement of the 1960s – or, further back, *The Futurist Manifesto* of Marinetti of the early twentieth century. Assange and company's precautionary narrative is cast, somewhat in the manner of Debord, as a series of aphorisms whose truth has to be empirically tested. It took a quarter century and more before Debord's propositions became central to the information society. It may take far less time in the digital age to discover whether the technology, and the political and commercial forces that operate on the cyberspace we populate will set us free, let us be, or, as Assange predicts, have us electronically profiled and stored, as actionable information, in the databanks of power.

Published in *Frontline*, 11 January 2013.

More to it than meets the eye

In the film *Viswaroopam*, a Faraday shield saves New York from being destroyed by a dirty bomb. It is something of a glib anticlimax, almost a narrative non sequitur. One feels a bit cheated as the denouement seeks refuge behind that shield. The trail of pounding action, blood and gore that leads us, along with the FBI and our own RAW agent Viswanath (Kamal Haasan), to this point seems so much wasted cinematic effort, when all it takes to save the day is for a metal cover of sorts, fortuitously lying around in the room to be slipped over the lethal contraption, like a tea-cosy, to shield it from the electronic signal that will trigger it. It is Viswanath's wife Nirupama (Pooja Kumar), a nuclear oncologist, who suggests this last-minute ploy to foil the Al-Qaeda plot to devastate New York. She has accompanied her husband to the room in the metropolis where the bomb is live and ticking, and where a Nigerian Al-Qaeda operative, shaven from head to toe, is ritualistically self-set to blow up the device with a remote. Neutralizing him is not enough; the device can be activated by a call from the mobile phone of the Al-Qaeda mastermind, Omar (Rahul Bose). As they desperately confer outside the door of the apartment on how to handle the situation, Nirupama comes up with the Faraday shield plan. Good science pips dark science at the post. The director in Kamal Haasan, it would seem, is trying to score a point over the action hero, but with unconvincing result. 'That's it?' you almost hear yourself exclaim as instead of climactic heroics, you get a primer on firewalling against nuclear detonation for the finale. Brain over brawn doesn't quite work here.

A Faraday shield is perhaps what Kamal Haasan and *Viswaroopam* needed to prevent the layers of distorted and cross communication that plagued the film from the moment its release was announced. There was first the confusion about DTH versus theatre release, which became an intra-industry issue. There was further confusion within this confusion about how far the threat of boycott by theatre owners, if the actor–director stuck to his initial DTH-first-and-theatres-next stand, and how far the rather modest bookings for the DTH premiering at Rs 1,000 per view (according to an industry source, fewer than 10,000 bookings had been made with two days to go for the scheduled beaming direct-to-home) were responsible for the compromise eventually worked out:

that the film would hit the theatres first and the DTH telecast would follow a couple of weeks later – of course at nowhere near Rs 1,000 per view.

One can't help wondering why Kamal Haasan got himself mired in this distribution tangle in the first place. He perhaps had a premonition of religious objection from Muslim groups holding up the film's release and sought to preempt it with a one-shot DTH show that would put the film out there in the public realm as a *fait accompli*. As it turned out, however, the film was held back from his core constituency and market of Tamil Nadu, and released, albeit in spurts and with interruptions, in some other states in the country and abroad. This staggered release, in turn, raised the danger of pirated DVDs of the film doing the rounds in Tamil Nadu before it formally opened in theatres across the state. The High Court asking the authorities to ensure there would be no video piracy while the matter was being disposed of seemed almost as naively hopeful as the protesters on the streets of Delhi holding up placards saying 'Ban Rape'.

What are the possible sensibilities the film offends? The anti-imperialist one, for sure. The film does not seem to concede even collateral damage, which after all would be the euphemism for innocent civilians killed when the US forces rain fire and death on swathes of the Afghan countryside from their flying machines. It does depict raw scenes of what bombing from the skies does to those on the ground, including dismemberment of bodies spurting out blood. But there is no presumption of innocence of the victims, even the non-combatants.

Al-Qaeda in Afghanistan, of course, deserve all that they get. Their kith and kin, weaned on their aggressive or suicidal or broadly jehadist ways, are not any less dispensable, and without too many pangs of guilt. The one instance of guilty remorse our RAW agent exhibits is when a Pakistani Sheikh in their company is lynched by the Al-Qaeda after they discover an electronic homing device in his bag, which betrays to the US forces their location in the Afghan mountain redoubts, and which actually belongs to RAW and had been unintentionally placed there by Viswanath's assistant (another RAW agent who has accompanied him as a mole in the group). But then, these are the occupational hazards of war, and there is just so much pity an Indian secret agent needs to feel for a dead Pakistani. There is an emotional dissembling here in terms of valorizing the lives of Afghans and Pakistanis vis-à-vis the rest, including the entire population of New York which has been saved (courtesy the Faraday shield, remember?), which is rather disturbing. Even more blatantly, when the US gunships are upon them, and the Afghan Al-Qaeda fighters are scrambling to defend themselves and their families, Viswanath runs about deflecting their aim – in one instance swiping at the hand of a veteran (an all-too-brief cameo appearance by the versatile Tamil actor Nasser) taking a shot with a shoulder-fired missile at an invading helicopter, so that he misses it. The good guys in the film, if one has got the drift by now, are the ones led by Viswanath, his RAW cohorts and boss (played by Shekhar Kapoor), who aid and abet the imperialist invaders.

The US action is, of course, just and legitimate, because it is to seek out – and take out – the terrorist Al-Qaeda and their paramount leader, Osama bin Laden, who is hiding out in the mountain fastnesses and who makes an epiphanic appearance that Viswanath witnesses with awe from a distance. With both right and might so overwhelmingly vested in the US, it is as if there is little need for any thought to be spared for those at the receiving end of its military might. So all we get by way of contextual reference is a one-liner from Omar to an American hostage kneeling, his back to a masked Al-Qaeda fighter behind him and before a video camera that will capture the grisly act to follow. Omar asks the American whether he thought what the US was doing (to the Islamic world) was right. The miserable man shakes his head to indicate that he doesn't. Then, says Omar, we must do to you what you have done to us (or words to that effect), and the masked man steps up from behind and slashes the American's throat. Put – and portrayed – thus, this singular act of throat-slashing is clearly meant to, and does, become more despicable and culpable in viewers' minds than the killings of tens of thousands of people in the region by the US war machinery, which is airbrushed away as amorphous background static.

The RAW currying favour with the FBI is not an edifying sight and ends up looking like, even if that was hardly the intention, a screen secret-service parable of the Indian government toeing the American line on its vaunted war on terror. Viswanath seems almost eager to ingratiate himself with his counterpart in the US secret service. It doesn't matter that the federal agency initially distrusts him, suspects that he might have something to do with Al-Qaeda himself and roughs him up in an interrogation room (lightly, and mercifully with no water-boarding or like treatment from the post-Iraq US torture manual), before the Indian consular car arrives with his RAW boss and a diplomat who bring the FBI up to speed on how, unbeknownst to the Americans, Viswanath has actually been fighting on their side and for the safety of the US. American interests here, we are left to infer, are *ipso facto* Indian interests. Otherwise it makes little sense to see this RAW agent go out on a limb, uninvited, to safeguard the interests of the US on Afghan and US soils, which Washington, with the hard and soft power resources at its command, is perfectly capable of handling itself.

Crony imperialism, then, is writ large on the film. But that is not why its release ran into trouble in Tamil Nadu. The burden of the objection from the fringe Muslim groups who have taken to the streets, from what one can put together from their disparate responses, is that the film is (or so they assume, because most of them have not seen it) a slur on Islam in its use of recitation of Quranic verses and the *kalima*, and plays into the stereotype that synonymizes religion with terrorism. This would be true if, and only if, their objection pertains to the portrayal of the Al-Qaeda, who do incorporate sacred verse and ritual into their killings and suicide bombings because they operate in a different moral universe, and what is terrorism for the rest of the world is holy jehad enjoined on them. And, as the poet and lyricist Javed Akhtar pointed out in a discussion on the subject on a television channel, this is indeed how Al-Qaeda goes about it in real life. What the film does is to show this abuse of and parasiting on Islam by the Al-Qaeda to wreak terror. Isolating this sacral behavioural detail from its Al-Qaeda context in the film (or in real life) and opposing it as anti-Islamic *per se* makes little sense, and may actually end up looking like acquiescing in or apologizing for the ways of Al-Qaeda; and surely that is not what the protesters mean. The film is substantially about the Al-Qaeda and what they do, and this critical element of how they distort their religion for their diabolic ends is so germane to the plot that removing it – as Kamal Haasan is under pressure to because he has so much, including his house and property, riding on the film, and failure to recoup in time from the box office will spell doom for him – may make them look like strange, gratuitous villains even more inexplicably Islamic.

It is by now clear that artistic freedom guaranteed by the Constitution, a censor certificate by the statutory body set up for the purpose, even repeated verdicts by the highest court of the land against films that are duly censored being prevented from being screened for the public, add up to nothing before random malcontents set to block a film from reaching its viewers. What makes the case of *Viswaroopam* more curious is the pussyfooting by the state government. The ostensible reason is intelligence supposedly available with the government about a law-and-order situation that could arise with the film's theatrical release. That seems a bit strange because the film has been exhibited, even if in fits and starts, in neighbouring states.

In Kerala, in particular, the government itself took the lead by releasing the film through its own chain of theatres; and, even if accompanied by some street protests and demonstrations, other private theatres followed. With nearly a quarter of its population being Muslim, Kerala could be expected to be even more sensitive to any slight to Islam. Moreover, in the precariously balanced coalition government that runs the state, the Muslim League enjoys strong representation and tremendous clout; and all it would have taken was for it to frown upon the film's release for it to be stalled. That this did not happen is a tribute to the dynamics of more enlightened politics in the state. But that the more comfortably placed government in Tamil Nadu could not do as much for the film begs reason. There is obviously more to *Viswaroopam* than meets the eye.

Published in *Frontline*, 22 February 2013.

Telling the Story and Spinning a Yarn

We hear that the Iranian counter to Ben Affleck's Oscar award-winning *Argo* is to be another film titled *The General Staff* by Tehran-based filmmaker Ataollah Salmanian, also set against the hostage crisis of 1979–81. Salmanian says the script is done and that it deals with the revolutionaries releasing twenty American hostages to the United States. That number doesn't quite tie in with the American narrative, and the current conjecture in the western media is that this must be about the twelve hostages, including African-Americans and women, who were freed soon after the takeover of the US embassy.

Be that as it may, a fanciful thought that offers itself in this situation is that such tit-for-tat films may be a better way than sanctions, nuke-baiting or nuke-rattling for the US and Iran to settle scores with each other – a variant, if you like, of ping-pong diplomacy. The one has the world's most powerful cinema hub, Hollywood, which ever so often comes to the rescue of the prestige of the US state; the other, arguably the best collection of new generation filmmakers, whose genius and prestige the state seems woefully unaware of or unimpressed by – and some of whom, like Jafar Panahi, the state in fact rewards with imprisonment, ban and house arrest for their creative expression, and who therefore make their mark in spite of the state.

Argo is both about a film within a film and a rescue within a rescue. The film-within-the-film part is trite and apparent enough. Ben Affleck, as a Central Intelligence Agency (CIA) operative, thinks up the ruse of a production team from Hollywood doing a reconnaissance for a sci-fi film, to smuggle six US diplomatic staff members – who had escaped from the US embassy in Tehran when the revolutionaries broke into it on 4 November 1979, and taken refuge in the house of the Canadian Ambassador – on a flight back to the US. This, as an article in the August 2007 issue of *Wired* magazine, which inspired Affleck to make the film, tells us, is more or less how it happened.

The CIA agent in real life, the same article informs us, was Tony Mendez, who was trained in the Agency's Office of Technical Service (OTS) – where, among other things, they worked on those explosive-laden cigars to get Fidel Castro. Mendez was an expert at 'identity transformation', and this is what Affleck is supposed to be doing in the film as he identity-trains each of the six Americans in their respective role-plays in the recce team, and fixes their false passports and documentation. But all of this is so cursory and routine that but for its real-life intimation, and meticulous recreation and evocation of the period, the film would have ended up looking like a plot with a hole for a bottom rather than, appropriately for a spy thriller, a false bottom.

Within the dramatic rescue motif seems embedded the real motive: to rescue and refurbish the American image from the beating it took through the 444 days of siege of the embassy under intense scrutiny of the international media by retrofitting it with the successful initiative of a side plot, at a time when Iran is again occupying mind and media space on a regular basis in the US. Other than this, there seems little reason for such a film appearing at this juncture, and for it bagging the top Oscar award. It is instructive that in the media speculation leading up to the Academy Awards, the wisest and most experienced voices were predicting a win for *Argo*, not necessarily because it was the best in the race but because it was the right film at the right place at the right time. The on-screen presence of the US First Lady to present the award only strengthened this impression of political expediency.

The casualness with which *Argo* combines fact and fiction makes it ethically discomfiting. The opening prefatory section itself, ostensibly meant to set the historical and political contexts, sets this hybrid tone. Running into a few minutes, it combines sketched imagery of the graphic novel with documentary photographs and snippets of archival footage to tell us, in a matter-of-fact narrator's voice, that in the land of Iran, which was once called Persia, where rulers called Shahs had been ruling for 2,500 years, a secular democrat, Mohammad Mossadegh, was elected Prime Minister in 1950 (in fact it was in 1951), who went on to nationalize the oil assets of the country; that the US and Britain, the affected parties, engineered a coup against Mossadegh in 1953 and restored effective power to Shah Reza Pahlavi, who was a despot leading an obnoxiously luxurious lifestyle while his people starved and were tortured by his dreaded secret police, Savak. The Shah, the narration goes on, took steps to modernize Iran and this turned the conservative Shias against him, so that he was deposed in 1979. Ayatollah Khomeini returned from exile abroad, and there was anarchy everywhere with mobs clamouring for the Shah, in asylum and dying of cancer in the US, to be returned to stand trial in Iran.

If Ben Affleck had taken the trouble to read Edward Said's fairly detailed critical analysis of the media depiction of Iran, written even while the hostage crisis was in progress and with no resolution yet in sight (he devoted a long, four-part chapter titled 'The Iran Story' to this in his work *Covering Islam*, published in 1981), he would have realized that in spite of the benefit of hindsight, he was falling into the same ethnocentric stereotype that the US media exhibited in their daily print and broadcast coverage during the period. As Said, himself a US citizen, put it: '[I]t seemed that "we" were at bay, and with us the normal, democratic, rational order of things. Out there, writhing in self-provoked frenzy, was "Islam" in general, whose manifestation of the hour was a disturbingly neurotic Iran.'

But then, perhaps, such typecasting was imperative to push the plot. Ben Affleck doesn't let truth get in the way of his story, as he himself admitted in response to the *SNAFU* about the reference in the film to the British and New Zealand embassies not offering succour to the six Americans before they were given refuge by the Canadian Ambassador, whereas in fact they did. 'I struggled with this long and hard', a report in *The Telegraph* quotes him as saying, 'because it casts Britain and New Zealand in a way that is not totally fair. . . . But I was setting up a situation where you needed to get a sense that these six people had nowhere else to go. It does not mean to diminish anyone.' In the same report the then British Ambassador to Iran, Sir John Graham, was piqued enough by this transgression of fact to deplore that 'the filmmakers should have got it so wrong. My concern is that the inaccurate account should not enter the mythology of the events in Tehran in November 1979.'

It becomes similarly convenient, even necessary, from the point of view of the given cinematic plot line, to project the revolution as all and utter mayhem, to paper over the timelines of the emerging new order, as well as the tensions and differences in the ideological positions of a Beheshti, Bazargan, Bani-Sadr and Ghotbzadeh, and reduce it all to a largely faceless, amorphous mass of antipathetic and agitating Iranians – essentialized in the austere, iconic visage of Khomeini on larger-than-life banners and posters – versus the six guileless Americans meant to be objects of our empathy, mentored by their CIA rescuer, finding their scripted way out of this mess.

The film is not about seeking to understand or about reconciling differences, but about reinforcing the 'othering' of Iran. Irrespective of their internal political shortcomings and differences, Iranians are unlikely to take kindly to such a civilizational taunt. The US attitude demonstrated in the film is faintly reminiscent of the Hollywood hatchet job of the Cold War era. To go back to Said, even in the thick of the hostage standoff it was clear to him that

> the world we live in is much too complex and much too different now and much too likely to go on producing unconventional situations (however little they may be to the United States' liking as a nation) to be treated as if everything could be translated into affronts or to enhancements of American power. Americans cannot continue to believe that the most important thing about 'Islam' is whether it is pro- or anti-American. So xenophobically reductive a view of the world would guarantee a continued confrontation between the United States and the rest of an intransigent mankind. . . . I suppose that such a policy could be considered active advocacy of the 'Western way of life', but I believe an equally good case could be made that the Western way of life does not necessarily involve provoking hostility and confrontation as a means for clarifying our own sense of our place in the world.

When a film is predicated on a well-documented historical context, when it is pitched against the backdrop of a vast political churning constitutive of a new and difficult nationhood as was Iran in 1979, there are limits to the liberties the filmmaker can take with what actually happened. *Argo* works as a credible, gripping narrative because it is referenced to the context every inch of the way, or so we believe. Remove the reference, and the film collapses like a deflated balloon. Faithfulness to the context then becomes a minimum ethical obligation.

If Ben Affleck had given to the film's ethical integrity even a fraction of the attention he devotes to its outward aesthetical aspect, he could have emerged with a film which was like a mnemonic bookmark in the pages on this transitional period in Iran. As it stands, fractional facts prop up a figment that misleads and disinforms. We do not know where he is telling the story and where spinning a yarn.

What transpires in the final scenes as the Americans pass through airport security before they board their Swissair flight out of Tehran – making it by the skin of their teeth – is as suspenseful as it is because we are not aware as we watch that it is all false. Unless, of course, we have learnt from the real Tony Mendez on the CIA website that the operation, 'exfiltration' as it is called, went without a hiccup even at the airport and was, as he describes it, 'as smooth as silk'. If anything, the construct, or reconstruct, of the tension in the final moments of the film has an opposite resonance post September 11, when reports of profiling and targeted scrutiny of Muslims travelling to, from or through US airports have become commonplace.

Postscript: Some five years after the real or make-believe (take your pick) scene at the airport in January 1980, I was there – in the real airport, that is – to take a return flight out of Iran. I had, a couple of days earlier, flown into Tehran via Dubai from Bahrain, where I was based as the West Asia correspondent of *The Hindu*, to interview Iranian Foreign Minister Ali Akbar Velayati. By then the revolution had consolidated around Khomeini; the Islamic Republic was firmly in place; Iran was on the offensive in the war against, and provoked by, Iraq; anti-Americanism continued to be on a high with stars-and-stripes as the motif on the large foot-mats at the entrance to hotels, so that one had to step on and across them to get into the lobby; and rifle-wielding Revolutionary Guards, many of them in their teens, were a common sight in the capital.

At the security check in the airport, the audio tape of the Velayati interview I carried in my inner jacket pocket caused a hubbub, with a group of Revolutionary Guards surrounding me and demanding to know why I had not declared it in the first place. When I explained that it contained my interview with their Foreign Minister they seemed mollified, but then wanted to check it on an audio player first. I had visions of the erase instead of play button being pressed, and decided to up the ante. I told them they could play the tape, but that if something happened to the recording, I would have to reproduce the interview from memory and they would be to blame for the consequences, if any. It worked, and they waved me on to the waiting flight.

Published in *Frontline*, 5 April 2013.

True Archivist of Cinema

An eight/nine/ten-year-old boy is already falling in love – with cinema. His father frowns upon the baneful influence of the silver screen, and so he has to wait until the household is asleep to sneak out and sprint the fifteen-minute stretch to the movie tent in Thiruvananthapuram, in order to catch the latter half or less of the night show. The cheapest ticket provides the most luxurious setting of seating, on the bare white sand carted in from Shankhumugham beach and evened out across the floor. The white sand, routinely used in rituals and on auspicious occasions, becomes the metaphor of the earthy beginnings of a lifelong affair that shifts from a sense of 'wonder and magic' into an 'obsession', and then into an enduring 'passion'.

But does the boy get to see the early parts of the films he missed in these nightly escapades? Yes – as, and perhaps more legit, matinee shows on weekends. One cannot help wondering whether this habit of reverse, staggered and repeat viewing of a film in his very early formative years did not endow him with a different, modular, reel-by-reel awareness of the medium.

As the boy grows older he has again to dodge his father's plans for him to study engineering, and move to Mumbai in 1955, hoping to find work as an assistant to any one of the legendary directors, Mehboob Khan, Bimal Roy, Guru Dutt or Raj Kapoor. He manages to contact Mehboob Khan who was then shooting *Mother India* and who already had six or seven assistants, and could only allow him to stick around, without any payment, keeping dope sheets. The famous cinematographer of the film and of the times, Faredoon Irani, too was virtually inaccessible, and our young protagonist, his exposure limited to layers of assistants, is hardly able to really cut his teeth in this very hierarchized industry. As he and some friends then dabble with scripting for a film, it probably begins to dawn on him that making a film does not excite him as much as a made film.

Around this time he meets Rammohan, the famous animator of later years, in the Films Division, who advises him to apply for a position in the new Film Institute – eventually set up in 1960 on the site of Prabhat Studios in Pune. Four years later the National Film Archive formally comes into being on the same location, and becomes, over the years, synonymous with the name of the young assistant curator who builds it up, as Shyam Benegal puts it, 'brick by brick' and, one might add, film can by film can, rising to the position of its director and beyond, to that of the master archivist of cinema in India, comparable, in peer appraisal (even if as a quieter and more unassuming version), to the formidable collector of cinema and co-founder of the Cinémathèque Française in Paris, Henri Langlois.

P.K. Nair, or Nair sa'b as he is called by succeeding generations of filmmakers, cinematographers and other technicians from the Film and Television Institute of India (FTII) and outside, is a very unlikely candidate for the lead role of a film; and a very reluctant one, to boot. As the director Shivendra Singh Dungarpur wearily admits at the very beginning of his adventurous biopic of an icon he is obviously in awe of, it took him eleven visits to Nair over a year before he could persuade him to feature in it. But the adventure paid off and *Celluloid Man* emerges as a long (all of 155 minutes), unblinking – but no less fascinating for it – Nair gaze.

For all that, there is little Nair himself does, or can do, because of his difficulty in walking, except hobble with the help of a crutch on locations germane to his occupation and preoccupation with cinema – in his native Thiruvananthapuram, or his home-is-where-the-heart-is Pune, or Nasik where he scooped a Dadasaheb Phalke film; or across and through dank, cobweb ridden rooms and corridors on the precincts of the Film Institute with film cans piled on the floors or stacked on a long line of shelves, pausing to examine a can here, a strip of film there; or seated alone amidst rows of empty seats in a preview or commercial theatre, viewing a sequence unspool on the screen – through it all recollecting, recounting in simple terms, the simple pleasures of his life, all of which have to do with his love for and acquisitions of films. It is the others, some of the country's best engaged with the art and the craft of cinema, who construct his image with the building blocks of their first-person experiences and interactions with him; their mostly real and occasionally apocryphal anecdotes surrounding him; their own sense of personal transformation through the films he led them through; and their evocation of a subculture of camp following, intellectual insouciance, and debate or drunken disagreement, all of it revolving around the treasure trove of films that Nair sa'b put at their disposal. At the end of it Nair's virtual and construed, rather than physical and palpable, presence dominates the screen and our minds.

Shivendra Singh accomplishes this impact by marshalling his vast and varied material in a grand sweep and herding all of it forward, at once particularly and comprehensively, so that no interesting facet or detail is left behind, and the Nair saga takes shape before our eyes with a degree of nuance and credible complexity. It is not a predetermined linear narrative – it cannot be that; it flits from idea to idea and person to person, all of which cohere in the underlying persona that the director seems to extract from the footage, rather than conjure up as a romantic portrait. This can be tough going and risky because he is letting the diverse shot stuff – impressionistic accounts, inconclusive threads – determine the structure and pace of the work. But it works; and in the few instances that the effort shows, it is because there is no attempt to hide it.

Early in the film, the Polish director and producer Krzysztof Zanussi compares cinema to a butterfly with a short life, which dazzles briefly and then vanishes. Archivists like Nair are those who preserve the butterfly for long after. Zanussi puts his finger on the temporal essence of archiving. In terms of its currency, whether at the box office, or in the festival circuit, or to a niche viewership, a film has an expiry date; as an archival entity it almost certainly does not. It has a relevance, even an immediacy, which has nothing to do with its period setting. Such presence of the past comes alive in one track of the film which fields the raconteurs – illustrious alumni of the Film Institute whose minds and creative energies were vivified by Nair's archives. The other track, featuring for a good part Nair in sombrely lit settings, bears the tone and tenor of loss and perdition as the materiality of celluloid yields to digital pixelation. The tension between the two tracks adds to the viewer's engagement with the work.

The categories of memory, nostalgia and archiving jostle with one another for our attention. There is a standard portrait of the archivist that emerges from many remembrances: one in the darkened auditorium while a film is being screened, making continuous notes about it with a pen and a pen-torch – 'a little light and a man with a pen making notes about the film', as filmmaker Saeed Mirza puts it. Girish Kasaravalli remembers taking to note-taking in the Nair fashion, and Ketan Mehta about some of them sneaking into his room to check what the notes said and discovering that they were meticulous entries including such detail as at what point the emulsion of the film stock wears thin.

There is then the widely shared memory of the Nair who carried an encyclopaedic filmic reference in his head. He could recall at will which film and which reel in it contained a particular song or important dialogue or sequence, and would reel off, on the phone to the projectionist, the reel numbers across different films in their screening order for an evening's session, leaving those witnessing this remarkable feat of memory awestruck. Where the memories turn into nostalgia they become more subjective, and to that extent less verifiable.

Where the nostalgia of one does not match the memory of another, Shivendra Singh just lets it be without attempting to smoothen it over. Filmmaker K. Hariharan remembers the *enfant terrible* of the Indian new wave, Ritwik Ghatak (who detested Ingmar Bergman, loved Alexander Dovzhenko and held that Satyajit Ray had made only one-and-a-half films: *Pather Panchali* and the first half of *Aparajito*), kicking up a shindy with Nair about screening Masahiro Shinoda's *Double Suicide* because it was based on puppetry and did not qualify as legitimate cinema. Nair, however, does not believe this happened and thinks Hariharan must be imagining it. The director's openness in letting that contradiction stay unresolved does not, however, detract from the credibility of other memory bites, or of the film as a whole. After all, as Oliver Sacks, citing the psychologist Donald Spence, points out in a recent article in the *New York Review of Books*, there is 'historical truth' and there is 'narrative truth', the latter being vulnerable to honest confusion, compounded by time, of hearsay with personal knowledge, so much so that you believe you remember something as directly experienced by you when in fact it was borrowed from or planted in you by another person. Such paradoxes, if anything, provide the interpretative and contemplative spaces that enrich a film on an archivist and archiving.

The combination of narrative and historical truth is what makes *Celluloid Man* tick. We travel with Nair to Nasik to revisit his trip there in 1969, in search of any footage available from the silent era films of Phalke. Nair remembers that first visit in a 'paper taxi' (that is, a taxi that carried the first morning edition of the daily *Kesari*, published from Pune, to Nasik) so that, should he find anything, he could bring it back in the vehicle that would normally return empty. Miraculously, he finds a wooden box in Phalke's house with rolls of film, and piecing them together with the help of notes also left behind in the box by the director, he reassembles them into *Kaliyamardan*, the only complete Phalke film now available.

We are with him on the historical location of *Raja Harishchandra*. We hear him remember how he went about doggedly collecting anything and everything he could lay his hands on from the silent era of 1912 to 1931; and yet, from over 1,200 films made in that period, only ten or twelve could be traced and archived. We listen on in dismay as he tells us about his attempt to procure the first Indian talkie, Ardeshir Irani's *Alam Ara*, only to learn from Irani's son that he had sold three reels of the film for the value of the silver that could be extracted from them. In one of the docufeature's riveting asides, dancer Sitara Devi recalls the shift in the experience of viewing cinema as movies transited from silence to sound. For viewers used to mouthing together in a subdued murmur the captions that conveyed each dialogue of a silent film, the arrival of sound was nothing short of devastating.

Nair then takes us through his pursuit of the productions of the big studios of the sound era – Bombay Talkies, Modern Theatres of Salem, Pancholi Studios of Lahore, New Theatres in Calcutta, Gemini Studios in Madras; his acquisition of the body of work of the mainstream and parallel Indian cinema in different languages, and of world cinema, until he had built up a collection of 12,000 titles, 8,000 of them Indian, by the time he retired. In this collection drive, the reputation of the film or the filmmaker made little difference to him. 'From an archival point of view,' he says, 'a Satyajit Ray film is as important as a John Cawas-Nadia stunt film.' His singleminded, nose-to-the-grindstone approach to the serious task of building the archive, and making it an organic part of the learning experience at the FTII in Pune, quickly won him the admiration and respect of successive batches and generations of students. It took the industry and film fraternity outside longer to recognize his pioneering work; and much of it may still not be aware of what he meant, or means, to cinema in India. But from those who know, the praise is fulsome. Veteran Sri Lankan director Lester James Peres calls him the 'custodian of Indian cinema'. Lyricist Gulzar sees in him no less a figure than Dadasaheb Phalke in his own right. For Balu Mahendra he is a father-figure. Shyam Benegal and Mrinal Sen equate him with Langlois. The list of those he touched and who recall it memorably goes on: Kumar Shahani, Adoor Gopalakrishnan, Naseeruddin Shah, Jahnu Barua, Mahesh Bhatt, Kamal Haasan, Dilip Kumar and Saira Banu, Rajkumar Hirani, Shabana Azmi, Jaya Bachchan, Vidhu Vinod Chopra, Kundan Shah . . .

Shivendra Singh does not allow such growing adulation to make his protagonist appear sanctimonious. In a defining, and perhaps defiant, moment of the film, he forces the issue on the matter of a rumour delightfully shared by Nair acolytes: that he would, like Langlois who had the same reputation, go to any extent, including pirating a copy, to procure a film he badly needed for the archive. As Nair is seated alone amidst rows of empty seats in a long shot of the interior of a cinema hall, a question is suddenly sprung to him by a voice off the frame. Does he steal films? Nair does not, or pretends he does not, hear the question. The question is repeated, but again it does not elicit a response and the shot is cut. We do not know what then transpired off-screen. But the next shot has him closer and includes the clapboard; and Nair begins his response saying 'stealing' is not a nice word to use. He then goes on to admit how, when he had the Argentinian film *The Hour of the Furnaces* at the archives for a festival, he kept it for an extra day or two to make a dupe copy, and did not put it on record that he had done so. 'I think', he concludes stoically, 'a true archivist should have the immunity to overcome all these legal problems.'

First published in *Frontline*, 31 May 2013.

Contemplative Triptych

The ship of Theseus is as old as conundrums go, harking back to the vessel in which the mythic Greek slayer of the Minotaur sailed. The poser, as it was first recorded by Plutarch, was: if the planks of the ship were replaced one after the other until nothing of the old timber was left on it, would the ship remain the same? Ancient philosophers, including Heraclitus, Plato and Socrates, took a shot at this riddle, and Hobbes in the seventeenth century raised the obverse scenario: what if all the old timber of the ship had been saved and used to build another ship? Which would then be the original ship? Variations of this theme have engaged others down the ages.

Now we have a young filmmaker, Anand Gandhi, who sets up the paradox afresh as the framework for his film of the same title. In the process, perhaps unknown to himself, he sets off a subset of a paradox himself because the entry point to the film with a loaded title like this is essentially cerebral; but its philosophical overlay seems overwrought and to distract, if not detract, from the three situations portrayed of being and becoming, where the heart and free will, as much as the mind, play decisive roles, and where the *gestalt* is not a sum of the body-parts.

The first in the triptych is about a blind young Egyptian photographer and her transformation with a cornea transplant that bestows sight to her. When blind, she is surefooted, instinctive, works within a monochromatic axis of black and white, is drawn by her other sensory faculties – and some electronic jigs attached to her camera that can read off distances – to zero in on her shot, and, driven by her keenly cultivated internal rhythm, to capture the moment as the vision clicks in her mind. Absence of eyesight virtually invests her frames with a cutting edge. All this dissipates with the corneal transplant, and the coming of sight and light in her life, and she finds herself faltering and struggling to cope with the abundance and disorder of what she sees around her.

Thanks to what seems a vague plagiarism charge – that this plot is modelled on another short film of a blind painter and the crisis of creativity that the gift of sight forces on her – Anand Gandhi has volunteered the information that the inspiration behind the character was the blind Slovenian photographer Evgen Bavčar, whose works of, and thoughts on, photography are seminal to an understanding of how the camera mediates between blindness and sight.

Bavčar makes a distinction between the visual as 'that which our eyes see', and the visible as 'that which our mind sees'. The camera view, for Bavčar, is 'the gaze of the third eye', and imagining images is existence itself. 'I can't belong to this world,' he says, 'if I can't imagine . . . in my own way. When a blind person says "I imagine", it means he too has an inner representation of external realities.'

It is no coincidence that the camera images captured by the blind young woman in the film bear a resemblance to those of Bavčar. They are, both, manifestly digital – light sources leave an incandescent trail as the shot is of movement or in movement; the compositions have an oneiric strangeness about them. As an aside it is interesting to note, in the larger context of the techno-cultural shift from the analogue to the digital, that as part of a write-up on Bavčar (titled 'The Blind Photographer'), the psychoanalyst and expert on blind photography, Benjamin Mayer Foulkes, observes that

> the main questions posed by the transition from analog to digital photography can be considered in relation to blindness. While analog photography tends to think of itself as not being blind, digital photography knows itself to be blind and operates accordingly. While analog photography equates the visual and the visible, digital photography presupposes their distinction. While the referents of analog photography appear to be ocular, digital photography demonstrates that pictorial referents are not merely the objects of sight, but essentially the objects of the gaze. In sum, blind photography is digital photography 'avant la lettre'.

There is no reason to infer that our blind protagonist with the camera, played with a delicate combination of ruminant restlessness and coiled-spring terseness by the Egyptian actor Aida El-Kashef, may be afflicted by a crisis of identity just because after the corneal graft, to put it rather plainly, she begins seeing with someone else's eyes. Her dilemma, rather, is one of identification, expression and creativity as she moves from a state of being blind to one of becoming visually enabled. She has literally to readjust her sights to the colour and light and forms of the visual external world. Without a history of seeing, it is perhaps a quantum leap into sight and into the attendant problems of adjustment that Oliver Sacks has recounted in his case study ('To See and Not See', *The New Yorker*, May 1993) of a middle-aged man he calls Virgil, who had been rendered blind from childhood by a form of complicated cataract; the cataract was surgically removed and he could then see, but he could never relate to his faculty of sight. But this is a different problem and the Theseus paradox seems far-fetched in her circumstance.

The film leaves her there, grappling with sight, and moves on to the second situation of a young Jain monk, winsomely affable but resolute in his ways, and fighting, even while observing the austerities enjoined on him by his faith, a legal case against experiments involving animals by pharmaceutical companies. When he is diagnosed with cirrhosis of the liver and finds that the cure entails a liver transplant and medication using products manufactured by the same companies, he resorts to the ultimate act of '*Santhara*', or death by starvation sanctioned by Jainism, but relents in the last minute and decides to submit to the surgery. Again, there are other paradoxes at better work here than that of the film's title, but by now the overarching intellectual hypothesis no longer nags. We are, we realize, into a resplendent film whose every moment needs to be savoured, irrespective of the theoretical constructs. And it is in this segment of the monk and his cause that the film is at its heart-wrenching best.

The actor and theatre director Neeraj Kabi puts body and soul into the role with devastating effect, stirring us with his infectious warmth, spurring us to keep pace with his hurried strides on his unending karmic path, drawing us into his utterly selfless humaneness, touching us with the poignance of his inner turmoil, and challenging us to behold him as he wastes away into skin and bones before our eyes. The physical, the emotional, the intellectual and the spiritual come together into lived daily routine and banter without ever becoming overtly profound. This stretch of the film is covered with masterly finesse by the director, with tightly engaging, peripatetic camerawork by Pankaj Kumar to match.

In the third and final act, we pick up the narrative thread in a hospital room where a stockbroker, played by the actor Sohum Shah (who has also produced the film), is recuperating from surgery for a kidney transplant. When he stumbles on a case, in the same hospital, of a poor bricklayer's kidney being stolen when he was being treated for some other ailment, he wonders and needs to find out whether he was the unwitting recipient. It turns out not, but by now his empathy for the bricklayer's plight is aroused, and setting aside his single-minded obsession for the stockmarket, he goes in search of the person who was the beneficiary – a journey that takes him to Stockholm and into an ethical quagmire.

Again, Sohum Shah transits the being-to-becoming curve with a consummate touch of ordinariness. The change in the one-dimensional stockmarket votary with little that is intellectual or creative to recommend him – the despair of his more cerebrally accomplished grandmother on this count hangs heavy in the air – is subtle and nuanced. In the end, his efforts to get justice for the bricklayer do not quite measure up to his own expectations. But he has actually accomplished a lot and redeemed himself in his grandmother's eyes.

Sohum Shah, Neeraj Kabi and Aida El-Kashef substantially carry their respective segments on their individual shoulders, but every other character too is flawlessly in place. It is a casting coup rare in Indian cinema. The film has the look and feel of a coverage of three stories that are happening even as the crew engages with them, rather than of a scripted plot being directed. All of this, of course, is the vision and execution of Anand Gandhi. It takes guts born of assurance and conviction to make a film like this. The title may be a bit of a philosophical red herring. But then it helps elicit a thinking response to the film which proceeds far beyond the sensory experience and appreciation of it. A straightforward, pared-down narrative structure and style, dialogues that are so true to form for those mouthing them that you think they cannot have a common author, a controlled visual treatment, editing that just about allows space and time for the reflexive, and location sound that adds to the sense of documentation, together make for a contemplative film for the seeker as much as for the viewer.

Given the set expectations of and from the box office, it is a surprise that the film finds commercial release at all. Even more surprising is the fairly robust response to it in the mainstream film bazaar. Past experience of films like this has been that they shuttle between the shelf and the film festival without access to the theatrical circuit. That may well be changing, as recent experience in some regional cinema indicates. The assumption that our film-goers are a dumbed-down lot obviously has to be set aside. There will be no doubt the formulaic spectator, just as pre-programmed as the formulaic film, as long as formulaic films dominate. There were the few deserters of *Ship of Theseus* too. At different stages, one or two would get up and leave, some of them making obvious their distaste for the unaccustomed sights and sounds to which they were being treated by stomping out. That is when you almost wish, no doubt undemocratically, that there were bouncers at the entrance who would send them right back to their seats for some compulsory educative viewing.

First published in *Frontline*, 6 September 2013.

Contemplating a Century

The social, cultural, moral and psychological registers of the conventional, popular, mainstream Indian cinema; its formulaic plot and narrative mode; its unique and trademark use of 'song picturization' as both a routine device for spatio-temporal shifts, and for abstraction and transcendence; its stereotypical categories of the hero, the villain, the comedian and the vamp who become, as a commentator of Tamil cinema put it, like actants on a chess board who move in a particular manner – all these speak to an informed and cultivated ritual of seeing. It is a cinema that taps into the cultural DNA of its viewers. It assumes in them an accreted mental lexicon and glossary of colloquial and epic references. It speaks to them as initiated viewers who instantly grasp what is implicit in the explicit; who, like spectators following a cricket match or wrestling bout, know the rules of the game, and therefore relate to it and appreciate it that much better, with that much more discernment.

This does not of course mean that the average cine-goer needs to be educated or even literate to be mentally or sensorially alive to these coded meanings and messages. They are imbibed, generation after generation, as part of a cumulative oral tradition. A foreigner accosted by an Indian screen potboiler for the first time must more than suspend disbelief; the whole syntax and structure, not to mention plot, appearance and characterization, must be quite disorienting. But for us, these are a given. With each new film we pick up the thread, as if from where we left off in some other film in the recent or distant past, and carry on. A mnemonic continuity underscores the varying tales of the grand Indian cinematic narrative.

On the other hand, the film scholar Sheila J. Nayar (in *Invisible Representation: The Oral Contours of a National Popular Cinema*) draws attention to the empathy Indian cinema evokes in a foreign viewer precisely because of this orality, which plumbs a common heritage of

> oral performance and orally transmitted narratives, conspicuously sharing traits with, for example, Homeric epic and the Indian *Mahabharata*. It is a cultural product that has been historically circumscribed by the psychodynamics of orality – that is, by the thought processes and personality structures that distinguish a non-writ-

ing mindset, and as such, it is a product that employs specific devices and motifs that are traditionally part of orally based storytelling.

When two of the brand-and-banner leaders of Indian cinema, Ramanand Sagar and B.R. Chopra, reduced the *Ramayana* and the *Mahabharata* respectively to the small screen, these cardboard cut-out versions became the universalized archetypes of soap-operadom that took over and continues to dominate television entertainment. They were bound to because, as the two producers knew only too well, the two epics have had a sway over the plot and theme of almost every commercial Indian film; G.P. Sippy, the producer of *Sholay*, believed that Rama and Ravana are implicit in every Indian film. The freewheeling filmic play of the epics has, however, been wide-ranging and heterodox, and not narrowly cast in a sacral mould that lends itself to be religiously or politically divisive and exploitative, as their television versions have been.

A similar attempt at sanctification may have overemphasized the Brahmin-priestly lineage of the one who pioneered the Indian feature film, Dhundiraj Govind Phalke, and projected his *Raja Harishchandra*, made in 1912, as a conventional mythological – glossing over, in the process, the rebellious, unorthodox nature of the man and his work. In her essay 'The First Cinematic Pauranik Kathanak' (in *Narrative Strategies: Essays on South Asian Literature and Film*, edited by Vasudha Dalmia and Theo Damsteegt), Brigitte Schulze challenges the approach of authors like Toeplitz (1964) and Barnow and Krishnaswamy (1980) in typecasting Phalke as a 'Shastri Brahmin', and the view of Chidananda Dasgupta that *Raja Harishchandra* was 'unmediated traditional mythology in a new vessel'. She points to Phalke's eclectic European influences, his 'inter-nationality', and the fact that he does not open and close the film in heaven, as was the norm in the stage treatment of mythologicals which were normally bookended by a paradisiacal prologue and epilogue, to suggest a spin by scholarship to claim him for caste, tradition and nation. She seems, though, to go overboard in her own attempt to divest Phalke of his 'nationalist' image, and the one quote from him she says has been used to this end actually works against her and does seem to evoke a stirring of national pride: 'I was determined to do my duty even at the cost of my life, i.e., to defend this industry even in the absence of any financial support, with the firm conviction that the Indian people would get an occasion to see Indian images on the screen and people abroad would get a truer picture of India' (from Phalke's series of four articles in *Bharatiya Chitrapat*,1917).

Phalke's struggle to make *Raja Harishchandra*, to find the money for it; his coopting his wife Saraswatibai and children and friends and technicians into a larger family enterprise dedicated to the project; his futile search, including in the red-light areas, to find a woman to play the female lead role of Taramati and his having to finally cast a man, Anna Hari Saluke, in the role; his casting his son Bhalchandra as the royal couple's son Rohitas in the film; his drawing on his familiarity with Raja Ravi Varma (for whom he had worked) for the costumes of his characters, and to frame his opening scene like the tableau of the king, queen and prince as rendered by the royal painter; his probably cranking the camera himself in good part; the quaint special effects; the bold (for that time) embrace of husband and wife as they come together after a stretch of separation – all these are now part of a legend that surpasses any cinema.

A recent Malayalam film, *Celluloid*, by the accomplished director Kamal, recreates to a good degree of period verisimilitude, the difficult circumstances faced by the first filmmaker in that language, J.C. Daniel, in making his *Vigathakumaran* (Lost Child). Made a good sixteen years after *Raja Harishchandra*, towards the end of the silent era, this film and the dire conditions in which it was shot are reminiscent of Phalke in more ways than one. J.C. Daniel, as portrayed in the film, actually goes to meet Phalke in Bombay and, reinvigorated by his example, sets out to make his film in his native Travancore. Like Phalke, he goes to great lengths to realize his cherished ambition, selling his land and his wife's jewellery, putting his family into the production, and himself playing the role of the protagonist. What proved fatal for the film, though, was his casting a woman from a lower caste, P.K. Rosy, to play opposite him as a Nair lady. An upper-caste boycott of the film meant that it had only limited and sporadic screenings, and it sank at the box office. Daniel never recovered from the blow; the film itself was destroyed in a fire and there is today no trace of it left, except for a few photographs and posters.

Raja Harishchandra had a slightly better fate with two (the first and the last) of the four reels of the film being salvaged and preserved. But the story of *Vigathakumaran* does not end with the destruction of the film reels. Caste prejudice, because J.C. Daniel was from the Nadar community, at the bureaucratic and political levels continued to deny the film, for a long time, its rightful place as the very first Malayalam feature. It is interesting to see how caste-based appropriation and denial determined the fortunes of the first Indian (or Hindi) and the first Malayalam film, respectively. The silent era was thus nowhere as quiet as the films themselves; even in terms of numbers, the National Film Archive catalogues as many as 1,313 silent films over a twenty-two-year period, pointing to a fairly active dawn of Indian cinema.

With the silver screen breaking out of its long silence, from the early 1930s, into spoken tongue, songs, background score and effects, the issue of the language of the 'national' cinema was quickly settled in favour of a mix of Hindi and Urdu, with the accent on the latter. It helped that the Punjabi producers and actors and writers, both Hindu and Muslim, who came to dominate the industry were already accustomed to lacing their language for social discourse with the sophistication of Urdu. By this time, as Rachel Dwyer and Divia Patel recount in their study, *Cinema India: The Visual Culture of Hindi Film*, the main categories of the box-office cinema had already crystallized into the historical, the mythological and the stunt; to this was soon to be added the social as a distinct type.

The studio system straddled the industry and studios privileged their preferred genres. The Prabhat Film Company of V. Shantaram and his colleagues had a flair for musicals, and produced one of Indian cinema's all-time greats, *Sant Tukaram* (1936). Bombay Talkies, set up by Himanshu Rai and his wife Devika Rani, showcased such talents as Saadat Hasan Manto, Gyan Mukherji, Kamal Amrohi, Ashok Kumar, Dev Anand and Dilip Kumar, and spun out socials like *Achhut Kanya* (1936), *Kangan* (1939) and *Kismet*(1943). B.N. Sircar's New Theatres in Calcutta hosted stars and actors like K.L. Saigal and P.C. Barua, Prithviraj Kapoor and K.C. Dey, and produced the quintessential Indian cinematic tragedy *Devdas* (1935), which Barua both directed and acted in as hero. There were, similarly, the stunt films of Fearless Nadia from Wadia Movietone and the historicals of Sohrab Modi's Minerva Movietone.

The industry lurched forward. Even by the late 1930s, India was the third largest film-producing country in the world, and by the beginning of the 1970s, the largest; by the 1980s, the output had risen to about 900 films a year, with about 15 million daily viewers in the 11,000 cinema halls across the country. And so it went well until 2000, when revelations of links between the underworld and Bollywood caused a temporary setback and a serious relook at the organizational structure of the industry and its financing mores.

The late 1930s and the 1940s fostered a revolutionary passion, with films like V. Shantaram's *Duniya Na Maane* (1937) and *Aadmi* (1939) – Khwaja Ahmed Abbas, who, teaming up with Raj Kapoor, was to carry this legacy forward, saw the first film, much like the chronic repeat viewer at the box office, eighteen times and the second twenty-four times. Abbas went on to script *Dr Kotnis ki Amar Kahani* (1946), which V. Shantaram directed in Hindi and English, himself donning the role of the Indian doctor in China. The fervour of the nationalist struggle, the sacrifices of the political leadership of the Quit India movement and the devastating Bengal famine seized the sensibility and creative imagination of a progressive group of activist–artists who formed the Indian People's Theatre Association (IPTA). K.A. Abbas made his directorial debut with the IPTA's only film venture, *Dharti ke Lal* (1946), an unblinking look at the Bengal famine. Balraj Sahni and Shombu Mitra, who acted in the film, and Pandit Ravi Shankar, who composed music for it, were among the leading lights of the IPTA in Bombay; others in the movement included Bimal Roy and the brothers of Navketan Films, Chetan, Vijay and Dev Anand.

The end of the decade saw the advent of the RK banner of Raj Kapoor, who brought a different, romantic fervour and intensity to the screen with his *Aag* in 1948 and *Barsaat* the following year. Nargis was his co-star in both the films and it was a romantic pairing that was to take the celluloid world by storm. It was a reflection of the liberal mood of the times that Raj Kapoor could acknowledge what Nargis meant to him and his cinema. 'Women have always meant a lot in my life,' he said, 'but Nargis meant more than anybody else. I used to always tell her, "Krishna is my wife, she is the mother of my children. I want you to be the mother of my films." And that is precisely what she was.' The logo of RK Films was an unabashed frozen moment from *Barsaat* with Nargis bending backward on Raj Kapoor's right arm as he, carrying a violin in his left hand, gazes intently at her. *Barsaat* also introduced the musical duo Shankar–Jaikishen, whose compositions went on to become hits, film after film. This was also the time when Lata Mangeshkar and Mohammed Rafi were getting their major breaks in Hindi film music, and poets like Hasrat Jaipuri and Shailendra began penning lyrics for the screen.

The 1950s began with a bang with Raj Kapoor and K.A. Abbas coming together to make *Awara* (1951), the film that put India sensationally on the world map. Abbas's story idea was developed for the screen by him and V.P. Sathe. Raj Kapoor directed it and, with Nargis in tow, acted in it. As he recapitulated three-and-a-half decades later, it was for him the complete film:

> *Awara* had everything. It had the theme of class distinction. It had the greatest juvenile romantic story wrapped in the poverty that the post-Independence era had inherited. It bloomed like a lotus in the mud and it went to the people as something they had never seen before. Could this ever happen to a young man in such circumstances? With a song on his lips and a flower he went through all the ordeals that socio-economic disruptions could bring about. The change that the people wanted, they saw in the spirit of the young man who was the vagabond, the Awara.

In his autobiography, *I Am Not an Island*, K.A. Abbas recalls the huge impact the film made on the then Soviet Union:

> From Moscow to Vladivostok, from the frozen icecap in the Arctic where a steel box containing the film was airdropped along with oranges from the south as a seventh of November surprise gift to the marooned group of scientists on a Polar expedition, to the ancient dusty lanes of Bokhara in the hot south, the film *Awara* (or *Brodgaya* as the Russian dubbed version was called) swept the land like a prairie fire.
>
> Within a few months all bands and orchestras in hotels and restaurants were playing the tunes from this film, Russian and Ukrainian and Georgian teenagers were singing 'Awara' songs in chorus.

Three powerful evocations, neorealist in varying degrees, of stark ruralness and deprivation as a lived condition dominated the artistic conscience, as much as consciousness, of the 1950s: Bimal Roy's *Do Bigha Zamin* (1953), Mehboob Khan's *Mother India* (1957) and, quite in its own class, Satyajit Ray's *Pather Panchali* (1955) in Bengali. There were also, at the same time, the stardom, acting prowess and signature styles of Dilip Kumar, Madhubala and Dev Anand, Guru Dutt and Waheeda Rehman, vying for attention and accolades at the box office. Dilip Kumar's inimitable, subtle, measured and controlled movements, gestures, expression and dialogue delivery remain exceptional to this day in a film world of contagious mannerisms and trademark postures.

Guru Dutt, whom his close associate Abrar Alvi – who scripted his hit films *Pyaasa* (1957), *Kaagaz ke Phool* (1959) and *Sahib Bibi aur Ghulam* (1962) – calls the 'Hamlet of films', was an ever-so-tentative, almost self-abnegating, brooding yet compelling presence on the screen. His composition of the frame, construction of the *mise-en-scène* and conjuring of mood in a shot are so distinctive that they bear the stamp of the auteur. He excelled in the art of song picturization, of languid takes and breathtaking close-ups (particularly of Waheeda Rehman), but, surprisingly, believed that songs were unnecessary – even if unavoidable – baggage that films had to carry for popular appeal. Rehman recalls Guru Dutt asking her to pray for the success of BR Film's *Kanoon* which had no songs in it, hoping that if it clicked, he could follow suit.

The 1950s, again, saw a churning of the regional language cinema. The Tamil studio system, which had the industry in its firm grip and had put up such mammoth visual extravaganzas like *Chandralekha* (1948), produced and directed by S.S. Vasan of Gemini Studios, began to reconcile to the fact that it was dependent on the star – represented by the trio M.G. Ramachandran, Sivaji Ganesan and Gemini Ganesan – as much as, or more than, the star was dependent on it. The Dravidian movement, which leveraged cinema to good effect as a vehicle to propagate its ideology, also inducted MGR and Sivaji into the cause, giving them an additional, independent mass following and political appeal.

In neighbouring Kerala, where left and progressive forces were on the ascendant, poet and lyricist P. Bhaskaran teamed up with Ramu Kariat to make *Neelakkuyil* (1954), based on a story by Uroob. Its crusading theme against untouchability and feudalism captured the new spirit of the times; its spoken language and catchy songs were freshly minted in the local idiom. It was a clear break from the trend of a surrogate Malayalam cinema whose look and feel and sound were fashioned after the dominant Tamil or Hindi types. Meanwhile, N.T. Rama Rao was becoming synonymous with the mythological roles of Rama and Krishna that he donned with androgynous assurance in Telugu and some Tamil films, and Rajkumar was being catapulted into stardom with his very first lead role in *Bedara Kannappa* (1954).

The transmogrification of the organic star who has a legitimate performative locus and role in the film, into the ritualized, fatuous superstar who runs away with the plot or becomes an ornamental peg on which to hang wild wish-fulfilment or fantabulous actions, begins with the rise of the phenomenon of Rajesh Khanna and his unbroken, nearly two-decade-long reign of the silver screen. In one of the saner, more human performances in his frenetic career, in Hrishikesh

Mukherji's *Anand* (1971), he faces off with the man who was to take over the mantle from him and push superstardom to more dizzying heights – Amitabh Bachchan, although neither he nor the critics or viewers could know it then.

And so on to the 'angry young man' of the 1970s and 1980s, of a newly concocted cinematic ethic of vigilantism and vendetta, of the aesthetic of mind-boggling violence and gore. A generation later, the superstars of today seem to shuttle between cathartic, orgiastic, collective choreographed dances and supra-human fisticuffs, where the fist packs such tonnage of power into the punch that the man at the receiving end goes flying in the air and crashes into a solid wall of brick and mortar, shattering it with the impact, and so on. The screen diva, meanwhile, has combined the attributes of the heroine and the vamp, and relies, by and large, on gyrating, erotic 'item numbers' to prove her worthiness. Superstardom, by definition male, has brought with it a greater commodification and subordination of the woman on the screen, albeit in the lead role opposite the star. There is less and less scope here for autonomy of will or purpose, less and less space for the independent performance that made Nargis, Waheeda Rehman, Madhubala and Meena Kumari stars in their own right.

In the normative sense, stars, as Christine Gledhill put it, 'signify as condensers of moral, social and ideological values'. But it is a moot point whether the star as the habitual offender and iconoclast; as the rogue cop who kills in staged encounters those who he believes will otherwise use the legal system riddled with loopholes to escape; as the homicide who lectures the contrite judge in the open court on higher laws of vengeance and justice; as the one who invariably sows, even if in response to a violent provocation, even more death and destruction all round, and walks away from all that he has laid low in slow motion, really fits that definition. It seems apotheosis of vendetta all the way, and morality, moral justification and social purpose are brought to bear on it.

There was a time when the cinema sold dreams, dreams that may have made a mockery of the viewers' real lives but provided opportunity of equivalence at least in terms of aspiration. 'How can I lose faith in the justice of life,' wrote Khalil Gibran, 'when the dreams of those who sleep upon feathers are not more beautiful than the dreams of those who sleep upon the earth?' The hyper-reality that rules the screen today estranges even as it stimulates. The viewer has been replaced by the voyeur.

First published in *Frontline*, 18 October 2013.

Requiem for Film

We have known for some years now that the days of film as film are numbered, that movies are being increasingly produced and delivered in the digital mode. But when the largest commercial film laboratory in the country, Prasad Colour Lab, formally begins to wind down its operations, the sense of finality, the reality of an epochal shift, suddenly hits us afresh. The closing montage of the century-old saga of celluloid will comprise a series of images and sounds that now lapses from physical existence into the realm of memory – the can of raw stock that disappears into the two-sleeved, lightproof changing bag and emerges as the loaded camera magazine, to be snapped into place on the Arriflex camera ready for the shot; developing baths in which the exposed stock are washed; white gloves handling the processed negatives; the working print being cut and spliced into sequence at the linear Steenbeck editing table; the rows of strips of chosen film hanging on clipboards above the bin on one side of the table and the rejected 'NG' footage discarded into it; the frame-by-frame grading of the final negative length for colour and tonal correction; the whirring bobbins, the constant winding and rewinding of rolls and reels of film, large and small, of positive and negative, of picture and sound; and finally, the married release print spooled into reels in cans and carried into the projection cabins of cinemas where they unreel, through the projector, at 24 frames a second, to give us cinematic temporality. Beyond these associations of sight and sound are those of smell and touch, of the chemical bath, of the feel of the film strip by expert fingers. For those involved with the production and post-production of film right up to its incarnation on the silver screen, an entire way of life stands altered. There is a digital erasure of celluloid materiality.

The sense of loss is not just personal. 'You really lose those wonderful silver halide images, that organic look, those tonal values, the emotion they create,' says S. Sivaraman, who joined Prasad Colour Lab at its inception in 1976. Sivaraman handled, with his colleagues, thousands of feature films, and the demands of a wide array of directors and cinematographers from across the country; rose eventually to head it; and now has to preside over this mega lab's dissolution before the onslaught of the digital. Unlike the pixels arranged in linear order which create the synthetic digital image, he explains, the silver halide grains are in random formation and better knit to provide the crystalline filmic image.

He breaks out of his film spell to a more objective appraisal of the digital as less time-consuming and more globalizing – with cloud-based technology you can upload data and disperse it to different locations so that, say, visuals can be edited in Chennai, sound can be worked on in Los Angeles, and so on – but still finds it wanting in many respects, at least in the way it is used. Although 'digital data are very malleable', the volume to be handled is enormous, especially when, as often happens, the shooting ratio is lax and sometimes of the order of 1:10, since scarcity or cost of raw stock is no longer a factor. This then generates a huge amount of data to be processed, driving up the post-production cost and neutralizing the digital advantage. The production costs too, and this is endorsed by independent producers, are not any less; in fact the hiring charges of the Arri Alexa or Red series digital cameras are more than double that of the best conventional film cameras.

If the role of the lab processor has been rendered redundant with the digital takeover, and that of the projectionist with satellite delivery of movies to cinema screens, there is a perception or impression that the cinematographer too may not be as central to digital image-making as he was in the film era. Sivaraman, for example, thinks that the 'DOP [Director of Photography] is no longer in command of the image', which is 'chopped, reorganized, goes into many mediums . . . is practically mutilated'. Also, the 'image may be created, even the colours manipulated, at the workstation . . . flaws can be fixed in post-production, so the care at the time of capturing [the image] is going down'.

However, the versatile cinematographer Madhu Ambat, who straddles art and commercial and celluloid and digital cinema with consummate ease, sees the digital camera shoot as more empowering, flexible and enhancing in terms of quality. The best digitally shot images, with resolutions of up to 4 k, may still be well short of the 6 to 8 k resolution that the medium of film can provide, but the difference is theoretical because, says Ambat, 'beyond 2 to 4 k, the human eye cannot distinguish the difference'. His work in *Adaminte Makan Abu* (Abu, Son of Adam), shot on Arri D-21 digital camera, which won him the Best Cinematography award in 2011, apart from the national award for Best Film, Best Actor and Best Music Director that year, certainly illustrates the point that the digital image can evoke no less organic and profound a feel than that captured to exacting standards on film.

There are obvious advantages to going digital: it is environment-friendly, whereas disposing of film waste can pose a hazard; there is no need to worry about dust specks and scratches as on film in the post-production chain; distribution through a combination of satellite simulcasts and on hard disks save the big banners the cost of hundreds of release prints on film stock and reduce delivery time. But when it comes to archiving or durable and reliable preservation, the digital is as yet an unproven medium before the century-old track record of the photochemical film. Constant format changes in the video and digital mode, driven by a rapid rate of technological obsolescence – kept going, no doubt, by the corporate need and greed to have newer products hit the market with regular frequency and keep the buyers coming – make it difficult to arrive at a standard specification in these media for archival preservation.

As we moved from videotapes of various gauges to DVD, briefly dabbling in between with laser discs, and into high definition (HD) and three-dimensional (3D) viewing, and as the prosumer market expanded, whetting the appetite for better and more multitasking digital electronics – an appetite met by the operation of Moore's law in this field – the emphasis has been on the qualitative and quantitative aspects of the production and dissemination and consumption of software, and not, at least not yet, on their preservation for posterity. Digital compression may offer vast storage capacity, but whether there is loss or distortion in the process apparently depends on the tool for compression and the format chosen.

Cinema going digital has unleashed a lot of youthful energy into the field. Nowhere is this more evident in as concentrated a manner as in Kerala's small but resilient, and ever-improvising cinema sector. A number of young directors, technicians and actors, many of them newcomers, are tackling refreshing new themes with varying unconventional treatments and are being received with success at the box office. The established producers are unnerved by this development because their own bigger-budget, formulaic, star-driven products do not get long enough runs in the theatres to recoup their costs. In a market with as narrow a base, as fragile and as delicately balanced as this, this new crop and generation of digital moviemakers are seen as spoilers by a petulant industry and the stars on which it rides.

In a more basic and crucial sense, digital technology in cinema can, it appears, at last undo the inequity that darker skin tones were subjected to in the medium, and the century, of celluloid film. The raw stock and technology of the film era were not skin-colour-neutral. Film emulsion, whether on Kodak or Fuji stock, and light metres were calibrated for the fair Caucasian skin, so much so that the face of a black American or African appeared featureless and characterless, especially when juxtaposed with that of a light-skinned person. There was the other infuriating image, common in films featuring a black actor in a dark suit, where only the white of the shirt and the teeth when the lips parted could really be seen. In an article this October in *The Washington Post*, Ann Hornaday quotes the director of the recent film *12 Years a Slave* (about the abduction from New York and enslavement of a free black man in 1840), Steve McQueen, recalling

> growing up and seeing Sidney Poitier sweating next to Rod Steiger in *In the Heat of the Night*, and obviously it's very hot in the south. But also he was sweating because he had tons of light thrown on him because the film stock wasn't sensitive enough for black skin.

Black skin, which absorbs over 40 per cent more light than fair skin, needed that much more compensation. A ploy cinematographers used to film black artistes was to daub their skins with Vaseline to reflect light. However, now, as Ann Hornaday points out, a clutch of films on African Americans (apart from *12 Years a Slave*, *Mother of George* and *Black Nativity*) capture the pigment of the black skin in all its nuances, thanks to a combination of digital cameras with better latitude to handle darker shades and shadows, and the possibility of digital post-production correction.

This technology shift represents the removal of a historical prejudice that dates back to the 1940s and Kodak's so-called Shirley cards (Shirley, a fair-skinned female model, was probably an employee with Kodak), which was the skin tone reference to which its colour film stock was standardized. Interestingly, but not surprisingly, it was only when its clients in the dark chocolate and dark furniture businesses complained about the dull and drab quality of the images of their products that Kodak began to look at how it might capture the darker shades and colours better.

When, in 1977, the pioneering French filmmaker Jean-Luc Godard was invited by the new Marxist Samora Machel government of Mozambique to help set up a telvision station with truly indigenous, as against western, programming values and content, he refused to work with Kodak film stock, calling it 'racist'. Although the project had to be abandoned, Godard has recorded his impressions of what it meant for a nation where 'eighty per cent of the population had never seen an image – only nature' to be initiated into the visual medium. 'It's like a child,' he continues, 'opening his eyes and there's no code, no sense, he's just looking. In Mozambique the image is the raw material. But in Hollywood, the images are so sophisticated you can't even read them anymore.'

In the days of apartheid in South Africa, a special Polaroid ID-2 camera, which had a boost button for extra flash light, was used by the state and its departments like the Bureau of Mines to take pictures of the black citizens for their pass-books and identity documents. An exhibition mounted last year by the London-based photographic duo Adam Broomberg and Oliver Chanarin revolves around some of these issues and their assignment to shoot in the Central African republic of Gabon. It is pithily titled 'To Photograph the Details of a Dark Horse in Low Light', which was the code used by Eastman Kodak Company in the 1980s for its experiment with colour film stock that could depict the darker skin colours and tones more faithfully.

Digital technology itself, unlike the proven role of film in this respect, may yet be a dark horse when it comes to preservation of cinematic work for the distant future. But it is today a liberator of the expressiveness long suppressed beneath dark skins.

First published in *Frontline*, 10 January 2014.

Colour, Light and Darkness

José Saramago's riveting novel *Blindness*, written in 1995, opens with cars waiting at a traffic light. When the light turns from red to amber to green, the car at the head of the line does not move. As it turns out, the driver has suddenly, inexplicably, lost his sight. Blindness rapidly spreads like a virus in the city and we are sucked into a dystopia of the unseeing. Imagine, instead, that the driver did not go blind, but that his colour references were suddenly all jumbled up and thrown out of sync, so that he saw green instead of red or amber instead of green, or any other colour at random instead of these three colours. Imagine a colour riot of a virus taking hold of the population. It would be the setting for anarchy of a different, seeing kind.

What you see or, as in the Saramago plot, do not see, need not be all what you get. What you name may get to be what you see, as in the case of another traffic light, this time outside fiction. Guy Deutscher, in his recent work, *Through the Language Glass: Why the World Looks Different in Other Languages*, notes that the green or 'go' traffic light in Japan has a bluish tint. It was not, he says, always so. In the 1930s, when these lights were imported from the United States, they were the same green as elsewhere. But the Japanese word for green (*ao*) was also the word for blue, and in time became more applicable to blue than to green. Green came to be known by another term, *midori*. However, *ao* continued to be used to characterize freshness, and, Deutscher explains, 'in common parlance the go light was dubbed "ao shingoo" perhaps because the three primary colours on Japanese artists' palettes are traditionally "aka" (red), "kiiro" (yellow) and "ao".'

So there was this problem of a mismatch of a light which is green, or *midori*, in colour being called *ao*, or blue, because of the latter term's association with the greenness of freshness. Deutscher says:

> Nations with a weaker spine might have opted for the feeble solution of simply changing the official name of the go light to midori. Not so the Japanese. Rather than alter the name to fit reality, the Japanese government decreed in 1973 that reality should be altered to fit the name: henceforth, go lights would be a colour that better corresponded to the dominant meaning of ao. Alas, it was impossible to change the colour to real blue, because Japan is party to an international convention that ensures road signs have a measure of uniformity around the globe. The solution

was thus to make the ao light as bluish as possible while still being officially green.

Deutscher launches into his discourse on how the perception of colour is mediated by the need-based vocabulary for colour in different cultures and periods by reaching back to the mid-nineteenth century to dip into the scholarly tome, *Studies on Homer and the Homeric Age*, by William Ewart Gladstone, the Liberal politician and four-time Prime Minister of England. Gladstone parses the use of colour by Homer and concludes that it is neither poetic licence nor blindness (Homer as a blind poet was, he held, a later construct) that drives the epicist to describe, in the *Iliad* and the *Odyssey*, the sea or oxen as wine-coloured, or the wool of sheep or iron as violet. Homer's sky, observes Gladstone, 'is starry, or broad, or great, or iron, or copper, but it is never blue'. Nor was such skewed attribution of colour peculiar to Homer. It was typical of his times: Pindar's poems of the fifth century BC refer to violet-coloured hair.

The burden of Gladstone's finding, concludes Deutscher, is that there was 'nothing less than universal colour blindness among the ancient Greeks', that 'they saw the world in black and white with a dash of red' (there was growing awareness and deployment of *eruthros* or the colour red), that 'violet' or 'wine-looking' were probably proxy terms to convey shades of darkness. As for the absence of any specific allusion to the abundant blueness of the sky or the sea, Gladstone's take was, according to Deutscher, 'a masterstroke of ingenuity':

> His theory was that colour – in abstraction from the object that is coloured – may start mattering to people only once they become exposed to artificial paints and dyes. The appreciation of colour as a property independent of a particular material may thus have developed only hand in hand with the capacity to manipulate colours artificially. And that capacity, he notes, barely existed in Homer's day: the art of dyeing was only in its infancy, cultivation of flowers was not practised, and almost all the brightly coloured objects that we take for granted were entirely absent.

The next protagonist in Deutscher's colour narrative is the philologist Lazarus Geiger who, in his lecture titled 'On the Colour Sense in Primitive Times and its Evolution', delivered to the Assembly of German Naturalists and Physicians at Frankfurt in 1867, dwells on why the preponderant blueness of the sky finds no mention in recorded artistic expressions or religious evocations of ancient times. Geiger draws the example of the Vedic verses:

> These hymns, of more than ten thousand lines, are brimming with descriptions of the heavens. Scarcely any subject is evoked so frequently. The sun and reddening dawn's play of colour, day and night, cloud and lightning, the air and the ether, all these are unfolded before us over and over again, in splendour and vivid fullness. But there is only one thing that no one would ever learn from those ancient songs who did not already know it, and that is that the sky is blue.

Geiger found that this was as true of biblical Hebrew, which had no word for blue. He moreover hazarded the idea that blue was an etymological construct and a combination of the colours black and green, and that therefore, in earlier cultural contexts, blueness was either included in black or was part of green. The description, then, in ancient literature and verse, of black sky or wine-coloured sea begins to make some sense. Similarly the colour green, he argues, although lexically anterior to blue, is younger than yellow, which in turn is derivative of hues of red. He was thus getting to an arrangement of a chronological awareness of colour 'according to the schema of the colour spectrum', where red came first, followed by yellow, then green, and then blue and violet.

It was Geiger who introduced the idea that the ancients may not have been deficient in their perception of the full range of colour as we see and know it today, but perhaps had a limited range of language to express colour. They anticipated, without of course being aware of it, Wittgenstein's wisdom (in his *Tractatus Logico-Philosophicus*) that 'the limits of my language mean the limits of my world'. It was a short step, although it took a century, from Geiger to Brent Berlin and Paul Kay's *Basic Colour Terms: Their Universality and Evolution*. Published in 1969, it became the definitive study on the sequence in which different cultures and languages discover, as in name, colours. They invariably begin with black and white, then proceed to red, then interchangeably to yellow and green, then blue followed by violet, and so on. This, suggests Deutscher, was what Geiger was already on to, and 'Berlin and Kay rediscovered Geiger's 101-year-old sleeping beauty essentially unchanged and woke it up with a smacking great kiss.'

The intervening decades had seen a few wild goose-chases in the direction of a nod by Gladstone to define the progressive acquisition of colour sensibility as a Lamarckian phenomenon of transmitting, like the classic misunderstanding of the evolution of the giraffe's neck, acquired characteristics down the generations. The retina's sophistication in distinguishing colour, roughly went the thought process, evolved over time and in keeping with the necessity to see the world in fuller colour, and was passed on, with improvement, from one generation to the next. But, as Deutscher sums up,

> by the first decade of the 20th century it had become clear that the tall story about recent physiological changes in vision had been a red herring. The ancients could see colours just as well as we do, and the differences in colour vocabulary reflect purely cultural developments, not biological ones.

In the realm of aesthetics, though, counterfactual thought and expression can be privileged. A wine-red sea or a black sky can be irresistible. A retreat from colour and light can denote artistic rigour. The Japanese novelist Jun'ichiro Tanizaki's ruminations on the Oriental and Occidental artistic and utilitarian approaches to sound and colour and light, published in the 1930s in a slim volume titled *In Praise of Shadows*, makes a refreshing study of differences and contrasts between the two. He ascribes to the western aesthetic a shine and glitter and brilliance and burnishing which is far removed from the look and feel of grime and dust and 'importance to age and patina' of the orient.

For him,

> the beauty of a Japanese room depends on a variation of shadows, heavy shadows against light shadows – it has nothing else. Westerners are amazed at the simplicity of Japanese rooms, perceiving in them no more than ashen walls bereft of ornament. Their reaction is understandable, but it betrays a failure to comprehend the mystery of shadows. Out beyond the sitting room, which the rays of the sun can at best but barely reach, we extend the eaves or build on a verandah, putting sunlight at still greater a remove. The light from the garden steals in but dimly through paper-panelled doors, and it is precisely this indirect light that makes for us the charm of a room.

And so he goes on, celebrating the shades of shadows and arrives at darkness made visible by candle light which is 'different in quality from darkness on the road at night . . . a repletion, a pregnancy of tiny particles like fine ashes, each particle luminous as a rainbow'.

This comes so close in ethos to the darkness of village homes in India before the electric light, a darkness so palpable that, as Tanizaki says, you almost blink to keep it out of your eyes. It is darkness that responds varyingly to the flickering pinpoint luminescence of fireflies, to the flaming torch of dried and bunched coconut palm leaves, the lit, oiled cotton-wick, the kerosene lamp or the petromax paraffin pressure lamp, the battery-powered torch or beam of electric light. In his Malayalam film *Oridathu* (1986), the filmmaker G. Aravindan deals delightfully with the arrival of electricity in a village wreaking havoc with the lives of its inhabitants. The film arrives, even if via satire, at the same lament as of the highly regarded poet, Akkitham: 'Light is sadness, son; darkness is bliss.'

The muted colours and lengthening shadows at the tail-end of day, the light flung like a parting shot by the setting sun and the quiet colourations it evokes in nature became the thematic *mise-en-scène* of Aravindan's earlier film, *Pokkuveyil* (1981), shot, to capture its natural tonal form, only in the short span of twilight each day of the filming schedule. There are, of course, the more formal experimentations of chromatic scaling in some of the best of European cinema, like the work on a colour axis by the masterly director, Robert Bresson. But the brooding colours and shadows at the cusp of light and darkness endowing a peculiarly Indian moment give *Pokkuveyil* a home-grown aesthetic feel. The ethos of that moment is perhaps also a subconscious derivative of a momentous mythos: that of the slaying of the demon king Hiranyakashipu by the Narasimha avatar of god Vishnu.

As the legend goes, Hiranyakashipu had protected himself with a boon against being killed by either human or animal, by any weapon, either inside or outside, either on the ground or in the sky, either during the day or at night. Vishnu takes the form of Narasimha (a combination of a lion and a man), drags Hiranyakashipu to the threshold (so that it is neither inside nor outside), places him on his lap (so that he is neither on the ground nor in the sky), disembowels him with his claws (so no weapon is used). All this happens at twilight so that the neither-day-nor-night stipulation of the boon too is not violated. Twilight, then, also portends a neither-nor time for wily, godly – and not very aesthetic – retribution.

First published in *Frontline*, 24 January 2014.